EUROPA

EUROPA

How Europe Shaped the Modern World

Julio Crespo MacLennan

PEGASUS BOOKS
NEW YORK LONDON

EUROPA

Pegasus Books Ltd.
148 W. 37th Street, 13th Floor
New York, NY 10018

First Pegasus Books edition July 2018

Interior design by Maria Fernandez

Library of Congress Cataloging-in-Publication Data is available.

ISBN: 978-1-68177-756-6

10 9 8 7 6 5 4 3 2 1

Printed in the United States of America
Distributed by W. W. Norton & Company

To Hugh Thomas, in memoriam.

To Catherine, Eduardo, and Sandra, as always.

Contents

Introduction

Europe over the last years has lived through very difficult times. The global financial crisis had a devastating impact on the European Union. The financial problems of the eurozone were so serious that many external observers ventured to predict an imminent collapse of the European single currency. The peoples of Europe have had to learn how to live under austerity programs that imperil their living standards. Emigration problems have been exacerbated by the Syrian refugee crisis and Islamic terrorism. While the first signs of recovery finally appeared in the EU, the next major challenge came: Brexit. The decision of the British people to leave the European Union not only implied that the European project would lose one of its four major economies, but something that was potentially more dangerous: that if people were given the opportunity to vote on membership of the European Union in a referendum they would reject it. European unification could be defeated by its worst enemy, which mainly inspired its birth: nationalism.

The last ten years have been a golden era for doomsayers and specialists in Western decline, and there have been many of these since the beginning of the twentieth century. Before every single problem that EU governments and institutions have faced, they have enjoyed warnings that the EU is doomed to disappear and that Europe on the whole is increasingly irrelevant in a new bipolar world mainly led by the United States and China, in which the latter is destined to gain the upper hand.

Yet the most recent crisis has not been exclusively European but a global crisis, and it does not seem so serious if we look at it from an historical perspective. For a continent that has survived two world wars, the problems faced by the Europeans over the last years seem quite manageable. Europe has assets that no other power or civilization possesses. Its most important legacy is the world in which we live and this in itself is enough to guarantee a very relevant role in the twenty-first century. For Europeans shaped the modern world, as this book will explain.

This book is written for readers from all walks of life and from any part of the world; all of you who have a passion for history, an infinite curiosity, and an eagerness to acquire knowledge, not to be confused with information, which is easily accessible in the Internet era. It will be particularly relevant to those who have asked questions like: What has Europe done for us? What historical trends explain the present? Who provided the essential elements of our contemporary society?

The aim of this book is to explain why Europe dominated the world from the sixteenth century to the twentieth century, in what way did it influence other continents and peoples, and finally, what were the consequences of this era of hegemony exerted by the Europeans.

The curiosity of the Europeans for other worlds, their wish for expansion and conquest, as well as their economic needs took them much further than they could ever imagine. On reaching the zenith of power, the Spanish Empire not only stretched across a great part of the American continent, but it was also a global empire over which the sun never set. Portugal also consolidated an empire that included territories in the Americas, Africa, and Asia. The British Empire at its height in the early twentieth century covered a fourth part of the globe and held sway over a fifth of the world population at that time. In that same era the territories under French dominion were also formidable, as they included almost half of the African continent. And of course a very notable example of terrestrial expansion was Russia, which managed to include a sixth of the earth in its frontiers. Holland in the seventeenth century created an empire of much more modest dimensions, but that was enough for this small nation to reach economic hegemony.

Territorial expansion was only one indicator of the power that Europeans exerted over the world. Political influence was a very important dimension due to the fact that many nations were created based on the model of the European nation-state. There was also an ideological influence as the ideas of the old continent propagated across the world. Economic power had paramount importance, for access to so many natural resources at global level was going to be essential to explain Europe's economic growth. Furthermore, European powers managed to create a global market. Last but not least, Europe was going to exert its hegemony from the cultural point of view, for thanks to the expansion of its powers Western culture prevailed in a great part of the world. There was even a spiritual aspect of European dominance as a result of the extraordinary propagation of Christian religion. Several governments considered that propagating Christianity was one of the main justifications for imperial expansion, and missionaries were going to play an essential role in this task.

A very important factor that contributed to European dominance of the world in all mentioned aspects was demography. Emigration of the European population and its permanent settlement in other continents accompanied the great powers in their expansion, especially in the Americas. One of the reasons why the empires reached so far was due to the migratory zeal experienced by Europeans and the networks of emigrants created by them, particularly between the nineteenth and twentieth century when the mass migratory waves took place.

Imperialism and European colonial expansion have not only been criticized by the people who considered themselves their victims but also by the Europeans, including the inhabitants of the old colonial powers, who were mostly to benefit from them. This is mainly due to the fact that these phenomena are identified with nations and cultures oppressed by the great powers, indiscriminate slaughters, and worst of all, genocide. Racism is also very much associated with European expansion of the world, and finally, slavery.

None of these evils is exclusively European, for unfortunately the history of infamy is universal; it took place before the era of European hegemony and it has continued after. But undoubtedly European imperial history is full of blood, submission, exploitation, humiliation, suffering, and injustice. This book will pay the attention that they deserve and the names of those who were primarily responsible for these evils will appear on these pages.

On the other hand, we will also examine the contribution made by Europe to the creation of the modern world by means of imperial expansion and European experiences that have usually been considered beneficial for the whole of humanity. This list would be led by the propagation of the system of government that is generally considered as the best, or at least the one that confers more powers upon the citizens: democracy. Also the ideas that enable its proper functioning, like the rule of law, the separation of powers, parliamentarianism and the principle of equality of all citizens, individual liberty, and finally, human rights. A very important European political contribution for all the peoples on earth was the nation-state. Another obvious contribution is that of the market economy that was inexorably implemented by people throughout the world as the best way of exchanging products between human beings and generating wealth. There is also a long list of benefits that many citizens in the world enjoy as a consequence of the propagation of European scientific and technological advances. These include more efficient agricultural methods that provided food for a rapidly expanding population and prevented famines, transport and communication technology that allowed a more rapid exchange of peoples, products, and capital, and finally, modern medicine that allowed many illnesses to be cured and has contributed to a general increase in life expectancy.

To summarize, we shall examine an epic history, as the expansion of Europe is, with its lights and shadows, its main representatives-so much those who inspired admiration as those who were despised-and the ideas that were propagated. With this aim in mind, we shall examine the expansion of several European countries by means of their military settlements, colonial empires, entrepreneurial projects, and migration of citizens. We will analyze one of the most fascinating chapters in the history of humanity, the arrival of Europeans in other continents. We will review the lives and works of sailors like Christopher Columbus and Vasco da Gama, Spanish conquistadors like Hernán Cortés and Francisco Pizarro, great figures of British expansion like Captain James Cook, Robert Clive, and Cecil Rhodes, and other extraordinary figures from France, Holland, Russia, and other countries.

On the other hand, this book will also pay attention to the experience of anonymous Europeans who arrived in other continents for very diverse reasons, from soldiers and civil servants, emigrants and fortune seekers, to prisoners and exiles. It will also deal with the confrontation with other peoples in conquered lands, how some of them were exterminated, and the clash of cultures. Finally it will also examine some of the literature that the European expansion bequeathed.

Europe not only shaped the world in the process of the rise of its great powers but also that of decline and dismemberment of its empires, as we shall see in the last chapters of this book. We will see how the crisis of imperialism and two world wars precipitated the end of the era of European hegemony. We will examine the impact that imperialism, taken to its extreme levels, had on European powers, and the birth of the postcolonial world, in which the European legacy provoked much controversy but was ultimately to be so influential. Finally, we shall see how Europe reinvents itself in the postwar era, and how the process of European unification and the internal organization of its society allow Europeans to continue exerting a very influential role and setting the main trends of the contemporary world.

A lot has been written about the era of European hegemony, about its empires and great powers. I would not have been able to write this book without benefitting from the contribution made by all authors that I mention in the bibliography. Nevertheless explanations about Europe's leading role in making of the modern world are very rare. One explanation for such an important gap in literature is that historians, political scientists, economists, and authors in general who are interested in the topic of imperial expansion or global dominance have approached it from a national but not a European perspective.

Until only a few decades ago, Europe was deeply divided into nations, and ancient rivalries were rife. This is one of the reasons why both authors and readers in general showed little interest in looking beyond their own national experiences. Fortunately, to compensate for this there have been an increasing number of historians who have specialized in countries that were not theirs, and made magnificent contributions. Increasing mutual comprehension among nations, particularly in the academic sphere, may account for the fact that we now have very good books on the contemporary history of Europe, capable of looking beyond the psychological barriers of national frontiers.

On the other hand, very few historians have been tempted by the challenge of comparing the experience of all the European nations that expanded throughout the world. Undoubtedly the bitter legacy of old rivalries and war have been very influential, contributing to make all factors that separated them be considered more important than what brought them together. There were empires like the Spanish, the French, or the British that were considered by themselves civilizations in their own right, especially in the case of France. All of them were aware of being part of a great Western civilization, but not so much part of a European civilization, for Europe was a geographic term and a vain cultural reference but nothing more.

Nevertheless in contemporary Europe, and particularly in the European Union, the meaning of the term European has changed radically as a result of an ever-increasing union between states and peoples. Not only do we need a narrative that explains to Europeans the history and the culture that they share, as it has been done over the last decades, but also one that may contribute with an explanation about the role that they have played in the world and what their legacy is. This is particularly relevant at a time like the present, when the members of the European Union have been building a common foreign policy and discussing global strategies to defend and promote EU interests in the world.

And it becomes urgent with the global crisis that we have suffered over the last years, when the whole process of political and economic union has fallen into disarray. Nationalist, xenophobic, and populist parties throughout Europe defy the existence of the European Union, reverting to ideas that actually led to the destruction of Europe in the first half of the twentieth century. Islamic terrorist groups break peace and security in several European capitals with increasing frequency, and mass migration that fails to assimilate undermines the values on which European society was built. Perhaps more than ever Europeans need to come to terms with their history, and the rest of the world needs to understand the nature of its relationship with Europe.

Ever since wars and barbed-wire frontiers in Europe were replaced by the free movement of peoples, services, and capital through Europe, there has been an increasing number of Europeans who are aware that their identity spans a space that is much wider than the nation to which they officially belong. This has specially been my case. As a result of my family background I was brought up between two countries that have been historically confrontational, Spain and Britain. From grade school to college, I have always been surrounded by classmates from diverse European backgrounds. My wife is French and Spanish, at home we speak in English, French, and Spanish, and my children have the blood of three great powers: Spain, France, and Great Britain, and they are being brought up under the influence of these three cultures. It will therefore be understood why for me, and even more for my children as soon as they are old enough to be aware of it, to be European means something more than a geographic term, as it clearly defines what our identity is.

This European identity, as well as my affinity toward several European nations, have deeply marked my academic trajectory. I have always been very interested in comparative history, not only of Britain and Spain, the countries that I know best, but also of other great European nations. In my travels through all these countries I have always asked myself about their similarities and their differences, and the extent to which the history that they have shared or that has confronted them marks their present.

As it generally happens with Europeans, I have become particularly aware of my European identity during my stays away from the old continent. The origins of this book can be traced back to the journeys I have made through the world over the last decade. On the beaches of Saint Lucia, the cafés of old Havana, strolling along the elegant avenues of Boston or Buenos Aires, or on the train from Delhi to Jaipur, the European legacy in all these places led me to ask many of the questions that I have attempted to answer.

In this book I have followed a chronological and thematic approach. Chapter 1 starts by answering a question of crucial importance: Why did Europe, rather than any other civilization, manage to reach global hegemony and shape the rest of the world? The Renaissance mainly provides the answer, a remarkable era that allowed the early development of the knowledge-based society, science, empiricism, and the market economy, all of which were going to give Europeans a crucial advantage over the rest of the world.

The curiosity about the limits of the earth and the desire to discover trade routes that would generate wealth—together with an adventurous spirit developed by navigators and explorers in that era—explains why some European powers acquired such an advantageous position from the sixteenth century. Chapter 2 will examine how European navigators laid the foundations of an era of European expansion, and how the most important explorer of all, Christopher Columbus, radically altered the fate of Spain and the rest of Europe with the discovery of America.

The Iberian pioneers in the European expansion divided the New World among themselves and consolidated huge empires there. They were soon followed by England, France, and Holland in the process of building overseas empires. Apart from the Atlantic powers other European kingdoms were soon to follow suit in imperial expansion, like Denmark and Sweden. Russia on the other hand played a very important role expanding toward the East and consolidating an immense land empire. Chapter 3 will examine this process and answer the following crucial questions: What kind of empires did all these nations create? To what extent was their expansion motivated by the same needs? How did they manage to control and administer such vast territories? Finally, what were the economic benefits of imperial expansion and how did they affect international relations?

The era of revolutions had enormous repercussions both in Europe and the imperial world. For this reason Chapter 4 is devoted to this topic. The French Revolution shook the European world, nevertheless, a few years before the old regime started to crumble on the other side of the Atlantic with the outbreak of the American War of Independence in 1776. This chapter analyzes the impact that the creation of the United States of America had, and the ways in which the principles of the enlightenment influenced the founding fathers of this great nation. It will then explain how the revolutionary wave spread across the American continent, dismantling the Spanish and Portuguese empires. In this chapter we will also analyze the great changes brought by this era, like the abolition of slavery and the creation of a new Atlantic world.

The expansion of European powers in Asia was crucial to reach global hegemony. Chapter 5 focuses on this topic. It will examine the colonization of India by several powers until Britain gained the upper hand, and the impact that the Indian subcontinent had on the British Empire. The European incursion into China will be treated in detail, and finally an event of great repercussion on the Asian world: the rise of Japan as a Westernized power.

European emigration is essential to understand the impact of imperial expansion. For this reason Chapter 6 is devoted to the great European migratory waves through the world. As we shall see, the development of American nations from the United States to Argentina cannot be understood without the contribution of European migration and the networks they created.

Europe experiences a golden age in the nineteenth century, as Chapter 7 explains. Imperial expansion and the Industrial Revolution are the main explanations for the phenomenal wealth that European powers acquired at that time. This is also an age of improvement in all spheres, and great intellectual creativity that led to the emergence of a new European way of life that was internationally admired. All major political ideas of our present-day world emerged in Europe at this time. This chapter also examines the global impact of major European technological innovations of that era.

For a long time Africa was hardly affected by European expansion. Nevertheless, as Chapter 8 will show, in no more than two decades the European powers distributed among themselves this great continent toward the end of the nineteenth century. The so-called scramble for Africa considerably increased rivalries among great powers, with deep consequences in the era of imperialism, and it was also to determine the future of Africa and the Middle East.

The two world wars were the most devastating way in which Europe shaped the world. Chapter 9 examines how was it possible that Europeans fought these wars despite the fact that they were going to be so self-destructive, how so many nations were dragged into them, and finally, how they precipitated the end of the era of European supremacy.

An unexpected way in which Europeans influenced other nations has been through exile. Chapter 10 focuses on this issue that has not received the attention it deserves. Citizens were forced to abandon several countries because of political, ethnic, or religious persecution. This was particularly the case among members of the Jewish community. For this reason the development of the Zionist movement is examined here, culminating with the creation of the state of Israel. This chapter also dwells on the consequences of what I describe as intellectual migration and the exodus of many of the great European talents of that era.

Were colonial empires doomed to disappear or was this another consequence of the world wars? Chapter 11 deals with these questions. It also explains the rise of the Third World and the extent to which it lived under the influence of former colonial powers and European culture. This chapter also explains another factor that played a crucial role in the Third World: the rise and fall of the Soviet Union, and communism as one of the most influential ideologies of the twentieth century.

The final chapter of this book deals with the rebirth of Europe in the postwar era through the creation of the European Union and the emergence of what has been called the European dream. It explains the factors that made possible the welfare state and its effect on European society. It analyzes how European integration managed to eradicate war between its nations, and embark on a process of unification that has allowed Europe to continue playing a very influential role in global affairs. It will also explain why, in spite of all its shortcomings and internal crises, the European Union has set some of the global trends that determine the twenty-first century.

What is the final outcome of more than four hundred years of European hegemony in the world? What is the most important legacy in Europe? Can the present global world be understood without referring to Europe? Does Europe have a relevant mission in the world of the twenty-first century? The reader will find the answers to these great questions at the end of this book, and after the journey that we shall make in these pages through five of the most fascinating centuries in universal history.

Chapter 1

Europa from Myth to Reality

How Renaissance Europe Gave Birth to an Expanding Civilization.

---

t was not until the Renaissance that the peoples of Europe acquired
the strength and capacity to expand their civilization. Europe is a small
continent with a loosely defined eastern border. That little promontory
of the Asian continent, as poet Paul Valéry defined it. As so many aspects
of its identity, Europe got its name from a Greek myth. Europa was the
mother of King Minos of Crete, who was abducted by Zeus and named
most of the land after her. The Greeks started to call their lands to the
west of the Aegean Sea Europa, to differentiate them from those in Asia
Minor. The earliest references that can be found to Europe as a geographical
term is in the eighth century, in relation to Charlemagne's empire, which
spanned across most of central and western Europe. It was not really until

the thirteenth century that the continent of Europe began to be identified by such a term by its inhabitants. Until then Europe was more commonly known as Christendom.[*]

Together with the legacy of the Greek civilization and the Roman Empire, it was Christianity that initially brought the inhabitants of this continent together. External threats and invasions have been an important contributing factor to make people become aware of their identity and strengthen their cohesion. For the peoples of Europe it was the rise of Islam and the Islamic invasions that provided them with a sense of identity and an awareness of belonging to the Christian world. In the year 1095 Pope Urban II called upon the Christians to defend the Byzantine Empire from the Turkish threat. This campaign was followed by three other so-called Crusades, which allowed Christians to go as far as Jerusalem to defend this holy land where their origins were. Despite the mixed success of the Crusades they did contribute to the rise of a sense of identity among the peoples of Europe. They also reinforced their determination to defend their faith and their territory from external invasions from Islam or any other civilization. But at that time the Christians in Europe were a civilization fighting on the defensive and lacking capacity for expansion.

The Arab civilization for a long time had proven to be stronger than the Christian-European one, and it also showed much better prospects for expansion. The Prophet Muhammad, the founder of Islam, had called upon the Arabs to spread this religion. Shortly after his death in the year 632 C.E. Arabs embarked on an extraordinary process of conquest and expansion, with the ultimate aim of spreading Islam and converting as many infidels (unbelievers) as possible, as the Prophet had ordered. From the Arabian Peninsula they conquered Syria in 634, Persia in 664, and from there Muhammad Bin Qasim led the first successful attack on India in 715. The Eastern expansion of Islam continued across the Indian Ocean, until it became firmly established in the Malay Peninsula by the fourteenth century.

Islam even threatened the frontiers of the Chinese civilization in 678, when Arab pirates looted Canton in 678.

---

[*] Norman Davies, *Europe: A History* (Oxford, England: Oxford University Press, 1996).

After spreading across the whole of North Africa Islam crossed into Europe and became the most imposing threat to the Christian world. By the eighth century, most of the Iberian Peninsula had been conquered by Islamic forces, and even then they threatened to continue moving toward northern Europe, through Gaul. In *The History of the Decline and Fall of the Roman Empire*, Edward Gibbon reflects on the consequences that the Muslim invasions could have had on European civilization, arguing that once they reached the Pyrenees they could have easily continued expanding all the way north up to Scotland, in which case, "perhaps the interpretation of the Koran would at present be taught in the classrooms of Oxford."

The success of this Arab empire was mainly based on the reconstruction of economic life, which had been inherited from the Roman Empire in the Mediterranean. This was particularly the case with Al-Andalus, in southern Spain, where Moorish invaders benefitted from the remainders of Roman and Visigoth splendor, and revived it. Córdoba became a great center of learning. Technology was another key answer. The astrolabe and the quadrant were invented by Arabs and used for celestial navigation. They also replaced the traditional square sail, which the Romans used, by a triangular one that could beat into an adverse wind. This explains the facility with which the Arabs traversed the Mediterranean and the Indian Ocean, and reached the Far East. The other key element to explain Islamic expansion is of course religious faith. Muslims were as convinced as the Christians that theirs was the true religion and that it was their moral duty to spread their religion to as many infidels as possible.

By the thirteenth century the Christians had reconquered most of the Iberian Peninsula from the Moors. But two centuries later Islam began penetrating into Europe from the east. In 1453 the Ottomans invaded Constantinople, and from there they continued a westward advance until in 1529 Suleiman the Magnificent attempted in vain to capture Vienna. While Islam was stopped in Europe it succeeded in its advance toward Asia. Turkish Muslim mercenaries led by Zehir Eddin and Muhammad Baber (a distant descendant of the great Turco-Mongol leader Tamerlane), seized Delhi in 1526. There they founded the empire of which Babur was the first great Mogul, and laid the foundations of an Islamic empire that was soon to dominate most of India.

Through its golden age, from the eighth to the twelfth century, Islam managed to dominate the Old World and until 1492, when Columbus reached America, it very much shaped this world according to its interests and values. Islam had brought together important parts of Asia, Europe, Africa and the Maghreb, and the Far East. Apart from religion, trade networks developed by the Islamic conquerors contributed to bring peoples from such diverse places together. Spices, silk, pepper, and pearls were brought from Arab merchants from the Far East into Europe. The first African slaves to reach Europe were brought by the Arabs.

The Arabs also contributed to the spread of knowledge acquired by the ancient Greeks. Aristotelian philosophy was revived in Córdoba by the Andalusian polymath Averroes.

Arabic numbers were one of the most enduring legacies bequeathed by the Arabs. The system of Arabic numbering reached Europe through Spain. Leonardo of Pisa, in his *Liber Abaci*, asserted in 1202 that the Arabic numbering system was better than the Roman one and contributed to a clearer thought. Once this numbering system was adopted by Europeans, it gradually expanded through the rest of the world.

The other civilization in the world that was much stronger than the European in medieval times was the Chinese. Europeans were introduced to the Chinese civilization through the writings of Marco Polo in the early fourteenth century. According to one of its fantasizing descriptions, both the Chinese and Indian civilizations had so much wealth that they had palaces made out of gold. From then it spread through Europe that this faraway civilization was not only richer than Europe, but also more advanced in all aspects.

While Europe was deeply divided into kingdoms, China had consolidated a strong state, ruled by an emperor who could trace his lineage back over a thousand years. It was administered by a genuinely meritocratic administrative corps, the Mandarins, who gained access to the Chinese administration through a selective examination system. By the thirteenth century, around ten thousand families belonged to the Mandarin elite. Not only were they a pillar of the state, but their values of hierarchy, public order, and Confucian ethics helped strengthen Chinese social cohesion in a remarkable way.

Scientifically and technologically China was also much more advanced than Europe. The blast furnace and cast iron were known by the Chinese long before the Europeans. They also used paper and the first printing techniques, almost one thousand years before Europeans. Gunpowder was also invented in China, and its first cannons gave it a military superiority that went unchallenged for centuries. From the establishment of the Ming dynasty in the thirteenth century, the Chinese consolidated a territory that was almost as big as continental Europe, and Chinese language speakers proliferated from the steppes of Siberia to the Himalayas and the tropical jungles in Southeast Asia. Last but not least, China was much more populated than any other region in the world; by the sixteenth century it had over one hundred million inhabitants, two times as many as Europe. The sense that they were superior to any other civilization and that they were very much the heart of the world explains why the Chinese referred to themselves as "the Middle Kingdom."

The feeling of being at the center of the world to a certain extent explains the lack of interest felt by the Chinese in exploring other regions. Nevertheless, a remarkable naval enterprise was launched in the early fifteenth century. The Chinese navy had 1,350 ships in the year 1420, and in the first decades of the fifteenth century Chinese sailors had discovered a good part of the southern Pacific and had even reached the town of Malindi on the eastern coast of Africa in 1414.* The theory that the Chinese discovered America several decades before the Europeans has even been defended by some researchers over the last years and received considerable attention, although convincing evidence has not been provided.

China had all the necessary conditions for exploring and discovering new worlds and benefiting from them long before the Europeans could reach them but it was not going to be the case. In 1436 an imperial edict forbade the construction of ships and a substantial part of the Chinese navy was dismantled. The reason for such drastic measure is the fact that the Mongols were threatening to invade the interior frontier. The emperor decided that in order to maintain the frontiers of his dominions it was imperative to focus on its defense and abandon vague projects of expansion across the seas. This was

---

* John Keay, *China: A History* (New York: HarperCollins, 2008).

a turning point in Chinese history. From then on China turned its back to the world, and the most advanced civilization became stagnant. The nation that for so long had the potential to acquire world hegemony as an imperial power merely became passive object of the great European powers.

For many centuries Europe was more backward than the Chinese and lacked the expansive capacity of the Islamic civilization. The key to explain how this relatively small continent mainly populated by backward peoples was transformed into a civilization that was to shape the world is in the Renaissance.

The Renaissance is the most extraordinary cultural movement in history. It led to the discovery of the human being in all its dimensions, and ultimately to the discovery of the world. It produced a new mode of thinking that was to distinguish European civilization and eventually give it a leading edge over all others. It allowed Europeans to use knowledge and culture as a means for self-improvement, growth, and expansion. The scientific inventions and technical innovations that it generated brought great improvements in peoples' lives and led to a more sophisticated level of civilization. The changes this movement generated in all spheres of knowledge have been influencing humanity until the present.

The Renaissance began in Italy in the thirteenth century and it gradually spread through a great part of Europe until the sixteenth century. For this reason, Italy can claim to be the mother of modern Europe. It fulfilled all necessary conditions for inaugurating this new era. Its people lived on the ruins of the great Roman Empire, their Latin language gave them access to the documents that held all the secrets of the Roman-Greek civilization. Italy also had the Papacy in Rome, which was to act as bridge between this ancient civilization and the emerging one in Europe. Pope Julius II who commissioned Michelangelo with the decoration of the ceiling of the Sistine Chapel in the sixteenth century was determined to recover the architectural and artistic splendor of ancient Rome. The cities where this movement mainly took place, such as Florence, Venice, or Genoa, were all prosperous trading cities with a financial elite that was willing to invest in the promotion of art projects. Finally Italy was rich in natural talent, for it was in these cities where the most significant figures of the Renaissance lived. At this time

Italian cities became magnets attracting ambitious and adventurous people from diverse parts of Europe. They were also responsible for spreading the news of the Italian Peninsula's civilizing influence.

Petrarch, a fourteenth-century poet and scholar, devoted much of his work to reviving the cultural splendor of the Romans that had been lost in the dark ages, a term which he himself first used. He is considered as the father of humanism, the philosophy that places human beings at the center of everything, not just as a passive element of God's will or natural forces, inspired by Protagoras's quote that man is the measure of all things.

Humanism inspires Giovanni Pico della Mirandola's *Oration on the Dignity of Man*, published in 1493 as one of the most important texts of this era, which develops the concept of human personality and emphasizes the uniqueness and worth of individuals.*

The acquisition of knowledge is very much at the heart of the Renaissance and as a result of it Europe lays the foundations of a knowledge-based society. From the early years of the medieval era the first universities were created in places like Bologna, Salamanca, Oxford, Cambridge, Paris, and Heidelberg. The first communities of teachers and scholars exclusively devoted to learning and independent thinking, to a certain extent free from religious or political pressures, had a substantial impact on European culture. As a result of this it gradually became accepted among the elites that knowledge was the key to human progress and prosperity. The new man that this era aimed to produce had to be educated from childhood until youth, and the proper intellectual training ought to be acquired for society's most important professions. In this way universities became one of the key factors that gave Europeans an advantage over the rest of the world.

Scholasticism, the method of promoting critical thought, spread among the first universities in Europe, and its followers started traveling in order to meet each other and exchange ideas. In this way the first universities and their most notable scholars contributed to the spread of ideas around Europe. The greatest of all was Erasmus of Rotterdam, who took humanist thinking further than

---

* Jacques Barzun, *From Dawn to Decadence, 500 Years of Western Cultural Life: A Cultural History of Europe* (St. Louis: Turtleback Books, 2001).

anyone in his time. Born in Rotterdam in 1466 he mainly lived in Basel and traveled frequently to London and Cambridge, for which he described himself as a man of the world. As an ordained priest he criticized the superstition and corrupt practices of the Catholic Church and advocated a new scientific study of divinity, in this way leading a new trend of Christian humanism. His *Adagia*, a compilation of Greek and Latin proverbs that was published in 1508 was the world's first bestseller. Such widely used proverbs like, "In the kingdom of the blind the one eyed man is king," or "Where there is life there is hope," were passed from antiquity into our modern era mainly as a result of Erasmus. No wonder that Erasmus was the first humanist to earn a living from his writings.

Humanism and all the notable personalities that it produced during the Renaissance were responsible for a new frame of mind, which was to shape European civilization in modernity. As a result religious faith gradually moved away from superstition and became more influenced by reason, tradition was revived but it cohabitated with a great degree of innovation, and an inquisitive spirit led to extraordinary scientific breakthroughs. Above all humanism generated the growing conviction that humanity was capable of mastering the world in which it lived and that all spheres of life could be both controlled and improved.

Humanism explains the extraordinary works of art produced by the Renaissance that have been admired ever since, like the Old Sacristy in Florence, the Sistine Chapel in Rome, or the *Mona Lisa*. Their authors, Brunelleschi, Michelangelo, and Leonardo da Vinci acquired a reputation and celebrity that had been unprecedented in their professions. From then artists began to be seen as special individuals that deserved a prominent role in society. This idea has played a very important role in Western civilization until the present. A proof of this is the fact that in 2017 *Salvator Mundi*, a long-lost Leonardo da Vinci painting of Jesus Christ was sold at a Christie's auction for a record $450 million.

Technological advancement played an essential role in this era. Around the year 1300 Venetians invented the convex glass mirror. A century later mirrors were rapidly spreading through Europe. Those who could afford it, initially only monarchs and aristocrats, paid substantial amounts for acquiring this expensive metal device, which allowed them the privilege of looking at themselves. Until the invention of the mirror, people had been able to see their faces vaguely reflected in bronze or other metallic surfaces, or simply in water. But from the early fourteenth century peoples of Europe began to see how they actually were. This had a great impact on individual identity. Until then a person's identity was mainly acquired through interaction with other people. Mirrors on the other hand allowed people to see how they actually looked, and this played an important role in the rise of a new individualism. The fact that people became aware of their uniqueness as human beings contributed to their proper identification. In the Renaissance every person, regardless of social strata began to be known by a surname as well as a personal name. This had been the custom in ancient Rome, but only the royals and the nobility retained it until medieval times. From the thirteenth century, particularly in Italy and France, every person regardless of social origin began to use a second name, a nickname, or the place they came from as a surname, and this became hereditary. Individual and family identification was to have a substantial impact on every European society from then on, a name and a proper identity was no longer the privilege of kings, nobles, or popes.

Another major European invention of the fourteenth century was the clock. Other civilizations had developed methods for measuring time, as the Chinese did with sundials, but they were not as precise and efficient as the counterpoise clock that emerged in Europe at that time. From then any European city could not feel proud of itself unless it had one of these great clocks, usually in the façade of town hall or the church tower. Clocks reminded people of the importance of time in their daily lives, contributing to better organization and productivity. Measurement of time was improved by the Gregorian calendar, introduced by Pope Gregory XIII in 1582. It was an improved version of the Julian calendar that had been used since the times of Julius Caesar, and it was eventually to become the standard international civil calendar. From then on, time could be measured efficiently, just as people's ages.

The fifteenth century brought the most important agents of change. Printing, gunpowder, and the compass were described by philosopher Francis Bacon as the three inventions that changed the world.

Around the year 1440 Johannes Gutenberg, a goldsmith from Mainz in the Holy Roman Empire, invented a printing press with moveable and replaceable metal letters. Until then Europeans had been printing texts using a form of woodblock printing, similar to the Chinese method. But with Gutenberg's invention the press could be used as many times as necessary in order to print many different books. Printing became the first means of mass communication, allowing the production of books, periodicals, and newspapers in great numbers. In this way knowledge could be spread to the bulk of the population. With the exception of writing itself, no other invention has had such an impact on the history of culture as the printing press.

In 1455 Gutenberg tested the efficiency of his invention with the publication of a book that every good Christian wanted to read: the Bible. But the major breakthrough in the publishing world came with the appearance of vernacular Bibles. Only the educated elite could read Gutenberg's Bible, which was in Latin, but people from all over Europe wished to read the Bible in their own language. The first Bible in German was published in 1466 and versions in major European languages were soon to be published. Vernacular bibles had a snowball effect in the publishing world. As people bought vernacular bibles they also became interested in reading books on other subjects; the demand for books steadily increased from the end of the fifteenth century, giving birth to publishing as a major industry.

Publishing had other important benefits in society. It acted as a catalyst to scientific advancement. Major scientific works like Nicolaus Copernicus's book *On the Revolution of Celestial Spheres*, published in 1543, could be widely read by members of the scientific community. It also greatly limited the church's censorship capacity as books allowed scientific ideas to be rapidly spread.

Printing also contributed to the spread of literacy. As so much knowledge was transmitted in book form, reading began to be seen as an essential skill that every person ought to have. As a result of the spread of literacy people gave greater importance to the written word, a factor that very much changed the nature of the relationship between citizens and authorities. From the early fifteenth century most European authorities began to keep records of people's births, marriages, and deaths. This also contributed to enhancing individual identities, among other advantages. Finally, a less obvious consequence was to strengthen the role of women in society and improve their relationship with men. Europeans had always given women a more important role than other civilizations. Such powerful positions as those of Queen Isabella of Castile, Elizabeth of England, or aristocrats like Caterina Sforza would have been inconceivable in China, India, or even less in the Islamic world. Even so, women were still generally considered inferior to men in medieval Europe, but this gradually began to change with the proliferation of books. This allowed women—the minority of them who could read, of course—the same access to knowledge as men. It also afforded the most talented ones the opportunity to write books, which explains why from the sixteenth century on women authors began to emerge in Europe.

Gunpowder could not rank in importance with the printing press, but it did play an essential role in the emergence of Europe before other civilizations. In its basic form it probably reached Eastern Europe from China through the Silk Road. From the fifteenth century Europeans transformed it into an offensive and defensive weapon, and it was one of the factors that later made the military revolution possible, which played such an important role in Europe's expansion. By the end of that century, European troops were experimenting with mobile artillery, which allowed lighter and more efficient cannons to be transported. The full impact of European gunpowder was appreciated for the first time when King Charles VIII of France invaded Italy in 1494, with what has been described as the first modern army. It included batteries of light mobile bronze field artillery, which fired iron cannon balls rather than stones. They destroyed every castle they aimed at. A new age of warfare had begun. From then on cities were no longer invulnerable behind walls.

The magnetic compass was the other great technological innovation of this time. Just like gunpowder, it seems likely that this was initially an importation from the East as both the Chinese and the Arabs had used rudimentary compasses. An improved version, consisting of a needle suspended over a compass card came into being in the fourteenth century and became widely used a century later. This magnetic compass allowed European sailors reach further than those of any other civilization from the late fifteenth century. But more than this tool, it was the proliferation of knowledge about the geography of the world that stimulated them to venture into the seas in search of unknown lands.

Scholars and savants proliferating in the Renaissance provided diverse explanations about the shape and the size of the earth, and the possible existence of other continents. From then on, Europe took the lead over other civilizations in the knowledge of geography and cartography.

The Catalan Atlas, produced by a Majorcan chartmakers' school in 1375, constituted a major improvement in cartography by giving India its proper shape. Europeans at that time gave names to the continents by which they were later universally known. Asia was named after the daughter of King Oceanus mentioned in a Greek myth, just as Europa was named after the daughter of King Agenor. Africa was the name by which the Romans referred to Tunisia and from this time it began to be used to describe the whole continent.

After Ptolemy's treatise *Geographica* was translated into Latin by Giacomo di Scarperia in 1406, the idea that the world was round was gradually to be accepted by the scientific community. Furthermore it prompted a debate on what lay beyond the borders of the known world. Particularly influential in this sphere was the work *Imago Mundi* written by the French cosmographer Pierre d´Ailly in 1410, which defended the theory that the world was asymmetric and that there were four continents in the world. This information began to be widely circulated when the first books on this subject were published toward the end of the fifteenth century. From then many poor sailors began to think of the fortune-making opportunities that could be found by reaching unknown territories. This eventually led to the first voyages that were to change the fate of Europe in the world.

The modern state began to be conceived during the fifteenth century. This was mainly thanks to Niccolò Machiavelli, another of the great minds of the Renaissance who has been considered the father of modern political science. Machiavelli worked as a senior official for the Florentine republic and also served as a diplomat in Rome. His magnum opus, *The Prince*, published in 1513, was very much inspired by the brutal methods of Pope Alexander VI and his son Cesare Borgia, which he witnessed when he was posted in Rome.

The Prince is basically a guide on how to acquire and maintain political power. As the first political empiricist, Machiavelli based his recommendations on how people actually behaved in real life. "It is much safer for the prince to be feared than loved, but he ought to avoid making himself hated."* Quotations like this explain why this book has become one of the great classics of all time. From Henry VIII to Napoleon and Stalin, a wide range of statesmen from all over the world have not only read *The Prince*, but they have used it as a basic reference book to guide their careers.

Machiavelli's *Prince* is one of the books that have been subject to most intense debate in history, as it is open to the widest interpretations. It is not clear whether it is a satire of the excesses of power or a compendium of good advice for potential governors on how to exert power.

Although Machiavelli was criticized for justifying duplicity and immoral behavior in politics, philosophers from Francis Bacon to Jean-Jacques Rousseau admired this work for describing the realities of statecraft and also exposing the faults of one-man rule. Above all Machiavelli made two essential contributions to modern politics: first, that politicians and their decisions have deep consequences on peoples' lives; and second, he defined the state as a territory in which an organized community exists under one government. Society was never the same from the moment people became aware that the way they lived was not a consequence of a divinely ordained plan, and that their community needed to be ruled by laws and regulations that protected the general interest from personal ambitions and human whims.

The economy had a leading role in the transformation of Europe during this era. The Renaissance could not have taken place without the contribution of bankers and wealthy philanthropists, opening up vast possibilities for the creation of beauty and the expansion of human knowledge. The financial world experienced a notable transformation from the thirteenth to the fifteenth century, laying the foundation of the market economy as we know it today. Some elements of the financial world that made this possible were imported from the East. Leonardo of Pisa (or Fibonacci) studied Hindi-Arabic numerals and introduced it in the book of calculation,

---

* Niccolò Machiavelli, *The Prince* (New York: Penguin Classics, 2011).

published in 1202. Fibonacci was not only responsible for giving Europe the decimal system, which makes calculation easier than Roman numerals, it also shows how it can be applied to commercial bookkeeping.*

Banking as we know it today emerged during the Renaissance. Venice, a great trading center open to Eastern influences, became the world's great lending laboratory. This explains why William Shakespeare was inspired by this city to create the most famous moneylender in Western literature: the Merchant of Venice. Here moneylenders made the transition to become bankers by developing the idea of credit, and propagating wealth in society as a result of it. One of the major obstacles for the emergence of modern banking was the fact that Christianity, just like Islam, condemned as usury the charging of interest. But shrewd lenders found ways of benefitting from lending money in a more subtle way by calling the benefit obtained from lending money *discrezione,* which was a compensation for the risk of lending money. It was in Venice where bankers began to be called by such a term, because they literally sat on a bench *(banco)* in front of a table, usually in marketplaces looking for customers. Bankers and merchants soon started using what became known in Genoa as the double-entry method, with credits and debits (*credito* and *debito* in Italian) arranged in a way that greatly increased accounting efficiency and eventually became universal.

A family that became particularly talented in all these skills associated with moneylending was the Medici, the first great banking family in history. The Medicis were originally foreign exchange dealers and moneylenders working in Florence. Among the customers of Giovanni de' Medici were several cardinals. He also betted on the return of the Papacy to Rome at the time of the great Western schism. He was rewarded by Pope Martin V, who appointed him his banker in 1417. The Papacy constantly needed more income throughout the fifteenth century in its determination to increase its power and influence. Financing the pope's wishes and needs was an extremely profitable business that allowed the Medicis to become Italy's richest bankers. By the time Giovanni passed the business on to his eldest son Cosimo, he had

---

* Niall Ferguson, *The Ascent of Money: A Financial History of the World* (New York: Penguin, 2008).

established a branch in Venice and Rome and later added branches in Geneva, London, and Avignon. The Medicis were the first family to win princely status not by warfare, marriage, or inheritance but through commerce. They were also pioneers in philanthropy. Their patronage was responsible for some of the most extraordinary works of art during the Renaissance and it very much helped to create an atmosphere where arts and humanism could flourish.

The person who really showed the power of money in the modern era was Jacob Fugger, who has been described as the world's first modern capitalist. The Fuggers, a German merchant family that made a fortune in the textile industry, was a very good example of how rapidly money could change a family's status during the Renaissance. Jacob Fugger went even further than the Medicis, for he became the banker of the Habsburg Emperor Charles V, who also inherited the Spanish crown and was therefore the most powerful man of his time. "It is well known that without me your majesty might not have acquired the imperial crown," Fugger dared to write to the emperor. This was no exaggeration, for he had financed the Habsburg family in their rise to power, and he was to finance everything from wars to castle building projects that consolidated the power of the Habsburgs. In this way Fugger was the creator of the sovereign debt, an essential instrument to finance the modern state, which was also to become a nightmare for future heads of government.

Fugger can also be regarded as one of the first venture capitalists, giving money to those who came up with risky but potentially profitable ideas in return for a share of the business. Such was the case of Ferdinand Magellan's first circumnavigation of the globe.* The relationship established between prominent businessmen like Fugger and navigators and explorers was to have a vital importance in Europe's ascendancy, for it made possible the discovery of the world.

Families like the Medicis and the Fuggers were the most notable examples of social climbing and acquiring power by means of financial success. At a

---

* Greg Steinmetz, *The Richest Man Who Ever Lived: The Life and Times of Jacob Fugger* (New York: Simon & Schuster, 2015).

much modest level, peoples of Europe during the Renaissance learned how to earn a living in the trading or financial spheres, and used money for improving their position in society. Money was the great equalizer that allowed different social classes to establish a relationship in which there were simply buyers and sellers or lenders and borrowers. Feudalism, in which it was almost impossible for members of the lower strata to improve their station in life, gradually gave way to a new society in which the rules of the market economy prevailed. This contributed to the proliferation of fortune-seekers who came up with money-making ideas in their own land, and were also particularly eager to travel the world in search of riches and open new markets. They were ultimately responsible for opening the trade routes that changed the fate of Europe.

The culture of the Renaissance led to a major event that had deep consequences in the history of Europe: the Reformation. In 1517 Martin Luther, a professor of theology and priest from Wittenberg, published the *Ninety-five Theses*, denouncing the corruption of the Catholic church. The *Ninety-five Theses* is one of the most influential documents in the history of humanity. In particular it criticized the Church's habit of selling indulgences, which according to Luther was nothing more than a ploy to make money. Luther went even further by asking uncomfortable questions like to what extent was the pope an example of Christian virtue, and ultimately how could he forgive people for their sins when only God could do so.

Luther was not only excommunicated by the pope due to the *Ninety-five Theses* but his writings were banned. Nevertheless he was not alone in voicing criticism of the church. The Protestant revolt rapidly spread across Europe. Proliferation of vernacular bibles and books that allowed people to acquire knowledge and think for themselves explains its popular appeal. The critical stage was reached when even monarchs supported Protestantism. In 1534 King Henry VIII declared himself head of the church in England, refusing to obey the Catholic Church's authority. Shortly after, Denmark followed the same path.

The schism in the church provoked by the reformation led to wars and persecution that lasted for over one hundred years. Christendom, which had already been divided into two halves, the Catholics and the Orthodox, was then further split into three with the rise of Protestantism.

Christendom ceased to be what unified Europeans, and as a result people no longer talked about Christendom in relation to the common territory where they lived, but about Europe. Catholicism, Protestantism, or one of the sects of Protestantism (and the Orthodox toward the East) became one of the key factors defining kingdoms and nations emerging in Europe. The fact that as a result of the reformation the pope was no longer recognized as an authority in several kingdoms in northern Europe had deep impact on the formation of the modern state. The Treaty of Augsburg in 1555 brought an end to hostilities between the Lutheran states in Germany and Charles V of Spain, who was head of the Holy Roman Empire. Peace was made under the maxim of *cuius regio, eius religio* (literally, who rules his religion), a recognition of the right of the sovereign of each country to chose the religion of his people. The power and independence acquired by rulers of Protestant territories because of this treaty had deep consequences in modern European history.

Deep rivalry among them played a very important role in the modern world. While the Protestant North struggled for independence from Catholicism, its peoples also showed increasing eagerness to create wealth, which explains the rise of the ethic of thrift and hard work with which the great sociologist Max Weber identified Protestants. Catholics reacted with the Counter-Reformation, which was an attempt to reform and reinvigorate itself. The Jesuits played a leading role in this process. This new religious order was founded by the Basque priest Ignatius of Loyola in 1540, an elite corps within Catholicism, focusing on education and missionary activity. Within a few decades after their founding Jesuits were all over the world, propagating Christianity and educating the young. In parallel, Protestant missions were also to proliferate through the world from then on. The European continent was deeply divided between nations competing against each other for power and influence. Not only did they struggle for supremacy in Europe but also in the rest of the world, as we shall later see. This was one of the major reasons why Europe was to shape the world over the following centuries.

The scientific revolution constitutes the definitive contribution to the modern world view. Nicolaus Copernicus initiated this drastic break with the ancient and medieval frame of mind and the entrance into modernity.

The great Polish astronomer and mathematician, born in Prussia in 1493, focused his career on proving that the Sun was at the center of the universe, rather than the Earth, as it had been widely believed until then. The publication of Copernicus's book *On the Revolution of Celestial Spheres* in 1543 marks the beginning of a long struggle between science and religious bigotry. Some decades later the Italian polymath Galileo Galilei took the Copernican model and scientific mind to new heights. Galileo was condemned to house arrest by the Inquisition for defending Copernicus's theories. But this constituted no impediment to his extraordinary career, for which he was to be known as the father of astronomy. He was one of the first scientists to use a reflecting telescope, made by him to observe the stars, and also made groundbreaking contributions to physics.

The revolution culminates with the English scientist Isaac Newton, who has been described as the greatest scientist of all time. His main work, *The Mathematical Principles of Natural Philosophy*, published in 1687, formulates the laws of motion and universal gravitation that were to dominate physics for over three centuries. Although Copernicus, Galileo, and Newton are the most conspicuous figures of this scientific revolution, several others made extraordinary breakthroughs in the spheres of medicine, biology, anatomy, chemistry, and geology throughout the seventeenth century.

European scientists in this era also contributed to the establishment of a very important principle: that religion and science ought to be separated, as they could not be made compatible. This principle was also to be extended to the affairs of the state and the realm of politics. This separation eventually became a characteristic of the entire Western world.

The rise of the first scientific academies in Europe also contributed to free and independent thinking. The first one was the Leopoldina, Academia Naturae Curiosorum, founded in 1652 in Germany; the Royal Society, founded in London in 1660; and the French Académie de Sciences, founded in 1666.

The scientific revolution would not have been possible without a new scientific method that emerged from the trends in philosophical thought in the seventeenth century. One of the main proponents of this method was the English philosopher Francis Bacon, the father of empiricism, who argued that science must be based on observation of facts, from which theory can be adduced. These ideas, which are commonplace now, were groundbreaking at that time. French philosopher René Descartes laid the foundations of rationalism, which regards reason as the chief test of knowledge. One of his most influential works, *Discourse on the Method* opened new paths in the search of truth. His famous proposition, *cogito ergo sum* (I think therefore I am), has been learned by every student of philosophy in the Western world, as an example of a truth that is incontrovertible. For all these reasons Descartes is considered as the father of modern western philosophy.

While these philosophers laid the foundations of the modern scientific method and philosophical thought, others began to conceive new forms of government that were to influence theorists and government practitioners until our day.

In 1516 the English statesman Thomas More published a book describing Utopia, an imaginary land with the ideal form of government, in which property is held in common, both men and women benefitted from universal education, and all religions are tolerated. *Utopia*, which became a European bestseller in the mid-sixteenth century, marks the beginning of a search for an ideal government that has existed in the public sphere in the Western world until today. More was also the first to describe a model of society in which there was no private property.

Over a century later, another Englishman, philosopher Thomas Hobbes, published *Leviathan* in 1651, in which he justifies a very different form of government: absolutism. His work was inspired by the chaos and the horrors that he witnessed during the English civil war. In his view, war where every man is enemy to every man is caused by the absence of a strong authority. He therefore justified the need for a king to exert his rights, which ought to be unlimited, to rule over the people. A Leviathan, "a monster composed of men," is his metaphor for the absolutist state—the only solution to prevent war and guarantee stability in society. With this book, however abhorrent to those who believed in individual liberties, Hobbes gave birth to the social contract theory and is also considered one of the founders of political philosophy.

While philosophers speculated on the ideal society and the role of the state, other authors gave free rein to their imagination, giving birth to national literatures of Europe. Italian literature, another great product of the Renaissance, begins with Dante Alighieri, who published his famous *Divine Comedy* in vernacular language. From then on authors began to express themselves in their own languages rather than in Latin. The printing press constituted a great encouragement for authors, and as a result of this, the sixteenth century saw the launch of full-blown national literatures in Europe. Consequently, popular literature became one of the essential attributes of any nation. Poetry and drama were the most popular literary genres. This explains the success of Christopher Marlowe and Shakespeare in England, or later Molière and Jean Racine in France. But memoirs and biographies also become fashionable very much as a result of the characteristic individualism created by the Renaissance. The autobiography of the Florentine artist Benvenuto Cellini, published in 1566, constituted a new way of expression and influencing people: simply telling about one's life and explaining why it was important. From then on, in the same way that notable personages commissioned a portrait of themselves to be remembered in posterity, those who were more intellectually gifted would write their memoirs.

A few decades later a Spanish author, Miguel de Cervantes published *Don Quixote* in 1604, which was an immediate success and was later translated into all major languages of the world. This book inaugurated a new genre: the novel, which eventually became the most popular literary genre in modern history. Fiction expressed in literary masterpieces became a very important channel by which Europeans were to influence modern minds throughout the world.

It is against the backdrop of the scientific revolution that Europe's military revolution took place. As a result, European powers acquired military potential and expertise that allowed them to dominate the world until the twentieth century. Technological advances gave way to remarkable improvements in gunpowder weapons and other military tools. The Swedes gained ascendancy in artillery techniques. During the reign of Louis XIV the French adopted the bayonet, and their infantry acquired an edge over the rest. England focused on navy improvements, which eventually allowed it to rule the waves. Innovations in galleon design allowed English ships to become faster and lighter, and at the same time have sufficient capacity to carry heavier guns. The first big battleships were made by the English and then imitated by rival European powers.

Military techniques radically changed due to technological innovations. The lance and pike were replaced by the arrow and musket, and gunpowder became the essential tool that determined military power. Armies increased in size by an extraordinary degree throughout Europe. Between 1600 and 1700 armies in most European countries increased over five times.*

The phenomenal growth of European armies would not have been possible without much greater wealth, as well as the increasing power and efficiency of state bureaucracies. In order to fund forces, taxes had to be collected on a much larger scale. The creation of a modern bureaucracy was fostered by the military exigencies of this era. Also the first permanent parliaments were to be justified by the needs of the armies, as sovereigns needed to justify both taxation and war before the nobles and the church. In this way the military revolution played a very important role in the emergence of the modern state.

There is an obvious reason why Europeans on the whole acquired this extraordinary superiority of weapons in the seventeenth century, for there were only three years in which there was no fighting, from 1669 to 1671. The rest of the time most of the European peoples were at war with each other and military innovations combined with the size of the armies determined who would emerge victorious. It is difficult to say which European country had the best army by the end of the century, but what is certain is that they were much stronger than those of other civilizations. This is proved by the last Turkish siege of Vienna in 1683. On that occasion a Polish-German force of 68,000 easily defeated the Ottoman troops of over 150,000. At the Battle of Zenta, on September 11, 1697, 20,000 Turks were killed, putting an end to the Turkish aspiration of expanding across Europe. It was no coincidence that 304 years later the notorious Al-Qaeda terrorist attacks on the United States took place on September 11. Islamic terrorists were hoping that this date would mark the return of Islam at the cost of Western supremacy.

---

* Geoffrey Parker, *Military Revolution: Military Innovation and the Rise of the West, 1500–1800* (Cambridge, England: Cambridge University Press, 1996).

The Renaissance changed the fate of Europe, from a relatively backward, inward-looking civilization, fighting on the defensive against incursions from south or east, to one that was secure of itself, proud of its achievements, and willing to expand all over the world.

The cultural revolution that takes place in Europe from the thirteenth to the seventeenth century places the individual at the center of society, promotes a limitless curiosity, and develops a new method of thinking. As a result the modern mind emerged. This led to an outpouring of intellectual innovation and creativity that has no precedent in history, allowing Europe to excel in all spheres of knowledge.

The market economy, the state, and the knowledge-based society are three major products of the Renaissance that allowed Europeans to take the lead over all other civilizations. The new era of geographic exploration that begins in Europe in the mid–fifteenth century is very much the consequence of all this. But it was an unexpected geographic discovery in 1492 that allowed Europeans to expand their power and influence beyond their wildest dreams.

Chapter 2

As Far as It Is Possible for a Man to Go

How Geographic Discoveries Laid the Foundations of European Hegemony.

On October 12, 1492, three caravels captained by Christopher Columbus reached an unknown island after sailing toward the west for sixty-nine days. Columbus had very good reasons to be exultant when he set foot on that island, for he believed that he had found a new route to Asia that would earn him the fame and fortune that he had been craving all his life. But his discovery was more important than he could ever imagine, for it was not a new path to Asia that he had discovered but a new continent.

Few dates have had deeper significance in the history of the world as the discovery of America. The discovery of this continent constituted the beginning of an era of expansion that would lead Europeans to enjoy world hegemony for several centuries. It was also a date that was going to mark the beginning of our modern era, an era in which Europe laid the foundations of our contemporary global civilization.

Columbus mainly owed this extraordinary achievement to his intelligence, perseverance, and knowledge, but also to the kingdom of Castile. Its sovereign aimed at expanding its frontiers and had the courage to endorse the very attractive but also extremely risky venture proposed by this Genoese sailor. It was the result of a combination of statecraft, patronage, technological innovation, and humanistic curiosity that the prodigious era of the Renaissance brought together. But why had Europe, and no other civilization before it, managed to reach and become aware of the existence of such a vast continent as America?

Europe is not as richly endowed with territory, fauna, flora, and mineral resources as other continents. But to compensate for this apparent geographic disadvantage Europeans had a very important asset in the race for world hegemony: they had more maritime communities than any other civilization. From the times of the ancient world diverse European peoples had grown and thrived around strategic coastal areas. City-states like Venice or Genoa, or kingdoms like Aragon and Portugal, owed their prosperity to maritime trade networks. After centuries profiting from voyages around the Mediterranean and neighboring seas, by the fifteenth century many of these peoples were eager to venture into further overseas exploration. The era of great geographic discoveries was set to take place in Europe.

The small kingdom of Portugal was going to be the pioneer in the movement of European expansion through the world. It was not as prosperous and powerful as France, England, or the rest of the kingdoms in the Iberian Peninsula, but it was more unified and cohesive. With an extensive Atlantic coast in the west and relative proximity to the African coast in the south, its geographic position gave Portugal a great advantage in order to lead what would later be known as the era of geographic discoveries. Their long maritime tradition contributed to their superiority in boat construction and sailing technology in the fifteenth century: the caravel was their invention, a lighter, highly maneuverable, and faster sailing ship that would allow them to reach further than any other nation. In 1415, under the kingdom of John

I, Portugal made its first incursion into Africa with the seizure of Ceuta on the northern African coast, and the establishment of a settlement there. It was hoped that this strategic enclave near the Strait of Gibraltar would strengthen their position vis-à-vis other Mediterranean commercial powers like Genoa and Venice. Shortly thereafter the Portuguese established agrarian colonies on islands like the Azores and Madeira. But this was only going to be the beginning of an extraordinary process of expansion that led Portugal to establish settlements in remote places and open horizons for the Europeans that would radically alter their destiny.

The rise of Portugal in the world took place mainly as a result of the initiatives of King John's son, Prince Henry, better known as Henry the Navigator despite the fact that he hardly ever left his country. Henry the Navigator was a typical representative of European royalty in the modern era: Portuguese, English, French, and Spanish blood ran through his veins. He was, as it could be expected from someone in his position, a good patriot and a devout Christian. But he was to stand out among the European royals due to his interest in the world of commerce, a topic that did not usually attract those who were born into ruling families. This made him support Portuguese expansion projects throughout the world with the eagerness of a present-day businessman. The reasons that led him to support expeditions to the south of the Azores were mainly commercial: obtain great benefits from the spice trade and discover new trade routes. But there were also religious and strategic reasons, for he wished to know how big the Muslim world was, and wanted to take Christendom to these lands, and at the same time find out if there were Christians with which he could make alliances.

In 1434 the Portuguese managed to sail around Cape Bojador in western Africa. One decade later, in 1444, Nuno Tristão reached the Senegal River, and shortly after Dinis Dias took possession of Cape Verde, which would become a colony of great importance for Portugal. Shortly after, Henry the Navigator was granted by the pope the right to exert sovereignty over all lands discovered by Portugal, from Africa to India.

As a result of this extraordinary success in journeys of discovery, and the papal blessings, it is not surprising that after Prince Henry's death in 1460 the crown continued to support the exploration projects with great enthusiasm. In 1469 King Alfonso V who would go down in history as "the African," granted trading and exploitation rights to a merchant named Fernando Gomes on the condition that every year he would explore one hundred leagues of territory. Gomes fulfilled his promise and reached the so-called Gold Coast in 1470. In 1481 Diego de Azambuja traveled with the aim of exploiting the west coast of Africa and founded San Jorge de la Mina, the first Portuguese settlement on the African continent. He was accompanied in this journey by two sailors that some years later would become much more famous than him: Bartolomeu Dias and Christopher Columbus. Particularly important were Diogo Cão's journeys through Africa. Cão delved into the heart of what was considered the dark continent, and reached the estuary of the Congo River, establishing the first contacts with the remote Congolese kingdom in present-day Angola. In this way the colonization of the most important Portuguese colony in the continent was going to start.[*]

In 1487 a Portuguese sailor marked another milestone in European exploration. Bartolomeu Dias managed to be the first European to sail across the southern border of the African continent through the Cape of Good Hope and reach the waters of the Indian Ocean. He failed in his aim of reaching India due to a water shortage and many harrowing experiences suffered on this long journey. He was forced by circumstances to give up and sail back home, but made a triumphal entrance into Lisbon in 1488, giving the good news that he had opened up a new route toward India from the south of the African continent.[**]

While Portugal had consolidated a leading position in the era of discovery, due to the formidable achievements of its most talented navigators, the neighboring kingdom of Castile experienced a meteoric rise in its status, mainly thanks to the contribution of Christopher Columbus.

Who was Christopher Columbus? Columbus was not only one of the great personages of his time but also the one who has inspired most literature due to the deep consequences of his discovery. He himself left several written works about his voyages and achievements. However, several stages of his life

---

[*] A. H. de Oliveira Marques, *History of Portugal* (New York: Columbia University Press, 1972).

[**] Roger Crowley, *Conquerors: How Portugal Forged the First Global Empire* (London: Faber and Faber, 2015).

have been subject to intense debate, among them his birth and origins. His son Ferdinand did not specify Columbus's place of birth in the biography that he dedicated to his father, which provoked all sorts of speculation about where the famous sailor was born. There are several peoples in Europe who have claimed to include Columbus among their prominent members. It has been said that Columbus was from Majorca, Catalonia, Greece, even France, Scotland, and Poland, while other sources claim that he was Jewish. But his most prestigious biographers seem to agree that he was born in Genoa in 1453, into a humble family.* He was the son of a weaver, and did not receive any formal education although he showed great eagerness to learn. He had delusions of grandeur from a very early age and always aimed to leave a deep mark in his time. This is why he decided to become a sailor, as it was one of the few professions that, in his circumstances, would allow him to climb the social ladder and make his dreams come true.

Columbus started sailing "from a very small age," according to his own account, and consequently by the time he was thirty he had acquired a broad experience as a sailor, having reached the coast of Guinea in the south and Iceland in the north. Just like many sailors of his time, he frequently asked himself about what there could be west of where his contemporaries usually sailed in the Atlantic. As he considered his profession a way of discovering the secrets of the world, he was particularly interested in the theories of the world's geography.

Columbus was familiar with the scientific theories about the shape of the earth that became a common subject of discussion among sailors meeting in taverns around ports. Particularly influential for Columbus was Pierre d'Ailly's work *Imago Mundi*, which defended the theory that the world was asymmetric and that there were four continents in the world. This knowledge, and above all his intuition as a sailor, would lead him to conclude that sailing toward the west it was possible to reach the Asian coast, and more precisely Zipangu, the land of God, the old name given Japan by the Europeans.

After conceiving such a bold and adventurous plan Columbus's next aim was to find a state willing to sponsor it, for sailors in those days, as well as

---

* Felipe Fernández-Armesto, *Columbus* (London: Oxford University Press, 1991).

artists, had no nationalist prejudices on looking for economic support that would make their projects possible. Any major European state could sponsor a journey of discovery, for all of them shared the same expansionist aims and also a very similar concept of civilization to promote in the rest of the world. The main candidates were Portugal, Castile, France, and England. Portugal, a pioneer in the era of discoveries and the first naval power, was the one that offered better prospects of success, so the Genoese sailor traveled to the court of John II in Lisbon, but he was turned down by the Portuguese king, for he was asking for too many rewards for such a risky venture. After failing with Portugal, Columbus contemplated the possibility of offering the project to other crowns, and even to his native Genoa, but he finally focused on the neighboring Iberian kingdom of Castile, and not only for reasons of proximity. The young and intelligent Queen Isabella of Castile, who was married to the ambitious King Ferdinand of Aragon, was eager to expand the power of her kingdom and was therefore likely to support Columbus's plans.

The aspirations of this foreigner with visionary airs and an arrogant tone did not have a positive impact on the court of Castile, but he would eventually be compensated for his perseverance. In 1492, Castilian and Aragonese troops conquered the last Muslim territory of the Iberian Peninsula. Shortly thereafter Columbus was summoned to Granada. In this city Queen Isabella decided to accept the project of the Genoese sailor, despite the reticence of her advisers, and she gave him what he demanded in exchange: the title of admiral and viceroy of the conquered lands, and ten percent of all benefits for him and his descendants. (Initially he had asked for twenty-five percent.) This was all a very high price to pay, but it must be taken into account that he, like the majority of the conquistadors who succeeded him, risked not only all that they owned but their own lives in such adventures.

Why did Queen Isabella decide to support Columbus? The euphoria of the Catholic kings after reconquering Granada must have influenced their decision, for after this success their dreams of conquering new lands on behalf of their kingdom and Christianity knew no limits. If Columbus's journey succeeded, Castile would obtain extraordinary benefits, and for this reason it was worth taking the risks despite the fact that their advisers disapproved of it.

On the other hand, sponsoring Columbus's journey did not imply a heavy burden for the crown of Castile. Despite the legend that Queen Isabella had to pawn her jewels in order to pay for it, the truth is that money did not come from the royal coffers but from the ship owner Vicente Yáñez Pinzón and his brothers. The Pinzon brothers not only provided the money for this great adventure but actually took part in it. Vicente Yáñez Pinzón was the captain of one of the three caravels in which they sailed, the *Pinta*.

As regards the crew, Christopher Columbus had considerable difficulty finding volunteers to embark on such a risky voyage. No soldiers or possible settlers were included, as this was a voyage of exploration, and a royal pardon to prisoners in jail who enrolled in this adventure allowed Columbus to recruit men from among the delinquent population.

The three famous caravels set out from the Andalusian port of Palos de la Frontera on August 3, 1492. Thanks to Columbus's habit of leaving written records of all his maritime experiences we know a lot about all that happened in this long voyage of discovery, including his thoughts and fears.* After a few weeks in the Atlantic a critical period was reached when some members of the crew started to express their concern that their foreign commander would not lead them to the promised land, but rather to death. Columbus had to impose his will on several occasions to prevent a mutiny on board. After all, the route that Columbus followed was based on his own intuition and the interpretation of scientific theories that had not been proved.

On October 12 Columbus and his crew saw for the first time land in what would be known as the New World, and shortly after that they disembarked on the continent that was to change the destiny of Western civilization. It was a small island situated in the present-day Bahamas, and was named San Salvador. It was in this island where the first encounter in recorded history took place between the white man and the indigenous peoples of the American continent. From then on they were commonly known as Indians, precisely because Columbus insisted that he had reached the Indies.

Columbus spent the first three months exploring the territories that he had discovered. One of the islands was named Hispaniola (the present-day

---

* Fernandéz-Armesto, *Columbus.*

Dominican Republic and Haiti), where he built a fort called La Navidad (Christmas), which constituted the first settlement of the Europeans in the New World. On March 15, 1493, Columbus made a triumphal entry into the port of Palos de la Frontera in southern Spain, and shortly afterward was received by Queen Isabella and King Ferdinand in Barcelona. He brought with him a few Indians, some parrots, and beads made out of gold to the court, with which he aimed to prove that the prospects for wealth creation in the lands he had reached were very considerable. After Columbus's return, the news of his discovery rapidly spread across western Europe. Nevertheless, the lands that Columbus had explored were subject to great controversy. Several people among the royal entourage argued that the Genoese sailor did not deserve much credit for having simply discovered a few islands toward the west of the Canary Islands. Be that as it may, for Queen Isabella the evidence provided by Columbus was enough to convince her of the importance of this discovery and grant him the rewards he had demanded. His dreams of wealth and glory and founding a dynasty as a result of his discoveries were going to come true.

On September 25, 1493, Christopher Columbus set out on the second journey to the New World, as the discovered lands were to be known. The admiral sailed south of his normal route, and this allowed him to discover the coast of present-day Venezuela and penetrate the delta of one of the great South American rivers: the Orinoco. Impressed by the immense landmass that seemed to have no end, on August 13 he wrote in his diary one of the most important sentences in the history of exploration: "I believe that this is a great continent that up to now has remained unknown."* He continued thinking that the islands that he had discovered previously belonged to Asia but, after sailing across the enormous coast of Venezuela, he reached the conclusion that he was before a new continent.

Columbus was authorized by the queen to make two more journeys to the New World. In the last one, in 1502, he explored the isthmus of Central America, from where he reached the province of Veragua, among present-day Panama and Costa Rica, which were especially rich in gold deposits. His aim

---

*   Fernandéz-Armesto, *Columbus.*

was to return to Spain with a great shipment of the precious metals, which would finally convince all his adversaries about the extraordinary prospects for wealth offered by the New World, but the tropical weather stood in the way. Storms prevented the members of this expedition from disembarking in such a promising land. A ship was lost and the fleet ended up shipwrecked in Jamaica. On top of this Columbus had to repel an attack of indigenous peoples in this island and suppress a mutiny among his men. In spite of all adversity, Columbus managed to explore the Central American coast to the northern limit, and prove that from present-day Honduras to Brazil, there was a great landmass. All this helped reaffirm his conclusion that he had discovered a new continent.

Christopher Columbus died in 1506 shortly after returning to Spain from his last crossing to the New World. By the time of his death he was a wealthy man and had managed to establish his family among the Castilian aristocracy, but he left this world with the sad feeling of not having earned sufficient recognition for his geographic discoveries. Nevertheless, his place in history was to become increasingly more important as time passed. In the early twentieth century October 12, the date when Columbus arrived in America, was officially established as Spain's national day, in this way the Spaniards paid homage to the man who changed the country's fate and allowed it to transform itself into a global empire. Long before Spain several countries in Latin America had been celebrating this date under the proud title of the "day of the race." It was later to be celebrated under the less controversial and more friendly name of the *Hispanidad*, "the day of the Spanish-speaking people." Yet for many people in Latin America, the day of Columbus's arrival in America did not deserve to be commemorated. For this reason in 2002 the Bolivarian Republic of Venezuela decided to rename this date as "the day of indigenous resistance," to honor the native peoples' resistance to European settlement that was to follow Columbus's arrival.

On the other hand in the United States the Genoese navigator is remembered every year on Columbus Day, which is celebrated with special enthusiasm by the Italian-American community, proud of the fact that a native from Genoa discovered America. A Latin American country received its name in his honor: Colombia. Nevertheless, for reasons that we shall see later, the continent was not named after the Genoese admiral but after a Florentine adventurer—much less talented as a sailor and discoverer—who arrived in the New World several years later: Amerigo Vespucci. Regardless of the recent attempts to vilify Columbus and make him primarily responsible for the decimation of the indigenous population, he must be seen as one of the most prominent figures of the Renaissance, whose vision contributed in a very special way to lay the foundations of the contemporary globalized world.

While Spain started to enjoy the benefits of having discovered America, Portugal was not lagging behind. The king of Portugal was outraged by Pope Alexander VI's decision to grant Castile all sovereignty over the discovered lands in the New World, for he argued that his kingdom had led the era of discoveries. To put an end to the dispute between the two Iberian kingdoms, on June 7, 1494, the Treaty of Tordesillas was signed, which established a dividing line between the Azores and Hispaniola. All territories to the west of this imaginary line would be Spanish and those on the east belonged to Portugal. In this way, the world beyond the European continent became a duopoly blessed by the pope. Apart from claiming a substantial part of the New World for Portugal, in 1498 a Portuguese subject managed to make a discovery that was almost as important as Columbus's, and it was to play a crucial role in the relationship between East and West: the route to India bordering Africa.

On July 8, 1497, a sailor named Vasco da Gama set out on one of the most fascinating and significant voyages in history. Da Gama had been born in 1460 in Sines, a city of great maritime tradition, and he inherited the project of sailing toward India from his father, a powerful man who had originally proposed it to King Manuel I.

Vasco da Gama set out with a fleet of four ships. On November 7 he reached a place that he named as St. Helena Bay, on the coast of South Africa, after having reached a record of ninety-six days at sea without seeing land. In January 1499 he managed to sail across the dangerous Cape of Good Hope with better fortune than his predecessor Bartolomeu Dias. From there his crew sailed in waters that were previously unknown to the Europeans. Present-day Natal was given this name by da Gama as he sailed past its coast on Christmas.

On March 2 the fleet arrived in Mozambique, and he was surprised to discover that the inhabitants were of mixed race and spoke Arabic. A month later Vasco da Gama reached a town, Mombasa in present-day Kenya, where he was received with hostility by the inhabitants. For this reason he had to leave in a rush and sail up the coast until they reached Malindi on April 23, a peaceful town of white buildings. There, the so-called raja who ruled over the territory welcomed them at the harbor, and Vasco da Gama responded to his hospitality allowing him to inspect the Portuguese fleet. In Malindi they also discovered that there was an Indian who had converted to Christianity, an encouraging sign for propagating their faith as they were meant to do.

From Malindi the Portuguese sailed toward the Arabian Sea, and after three weeks without seeing land, Vasco da Gama and his fleet became the first Europeans in recorded history to see the southwestern coast of the Indian subcontinent.[*]

On May 20, after a journey of ten months and two weeks, Vasco da Gama fulfilled his aim and the ships dropped anchor at the city of Calicut. The Portuguese were given a warm welcome in the city that included a grand procession of upper-caste Nairs, and da Gama was soon received by the sovereign, the Zamorin of Calicut. In the interview with the Zamorin, de Gama offered him several gifts on behalf of King Manuel, which included cloth, hats, barrels of oil, and a cask of honey. But the king of Calicut and his entourage were not impressed. Just as many other European travelers were to find out over the coming centuries in their first encounters with Asian civilizations, Western products were not highly valued. Instead the Indian sovereign demanded the Portuguese to pay a customs duty in the universal currency: gold. Da Gama was offended by this, and the relationship with their hosts was dramatically strained from then on. But in spite of the frustrating negotiations for initiating trade relations with Calicut, da Gama left India pretty satisfied for having discovered such a promising market.

Vasco da Gama took 132 days to return to Lisbon, and he lost half of the crew in a very dangerous and unpleasant journey. But when he finally arrived

---

[*]   E. G. Ravenstein, *A Journal of the First Voyage of Vasco da Gama, London, 1497–1999* (Cambridge University Press, 2002).

he not only gave the good news about a new route to India but he brought a cargo that was worth several times the cost of the expedition. Consequently, he was rewarded in a similar way to Columbus, including the title of admiral of the Indian Seas.* Vasco da Gama's achievement contributed to a large extent to transform Portugal into an imperial nation, well aware of its power in the world. From then on King Manuel made himself known by the grand title of, "King of Portugal and the Algarves, Lord of Guinea, and of the conquest, navigation, and commerce of Ethiopia, Arabia, Persia, and India."

Having discovered a new sea route to the east the next step was to establish the first settlements in these remote lands. On March 9, 1500, the Portuguese monarch sent a new fleet of thirteen ships to India, captained by Pedro Álvares Cabral, who traveled not as an explorer but as a conqueror. He was accompanied by Bartolomeu Dias, who was going to be in charge of founding a commercial settlement of Sofala, in what became present-day Mozambique. This expedition marked the history of European expansion for very different reasons to what they expected. Cabral decided to sail toward the southwest. Maritime currents and a great tempest diverted him to the point of casually reaching an unknown area in the coast of the American continent on April 22, 1500. Cabral named this territory as Vera Cruz.** The Portuguese were well received by the indigenous people who inhabited the region, and they helped them explore the area, but they did not find anything particularly valuable. Discouraged by such modest results the Portuguese fleet resumed the journey to India, and Cabral did not attribute any importance to the discovery for which he was going to make history, he simply sent a ship to Lisbon notifying them of the existence of Vera Cruz.

In 1501 the king of Portugal commissioned a Florentine navigator and merchant named Amerigo Vespucci with the mission of sailing across the coasts of the lands discovered by Cabral. Vespucci had emigrated to Seville in 1492, one of the most advanced cities in those days, and it was there that he

---

* Ravenstein, *A Journal of the First Voyage of Vasco da Gama, London, 1497–1999.*
** Martin Page, *The First Global Village, How Portugal Changed the World* (Lisbon: Casa das Letras, 2002).

was offered the great opportunity of his life: to travel to the New World.* A man of great ambition, his ultimate aim was to succeed where Columbus had failed: finding a western route toward India. In 1499 he set out to the New World in a ship captained by the Spanish conquistador Alonso de Ojeda. In this journey they reached the coast of present-day Venezuela's Maracaibo, where they discovered that the indigenous people lived in huts that had been built on the water. This reminded Vespucci of Venice, and led Ojeda to call this land Little Venice, or Venezuela.

Having consolidated a solid reputation as a navigator under the orders of the Castilian sovereign, Vespucci was recruited by Portugal for the most important mission of his career. Between 1501 and 1502 he sailed across the coast of present-day Brazil up to Río de la Plata, an area of Spanish influence. The Florentine wrote that "nothing of value was found except an infinity of tainted trees." Nevertheless, on returning to Lisbon he wrote a letter to the Medici family, for whom he had worked at an earlier stage of his career, commenting that in his view the lands traversed in the expedition were a new continent.

Vespucci's comment in a private letter was to have deep consequences in the history of the New World. For this letter reached the hands of Martin Waldseemüller, a Swiss cartographer who published a new edition of Ptolemy's cosmography in 1507, with a world map that included the most recent discoveries. The Swiss decided that the lands of the New World should be known as America in honor of the person who had reached the conclusion that a new continent had been discovered.** With this he did not wish to tarnish the reputation of Columbus, whom he considered the discoverer of new lands in Asia, but not of a continent, like Vespucci. Nevertheless, some years later, when it became evident that the discoveries of Columbus and Vespucci were part of the same continent, Waldseemüller tried to correct his error. In a map published in 1513, he attempted to rename the New World as "the unknown land"—but it was too late. The name America had spread

---

* Felipe Fernández-Armesto, *Amerigo: The Man Who Gave His Name to America* (New York: Random House, 2006).
** Ibid.

across both sides of the Atlantic, and even though both the Spaniards and the Portuguese continued talking about the New World, or the Indies, the name with which the recently discovered continent was going to be known both in the West and in the rest of the world was America. In this way Vespucci achieved universal fame not for his merits as explorer but thanks to the power of publicity.

What was going to make the eastern coast of the New World attractive for European trade was brazilwood, a tree that grew plentifully in that area and from which present-day Brazil got its name. In 1503 six ships set sail from Lisbon under the command of Gonçalo Coelho, one of which was captained by Amerigo Vespucci, and the two returned with great shiploads of the beautiful hard red timber that was going to be increasingly demanded in the old continent.

Brazilwood was not monopolized by Portugal despite the fact that it grew in a territory that was under its sovereignty. While the first Portuguese ships arrived in America, a French mariner known as Paulmier de Gonneville arrived on the coast of Brazil by accident, just as it had happened to Cabral, and he took a shipload of the coveted trees to France. The success with which Gonneville introduced brazilwood to his country encouraged many European merchants to send expeditions to this region, especially from the ports of Honfleur and Dieppe, to the point that Brazil started to be known as Equatorial France. With this incursion in Brazilian territory the French had timidly begun their overseas expansion.

Despite the increasing demand for brazilwood, Portugal paid little attention to the American possessions, considering them much less important than the Asian or African ones. But the growing presence of French ships on Brazilian coasts convinced the king of Portugal that in order to keep them under his sovereignty their colonization would have to be promoted.

In 1526 a squadron of six warships was sent from Lisbon to America, and as it approached the coasts of Brazil it sank three French ships. Five years later another armada of five ships was sent under Martim Afonso de Sousa, who founded at Pernambuco one of the first European settlements. In this way the official history of Portugal's largest and most cherished colony was to begin: Brazil.

After initiating the settlement in the islands of the Caribbean as a result of Columbus's discoveries the Spanish crown was to expand its possessions in the mainland, where the most famous adventures of the Spanish conquistadors were going to take place. A small group of men not only managed to conquer vast territories for their crown but even continued making extraordinary discoveries. Such was the case of Vasco Núñez de Balboa.

Vasco Núñez de Balboa emigrated to Hispaniola in 1501, the first major Spanish settlement in America. In 1509 he decided to join an expedition to the province of New Andalusia, in present-day Colombia. His great charisma soon led him to become one of the leaders of the expedition. After arriving on the mainland, Balboa led his men to victory in several battles against the indigenous people, and he founded the first permanent settlement in American continental lands, Santa María. He was appointed mayor and governor of Veragua, but Núñez de Balboa was more of a conqueror than a governor, and in 1513 he led an expedition to the Isthmus of Panama in search of gold and a place for a new settlement.

Balboa reached a region where he was told about the existence of another sea toward the south, which theoretically had gold in abundance. After this revelation on September 1, 1513, he set out with 190 Spaniards and several indigenous people who knew the territory. On September 25 he climbed up a mountain that would give him a better perspective of the area. On reaching the summit he saw for the first time the waters of a sea that was unknown until then by Europeans. Three days after that, he reached the beach with the rest of the members of the expedition and he took possession of this unknown sea on behalf of the sovereigns of Castile, naming it the Southern Sea.

This event marked the beginning of the European exploration and discovery of the Pacific Ocean. In this expedition, the conqueror also discovered lands that were especially rich in gold, which he named as Pearl Archipelago, for obvious reasons. In January 1514, Núñez de Balboa returned to Santa María with a great booty. He sent an emissary to Spain so that he would hand in a part of the accumulated wealth and notify the court about the new sea that from then on would be under Spanish sovereignty.

The news of the discovery of the Southern Sea led Emperor Charles V to send an expedition of 1500 men and seventeen ships, the most numerous and best equipped that had so far been sent to America. But it was sent under the command of Pedro Arias Dávila, better known as Pedrarias, whom he had named as governor of the province of Golden Castile.

Balboa received with great disappointment the news that he would have to submit to the command of a new governor. Nevertheless, the crown decided to reward him for his extraordinary services with the appointment of the honorary title of *adelantado* or commander of the Southern Sea and governor of Panama and Coibú.

As it usually happened with the relationships between the Spanish conquerors, it was only possible to consolidate power by means of eliminating others. Pedrarias distrusted Balboa from the outset, and sent a group of men led by a soldier named Francisco Pizarro—who was later to make history with the conquest of the Inca Empire as we shall see—with the aim of arresting him under the charges of treason and attempting to create a separate government in the Southern Sea. After being captured Balboa was sentenced to death. "I have served the king with loyalty thinking only of increasing his dominions," he shouted from the executioner's platform shortly before being beheaded.* This was the ignominious end of the European who discovered the Pacific.

After getting rid of his great rival, Pedrarias founded Panama on August 15, 1519. Despite the spitefulness with which he had put an end to Balboa's life, Pedrarias managed to be confirmed as governor. Nevertheless history gave Vasco Núñez de Balboa his due, for he was going to be remembered as one of the great discoverers, especially in Panama, where avenues, monuments, and even the official currency bear his name.

Meanwhile, the western route toward Asia continued to be the great aim in the era of discovery. It was finally achieved, curiously, as a result of a joint Spanish-Portuguese endeavor. In 1518 a Portuguese captain, Ferdinand Magellan, proposed a voyage with the aim of finding the strait that would lead to the Southern Sea, and from there to the Moluccas, the archipelago in Indonesia that was particularly rich in spices. Magellan had a bad relationship

---

* Salvador de Madariaga, *El Auge y el Ocaso del Imperio Español en América* (Madrid: Espasa-Calpe, 1977).

with the Portuguese king because of a personal dispute, and for this reason he offered his project to the Spanish sovereign, who enthusiastically supported it. He set out on September 20, 1519, with five ships and around 250 men.* His warrant officer was a Basque sailor known as Juan Sebastián Elcano. A third of the members of the crew were not Spanish, and fifteen were Portuguese. Over eighty percent of the expedition's cost was paid by the king, for which it could be considered a royal venture. A substantial part of the royal contribution came from the gold imported from the Indies.

In the long journey to the southern Atlantic, Magellan had to face a mutiny that he managed to suppress with great difficulty. Finally after sailing across the southern coast of the American continent, he went into a strait that was later going to bear his name. After crossing it with strong winds and a very rough sea, on September 28 he was thrilled to sail into the sea which he named the Pacific, due to the remarkable tranquility of its waters.

After traversing the coast of present-day Chile, Magellan and his crew sailed toward the northeast with the aim of exploring the unknown Pacific Ocean. It proved to be an infernal trip because they ran out of water and also experienced a food shortage, but finally they reached the Mariana Islands, south of Japan, in March 1521, and in this way Columbus's old ambition was finally achieved three decades later. After recovering in Asian lands the crew sailed to the archipelago that was later to be known as the Philippines. In one of the islands Magellan established a good relationship with the king of Zubu and managed to convert him to Christianity. In order to please him, he acceded to help him in his struggle against a neighboring tribe, a tragic mistake, for he paid for his generosity with his life when he was killed by the enemy tribes in combat. In this way, the arrival of Europeans not always brought misfortune to the natives, nor is it true that the Europeans only thought of their own benefit.

Juan Sebastián Elcano substituted for Magellan and completed the journey with success, although paying a very high price for it. Only one ship out of a total of five that initiated the voyage managed to reach Cádiz in southern Spain. It was on September 6, 1520, and only eighteen men were

---

* de Madariaga, *El Auge y el Ocaso del Imperio Español en América.*

on board. The king conceded the Basque sailor a coat of arms with a globe under which the motto *Primus circumdedisti me* ("You went around me first") could be read. With this great feat, the theory that the earth was round was proved beyond any doubt and finally, the route toward the Far East through the Pacific was open.

Spain and Portugal took the lead in the era of discoveries and even managed to obtain the papal blessing to divide the New World exclusively between themselves. What was the reaction of the rival powers in Europe? The news spread rapidly of Columbus's voyages and other great discoveries made by the kingdoms of Castile and Portugal through most of Europe, in spite of the era's poor communications. Sailors rapidly spread the news of the Iberian major discoveries through the ports of Western Europe, while Ambassadors, special envoys, and spies duly reported to their courts on the Castilian and Portuguese expansion plans that could threaten their interests. The news about the existence of a New World to the west rapidly stimulated the imagination of navigators, fortune-seekers, sovereigns, and statesmen in all major European states, and consequently the Iberian kingdoms were soon to find rivals in its exploration and settlement.

Just as those of the Spanish Empire the origins of the British and French Empires are also linked to the voyages of Italian navigators. It is not surprising that some of most important contributions to the discovery of the New World came from the Italian Peninsula. Citizens of city-states like Genoa or Venice enjoyed the benefits of a great maritime tradition and a formidable entrepreneurial spirit after centuries of wealth-creation from trade in the Mediterranean. But from the late fifteenth century the opportunities for developing new markets were no longer in the Mediterranean Sea but in the Atlantic Ocean. The most innovative projects to discover new trading routes beyond the confines of the western world required the backing of the major Atlantic powers, and this is why together with Christopher Columbus or Amerigo Vespucci several Italian navigators were eager to approach the courts of Western Europe that had the capacity to expand through the Atlantic.

The life of Giovanni Caboto, or John Cabot, as he was going to be known in English, bears similarities to Columbus. He was born around 1450, it is not clear whether it was in Genoa or Gaeta. He relocated to Venice when he was very young in order to start earning a living as a merchant, and in the 1490s he emigrated to Valencia. It was there that Cabot found out about the great feat of his countryman Columbus. As a result of it he decided to devote his career to find a shorter route to Asia than the one that the Genoese sailor had discovered, by setting out from farther north.

Neither the Castilian nor the Portuguese courts were interested in Cabot's offer, and for this reason he moved his permanent residence to England in 1495. A very wise decision, for King Henry VII, who had been eagerly promoting trade links with several Italian cities, was well informed about the extraordinary contributions made by Italian navigators to the Iberian kingdoms. For this reason, when the king of England heard of Cabot's proposal he duly commissioned the project granting him five ships that would sail under the English flag with as many sailors as he could recruit.

Cabot failed in his first voyage and was forced to return from Iceland due to problems with the crew. Nevertheless a year later, in May 1497, he set sail with a ship known as the *Matthew*, and a small crew of eighteen. The *Matthew* reached the coast of Newfoundland several weeks later, in this way became the first ship in British history to reach America.[*] Cabot only landed briefly in what he thought to be the possessions of the great Khan. On his return to England in August 9, he was generously rewarded with a substantial sum of money and the title of admiral, and most important of all, he was authorized to make another voyage. He set out again in 1498 on the journey that put a tragic end to his promising career: his ship never returned, and was probably shipwrecked in Greenland. Many other European sailors were going to have the same tragic end as Cabot on crossing the Atlantic in the coming centuries. But above all Cabot earned an important place in British and European history, for although the exact point on the Canadian coast where he landed with his crew in 1497 is not known, he was to be remembered as the discoverer of the route to North America that eventually made the first British Empire possible.

---

[*] Winston Churchill, *A History of the English-Speaking Peoples: The New World*, vol. II (London: Cassell, 1957).

A few years later, in 1508 John Cabot's son Sebastian led an expedition to the New World with the same mission as his father, and it is generally believed that he found the entrance to what was later to be known as Hudson Bay. This was only the beginning of a very outstanding career as a sailor but the British crown was not to enjoy the benefits of exclusivity, for Sebastian Cabot was later to offer his services to the Kingdom of Castile due to the fact that Emperor Charles V offered more opportunities. He was appointed captain general by the Spanish crown and in 1525 was entrusted with the important mission of establishing the exact demarcation of the Treaty of Tordesillas, and also to sail to the Moluccas in Asia, where Castile eagerly wanted to expand. He even secretly negotiated the possibility of leading an expedition to China for Venice. This shows the extent to which there was stiff competition between European states to recruit the best talent and support the most ambitious projects of exploration.

In fact Sebastian Cabot returned to England toward the end of his career when he received an invitation from King Edward VI, who proved to be very interested in opening trading routes and even creating settlements. Cabot's last major project was the formation of a company with Sir Hugh Willoughby and Richard Chancellor, with the aim of opening a trade route to Asia through the Arctic—a brilliant idea, as that area was then totally unexplored.

In 1553 three ships set sail under the command of Willoughby and Chancellor. Willoughby penetrated the waters of the Arctic with two ships but his men were trapped by winter in Lapland and died there. They were not to be the last Englishmen to perish exploring the coldest parts of the Earth.

Richard Chancellor had better luck. He managed to reach the small sailing village in Archangel and from there he continued his trip overland until he reached Moscow. Czar Ivan IV welcomed the brave Englishman and granted his company the rights to trade with Russia, a country about which hardly anything was known in those times—in England or the rest of western Europe. On his return to England, Chancellor convinced Cabot to grant the company a new name, the Muscovy Company of Merchant Adventurers. Unfortunately Chancellor died on returning from his second voyage to Moscow in 1555, but his work was to continue. The

Muscovy Company existed until the outbreak of the Russian Revolution and provided a very lucrative market for the English traders.

France was to benefit from the talent of Italian navigators in a similar way to its rival kingdoms. A notable Florentine sailor, known as Giovanni da Verrazzano settled in the French town of Dieppe where he acquired a solid reputation as a navigator. Just like other major navigators of his time Verrazzano also aimed at finding a new western route toward Asia. In 1523 he finally obtained support from King Francis I of France. The Florentine set sail in 1524, and although he did not fulfill his mission he became the first European to navigate through the eastern coast of North America, from present-day Maine to North Carolina, and he named this extensive area as Francesca. In the second voyage to America a year later Verrazzano accidentally reached the coast of Brazil, and he took advantage of this unexpected discovery by returning to France with one of the first shipments of brazilwood.* He died on this third voyage, when he was attacked by indigenous peoples on stopping at a Caribbean island, but with him France timidly began its expansion through the world.

King Francis I took a great interest in the European discoveries of America and focused on the promotion of French navigation and colonization, well aware that apart from Spain and Portugal, England was also starting to make progress. Trade routes to the New World had become a source of wealth, apart from a symbol of prestige which none of the great European states could afford to ignore. Determined that France should have its northwestern route to America he entrusted this mission to a Frenchman known as Jacques Cartier.

Cartier set out in 1534 with two ships. On reaching Newfoundland, he entered the gulf that he named the St. Lawrence. Cartier and his men were to be the first Europeans in recorded history to meet the people of that area. They learned from them the word *kanata*, which meant "little village," and Cartier started to use the word Kanata, or Canada, on referring to the whole area.** As a result the term started to propagate until it gave its name to the

---

* Samuel Eliot Morison, *The European Discovery of America: The Northern Voyages* (Oxford, England: Oxford University Press, 1971).
** Ibid.

huge North American country. Nevertheless, even in the 1530s Cartier was still making the same mistake as Columbus, thinking that he had reached the eastern coast of Asia.

Cartier placed a cross in the place where he settled with his men, and he took possession of the territory on behalf of the king of France. In 1541 Francis I named him captain general of the new lands. He sent him there with the aim of initiating the colonization and also propagating the Catholic faith, just as the Spanish and Portuguese had been doing wherever they reached.

During the reign of Elizabeth I England became a particularly serious contender in the race for maritime exploration. The crown no longer needed to recruit foreign talent, as an increasing number of Englishmen proved determined to contribute to the era of great discoveries. Such was the case of the explorer and adventurer Sir Walter Raleigh. In 1584 he planned the foundation of a colony in the New World that would be named Virginia, in honor of Elizabeth I, the Virgin Queen. He managed to raise funds and recruit potential settlers for the colony in North America, but all this was not enough for such an ambitious project, and eventually he had to give up the idea.

Raleigh was attracted by the myth of El Dorado, an imaginary city of gold that spread from the Spanish Empire, and he led a daring expedition in 1595 to present-day Guyana. He sailed through the Orinoco River, penetrating territories of the Spanish Empire. This adventure inspired his book *The Discovery of Guiana,* published on his return to England, in which he claimed to have discovered the region where the mythical El Dorado was. Nevertheless his proposals for further exploration and colonization of Guyana obtained no support from the crown, as they would inevitably lead to clashes with Spain. In fact another expedition that he led to Guyana some years later provoked his arrest and execution by the peaceful King James I, who was determined to avoid conflicts with Spain.

Elizabethan England also obtained considerable benefits from the maritime explorations of the famous privateer, sea captain, and navigator Francis Drake. He was to go down in history for his role commanding the English fleet against the Spanish armada in 1588 and numerous exploits against the Spanish Empire, but he was also to be hailed in his time as the first Englishman—and the second European after Elcano—to have circumnavigated the world.

In 1577 Queen Elizabeth I sent Drake on an expedition along the Pacific Coast of the Americas in order to challenge Spanish interests. Drake set sail with five ships; his crew stopped at various points on the south and central American western coast, making important geographic discoveries for England and obtaining great treasures from Spanish ships that were captured and ports that were looted. On reaching the coast of California in 1579 Drake claimed the land on behalf of her majesty the queen, which he named as New Albion.*

From California Drake's expedition sailed along until it reached the Moluccas in the southwest Pacific. From there he bordered South Africa through the Cape of Good Hope and reached England in 1580.

The cargo of spices and treasures accumulated from the journey around the world was so great that the queen's fifty percent share was worth more than the crown's income for a whole year. Apart from bringing home considerable wealth, Drake managed to open up the Pacific Ocean for England. Until the voyages of Captain Cook two centuries later, no Englishman was to broaden the horizons for Britain as much as Francis Drake.

While the leading kingdoms of Western Europe made progress with the discovery of territories in the New World the Dutch, still under the sovereignty of the Hispanic Habsburg monarchy emerged as imposing rivals. A long maritime and commercial tradition, as well as the growing awareness shown by the Dutch that the key to their prosperity was in the seas, all of this explains why the Dutch ports of Amsterdam and Antwerp were considered among the most important in the world by the middle of the sixteenth century. Against this background great navigators emerged who pioneered Dutch expansion. One of them was Jan Huygen van Linschoten. In 1580 as a young sailor he went to work in Lisbon, where he is alleged to have obtained confidential information about trading routes that allowed him to break into territories where the Portuguese enjoyed a monopoly. In 1583 he made the first Dutch expedition to the Far East. On his way there he stopped in

---

* Morison, *The European Discovery of America.*

India where he founded the first Dutch enclave in Asia.* He also made a name as a writer: in 1596 he published *Itinerario,* a manual about maritime routes through the world with explanations about how to trade with other people, which was not only extremely useful for aspiring merchants and sailors but it also contained vivid descriptions of exotic worlds. But it was the cartographer and seafarer Willem Janszoon who was to open up another major frontier in European maritime history. In 1606 he led an expedition from the coast of New Guinea in search of new trading routes. The winds took him to the shores of present-day Queensland, as a result of this his crew made the first recorded European landing on Australian soil. Janszoon was not impressed by this barren land, and his reports did not transmit much enthusiasm for his discovery. As a result of this the Dutch gave up the opportunity of leading the colonization of Oceania. It was not until two centuries later, in 1770, that the European colonization of this remote island began when Captain James Cook reached southern Australia and took possession of it on behalf of the British crown.

While Dutch exploration made progress in Asia an Englishman opened a frontier for the Netherlands in the New World. Henry Hudson started his career in his country's service, sailing for the Moscow Company. Due to his great experience in the Baltic Sea in 1609 he was selected by the recently founded Dutch East India Company to find a northeastern route to Asia. Hudson sailed through the Baltic Sea, but instead of confronting the frozen waters of the Baltic he turned around and decided to take the risk of looking for a route to Asia through the northwest. In this way he reached the coast of Cape Cod, where the English had already arrived. Further south he discovered Manhattan Island, where centuries later the great city of skyscrapers was to emerge, and sailed through the river that would eventually be named after him. As a result of this, a few years later the Dutch founded a trading post to be known as New Amsterdam, and Holland became one of the colonizing powers of the New World.

Captain James Cook, one of the greatest navigators of all time, who occupied southern Australia on behalf of the British sovereign, wrote that the

---

*   Felipe Fernández-Armesto, *Millennium: A History of the Last Thousand Years* (New York: Scribner, 1995).

purpose of his career was "to voyage not only farther than any man before me but as far as I think it is possible for a man to go." Almost three centuries before Cook, a series of European sailors, guided by the same aims, laid the foundations of the era of European supremacy as a result of their geographic discoveries.*

The curiosity about the world's geography, an adventurous and entrepreneurial spirit, and improving sailing technology—all of these factors explain why the era of great discoveries took place in Europe. The era that began with the occupation of strategic enclaves in Africa by the Portuguese pioneers eventually led to the discovery of new continents and seas. The most important of all, Christopher Columbus's discovery of America allowed Spain to transform itself into the first global empire. But as we have seen, several other navigators made it possible for other European powers to follow a similar path of overseas expansion in America and the rest of the world.

"It is always the adventurers who make great things, not the sovereigns of great empires," wrote the French thinker Charles de Montesquieu in the eighteenth century. Had it not been for adventurers like Columbus, Vasco da Gama, or the rest mentioned in this chapter, the role of the kingdoms they represented in modern history would have been very different, and certainly would not have been as outstanding. They opened up the paths to expansion that would allow Europe on the whole to obtain an advantageous position over the rest of the world, as we shall see over the next pages, and propagate their civilization more than any other.

---

* Fernández-Armesto, *Millennium.*

Chapter 3

The World Is Not Enough

The Rise of the Great European Empires.

I n 1516 a young prince traveled to northern Spain from Ghent in order to be crowned as king of Castile, Aragon, and Naples. He was also to rule over the Low Countries, Austria, Bohemia, and rapidly expanding possessions in America. Three years later, he was elected Holy Roman Emperor. Emperor Charles V as he was to be known, could genuinely claim to be a European monarch with a mixture of Castilian, Aragonese, Flemish, German, and Burgundian blood, and a command of German, French, Spanish, and Italian— apart from what was then known as the international language: Latin. A Spanish bishop had proclaimed Charles V "King of Kings" and "Emperor of the World." With such grand titles, backed by extraordinary wealth, it can be understood why Charles V genuinely believed that he had been chosen by

God to consolidate a universal monarchy, under the Catholic faith. This belief kept him fighting against the Protestant Reformation throughout his reign. His son King Phillip II loyally followed his father's aims with such efficiency that he consolidated the first global empire in history. Quite appropriately the motto of his coat of arms was *Plus Ultra* (Even Further). On occasion of the union of the crowns of Spain and Portugal in 1540, which was one of the highlights of King Philip's reign, a medal was minted to commemorate it with the words, *Non suffic orbis* (The world is not enough). No better words to summarize the dreams of grandeur of the Spanish Habsburg monarchy.

The Spanish Habsburgs were not the only sovereigns in Europe to be inspired by the idea that the world was not enough. While Spain and Portugal also consolidated vast overseas empires, several neighboring kingdoms in Western Europe followed similar trends of expansion, although initially at a much more modest level. Kings and ruling elites had diverse reasons for supporting the conquest and colonization of new territories. For all of them it seemed the obvious way of acquiring wealth, particularly after the discovery of the New World. For England, Holland, and France, building an empire seemed to be the only way of counterbalancing the hegemony of the Spanish Habsburgs. With the rise of the Protestant reformation there were also religious reasons for occupying the New World, to defy the papal will that had granted it all to the Catholic Iberian kingdoms. But not all expansion was motivated by Western European politics and religious conflicts.

The early settlement and colonization of the New World owes a lot to the expansionist ethos established by the Iberian monarchs in the fifteenth century. We have already seen the great contribution made by John I of Portugal and Henry the Navigator to the era of discoveries. The Portuguese laid the foundations of the European expansion through the world.

From the mid–fifteenth century, Portugal started to enjoy the benefits of a network of settlements created between the Azores and Central Africa. These overseas possessions were not meant to become settler colonies that would attract migration, but rather trading bases. Two prosperous businesses emerged from these early colonial adventures that had a great impact on the Portuguese economy and the great Atlantic powers. The first was the sugar industry. It started in Madeira and soon expanded to the Canary Islands.

Dutch traders contributed to its expansion around Europe. In the early sixteenth century both Portugal and Spain took sugar cane to their possessions in the New World contributing to its rapid expansion.

The sugar industry, like many other businesses that emerged in the colonial world, required plenty of labor. This led to the development of an equally lucrative business that eventually became very controversial: the slave trade. The Portuguese discovered on the coasts of Africa an abundant commodity for which there was going to be an increasing demand: human beings. These could be bought from African tribes or even kidnapped, and were subsequently sold in Lisbon or other ports.

However scandalous and unacceptable it may be considered from our contemporary perspective, slavery had existed both in the West as well as in other known civilizations from time immemorial without questioning it from a moral or ethical perspective. As Aristotle wrote "humanity is divided into two: owners and slaves." Nor did the Christian church condemn slavery as long as the slaves were not Christian. With the European expansion the slave trade became a very profitable business without which the development of occupied territories would not have been possible. Of all the enslaved races Africans were singled out, and suffered the most from this scourge.

The first shipment of African slaves reached Lisbon in 1441. In 1448 around one thousand slaves reached Portugal and the Portuguese islands.[*] From then on the arrival of shipments of slaves in Portuguese territories became increasingly frequent, and the unfortunate Africans were employed mainly in the sugar plantations, but also in diverse trades as well as the domestic service in Lisbon. The demand for slaves spread to neighboring Castile and Aragon, and to the Italian Peninsula. But these were all very modest figures in comparison to what European colonial settlers and many of their descendants requested in America.

In the meantime the neighboring Iberian kingdoms initiated an extraordinary period of expansion that allowed them to transform themselves into the first world power within less than three decades. The key factor to

---

[*] Hugh Thomas, *The Slave Trade: The Story of the Atlantic Slave Trade, 1440–1870* (New York: Simon & Schuster, 1997).

understand this fabulous transformation was the marriage between Isabella of Castile and Ferdinand of Aragon in 1469, by which much more than the unification of two kingdoms was achieved.

King Ferdinand of Aragon had extraordinary military gifts but above all he excelled in politics and diplomacy. He configured the marriage alliances of his own children, creating unions among dynasties that were going to determine the future of several European nations. Queen Isabella was not destined to be queen of Castile from her birth but she reached the crown thanks to her intelligence and wise alliances with nobles. She was to achieve the most ambitious targets for her kingdom, eagerly supporting the overseas expansion of Castile. A major Castilian achievement was the conquest of the Canaries, which allowed the first overseas expansion.

In 1492 the Catholic kings made a fundamental contribution to the history of Spain and Europe: the conquest of the Islamic Emirate of Granada, with which the Muslim presence in the Iberian Peninsula came to an end. It had deep consequences on the religious character of Europe over the subsequent five centuries, for until the creation of the state of Albania in 1925, there was no independent state in the European continent with a Muslim majority.[*]

The culmination of the reconquest of the Iberian Peninsula from Moorish power had great importance in the rise of an expansionist mentality that was predominant in the crown of Spain for over three centuries. Queen Isabella, emboldened by this success, aimed at conquering North Africa and in this way achieve its Christianization, as she wrote in her will. Nevertheless, this glorious year of 1492 gave her kingdom the opportunity to expand across a world that had never been imagined, thanks to Christopher Columbus.

The discovery of the New World did not generate much enthusiasm among the Castilian royal entourage. Nevertheless Queen Isabella fully supported all exploration and settlement projects of these territories, convinced that this could be the key to her kingdom's expansion.

The first settlement in the island of Hispaniola that was to be governed by Christopher Columbus constituted a good example of how complicated

---

[*] Felipe Fernández-Armesto, *1492: The Year the Modern World Began* (San Francisco: HarperOne, 2009).

European colonization of the New World was going to be. On his second journey to the New World the admiral traveled with twelve hundred men, which shows the determination of the Catholic kings to found a permanent settlement in their new territories. Nevertheless, on his arrival in Hispaniola he found that the locals had destroyed the fort he had originally founded and massacred the contingent of men that he had left behind. This constituted the beginning of the clash between the Europeans who pretended to impose their customs on the discovered continent, and the native people who refused to submit, let alone give their homeland away.

Columbus had a very clear idea of what he should do with the indigenous peoples: Christianize the members of the Arawak, who inhabited Hispaniola. Conversion to Christianity was one of the main aims that justified the conquest of new territories for the kingdom of Castile. As regards the cannibal tribes of those who were considered too savage to convert into Christianity, as well as those who rejected the Christian doctrine, they were all to be enslaved. On the whole the cruelty with which the indigenous people were treated outraged the early missionaries, and this became another source of internal conflict.[*]

The other major problem that Christopher Columbus encountered was to govern the new settlement in accordance with the laws of Castile. He was incapable of motivating men for the hard task of exploiting the land under the tropical weather, nor did he manage to impose order among people who considered the New World as an opportunity to make a fortune without the need to submit to any authority. Shortly after Columbus's arrival a rebellion broke out, and his inability to restore order led the court of Castile to take the drastic measure of sending Francisco de Bobadilla, who replaced him as governor of the Indies.

In the early sixteenth century sugar plantations and extraction of mineral deposits became the main sources of wealth in Hispaniola. But the scarce workforce became a serious problem. The indigenous population that Spaniards had initially employed declined at an alarming rate. According to Bartolomé de las Casas, of a population of approximately 250,000 Indians

---

[*] Bartolomé de las Casas, *A Short Account of the Destruction of the Indies* (New York: Penguin Classics, 1999).

living in Hispaniola in 1492, there were only 14,000 left in 1517.* Apart from the harsh treatment they received from the settlers, the main reasons for the extinction of the indigenous people were diseases brought from Europe. It was in these circumstances that the conquistadors decided to import African slaves. In 1501 the first shipment of slaves arrived in Hispaniola, with which the history of the Africans in the American continent began.**

In 1509 Christopher Columbus's son Diego was appointed governor of Hispaniola. Under his mandate Hispaniola was consolidated as a prosperous colony for the Spanish crown. For this reason the conquistadors focused on further expansion in the Caribbean. Juan Ponce de León conquered the island of Puerto Rico, and shortly afterward he discovered the peninsula of Florida. Diego Velázquez de Cuéllar was put in charge of an expedition to take possession of what was going to be the most important Spanish colony in the Caribbean: the island of Cuba.

While the colonization of America started making progress, important measures were taken to supervise and keep as much control as possible over those who were going to settle in territories on behalf of the crown of Castile. In 1503 the *Casa de Contratación* (House of Trade) was founded in Seville, with the aim of promoting and regulating commerce and navigation in the New World. After the death of Queen Isabella her husband King Ferdinand created the Council of the Indies in 1511. Its mission was to plan and propose the king's policies for the New World, and supervise everything in relation to the administration of the Indies. Its responsibilities were very broad: from appointing viceroys and posts in the high echelons of the administration to validating emigration permits. In this way, Ferdinand of Aragon, the king who had so successfully expanded his kingdom, managed to lay the foundations of the Spanish Empire's administrative structure. As a result, the Spanish Empire was more closely supervised from the metropolis than any other European empire. It required plenty of bureaucracy and a broad network of crown servants scattered around all overseas territories, but it served King Ferdinand's purpose if we take into consideration its rapid expansion.

---

*   de las Casas, *A Short Account of the Destruction of the Indies.*
**   Thomas, *The Slave Trade.*

During the reign of the King-Emperor Charles I, the Spanish Empire in America experienced the most extraordinary growth. He consolidated an empire that was larger than any other known until then. And this was largely thanks to the ambition of two adventurers with which the name of conquistador is most closely associated: Hernán Cortés and Francisco Pizarro. The conquest of Mexico, led by Hernán Cortés, is undoubtedly one of the great feats of history. Due to his victories in the battlefield and the size of the territories that he acquired, Cortés was going to become one of the most important conquerors in European history. As founder and governor of several cities, he laid the foundations of the viceroyalty of New Spain, the largest and richest territory of the Spanish empire. He led the first encounter between the Europeans and one of the great indigenous American civilizations: the Aztecs. He was responsible for their defeat and submission, and he also contributed to the rise of intermarriage that was going to predominate in Mexico, the most heavily populated country in Latin America. A man of great ambition and extraordinary achievements, loyal to the king and a devout Christian, he was also cruel, bloodthirsty, and covetous. With his virtues and his defects, he left a controversial legacy and became one of the great symbols of the Spanish Empire in America. As the twentieth-century Mexican poet Octavio Paz wrote about Cortés: "It is not easy to love him, but it is impossible not to admire him."

Hernán Cortés, who was born into a noble family in southern Spain, arrived in the New World in 1502. Initially he worked in Hispaniola as a public notary, but he soon decided to follow his vocation as a conqueror. In 1511 he took part in the conquest of the island of Cuba. Seven years later Cortés was put in charge of a flotilla to help an expedition that had been shipwrecked on the Mexican coast, and it was there that Cortés found the opportunity that would allow him to make history.

In 1519 Hernán Cortés traveled from Cuba to the Yucatan Peninsula with an expedition of 20 ships, 580 men, 16 horses and 10 cannons.* The first fight against the Maya civilization took place in present-day Tabasco. The defeated Maya were declared subjects of the king of Spain and several

---

* Hugh Thomas, *The Conquest of Mexico* (London: Hutchinson, 1993).

gifts were handed over to Cortés including La Malinche, known in Spanish as Doña Marina, who was going to become an interpreter and rendered exceptional services to the Spaniards who aimed at conquering the Aztec Empire. The beautiful indigenous woman was also Cortés's most famous lover, and Martin Cortés, who was born from this relationship, was one of the first prominent examples of a mixed race person that the Spaniards and Indians bequeathed in these lands. Cortés founded the city of Vera Cruz, and defying the authority of the governor of Cuba, he proclaimed himself captain general of the new lands.

Cortés aimed at conquering Tenochtitlan, the capital of the Aztec Empire, a city that was bigger than most European cities of that time. On his way he discovered that the Aztecs had enemies in neighboring territories, and formed alliances with them, strengthening his position. Finally he received emissaries of the Aztec Empire with the message that he would be well received.

On November 11, 1519, the historic meeting between Cortés and Emperor Moctezuma took place, which has inspired so much literature. Moctezuma identified the Spaniards as descendants of the great lord who had been expelled from the country of the Nahua. On hearing Cortés explain who he was he acceded to submit his people to the king of Spain.[*] Never in history was an empire given up so easily, although it is likely that Moctezuma was deliberately misinterpreted by the Spaniards and his apparent voluntary submission was simply an expression of courtesy. Soon after becoming a subject of the king of Spain Moctezuma became his prisoner.

Despite the relative ease with which Cortés and his men took the capital of the Aztec Empire, his problems had only started. The conqueror not only had to fight against the Indians but also against the Spaniards, for in January 1520 Governor Velázquez sent an expedition with the order of arresting him for having disobeyed his orders. This gave way to the first war between Spaniards in America, in which Cortés was to defeat his former governor. After fighting the battle against his fellow countrymen Cortés returned to Tenochtitlan in order to face a rebellion led by Prince Cuautémoc. On the

---

[*] Thomas, *The Conquest of Mexico.*

night of June 30, that became known in Mexican popular mythology as the "Sad Night," the conquistador suffered the most humiliating defeat, which forced him to retreat to the neighboring territories. But on August 13, 1521, Cortés and a troop of 20,000 warriors who were mainly recruited among the indigenous groups to inspire one of the classic works of the Spanish Empire in America: *The True History of the Conquest of New Spain*, written by Bernal Díaz del Castillo, one of the men who accompanied Cortés in this exploit.

Thanks to Hernán Cortés, Emperor Charles V became the sovereign of the biggest empire on the American continent, and the conquistador was compensated with the title of governor and captain general of New Spain.

In the 1530s Cortés continued making notable contributions to the Spanish Empire. He began the conquest of present-day Guatemala and founded the cities of Guadalajara, Chihuahua, Zamora, Mérida, and Valladolid. He also explored lower California. In 1540 he traveled to Spain with the aim of winning support for new ventures but, as it happened so often, his conquering mentality clashed with the narrow-mindedness of the members of the court. He died in 1547 when he was about to return to the lands of New Spain, where he had become a legendary figure.

While Hernán Cortés made such great contributions to the Spanish Empire that they extended from present-day Guatemala to California, another native from Extremadura, known as Francisco Pizarro, was to replicate his achievement with the conquest of another great empire in America, that of the Incas.

Francisco Pizarro's childhood and youth was much more difficult than those of the rest of the conquistadors: he was an illegitimate son of a nobleman, did not receive any formal education, and survived his early years looking after pigs. With such poor prospects for earning a living in his native land, the news of the New World, where he could try and make his fortune, attracted him from the outset. He arrived in America with the expedition of Nicolás de Ovando in 1502, just like Hernán Cortés.

Pizarro quickly understood that the great opportunities to make a fortune were in the mainland. He participated in the expedition of Alonso de Ojeda through present-day Colombia and Central America. There he conceived a much more ambitious plan with which to reach glory and make a fortune: the conquest of the Empire of Peru.

In 1524 Pizarro allied himself with Diego de Almagro and a priest from Panama, Hernando de Luque, to explore the western coast of America. He led two expeditions between 1524 and 1528 that proved to be a failure, but they served to obtain references about the vast reach and wealth of the Inca Empire in Peru. In 1529 Pizarro decided to travel to Spain with the aim of asking King Charles I for his support for an ambitious plan of taking over the Inca Empire. The journey had the expected results, for he was appointed governor and captain general and of the new lands that he could conquer, and in 1531 he set out with a contingent of 180 men and 37 horses toward Peru.[*]

Despite the fact that the forces with which Pizarro aimed at conquering the Inca Empire were very limited, he had the advantage that the Incas, just as the Aztecs, did not offer any resistance to the invader. On entering the Inca Empire, Pizarro was received at the city of Cajamarca by Emperor Atahualpa in 1532. Atahualpa was not as submissive as the Aztec emperor was with Cortés, and when Pizarro demanded that he accepted the sovereignty of Charles I and convert to Christianity, he refused. As a result of this the conquistador decided to make him his prisoner. A year later, he decided to execute him, alleging that he was preparing a revolt against the Spaniards.

As if he were inspired by Machiavelli, Pizarro took advantage of the internal divisions among the Inca elite and allied himself with the Inca nobility that had been confronting the emperor for a long time. This enabled him to conquer Cuzco, the capital of the Inca Empire (today called Cusco, Peru). To culminate the operation successfully, he appointed the Inca Manco Capác who was theoretically on his side, as the new emperor. Then he strengthened his power by appointing his brother Juan Pizarro governor of Cuzco, and he married the daughter of the Inca emperor, Huayna Capac. The offspring of this marriage was a daughter called Francisca Pizarro, known as the first child of intermarriage in Peru.[**]

---

[*]   de Madariaga, *Imperio Español en America.*
[**]   Ibid.

Once more, as it happened with Columbus, Balboa, or Cortés, Pizarro had to defend himself not only from his indigenous enemies but from rival Spaniards. De Almagro confronted Pizarro over the possession of Cuzco to the point of declaring war and fighting against him at the Battle of Las Salinas in 1538. Pizarro won and ordered Almagro's execution. From then the conqueror focused on the administration of the empire that he had conquered. He founded the city of Lima, future capital of Peru, and built a great palace for himself. But despite the fact that he managed to submit and govern the Inca subjects, he was not so successful with the Spaniards. The supporters of Almagro, led by his son, took revenge on June 26, 1541, bursting into his palace and murdering him.

While the Pizarros consolidated their power in the Inca Empire, the possessions of the Spanish crown were also expanding toward the south. The Spaniards decided to conquer the region around what was called River Plate for two reasons: first because they hoped it would be particularly rich, and secondly to prevent the Portuguese from advancing toward it. In 1534 a soldier called Pedro de Mendoza obtained royal permission to lead an expedition to this region. He founded a port known as Our Lady of Buen Aire, from where the future capital of Argentina took the name of Buenos Aires.

In 1541 another conquistador who had served under Pizarro named Pedro de Valdivia set out on the conquest of a region known as *Chili* by the Indians, from where the future nation of Chile got its name. De Valdivia opened up this new frontier for the Spanish Empire with a small contingent of 110 men, and he founded the city of Santiago. Shortly afterward another of Pizarro's men, Francisco de Orellana, marched toward the north and founded the settlement of Guayaquil in Ecuador. The empire's frontiers were also to expand toward the north of New Spain. In 1565 Pedro Menéndez de Avilés formally took possession of the peninsula that was later to be known as Florida, and founded the settlement of St. Augustine. From there the city of St. Augustine was to emerge as the oldest settlement founded by Europeans in the United States.[*]

---

[*]   Felipe Fernández-Armesto, *Our America: A Hispanic History of the United States* (New York: W.W. Norton, 2014), p. 28.

From the discovery of America, the exploration and conquest of the New World offered the Spaniards opportunities for acquiring wealth and glory beyond their wildest dreams. In this way, toward the middle of the sixteenth century, the crown of Spain had established its sovereignty over territories that spanned from present-day California to Argentina, and laid the foundations of the biggest empire that humanity had known until then.

Even though the conquistadors managed to take possession of a great part of the immense American continent, their control over the territories was very limited, for the human resources that they had were scarce. A great part of the occupied territory was composed of tropical land, rain forests, deserts, or uninhabited mountains—and also regions inhabited by indigenous peoples. Transforming the settlements into cities, sowing fertile lands, exploiting the resources, and consolidating a harmonious relationship with the locals constituted a huge endeavor that would take several generations. Especially harsh was the task of the first settlers.

Where did the first settlers of Spanish America come from? Initially they came from Castile, since the discovery of America was a Castilian initiative, and especially from Andalusia or Extremadura, where Cortés, Pizarro, and Balboa were born. They usually came from the lower nobility or from plebeian families with some fortune, for the poorest did not have the means to travel to the Indies except as servants of the noblemen. Nevertheless, soon there were going to be people from the crowns of Aragon and Navarre, and emigrants from the poorer classes also began to arrive.

Out of all settlers who came to Hispaniola in the first ships, only three hundred survived when Nicolás de Ovando arrived in 1502. For this reason, the 2500 settlers who arrived with him were going to be essential to allow the colony to thrive.* The majority came on their own without family and did not have the intention to stay there permanently, for unlike migrants from Northern Europe those from the Iberian Peninsula usually aimed for returning home as soon as they could afford it. In 1517 the Spanish judge Alonso de Zuazo wrote from Santo Domingo to the king of

---

* Henry Kamen, *Empire: How Spain Became a World Power, 1492–1763* (New York: Harper Perennial, 2004)

Spain informing him that the problem with Spanish emigration was that the men were generally not married, and for this reason they refused to settle permanently. He therefore proposed that emigration should be promoted from other parts of Christendom.*

European participation in the Spanish conquest was more significant than what is generally assumed. The news of the discovery of the New World spread rapidly though the old continent and attracted many Europeans. Among those who left to American lands who were not Spanish. Many came from Genoa, as it was no coincidence that the discoverer of America was from Genoa. As de Ovando comments in a letter to the king in 1504, the commerce between the Caribbean and Spain was in the hands of the Genoese and foreigners. Many Genoese settled in the New World in order to develop their business interests from there. For example, Jerónimo Grimaldi, member of a powerful family of Genoese financiers, lived in Hispaniola from 1508 to 1515. Then the Genoese expanded their business through Cuba and the mainland.**

Gonzalo Fernández de Oviedo commented in his famous *General History and Nature of the Indies* about the diversity of people who had gone to America. He wrote that in the city of Santo Domingo one could hear, "languages from all parts of Christianity, from Italy to Germany, Scotland and England, with people from France, Hungary, Poland, Greece, Portugal, and other nations from Asia, Africa, and Europe." Among those who conquered Mexico with Cortés, over ten percent were Portuguese, Genoese, Dutch, and Greek. In Pedro de Mendoza's expedition there were around one hundred Germans and Belgians.

Not only did European migrants participate in the Spanish conquest of America but also venture capitalists. The need to attract private capital to invest in the New World was going to make businessmen beyond the Iberian Peninsula invest in the Spanish Empire. Charles V encouraged several German financiers to invest in the New World. In 1528 he reached an agreement with the Welsers, a powerful German family of bankers, with the aim

---

*   Kamen, *Empire.*
**   Ibid.

of allowing them explore, develop, and settle in Venezuela. The first settlers sent by the Welsers arrived in 1529 and focused on the exploration of the Orinoco River Basin. The Welsers also opened a factory in Hispaniola with other German business partners.* The banker Jacob Fugger, the wealthiest man in early sixteenth-century Europe, also made handsome profits financing projects in America.**

As regards the professions of the colonists, the Spanish conquest of America has been identified with a cliché of greedy conquistadors with limitless voracity for gold. But this was only one part of the story. A very important institution in Spanish colonization was the so-called encomienda. The encomienda was a tract of land or a village, together with the indigenous living in it, that was officially granted to a colonist by the crown of Castile. It was created with the double aim of encouraging the conquistadors to settle and exploit the land, and also of Christianizing the Indians.*** In this way, the encomienda was a feudal system by which the Indians would lead the unenviable life of a peasant in Europe. But in practice it was much worse, for many settlers did not comply with their obligations and simply enslaved the Indians. As a result of this the encomiendas ended up being one of the most controversial aspects of the conquest of America and they were eventually abolished in the mid–seventeenth century.

The majority of conquistadors arriving in the New World soon realized that the only way of prospering there was by cultivating the land. They were responsible for the introduction of farming methods and livestock to America. Spaniards brought horses and dogs with them, and farms started to expand with cows, pigs, chickens, geese, and other animals that proliferated in any rural entourage in the European continent. Hernán Cortés introduced vineyards as well as sugar and silk in his lands, and wheat and sugar plantations were going to proliferate wherever the Spaniards settled. The farms and the agricultural methods introduced by the Spaniards became a new way of earning a living for many Native Americans, and were also going to eradicate famine in many

---

*   Kamen, *Empire*.
**   Steinmetz, *The Richest Man Who Ever Lived*.
***   de Madariaga, *Imperio Español en América*.

regions.* While a lot has been written about the destruction of indigenous life by the conquistadors, there is remarkably little about how Spaniards actually contributed to save lives and help Indian communities thrive in their native land by these methods and livestock imported from Europe.

Another profession that attracted many emigrants was that of colonial administration, as the Spanish Empire was also going to be a bureaucratic empire that required a broad network of crown servants. Then there was trade and defense. For one of the great paradoxes of the Spanish conquest was that it took place without the crown contributing an army. Even though the expedition leaders were usually professional soldiers, troops were recruited among the settlers in the colonies, who aimed at settling in the conquered lands and prospering there.

The Portuguese Empire evolved in a different way from the Spanish for several reasons. While the kingdom of Castile focused on establishing settlements in the New World, Portugal on the other hand was building a network of trading posts. For a long time Asia was much more attractive for Portuguese colonization than the New World, primarily because it was much more profitable. After the establishment of forts in Goa and Malacca the Portuguese culminated their rapid expansion in Asia by setting up a trading base in Macao in 1554, in this way becoming the first European power to have access to the hermetic Chinese market. With such prospects for growth in Asia it can be understood why the crown neglected the coasts of Brazil.

The Portuguese crown divided the coasts of Brazil into seven hereditary captaincies in 1523. It hoped that those in charge would manage to consolidate these settlements but this was not the case. Out of the seven only four of them made progress, a setback mainly due to lack of settlers. Toward the mid–sixteenth century the most prosperous captaincies, Porto Seguro, Ilhéus, San Vicente, and Pernambuco did not have more than six hundred settlers, excluding slaves and natives. On the whole the European population living in the coast did not exceed 10,000.**

---

*   de Madariaga, *Imperio Español en América*.

**   E. Bradford Burns, *A History of Brazil* (New York: Columbia University Press, 1993).

One of the reasons why Brazil attracted very little migration was because unlike in Spanish America, all attempts to find gold and silver initially failed. As a result settlers had no option but to cultivate the land, and tobacco, cotton, and sugarcane became the main products exported by this colony.

The captaincies did not give the expected results and it was also feared that those who inherited these territories would end up defying Lisbon or perhaps falling into the hands of the neighboring Spanish Empire. For this reason in 1548 the Portuguese crown radically altered the colonial administration, the hereditary captaincies were all dismissed and replaced by a governor general who would administrate the colony on behalf of the crown. In 1549 the first governor, Tomé de Sousa, arrived in Bahia. From then on the colony experienced major changes. Tomé de Sousa was ordered to found the settlement of San Salvador, and a contingent of three thousand men that were sent from Portugal became its first inhabitants.* San Salvador was soon transformed into a port of great importance for the sugar industry and the slave trade. Not only did it become the capital of Brazil for the next two centuries but also one of the largest cities of the New World. Another governor who left a deep mark on the formation of Brazil was Mem de Sá, who expelled the French from the Brazilian coast and founded Rio de Janeiro in 1567.**

In 1578 King Sebastian of Portugal died without leaving any legitimate heir. As a result of this his nephew King Philip II of Spain was crowned king of Portugal. Ever since he inherited the Spanish crown in 1556, Philip focused on expanding his vast empire, with considerable success. Not satisfied with the formidable growth experienced in the New World in 1564 he sent Miguel López de Legazpi on an expedition to southern Asia. As a result of this the archipelago that was to be known as the Philippines was occupied. From then Philip II could claim to rule over a global empire; a few years later he was able to enlarge it even further on inheriting the Portuguese crown and consolidated in this way the first empire in history where the sun never set.

Due to the historic rivalry between Castile and Portugal, and the reticence with which Portuguese elites received Philip II as their new king,

---

*   Burns, *History of Brazil*.
** Ibid.

important measures were adopted so that this union would not be seen as Castile taking over Portugal. Portugal kept full autonomy and control over its colonies. The king even contemplated the possibility of transferring the capital of his empire to Lisbon, for after the fusion of his kingdoms this had become the most important city on the Atlantic. But obviously this idea was badly received in Castile and it could not be put into practice.

Unlike his father Charles V, Philip II was well aware that the key to the power of the Habsburg monarchy was in the progress of its empire in the New World. For this reason he paid particular attention to improve colonial administration. The great viceroyalties of the Spanish Empire were created during his reign. The Portuguese Empire experienced steady growth and no interference from Castilian authorities, which partly explains why the Iberian union was to survive for eighty years. It was during his reign that America became synonymous in both Spain and Portugal with wealth and power, and it was going to attract the most ambitious and adventurous.

For a long time, until well into the sixteenth century, empire building seemed to be the exclusive privilege of the Iberian pioneers. For let us not forget that the Americas had been distributed between Spain and Portugal at the Treaty of Tordesillas in 1494 with the Pope's blessing, and other powers could only trespass on these domains by disobeying the maximum authority of the Christian world. The first European sovereign to openly defy the Pope's authority was the English King Henry VIII. During his reign, which marked the history of the English in so many ways, the word *empire* started to be openly used in association to England's territories. In the 1530s he proclaimed his realm an "empire," with the aim of demonstrating that he owed no allegiance to the Pope, nor would he allow any interference from the Habsburg monarchs who were the most determined supporters of the papal will. King Francis I of France was equally outraged by the Pope's favoritism toward the Iberian kingdoms. To protect French interests against this he initially sought an alliance with Henry VIII. Then he went as far as to sign an alliance with the sultan of the Ottoman Empire, Suleiman the Magnificent—quite a controversial decision for a Christian king, as it seemed to imply that national interest was above religious allegiance.

While these monarchs used diplomacy to protect their kingdoms against Iberian expansion, ordinary Europeans utilized diverse subterfuges to gain access to the wealth of the New World.

The quickest and easiest way of obtaining benefits from the New World for those who were not subjects of the Iberian kingdoms was through piracy. Initially the French corsairs were the great masters in the business of intercepting Spanish and Portuguese ships that transported gold, silver, and other treasures from America to Europe. Many of them came from the French port of Dieppe. Particularly famous was the case of the corsair Jean Fleur, who captured two Spanish galleons with treasures sent by Hernán Cortés from the conquest of Mexico. Other European rivals used the same method for snatching bits of wealth from the New World.

Elizabethan England started to use piracy as a legitimate way of reaping rewards from the Spanish Empire and promoting its interest against Catholic Iberian empires. Francis Drake and John Hawkins made very lucrative careers in this sphere. In his first voyage to the Caribbean John Hawkins attacked a Portuguese ship full of slaves that were later sold at a great profit in the Caribbean. As a result of this he became the wealthiest man in Plymouth, his hometown. He also became a pioneer in the notorious slave trade triangle between England, Africa, and America. Few years later he made a second voyage to the Caribbean, which allegedly transformed him into the richest man in England.*

In its eagerness to find new markets that could rival those of the New World Elizabethan England set its eyes on the Far East. In 1600 Queen Elizabeth I signed a royal decree by which the East India Company was created. The company was not only the pioneer in European commerce with India but also the first joint-stock company in the history of European colonialism. It was a very innovative way for promoting a state's economic expansion, as it was financed by private investors looking to develop new markets. The writer Richard Hakluyt was among the company's shareholders. Hakluyt became famous for his book *The Principal Navigations, Voyages and*

---

* Arthur Herman, *To Rule the Waves: How the British Navy Shaped the Modern World* (New York: HarperCollins, 2004).

Discoveries of the English Nation, in which he urged the Protestant nations to set up colonies with which to counterbalance Catholic influence in the New World. He was to put his theories into practice as the founder of the Virginia Company, which aimed at creating the first permanent settlement in North America. In 1607 the Virginia Company sent its first three ships with 105 men under the command of Christopher Newport. On his arrival in the New World, Newport founded Jamestown on the present-day coast of Virginia, laying the foundations of the colony that would bear the same name. A few decades later it would become the most populated and prosperous colony in British America.

The beginnings of this colony were extremely difficult. One year after their arrival half of the settlers had died of sickness, cold, and hunger. The rest survived thanks to the strict discipline applied by Captain John Smith, who emerged as the colony's leader. Unlike the Spanish conquistadors who were to find vast sources of wealth from territories where silver and gold was abundant, the English settlers initially found no other way of earning a living in the New World than by cultivating the land. It was only after one of the first settlers, John Rolfe, decided to try his luck by planting tobacco that the settlement's economy gradually started to take off.

Tobacco was initially brought into Europe by the Spaniards from America, and ever since the habit of smoking made progress first in Europe and gradually in the rest of the world. Sir Walter Raleigh is alleged to have introduced it in England. From the early seventeenth century, addiction to this drug expanded rapidly. John Rolfe had a brilliant idea of planting tobacco seeds in Jamestown. His experiment was so successful that tobacco became the colony's main export. Rolfe not only made a fortune with his tobacco plantations but he can be considered as the pioneer in an industry that was going to have crucial importance in the development of British Empire in North America and subsequently of the United States.

With the benefits from the tobacco exports and the harsh discipline imposed by John Smith, the colony started to make progress and expand into neighboring lands. Smith, who returned to England in 1614, was the first one to describe the coast between what was later going to be known as Maine and Massachusetts as New England.* In a book that was published under the title of *A Description of New England*, he described it as a land of opportunity where every settler can work in his own land and rapidly make a fortune.

Less challenging than continental America and also much more lucrative was the early colonization of the Caribbean. England occupied the islands of Saint Lucia, Granada, Barbados, and Saint Christopher and Nieves (Saint Kitts and Nevis today) between 1605 and 1628. Particularly important was the occupation of Jamaica in 1655, which had been a Spanish colony until then, and eventually became the most important possession in the Caribbean. The first settlers of these paradise islands mainly earned a living with sugar plantations, where slaves would work, as in the Spanish and Portuguese neighboring colonies. With the soaring demand for sugar in Europe Caribbean colonies became very profitable, which explains why they were to be initially more attractive for migrants than North America.

Overseas colonization also emerged as a solution for England's religious tensions, for let us not forget that Protestants not only provoked bitter confrontation against Catholics but also among different branches of Protestantism. Puritans were expelled from the Church of England toward the end of Elizabeth I's reign, and many of them decided that only by emigrating abroad would they be able to practice their faith. This was the case of the Pilgrim Fathers. In 1620, 102 members of the Puritan community set sail in the *Mayflower*, a ship that was to become legendary in the history of the United States. On reaching the eastern coast of the United States the Pilgrim Fathers (or simply, Pilgrims) founded a settlement that was to be known as Plymouth. After many disputes they signed the Mayflower Compact, a historic document by which they set the rules under which they were going to be governed as a community. They also agreed to elect by democratic vote the person in charge of governing them.

The colony founded by the Pilgrims who arrived on the *Mayflower* was one of the first European settlements in North America and one of the

---

* John H. Elliott, *Empires of the Atlantic World: Britain and Spain in America 1492–1830* (New Haven, Conn.: Yale University Press, 2006).

most fabled. It came to symbolize the effort and spirit of sacrifice implicit in emigration, and the main principles on which the United States was built: work, family, property, democratic government, religious faith, and liberty.

The British Empire in North America continued to expand in the sixteenth century, for religious reasons among others. The atmosphere of confrontation and persecution that prevailed among different branches of Protestants and Catholics contributed to make many of them opt for emigration, just like the Pilgrims, in order to practice their faith.

In 1629 George Calvert, an influential Catholic politician, requested a royal decree from Charles I in order to found a Catholic colony in America for Catholics persecuted in Protestant Europe. As a result of this the colony of Maryland was founded. Some decades later, in 1681, the Quaker philosopher, constructor, and promoter of religious tolerance, William Penn, requested from King Charles II a concession of land in North America in order to found a colony where all Christians would be allowed to practice their religion. The king granted him a total of 120,000 square miles, which transformed him into one of the greatest landowners in the world, and he named it Pennsylvania. In return for such generous concession, the crown demanded a fifth of the benefits from the extraction of gold and silver, but to their disappointment metal deposits in Pennsylvania were going to be very scarce.

William Penn had absolute power to develop the colony according to his own aims and ideas. Religious tolerance, one of the founding pillars of the colony, helped attract not only Quakers like the founder but also members of other branches of Protestantism, Catholics, and Jews. Migrants arrived in Pennsylvania not only from the British Isles but also from Finland, Holland, Germany, and Scandinavia. The generous land concessions offered to the settlers contributed to the increasing popularity of the colony in Europe. By the year 1700 Pennsylvania already had 180,000 inhabitants.[*]

William Penn also founded the colony's capital, Philadelphia, the city of brotherly love. In contrast with the rivalries and confrontations that

---

[*] Kathleen Burk, *Old World, New World: The Story of Britain and America* (London: Abacus, 2007).

proliferated among the first British colonies in America, Penn promoted its unity based on democratic principles. These contributed to make Pennsylvania the main example of a "melting pot" between Europeans of different religious faiths that characterized the future United States.

As regards the origins of the early settlers of British America, the overwhelming majority came from England. The fact that there was plenty of land but very few people to work on it led to the introduction of indentured servitude; by this system emigrants without means would pay for their passage to America by working for an employer without receiving a wage for a certain number of years. This form of provisional serfdom allowed members of the poorest strata of society to reach America, and it was very popular if we take into account that approximately half of the white emigrants who settled in the New World in the seventeenth century were indentured servants.

The reward for many of the indentured servants, as well as most of the early settlers in America, was to be able to become landowners in the long run. For land was the main and very often the only available source of wealth. This explains why they were collectively known as planters. Quite a humble term in comparison with their Spanish contemporaries who crossed the Atlantic, who were to be known as conquistadors. The English dreamed of discovering similar riches in North America to those found by the conquistadors in Spanish America, but the lack of gold and silver deposits left them no option but to earn a living by cultivating the land. Yet this initial disappointment ended up being a blessing in disguise, as we shall see later, for it laid the foundations of a very prosperous economy.

Another great player in Europe's colonial expansion to emerge in the seventeenth century was Holland. Toward the end of the sixteenth century Holland was a small territory with poor natural resources and barely two million inhabitants living under the sovereignty of the Habsburg monarchy. Nevertheless, Dutch overseas ventures were to transform it not only into a great colonial power, but eventually into the wealthiest nation in Europe.

In 1568 seven provinces of the Low Countries rebelled against Philip II, leading to a war of independence that lasted for over eighty years. The Protestant reformation played a very important role in this war, for Protestantism became a sign of identity of the Dutch people, contributing to their determination to break away from the Catholic Empire of the Spanish. This war provoked the exodus of many Protestants who lived in Flanders under Habsburg dominion, especially of those in the port of Antwerp who migrated to Amsterdam. Receiving so many merchants who had prospered in Antwerp helped transform Amsterdam into one of the most important ports in the world. Most of them were aware that the key to creating wealth and asserting their independence was by developing overseas trade routes.[*] This was particularly the case of Jan Huygen van Linschoten, who can be considered as the pioneer in the Dutch expansion.

When he was a young sailor in 1580 Jan van Linschoten emigrated to Lisbon and served in the Portuguese Asian empire as bookkeeper to the archbishop of Goa. On his return to the Netherlands he published two books that played a very important role in breaking the Portuguese monopoly of trade in the Far East. His book *Itinerario* provided very valuable information about maritime routes and India that was to encourage both the Dutch and the English in their early incursions into Asia.

In 1594 nine merchants set up the Long-Distance Company with the initial aim of opening up Dutch trade in Asia. Few years later the Estates General of the new Dutch nation decided that this private initiative deserved better official support and organization. In this way the Dutch East India Company was created in 1602, which led colonial activities in Asia. This can be considered as history's first multinational: it was granted absolute power to found settlements wherever it wished, and even use force if it considered it necessary.

The Dutch East India Company settled in Ceylon in the year it began its overseas operations. Admiral Peter Booth was appointed governor. He was also known as the viceroy, and even though his power was far from being the equivalent of a Spanish viceroy, the title gives an idea of how highly esteemed this post was. The company's fourth governor, Jan Pieterszoon Coen occupied Jakarta. Shortly thereafter, in 1621, he renamed it under the Christian name of Batavia and transformed it into the capital of the Dutch Empire in Asia.

---

[*] Jonathan Israel, *The Dutch Republic: Its Rise, Greatness, and Fall, 1477–1806* (Oxford, England: Oxford University Press, 1998).

From Batavia, the Dutch merchants and sailors managed to oust Portugal from its hegemonic position in the spice trade, which they controlled in the Moluccas. They also posed a challenge to the East India Company of Britain. Batavia emerged as the strategic point from where the Dutch established trade networks through Asia.

Holland also broke into the New World with great success. In 1621 the Dutch Estates General officially granted permission for the creation of a West India Company, with a monopoly of trading and establishing colonies in the eastern coast of America.* In 1624 a ship arrived with thirty families, in order to create the first colony in present-day Albany, New York, which was named Fort Orange. Peter Minuit, the first governor of this colony took a very important decision that would facilitate its expansion: the purchase of the island of Manhattan from its indigenous inhabitants. There has been much speculation about the price that Minuit paid for the island that was to become the epicenter of New York City, where centuries later the most famous skyscrapers in the world would be built. Dutch sources mention that it was bought for trade goods that were worth sixty guilders, approximately twenty-eight dollars, according to American storybooks.** A fort was established there called New Amsterdam. Initially populated by approximately 270 Dutch immigrants, it grew steadily until it became one of the most important cities in North America.

The Dutch company also became a great threat for the interests of the Spanish and Portuguese in America. In 1628 the sailor Piet Heyn attacked the Spanish fleet and took all its treasures, allowing the company to offer a 70 percent dividend to its shareholders. Two years later, it occupied the Portuguese settlement of Pernambuco. At that time, the Dutch occupied the Caribbean islands of Saint Martin, Aruba, Curaçao, and Bonaire, thus consolidating its American Empire.

In this way, in no more than four decades, a small northern republic proved capable of creating an empire that would seriously affect the interests of Spain, Portugal, and other European powers in their overseas expansion.

---

* Israel, *The Dutch Republic.*
** Burk, *Old World, New World.*

Holland not only consolidated a colonial empire in four decades but it was also to make it more profitable than any other. The government of the Dutch United Provinces supported its creation by granting commercial monopolies to the East and West India Companies, but it was the shareholders of these companies who provided the capital to finance their activities. In this way the Dutch Empire managed to be a public initiative but without being a burden to the taxpayer. The extraordinary entrepreneurial spirit in Amsterdam and the main Dutch ports also played a very important role. Dutch capitalism not only made it possible to build an empire but also to expand the nation's frontier by reclaiming territory from the North Sea. A sophisticated technology backed by a great amount of invested capital allowed the Dutch to claim about 200,000 acres of land from the sea between 1590 and 1640. A group of 123 investors from Amsterdam launched a project of building farms and pastoral lands in the territory that had been the sea. On their completion, 207 farms had been created that earned substantial wealth for the investors. The Dutch example was going to inspire many small nations and city-states throughout the world on how to confront problems caused by scarcity of land and natural resources.

Holland not only obtained great benefits from its new empire but it also created rapidly expanding markets throughout the world. Amsterdam emerged as a great financial center in the seventeenth century. It became the main market for precious metals. The Dutch Republic also managed to control from its capital the triangular slave trade between Africa, Europe, and America, and become the main supplier of African labor in the West Indies. It took advantage of the shipments of sugar and tobacco that reached America to become its main distributor through the European continent. Prussia, Denmark, Sweden, and Russia were among its main buyers.

In the seventeenth century Holland also took the lead in the European colonization of the African continent, although this, as with so many other episodes of European expansion, was not the product of a carefully designed plan. The East India Company was capable of overcoming all obstacles to establish itself in Asia, except for one: scurvy. This illness, produced by the lack of fruit and vegetables, caused many casualties in the long voyage to Asia. For this reason it was decided that a way station should be built on the coast of the Cape of Good Hope, where the fleets would stop and obtain fresh provisions on their way to the East Indies.

Jan van Riebeeck, a prominent merchant of the East India Company, arrived in Cape of Good Hope with three ships, eighty-two men, eight women, and his own wife. The Dutch managed to set up a fort there, and after discovering the great possibilities that the South African coast offered, van Riebeeck requested the East India Company to send free settlers. Although there was no official interest in colonizing this remote land, in 1657 the Company sent its first group of employees. As the settlers started to exploit the land around Cape harbor, it became necessary to employ new labor, and the first shipment of slaves arrived from Batavia and Madagascar on that same year.

Soon the new settlers started to expand toward the north in search of arable land, which provoked the first clash with the indigenous tribe of the Khoikhoi. In 1659 the Khoikhoi rebelled against the white settlers but were defeated and forced to withdraw from the lands where they lived. This constituted the beginning of a traumatic conflict between whites and blacks in South Africa that would last for more than three centuries.

In 1662 van Riebeeck was appointed governor's secretary in Batavia and set out from South Africa, leaving a community of 134 officials, 35 settlers, 15 women, 22 children, and 180 slaves. But this was only the beginning of the colony's growth, for in those days the repressive policy of the king of France against the Protestant population provoked the exodus of around 300,000 Huguenots. Many of them settled in Holland, and there the East India Company offered them an agreement by which they would be transported to South Africa and granted land there in return for their loyalty to Holland. This is how, in 1688, the first Boers, meaning *farmer* in Dutch, arrived in South Africa.[*] The Boers, pious and hardworking Protestants, settled in Africa with the determination to build a community that would live according to its religious beliefs.

The time when van Riebeek was in South Africa coincided with the imperial apogee of Holland. In 1648 the Treaty of Westphalia put an end

---

[*]   Martin Meredith, *The Fortunes of Africa: A 5000-Year History of Wealth, Greed, and Endeavor* (New York: Simon & Schuster, 2004).

to eighty years of war against Spain, and also the Thirty Years' War, which had confronted several powers mainly because of religious reasons. Holland was recognized as an independent nation and also Switzerland emerged as a nation independent from the Holy Roman Empire. This treaty led to a new world order based on the respect to the sovereign estate. In this way Europe created a term that would constitute the essence of international relations from then on: the nation-state.

In the mid–seventeenth century the young Dutch nation was going to emerge as the best example of the virtues of the nation-state in the world, and of the principles that could make it prosper. Its overseas empire had provided the Dutch people with the wealth to expel the Habsburg monarchy, and trade networks eventually allowed them to overtake Spain as the wealthiest power.

What about France? France had been the most powerful kingdom in Europe before the rise of Spain, and joined the race for overseas expansion in the early sixteenth century. It began making timid incursions into America in the sixteenth century, eventually managing to become one of the great four colonizing powers in the seventeenth.

The French began fishing off the shores of the North American coast from the times of Jacques Cartier in the early sixteenth century, and began exchanging hides with the locals. They eventually reached the conclusion that in order to obtain benefits from this continent, the foundation of permanent settlements was essential.

The sailor and explorer Samuel de Champlain was primarily responsible for the creation of the new French Empire in North America. After navigating along the eastern coast he took part in the founding of Port-Royal in 1605, which was the first permanent European settlement in northern Florida. Shortly after, he persuaded Louis Hébert, who had accompanied him on the voyage to Port-Royal to settle with his family on the coast of Canada. In 1608, Champlain obtained permission from King Henry IV to found the villa of Quebec in the territory where Louis Hébert had settled. From then on Quebec (which according to an Indian word means "where the river narrows down") became the center of the fledgling overseas possession, which was soon to be known as New France. Three years later, Champlain established a base in the island of Montreal to develop fur trade and this was to be the origin of the second great city founded by the French in present-day Canada.*

The French crown was going to play a very special role in the creation of its colonial empire. Not only Henry IV and Louis XIII, who ruled France at that time, but the person who knew better than anyone else how to defend the interests of the French: Cardinal Richelieu. Louis XIII's prime minister from 1624 until his death in 1642, he was responsible for the transformation of the French monarchy into a great centralized state, and his initiatives had crucial importance in the French rise to supremacy.

The main obsession of "the red eminence," as Cardinal Richelieu was known, was to counteract the power of the Habsburgs in Europe. For this reason he decided that it was not only necessary to expand the power of France in the continent but also to promote the creation of an overseas empire. Apart from supporting Samuel de Champlain's initiatives, Richelieu created in 1627 the New France Company with the aim of promoting trade and colonization in America.** The company was created with capital from one hundred private investors, for which it was also to be known as the Company of the Hundred Associates. The cardinal was one of the company's main shareholders, and for this reason, among other powerful reasons of state, he always kept a close eye on it.

Richelieu also promoted the French colonization of the Caribbean. In 1635 he was instrumental in the creation of a great company, the *Compagnie des Îles de l'Amérique*, and also became one of its main shareholders. As a result of this initiative, Pierre Belain d'Esnambuc and other adventurers occupied the islands of Saint Christophe (Saint Kitts), Martinique, Guadalupe, Tortuga, and Maria-Galante on behalf of France.

During the first years of the long reign of Louis XIV France enjoyed a golden era. France was consolidated as the most powerful state in Europe with the largest population, the best army, and an efficient centralized

---

* Samuel de Champlain, *Le Voyages de Samuel de Champlain au Canada, de 1603 à 1618* (London: Forgotten Books, 2017).
** Raymonde Litalien and Denis Vaugeois, eds., *Champlain: The Birth of French America* (Montreal: McGill-Queen's University Press, 2004).

administration. The success with which France was transformed into the arbiter of power in Europe, as well as the splendor of its court and its flourishing culture, contributed to make French the language of diplomacy that every good statesmen or educated person should speak. In this way France had all that was necessary to expand its power through the world.

The Sun King, who observed the world from the splendor of his palace in Versailles, did not have much enthusiasm for colonial adventures. In his view the key to French supremacy was in the European continent, and whoever dominated Europe would dominate the world. Nevertheless, his chief minister Jean-Baptiste Colbert, was very much in favor of overseas expansion. He was mainly responsible for convincing Louis XIV of the need to build an empire.

Under Louis XIV's scepter, France was going to consolidate its first colonial empire. In 1659 sailors from Dieppe established the first colonial base in Senegal, known as Saint-Louis. This was going to become the first settlement founded by Europeans in Western Africa, and it played an important role in the French economy. From this Senegalese base the French traded in rubber, ivory, gold, precious stones, and slaves.

In the Caribbean Louis XIV promoted the creation of the colony of Saint-Domingue in 1659, in the western half of Hispaniola where French buccaneers had arrived a few decades before. The establishment of this colony was a great idea from the economic point of view, as it became one of the main sugar producers.

Finally, under the reign of the Sun King, France managed to reach Asia. After the creation of the French East India Company in 1675 the French reached Madagascar, and from there they sailed to India where they founded their first trading bases in Asia.

The French crown was not only directly involved in the promotion of French colonization, it also managed to keep strict supervision over its development. This was largely thanks to Colbert, who was to go down in history as the founder of Colbertism, a doctrine believing in state supervision in order to ensure that the economy served the state's interests. "The colonies must serve the kingdom and must not develop beyond the French industrial control," he stated on one occasion.

With the aim of ensuring that the crown would have a closer supervision over the colonial expansion in America, the Sovereign Council of New France was created in 1663. Most important of all was the creation of the post of Intendant of New France, by which a senior government official would be in charge of the colony's administration on behalf of the king, in the same way that the viceroy did this in the Spanish empire.

The first Intendant of New France was Jean Talon, who took important measures to promote the development and prosperity of French America. An important initiative for which he was to be specially remembered were the so-called *filles du roi* (the king's daughters)—over nine hundred young women who were sent to New France with the aim of marrying settlers, hoping in this way that their offspring would lead to the population increase that the colony desperately needed.*

Just as it happened with Spain and Portugal, the difficulty to populate the colonies led the French crown to accept the fact that many of its citizens would not be white. As a result of this, intermarriage was promoted. According to the founding charter of the Company of New France, every descendant of French settlers who had been baptized would be considered a French citizen. Later on, the French authorities encouraged the settlers to build families with the indigenous people. Nevertheless, the fact that the Indian tribes in North America were much wilder and indomitable and also less numerous, prevented the emergence of a large mixed-race population as had happened in Spanish and Portuguese America.

In spite of all these measures to promote procreation of French citizens in America, population growth continued to be disappointing: New France, which had around 8000 inhabitants in 1660 did not have more than 17,000 settlers in 1700, an insignificant figure compared with the over 240,000 white settlers in the English colonies of North America.** Despite the fact that France had much more population than England or the Iberian Peninsula, promoting emigration to the colonies constituted a great challenge.

---

* W. J. Eccles, *The French in North America, 1500–1783* (East Lansing: Michigan State University Press, 1990).
** *A History of Canada's Population*: www.statcan.ge.ca

The economic, religious or personal motives that made so many Europeans wish to start a new life in America did not seem to be so powerful among the French.

The French Empire in America had several disadvantages in comparison to the other European empires and for this reason very few Frenchmen seemed willing to settle permanently there. In first place the geography and climate of New France were much harsher. Nor did the system that was established for colonizing the new lands give the expected results. The *seigneuries* (lordships) were an almost feudal system of land tenure. The company granted land to the *seigneurs* and in return they would look for settlers and cover the cost of their voyage to America. The settlers for their part would have to pay rents to the seigneur and work for him for a certain period each year. The main problem of this system was that all the settler's obligations toward the seigneur prevented them from prospering. The strong presence of the French state was also another obstacle: the Intendant enjoyed absolute power to raise taxes and recruit settlers for defense.

One of the main incentives for emigrating to America was precisely to get rid of the political and administrative controls exerted by the European states. The settlers in the English colonies felt relieved from many of their obligations as subjects of the crown, and they could also influence their government through democratically elected colonial assemblies. But this did not happen in the French colonies, where its inhabitants were submitted practically to the same hierarchical society as in France.

Unlike ordinary French citizens, the religious orders were particularly motivated to migrate to America, particularly the Jesuits. The Jesuits not only played a very important role propagating Christianity but also in the expansion of French America. The explorers Louis Jolliet and Robert de La Salle had been raised as Jesuits although after their arrival in America they earned a living trading in furs. Jolliet, in his frequent contacts with the indigenous population, heard them talk of a great river called the Mississippi, and he sailed along the upper reaches of this great river. La Salle went much further in his explorations.

On learning from the Mohawk tribe about the existence of a great river known as the Ohio, la Salle devoted himself to exploration. Greatly influenced by contemporary traveling myths he hoped that by sailing along the Ohio River he would reach the Pacific Ocean, and from there he would find a western path to China. He was soon proved wrong but in compensation he managed to explore the Great Lakes of North America. Shortly after he canoed down the Mississippi and claimed the Mississippi basin for France, naming it Louisiana. In his final expedition he founded Fort St. Louis in Texas.

La Salle made the most important contribution to French expansion in America, allowing him to consolidate a huge territory in North America that stretched from present-day Canada to the Caribbean. The territories around Illinois to Ohio were particularly appropriate for the fur trade. The sources of wealth offered by the lands around the Mississippi were immense, and the Louisiana expanse had much better weather for agriculture and the cultivation of products like sugar, cotton, and tobacco.

After la Salle other great adventurers started colonizing the discovered territory. Pierre Le Moyne d'Iberville founded the colony of "Luisiana" in 1699. In 1718 his brother Jean-Baptiste Le Moyne de Bienville founded the city of New Orleans. Another great contribution was that of Antoine de la Mothe Cadillac, who in 1701 founded the city of Detroit on the border of the American Great Lakes in present-day Michigan.[*]

With the founding of these cities and the occupation of the immense territory that stretched from Detroit to New Orleans, toward the end of Louis XIV's reign France had managed to consolidate the largest European empire in North America.

Rivalries between great powers increased as their empires expanded, and very often the territories held by some would expand at the expense of the others. This was certainly the case with England, whose empire considerably grew at Dutch and French cost.

A policy that was going to be narrowly associated with European imperial expansion was that of mercantilism, based on the idea that colonies should be forbidden to trade with rival nations and that incursions of foreigners into a country's national market should be protected by tariffs. England was to take drastic measures in order to protect the expanding market in

---

[*]   Eccles, *French in North America*.

its possessions, and this led to the first Anglo-Dutch War in 1652, which broke out as a result of the interception of Dutch ships that were found in English territorial waters. Holland was defeated and was forced to respect England's Navigation Acts. But this did not put an end to territorial clashes between the two countries. In 1664 King Charles II decided to put an end to the disputes with the Dutch by invading New Amsterdam. The territory succumbed to the British forces that were led by the duke of York, and it was duly renamed as New York. From then, the inhabitants of the Dutch settlement became British subjects.

Once Holland was expelled from North America the British managed to consolidate a solid colonial empire composed of what came to be known as the Thirteen Colonies. But frontier disagreements with the neighboring French Empire in America led to a new conflict in 1654, which in America was going to be known as the French and Indian War.

This colonial war between France and Britain contributed to soaring tensions between great powers in Europe to such an extent that it led to the outbreak of the Seven Years' War in 1756. Britain, Portugal, and Prussia fought against France, Austria, Russia, and Sweden in this first global conflict, which some historians have insisted on calling the First World War, as it was fought on four continents. This war showed how far European interests had spread across the world by the eighteenth century. The territorial aspirations of each nation fighting in this war could no longer be decided exclusively on the European continent.

France was the great loser in this war, and the Treaty of Paris in 1763 confirmed its disappearance as a great colonial power. It ceded practically the whole of New France to Britain, except the islands of Miquelon and St. Pierre, and it also lost Louisiana to Spain. Britain managed to oust France from India, in this way initiating the era of hegemony over the Indian subcontinent that was so important in its imperial destiny.

The key to Britain's victory in this war was twofold: first, naval supremacy. From the times of Elizabeth I there was increasing awareness that naval power was the key for the security of the British Isles and overseas expansion. In 1755 Prime Minister William Pitt embarked on an ambitious shipbuilding program by which the British fleet was to be twice as big as the French. Second, financial supremacy. From the reign of William II, Britain had implemented the Dutch method of financing wars by selling bonds. In this way, while the British government had a great capacity to raise money, the French had to accept defeat once their state coffers were empty.

Colonial expansion and victories on the battlefield made the British become increasingly conscious of their global power. The term British Empire started to be used in the mid–eighteenth century, especially after the Seven Years' War. Even before the reign of George III, after the union of the kingdoms of England and Scotland in 1707, the term British Empire became increasingly frequent in reference to the political union of Scotland, England, and Wales—and Ireland. But in the second half of the eighteenth century as a result of the increase in overseas possessions, the country's political elites started to describe their colonial power as "the British Empire."

As the empire grew, the British government and crown also took measures in order to consolidate their power over the territories and ensure a more efficient administration. The colonial governors became a key institution. Just as the Spanish viceroy or the French Intendant, they enjoyed absolute power wherever they were sent. As a result of this the colonial governor became a very prestigious position providing great opportunities for wealth and social promotion.

Nevertheless, British colonial governors were not surrounded by the pageantry of the Spanish viceroys, nor did they have such broad means to exert power. While the colonial government in Spanish America was financed by the extraction of precious metals, and also by the tax on the Church and even the Indians, in British America it could not count on any of these sources and depended exclusively on the contribution of its own settlers. In order to raise taxes and also maintain law and order in the American settlements, some of them were divided into counties, as in England, and the old English local authority of the sheriff was introduced. Nevertheless, as they had to pay taxes for the colonial government, the settlers demanded that their views on how to spend public money should be taken into account. Local assemblies represented by colonists became influential institutions from the early days of British America. As the colonies expanded, the clashes between the interests of the colonial people and the crown became increasingly frequent.

The combination of naval power, armies, and wealth made it possible for some European powers to expand their influence at the expense of others. But this was not always the case; there were still plenty of unexplored areas around the world that could easily be occupied without interfering with the interests of a rival power. For this reason Europeans continued investing in exploration and organizing journeys of discovery.

Portugal gradually expanded its territory in the seventeenth and eighteenth centuries as a result of exploration through the vast and often impenetrable jungles of Brazil. This was mainly due to the *bandeirantes,* groups of settlers who formed paramilitary groups in order to explore the interior of Brazil. Their most important achievement was their discovery of gold and diamonds in Minas Gerais in 1693. From then this remote region was transformed into the new economic center of the empire, attracting a large influx of migrants.[*]

Exploration allowed France to obtain some compensation from the dramatic losses of the Seven Years' War. In 1766 Admiral Louis Antoine de Bougainville led an expedition around the world and landed on the island of Tahiti, with which French influence in the southern Pacific began. Particularly influential for Britain were the explorations of Captain Robert Cook, one of the great navigators of all time.

Like so many Europeans of humble origins, James Cook joined the merchant navy as a teenager, as this was the only available way to avoid a life of poverty and mediocrity. He made his name as a sailor and cartographer in the Royal Navy in the Seven Years' War, and this led him to make three major voyages across the Pacific that were going to be remembered both for their scientific and geopolitical impact. In 1768 he was commissioned by the Royal Society to lead an expedition to the southern Pacific. He reached New Zealand and Australia and took possession of this land on behalf of the King George III, thus laying the foundations of British colonization in this part of the world.

The colonization of other continents and the occupation of remote lands was not the exclusive mission of the great Atlantic European powers that we have examined. Scandinavian nations also made an important contribution.

---

[*]   Burns, *History of Brazil.*

The kingdoms of Norway, Denmark, and Sweden opened up the frontiers of the northern lands that were apparently inhospitable due to the glacial cold and perennial snows. But not satisfied with expanding their influence throughout the North, they also embarked on the colonial adventure in America other continents.

The inhabitants of Scandinavia were not as cultured and advanced as the people of the Latin world but they were much more resilient before adversity. Having to survive in lands covered by snow for a good part of the year contributed to the development of a great conquering spirit and an expansionist ethos among their peoples, as they demonstrated several centuries before the era of discoveries.

The Vikings had one of the most extraordinary seafaring traditions in Europe. Archaeological remains have proved that they reached the shores of North America, although they were never aware of having discovered a new continent. With this background it is not surprising that their descendants in the Scandinavian kingdoms of Norway, Denmark, and Sweden made a substantial contribution to European expansion.

The first Scandinavian migratory waves settled in Scotland, Ireland, Iceland, and even Greenland. Norway emerged as the hegemonic kingdom in Scandinavia as a result of this network of northern settlements. Nevertheless, in the sixteenth century Denmark became the dominant state. Sweden, Norway, and Denmark had spent two centuries unified under the same monarch, but Swedish dissatisfaction under Danish dominion led to the end of this union in the sixteenth century. Denmark, on the other hand, was not going to allow Norway become independent. In 1536 the Danish Council officially merged with Norway and from then on the Norwegian overseas possessions were to be directly controlled from Copenhagen.

From that time, Denmark was also known as Denmark-Norway as a result of the union of the two kingdoms, strived to consolidate its position as a Protestant state in Europe. It did not achieve hegemony in the Baltic due to the opposition of Sweden and the German principalities, but in compensation for this it achieved formidable overseas expansion.

The Danish Empire was another European example of close cooperation among sailors and adventurers, private investors, and the crown. The Danish

East India Company was granted an official concession to trade in Asia during the reign of Christian IV. It built its first fort in Tranquebar, in southern India in 1620, and later other small enclaves in the Indian subcontinent. On their way to Asia, the Danish also built forts on the coast of Central Africa, in present-day Ghana.

The third pillar of the new Danish Empire was going to be the Caribbean. The Danish West India Company took possession of several small islands that became known as the Danish Antilles. Just as other powers in the region, the Danes made these possessions profitable through the exportation of sugar and cotton.

Much more challenging than the tropical possessions were the northern ones that had been originally occupied by Norway. In Iceland a small Scandinavian population started to thrive from the sixteenth century onward. Nevertheless, the harsh living conditions prevented the population from growing steadily. In the eighteenth century around a third of the inhabitants perished from a strain of smallpox.

The colonization of Greenland proved to be even more difficult. In 1721 a Lutheran missionary known as Hans Egede obtained the authorization of King Frederick IV to found a settlement of Gothab, meaning "good hope," which was later to become Greenland's capital. Migration to this largely inhospitable land was deemed as a punishment by ordinary Danish citizens, for this reason the first ships that were sent there in order to start populating the settlement were partially filled with ex-convicts who were forced to migrate. In spite of the hardship, the settlement, mainly composed of the Inuit and Scandinavians, has survived until the present.

While Denmark built an overseas empire, its Scandinavian rival Sweden rose to prominence. In medieval times Sweden emerged as a strong state in Scandinavia. The golden era of Swedish history took place in the mid–seventeenth century, under the reign of King Gustav Adolf the Great. During the Thirty Years' War, Sweden conquered a substantial part of the Holy Roman Empire. Under the Treaty of Westphalia, which put an end to this war in 1648, Sweden obtained vast territories of present-day Germany.

While the frontiers of Sweden expanded across Europe, the Scandinavian kingdom also built an overseas empire. In 1638 the first Swedish settlers in

North America founded a fort in what is now Delaware. The fort grew rapidly with the migration of several hundred Swedes and Finns, and it became known as New Sweden.* In the 1650s a few forts were founded in Central Africa, the Swedish Gold Coast. Nevertheless this period of imperial expansion was to be very brief. Holland invaded New Sweden and made it part of New Amsterdam. Similarly, Denmark ousted Sweden from Central Africa and transformed its territories into the Danish Gold Coast. A few decades later its hegemonic position in Northern Europe was successfully challenged by a rising power: Russia.

In 1700 Czar Peter I of Russia led a coalition of countries with the aim of putting an end to Swedish supremacy in Northern Europe. Russia, Denmark, Prussia, Poland-Lithuania, and Saxony were all allies in a war against Sweden that was going to be known as the Great War of the North. Sweden was finally defeated and with the exception of Finland and Pomerania, it lost all the territory that it had gained in its years of expansion.

Among the members of the alliance against Sweden that distributed the lands of its empire the main beneficiary was Russia, gaining territory in the Baltic as well as access to the sea. This culminated one of the most extraordinary processes of territorial expansion in world history, which also constituted an important chapter in the rise of Europe in the world.

The rise of Russia as a nation-state was very complicated, mainly due to its geographic location in the eastern end of Europe where the continent is only separated from Asia by the natural barrier of the Ural Mountains. This territory was constantly exposed to the attacks and ravages of the Mongols and Tartars. The early Russians were victims of formidable Mongol expansion. From the time of Genghis Khan in the thirteenth century, the Mongols managed to conquer so much territory that they became the largest land empire that has been seen in history. It was only after its decline in the fourteenth century that the Russian people gradually emerged.

The Russians started to thrive around a settlement known as Muscovy in the fifteenth century. During the reign of Ivan III, the principality of Moscow managed to triple its territory, forcing the Mongols to withdraw. The Russian

---

* Morison, *European Discovery of America.*

Orthodox Church established the seat of its patriarch in Moscow, which allowed it to forge a close alliance with the ruling dynasty.

The fall of Constantinople in 1453 and the death of the last Orthodox emperor allowed Moscow to become the main center of the Orthodox Church. From then Moscow was often referred to as the third Rome, and this helped make the Russian sovereign start to be called Czar, which derives from Caesar. The emperor of the Holy Roman Empire, Maximilian I, recognized Ivan III. Until then Ivan had been known as a Russian prince, but becoming emperor would deeply mark the destiny of his successors. The first one to be formally crowned as Czar of all Russias was the son of Ivan III, who reached the throne as Ivan IV and went down in history as Ivan the Terrible due to his brutality and despicable character. The Czar was determined to ensure that his title would not be symbolic; an emperor needed to govern over an empire and he devoted his reign to the task of building it.

Czar Ivan IV interpreted the history of the Russian people in very simple terms: the Russians had constantly submitted to external invasions from the east until they became strong in Moscow and began to expand through the territories that had been controlled by their enemies. The key to Russian strength was in its eastward expansion.

The power of the czars rested on two pillars: on the one hand the boyars, the landowning nobility, which was granted land in the conquered territories in return for its exploitation and loyalty to the czar. The second pillar was the Cossacks. The Cossacks, a Turkish term that means free men, were originally tribes of hunters that proliferated along the Don and the Dnieper Rivers. They were great horsemen and warriors who became the terror of many Eurasian peoples, for apart from hunting they lived on pillaging, and were to become the main symbols of Russian expansionism. Napoleon left it clear on invading Russia: "The Cossacks are the best light troops. If I had them in my army I would go around the world with them."

Ivan IV was the first czar to understand that an alliance with the Cossacks would be crucial to expand into Asia. For this reason, he reached an agreement with the Cossacks by which they would serve as frontier troops in return for payment of money or permission to plunder the conquered territories. This agreement made it possible for Ivan the Terrible to embark on the most ambitious conquests of his reign.

In 1552 Ivan IV, helped by the Cossacks, managed to conquer Kazan and expel the Mongols. This victory constituted a turning point in the Eurasian balance of power. With the conquest of Kazan, Russia annexed for the first time a non-Slavic state. In order to control it, Ivan expelled a good part of its Muslim population and sent Russian merchants and artisans to settle in this city.*

After Kazan, the next of Ivan IV's great conquests was Astrakhan, with which the Russian Empire reached the Caspian Sea. Once the Khanate of Astrakhan was occupied Russia managed to control the whole Volga River region. This enormous territory provided great possibilities for the Russian boyars to expand their wealth. Among them a family that was going to benefit in particular were the Stroganovs. The czar granted Anikey Stroganov great tracts of land in the Urals. As a result of this the Stroganovs became one of the most powerful noble families in Russian history, not only because they were the largest landowners but also as a result of their activities as industrialists. Stroganov promoted Russian immigration on a grand scale to these enormous territories. He provided incentives for Russians to found settlements. Due to this migration, civilization was brought to the Eurasian barren lands.

The Stroganovs also played a leading role in the occupation of Siberia, this apparently endless region in northern Asia that was to have such an important role in Russian history. Toward 1577 the Stroganovs entrusted a Cossack leader known as Yermak Timofeyevich with the protection of their lands from the attacks of Kuchum, the great khan of Siberia. In 1588 Yermak led an army of Cossacks on an expedition through Siberia with the aim of defeating the enemy tribes once and for all.**

This expedition also allowed the Russians to start exploring Siberia. Yermak finally captured the city of Qashliq, the capital of the Siberian Khanate. Over the ruins of this city the Cossack founded Tobolsk in 1585,

---

* Geoffrey Hosking, *Russia and the Russians: A History* (Cambridge, Mass.: Harvard University Press, 2001).
** Ibid.

which was going to become the historical capital of Siberia. Shortly after that he finally found Kuchum, but the cunning khan attacked the Russian troops at night and Yermak lost his life in the ambush. He failed to achieve his final aim of capturing Kuchum, but he went down in history as the pioneer in the exploration of Siberia, and his adventures were going to inspire many Russian songs and chronicles.

Yermak explored the main Siberian rivers, opening up the access to this immense region for the Russians. Ivan the Terrible took great interest in lands conquered by the Cossacks and supported the expeditions with which the Russians definitively occupied Siberia. Kuchum was finally defeated in 1598, putting an end to Muslim dominion in this region. As a result of the Russian expansion toward Siberia, many Tartar people who were also practicing Muslims became subjects of the Russian czar and the Russian Empire. It had began simply as a union of Slavic people, but was transformed into a multiethnic and interconfessional empire.

Ivan the Terrible deeply marked Russia's fate, as his reign constituted a bold attempt to transform his kingdom into an imperial power, controlling Eurasia. Nevertheless, his empire was excessively based on his authority; it lacked institutions or a system of government that would guarantee its continuity. After his death Russia went through a long period of instability and internal struggles for the crown. In 1613 a nobleman known as Michael Romanov emerged as winner in the struggle for power and was crowned as the new czar of all the Russias. Czar Michael I managed to authoritatively put an end to the times of political instability and found a dynasty that would rule over Russia for over three hundred years, consolidating his country as a great empire that was to play a very influential role in the international sphere.[*]

Throughout the eighteenth century the Russians rapidly advanced toward the East in the exploration and colonization of Asian lands. Above all they transformed Siberia into an integral part of Russia, making it possible for the Europeans to start having news of this previously unknown land.

---

[*] Simon Sebag Montefiore, *The Romanovs: 1613–1918* (New York: Alfred A. Knopf, 2016).

The Cossacks were to have, on one more occasion, a very important role in this extraordinary adventure. One of the most famous was Demid Pyanda. According to the Siberian chronicles, in 1620 Pyanda went to Siberia with a group of men on a hunting expedition, in order to trade later with animal furs in that region. He was the first Russian to descend the Tunguska River and reach the Lena, one of the largest rivers of the world, and he also contacted with the Yakuts and the Buriats, people that inhabited eastern Siberia. The Cossack explorations were followed by expeditions of Russian troops with the mission of building forts to ensure that the territories would continue under the czar's sovereignty. In 1627 they founded a fort in Krasnoyarsk, and another one on the Lena River; a decade later the troops reached the great Lake Baikal for the first time. Finally in 1648 one expedition reached the Bay of Okhotsk, on the Pacific Ocean. In less than one hundred years the Russian nation expanded its frontiers from Eastern Europe to the Far East.

The main factor that allowed Russia to achieve such a formidable expansion was not just the ambition of the czars but the determination of the common Russians to settle in what were known for several generations as the lands of darkness. As it happened with the Atlantic empires, the fortune-seekers and adventurers were going to lay the foundations of the Russian Empire. The main source of wealth that was initially discovered in Siberia was the fur trade, based on its abundant fauna. As a result of this fur became the most important business in eighteenth–century Russia. From the seventeenth century Russia experienced a sudden rise of demand for furs similar to the gold rush in the United States in the nineteenth century, and many ventured into the Russian steppe in search of this increasingly profitable product. For the czars the furs in Siberia constituted a source of wealth almost as important as the silver and gold of America for the Spanish monarchs. Just like the Spanish sovereigns, the czars received a percentage of the profits earned in the fur trade, and they also demanded the Siberian natives pay their taxes in furs as new Russian subjects.

The process of imposing Russian sovereignty and forcing the natives from the conquered lands in the eighteenth century to pay taxes was generally easier for the Russians than for the Atlantic empires, for various reasons. First,

Siberia and the Caucasus were scarcely populated by very backward peoples who did not have sufficient means to resist the arrival of the Russians. Second, the tax that was demanded from them did not constitute such a burden, as furs were abundant. And finally, the natives were generally not employed as cheap labor. Nevertheless, there was obviously plenty of resistance from many of the conquered peoples to becoming Russian subjects, and the resistance grew as they marched toward the East. The Buryats and Koryaks fought for their independence until they were finally subdued by force.

Another great advantage that the Russians encountered in the process of colonial expansion toward the East was that unlike the Atlantic powers, they did not have any significant rivals. While European powers rivaled and often clashed over the possession of lands in America and other continents, none of them showed any interest in northern Asia, leaving Russia comfortably alone in this huge territory.

On the other hand the Russian advance into southern Siberia proved much more challenging, as they were to interfere with the interests of two formidable nations: Mongolia and China. Mongol and above all Chinese resistance, starting in the seventeenth century, would define the southeastern frontier of the Russian Empire.

Russian territory increased from 2.1 million miles in 1600 to around 5.9 million a century later, when it was poised to become one of the largest empires in history.* To take possession of all these territories by the construction of forts was not going to be that difficult, but the real challenge was going to be to colonize, administrate, and extract the wealth of all this territory.

Despite the fact that the Volga and Siberia regions were a kind of El Dorado for the Russians, initially very few of those who ventured into these territories in search of fortune really aimed at definitively settling in lands that seemed so inhospitable. The fertile lands to the south of Siberia attracted many Russian peasants, but in general, the lack of migrants to populate such vast territory constituted a problem for the government in Moscow, and it

---

* John Darwin, *After Tamerlane: The Rise and Fall of Global Empires, 1400–2000* (London: Bloomsbury, 2008).

also explains its slow development. According to a 1740 census, the male Siberian population in that year was only 400,000.*

Russia expanded not only through the Asian mainland. Just like the other great European powers it also achieved territorial expansion as a result of naval exploration. Shortly before his death Czar Peter the Great sent a distinguished Danish sailor known as Vitus Bering on a mission to explore the eastern border of Siberia.

In 1741 Bering led an expedition of over six hundred men, with the aim of charting a map of eastern Siberia and reaching North America. The expedition discovered the coast of Alaska. Bering died on that voyage without having found out that he was the first explorer in recorded history to travel to America through the strait which was to be known as the Bering Strait. Thanks to this discovery Russia acquired a great possession in the American continent.

Especially notable in the consolidation of Russia as a great power were the territorial conquests achieved during the reign of Catherine the Great. Under her reign Russia gained almost half a million miles of territory at the expense of the Ottoman Empire and Poland.** It managed to acquire Crimea, the territory around present-day Belarus, Ukraine, and a good part of Poland. It put great emphasis on expansion toward the Caucasus, and during its reign plans were made for the campaign against the Ottoman Empire, which culminated with the expulsion of the Turks from Constantinople. The expansion of the Russian Empire reached its zenith during the reign of Nicholas I, who ruled from 1825 to 1855. By that time the Russian czar managed to rule over territories that stretched across three continents and covered approximately a sixth of the Earth.

Three centuries after the beginning of the era of great discoveries, the European powers that we have described here managed to create empires that spanned five continents. The reasons for this unprecedented movement of conquest and colonization in history are diverse; the acquisition of wealth was an obvious one that they all shared, as well as the power and the glory

---

*   Hosking, *Russia and the Russians.*
**   Montefiore, *The Romanovs.*

associated with the occupation of territories. Rivalry was also an important driving force. Let us not forget that the wish to emulate Portugal explains the Castilian strategies that led to the discovery of the New World. Of course, rivalry and resentment against the Iberian powers was a major motivation for the English and French monarchs for opening markets and settling overseas.

The pressure to survive in very adverse circumstances also explains the expansion of the Scandinavian powers as well as Russia. For all of them occupation of other territories seemed both the solution to many of their existential problems as well as the only way of prospering.

There were of course, important differences in the empire-building strategies used by European powers. Spanish conquistadors led conquering ventures that usually—but not always—counted on royal support. In the case of England, Holland, and the Scandinavian powers, settlements were created mainly through joint-stock companies and private initiatives that counted on royal endorsement, but were financed by citizens who generally hoped to obtain profits from these ventures. But in all cases, what the *conquistador,* *bandeirante,* planter, settler, or Cossack had in common was that they were all leading projects of expansion in which they put their lives on the line and risked all their possessions.

The first major consequence of the rise of European empires was the creation of a new Atlantic world. It started making progress with the arrival of the Spaniards and the Portuguese in the New World, followed by the British, French, Dutch, and Scandinavians. The first trade routes between the Iberian Peninsula and Central America gradually expanded toward the north and south of the continent. By the end of the seventeenth century all major ports of Western Europe were incorporated into these Atlantic trade routes, as well as certain enclaves on the coast of Africa. As a result, the Atlantic became the fastest-growing market in the world, and the European colonial powers were the main beneficiaries.

But as we have seen, the colonization of the Americas implied much more than the development of profitable markets. It entailed the creation of populated European settlements. This trend of migration that was initially small gradually increased until it became a mass movement, as we shall later see. Through these settlements Europeans were able to propagate their customs and institutions, their languages and religions. As a result of this Western culture became firmly entrenched in the Americas.

Until the fifteenth century the Western world, exclusively represented by the Europeans, was losing ground before the East, which was expanding at its cost. This situation radically changed after the discovery of America in 1492. From that year the Europeans gained the privilege of expanding into a vast continent and shaping it according to their beliefs. The ultimate consequence of this discovery was that Western culture was now represented on both sides of the Atlantic.

The rise of European empires had very important consequences that explain the hegemonic position that Europe was going to enjoy for over four centuries. Trade networks were established throughout the world that not only allowed European powers to obtain large economic benefits, but they also explain the steadily expanding gap of economic development between Europe, the West, and the rest of the world. Finally, the rise of empires had a deep impact on European collective mentality. In consequence, Europeans on the whole became increasingly convinced that the key to their power and prosperity was beyond the confines of their continent.

Chapter 4

Revolution Versus Empire

The Impact of the Era of Revolutions on European Empires and the Western World.

The revolution is one of the great products of modern Europe. If Europeans managed to propagate their interests through their empires, it was due to revolutions that some of the most influential ideas born in Europe have spread across the world. The term revolution has been used in excess in relation to European modern history. Not only has it been applied to describe Europe's most abrupt political changes, but also those in the economic, social, and the most diverse aspects affecting human lives. But revolution is not just a political upheaval that provokes a change of regime. It must lead to the complete overthrow of a system of government as well as its social, economic, and cultural foundations. Above all, a revolution must be supported by new ideas capable of changing peoples' values. For this reason it was the French Revolution that gave this term its full modern meaning. The French Revolution brought the country's old order to an abrupt end, and it gave way to a revolutionary era that radically transformed Europe and the entire Western world.

We are still living under the long-term effects of this revolution. In 1972, during a historic visit to China, U.S. President Richard Nixon asked the Chinese Prime Minister Zhou Enlai, who was an avid reader of French history, what he thought had been the impact of the French Revolution on Western civilization. "Too early to tell," answered Zhou Enlai.

"Whoever has not lived before 1789 does not know what the pleasure of life can be," said Prince Talleyrand. Despite making a phenomenal political career in postrevolutionary France and becoming Napoleon's foreign minister, Talleyrand evoked in this nostalgic statement an idyllic aristocratic life that disappeared with the revolution.

"The era of chivalry has gone. That of sophists, economists, and calculators has succeeded and the glory of Europe is extinguished forever," wrote the Irish conservative author Edmund Burke in his book *Reflections on the Revolution in France*. Others considered that the revolution offered great opportunities for creating a better world. Thomas Carlyle, who wrote a famous history of this revolution, described it as: "the great poem of our time."

"In order to conquer we must dare," demanded the revolutionary Georges Danton. Napoleon Bonaparte, who became the most conspicuous representative of revolutionary values, was very clear about what this term should represent: a fairer and more equal society where careers would be, "open to talent without distinctions of birth." According to his famous quotation, it would be where citizens could climb up the social scale as high as their talent and ambition would take them, without facing the insurmountable obstacle of a closed elite that monopolized power and accumulated so much wealth and hereditary privileges. As the principles of the revolution were universal, Napoleon aimed at creating an empire in order to spread them around Europe and the rest of the world. To a certain extent his aim was achieved, for after his downfall the continent was never the same, and the old world that fell before the revolutionary crowds and Napoleonic troops was never to return.

The great upheaval that the French revolution provoked throughout the European continent also reached America making the Iberian empires and a part of the French Empire collapse. But their downfall was also a long-term consequence of the event with which the revolutionary era began: the American Revolution that broke out in 1776. The American settlers who inhabited the British thirteen colonies successfully defied the principles of the old regime in Europe long before the French. For apart from aiming at independence from Britain, the American rebels aimed at creating a new society based on principles—like equality before the law and democratic representation—that would later revolutionize Europe. How did this conflict begin? Why was it in America that these European ideas triumphed for the first time?

The origins of the American War of Independence can be traced back to the problems and confrontations that emerged after the Seven Years' War. On defeating France, the British crown took measures that were going to be very unpopular in the thirteen colonies. In first place, frontiers were marked out with territories inhabited by Indians; a decree in 1763 strictly prohibited their occupation in order to avoid future conflicts. This prohibition was unacceptable for the colonists, as it implied setting limits on their desires for possessing and accumulating land. For this reason many refused to obey, and continued expanding into Indian territory. Among them was a landowner from Virginia named George Washington, who was to acquire great fame a few years later. Washington himself regarded the decree as "a temporary expedient to quiet the Indians," that was doomed to fail when "the Indians consent to our occupying the lands."*

But above all, the main cause of the confrontation between British colonists and their king was going to be the increasing taxation. The Seven Years' War doubled the British national debt, and as a result taxes rose dramatically, especially in the thirteen colonies, where the government decided that as British subjects the inhabitants of the American Empire had the obligation of paying a part of the administrative and defense costs.

In 1765 the British parliament passed the first direct tax that was going to be levied on the inhabitants of the thirteen colonies: the Stamp Act, which

---

* Burk, *Old World, New World.*

compelled traders to pay the rights for every product that was dispatched at customs. The tax caused so much outrage that it proved impossible to collect; very few dared to impose it, fearing reprisals. A very important consequence of the colonists' anger was that it gave way to a long debate on their rights and how to defend them. "No taxation without representation," was the main slogan by which the colonial assemblies that emerged in these years were going to coordinate their defense. It was certainly not easy to refute in the era of enlightenment, when the citizens' rights and obligations were being debated among political and intellectual elites throughout the Western world. The crown had decided that the inhabitants of America should comply with their fiscal duties like the rest of its subjects, but unlike the citizens in the British Isles they had not been granted any rights to be represented in parliament and defend their interests.

Benjamin Franklin, a scientist, politician, journalist, diplomat, and one of the most outstanding men to be born in the thirteen colonies, was sent by the colonists to London in 1765 in order to explain before the House of Commons the reasons why this tax should be abolished. Franklin argued that unless the tax was voted down a colonial rebellion was inevitable, and on this occasion he achieved his aim. But the crown did not give up the intention of increasing fiscal pressure on its American subjects, nor did it accede to grant them the parliamentary representation that they demanded. In 1767 new taxes were levied on basic products, including the notorious Tea Act, by which the crown aimed at defending the interests of the East India Company and preventing contraband in North America. On this occasion the colonists' collective anger was so great that many of them not only refused to pay but also decided to challenge the authorities directly.

On December 16, 1773, spokesmen for local merchants demanded that the tea shipment brought by the East India Company ships should be sent back to England, as they opposed not only the company's monopoly on tea importation but above the fact that American colonists had to pay a tax for which they did not obtain any benefit. After the authorities refused, a group of colonists disguised as Indians boarded the tea ships anchored at the port and threw the tea cargo overboard. The incident of the so-called

Boston Tea Party was to become one of the great episodes of American history, and triggered the outbreak of the thirteen colonies' rebellion against the British crown.

The government's reaction to the Boston Tea Party was to pass what became known as Coercive Acts, with the aim of punishing the colonists for their defiance. Among them was the decision of closing down the port of Boston until the East India Company was compensated for the tea cargos that had been chucked in the sea. At the first Continental Congress, in which representatives of the thirteen colonies gathered for the first time in September 1774, the withdrawal of these measures was demanded. From this point reconciliation between the two parties seemed increasingly difficult, and at the second Congress, convened on May 10, 1775, the majority of representatives voted in favor of armed struggle.

It was not the first time in the history of colonial empires that the colonists rebelled against their government. In fact the Spanish crown and Portugal as well faced several rebellions in its American Empire that it always managed to suppress by military force. But several factors contributed to make the rebellion in British America a success, and as a result of it alter the course of Western history.

In January 1776 the radical journalist and thinker Thomas Paine published a pamphlet under the title of *Common Sense*, in which he explained in plain language that all readers could understand, the reasons why America should break with the British crown and fight for independence. The pamphlet became a bestseller, proving how popular the cause of independence was. But not all American colonists agreed with the need to break links with the British crown; in fact the attempts to propagate the rebellion into Quebec and Florida failed. It has been calculated that at least twenty percent of the white settlers, and most of the nonwhite populations, supported the British.[*] Nevertheless it was clear from early 1776 that the aim of those who claimed to represent the thirteen colonies was independence. The majority of congressional representatives ratified this, on the historic date of July 4, 1776, when independence was officially proclaimed.

---

[*] Burk, *Old World, New World.*

In June 1775, when hostilities against Britain broke out, Congress's representatives took the crucial decision of appointing George Washington commander in chief of the American troops. Washington, a soldier and land-owner who came from a prosperous family from Virginia, had fought in the French and Indian War. His experience leading the Virginia Regiment, the first American regular army, proved very useful to organize colonists with hardly any military experience to fight against the professional British army. But apart from Washington's leadership and the determination of his troops to win independence, the key factor that allowed the thirteen colonies to defeat the British was the support of other European powers.

For France, the American War of Independence constituted a unique opportunity to take revenge on Britain for the defeat in the Seven Years' War and weaken its military power. On February 6, 1776, France signed a treaty by which it recognized the independence of the United States of America and promised to provide military support and promote trade with the new nation. Shortly after that it declared war on Britain. France was not going to be the only European power to use the War of Independence to weaken the British Empire and obtain benefits in return. Spain was initially reticent to support the American rebels, fearing that the same wishes for independence would spread to its American Empire. But, on the other hand ousting the British from North America would benefit Spanish imperial interests, and for this reason the Spanish crown eventually decided to join France in the war against Britain. Finally Holland, which had lost its American colony as a result of the British invasion, was also eager to contribute to the independence of the thirteen colonies. George Washington's troops counted on the support of three great European powers, making it possible to defeat Great Britain and create the United States of America.

In 1783 the Treaty of Paris was signed, by which Britain recognized the independence of the United States, a new nation that encompassed a territory from present-day Canada to Florida in the south and the Mississippi river in the west. In this way Britain lost a great part of its empire, and on top of this had to cede territory in the frontier with Florida to Spain, as well as return the island of Minorca. France was also compensated, winning the colony of Tobago and recovering Senegal. But above all, the most important consequence of this treaty was that the United States was born.

The United States constituted the first independent republic created on the American continent. It was much more than a new nation founded by European colonists in America, for it was founded out of defiance of many of the ideas and customs by which Europe was ruled.

Whereas the war that led to the creation of the United States was known as the War of American Independence in Britain and the rest of the European continent, on the other side of the Atlantic it was named as the American Revolution. Its leaders considered that they were not simply fighting for their independence, but to create a nation that would be very different from the rest, and that it would be governed by the most advanced principles in civilization. This new society would overcome the defects and injustices of the old one, in which the citizens would be free to work and make their dreams come true, where they would live in harmony with each other, and the causes of oppression and the abuses of power would be eradicated.

Where did the ideas that inspired the American Revolution come from? Mainly from the interests and the principles of the American colonists that led them to confront the British crown. But at a more theoretical level, the leaders of this revolution, who would become the founding fathers of the United States, sought inspiration in the ideas of the Enlightenment that were undermining the foundations of power in Europe.

The American enlightenment that was born in the political and intellectual circles of the thirteen colonies was specially influenced by English and Scottish thought, particularly that of John Locke, Francis Bacon, and David Hume. They were the source of ideas like respect for individual liberty and property as pillars of the American society, as well as the ideals of republicanism and liberalism.

Thomas Jefferson, the main author of the American Declaration of Independence, and the third president of the United States, admitted that the main source of political inspiration for him had been the British empirical thinkers, especially Locke, whom he considered one of "the three greatest men who ever lived."[*] Unconsciously, Jefferson was also influenced by European expansionist ethos. His famous quote of wishing

---

[*] Jon Meacham, *Thomas Jefferson: The Art of Power* (New York: Random House, 2012).

to make the United States "an empire of liberty," gives the impression of adapting the European powers' imperialist ideals to the dreams of the American founding fathers who aimed at broadening the frontiers of their young country and firmly believed that wherever they would be, freedom and prosperity would flourish.

"The constitution is the guide which I will never abandon." Such famous quotes clearly inspired by the Enlightenment contributed to Washington's popularity among the most advanced thinkers in Europe. His decision of giving up command and returning home once the war was over, instead of taking advantage of his position as commander in chief in order to take power, surprised many European observers and showed how deeply the spirit of the Enlightenment had influenced the Virginian general, for he understood that the army should always be at the service of a nation, and the limits of power should be clearly defined in a democracy.

Benjamin Franklin, the spokesman for the thirteen colonies in London and the first U.S. ambassador to France, defined the American spirit as "a union between practical virtues like thrift and a hard working and entrepreneurial spirit with the democratic ideas of equality, self-government, community spirit, and specially opposition to any kind of political or religious oppression."*

As regards religion, the very critical attitude of the enlightenment thinkers toward the power of the church, and especially Voltaire's morbid anticlericalism, took longer to penetrate the minds of the very religious and puritan North America. Nevertheless, it did contribute to convince the US founding fathers that the separation between church and state and the freedom of worship were essential for their country's progress. As the fourth president of the United States and author of the U.S. Constitution James Madison stated: "Conscience is the most sacred of all property."

The American Revolution produced texts that were clearly inspired by the spirit of the Era of Enlightenment, or what Thomas Paine defined as the Age of Reason. They were going to become models in America, Europe, and the rest of the Western world, and would inspire many constitutionalists and political leaders over the following two centuries.

---

* Benjamin Franklin, *The Autobiography of Benjamin Franklin* (New York: Henry Holt, 1916).

"We hold these truths to be self-evident, that all men are created equal, that they are endowed by their creator with certain unalienable rights, that among these are life, liberty, and the pursuit of happiness."

This statement written in the Declaration of Independence has been considered one of the best-known sentences in the English language, as well as one of the most important in American history. Thomas Jefferson, the main author of the Declaration of Independence, does not exclusively deserve praise for writing such a powerful statement, for he himself confessed that the declaration did not have any original ideas, but feelings that united all those who contributed to write it.

The other very influential document produced by the American Revolution was the U.S. Constitution, passed on September 17, 1787. The text laid down the rules of American democracy, it specified the powers of the states that formed the new nation and the federal system of government, and it had the virtue of doing it in seven articles that can be understood by any citizen. Such a simple text with virtually no legal jargon has served the purpose of governing the United States until the present, and has also been a key reference for many constitutions that have been written since then.

The political and economic consequences of the loss of the thirteen colonies were enormous for Great Britain, and psychologically it had a devastating effect. After signing the treaty that recognized the independence of the United States, Lord Shelburne's government fell and King George III seriously considered abdication. The British were going to take a long time to assimilate the loss of the first empire, as the thirteen colonies were known. For a long time they continued treating the United States as a colony, and their inhabitants with contempt and even hatred. Biographer James Boswell recorded Samuel Johnson's quote: "I am willing to love all mankind except an American."[*] Such comments were frequent among the British in those days.

To compensate for losing exclusive rights over the North American market, the British government retaliated against the U.S., forbidding its ships to trade with their colonies in the West Indies, inflicting considerable damage on the emergent American economy. Hostility prevailed in their

---

[*] James Boswell, *The Life of Samuel Johnson* (New York: Penguin, 2008).

relations for a long time, and the most dramatic point was reached in 1812, when the United States declared war on Great Britain, and the countries fought again in North America for two years. On the other hand, once this brief war was over, the relationship between the two countries gradually improved, particularly from the second decade of the nineteenth century. A common language, culture, and historic legacy were going to compensate for clashes in the political sphere. From the late eighteenth century over half of US exports went to Britain, and commercial exchange steadily increased through the nineteenth century.

Not everyone regretted having lost the thirteen colonies. Some British intellectuals thought that their loss was a blessing in disguise for the country's interest. This was the opinion of prominent Scottish economist Adam Smith, who had been urging the British government to abandon North America since long before the War of Independence broke out. In an essay published in 1788, Smith argued that the American colonies had been economically unproductive, an endless source of expenditure, and a problem for the British government that was certainly not compensated by the scarce economic benefits.[*]

As a result of the American experience the famous Scottish economist concluded that the colonial empires that implied exporting population and submitting them to the British government were undesirable; only mercantile empires based on commercial exchange were worth the effort. Edward Gibbon, one of the Britain's most respected men of letters, was relieved by the independence of the thirteen colonies, as was even former prime minister William Pitt.

While Europe assimilated the emergence of the first independent nation in America, a revolution broke out that not only shook the pillars of its societies but it was also going to have a dramatic impact on its role in the world: the French Revolution.

A lot has been written about the causes of the French Revolution, and what triggered such a drastic break with the system of the *Ancien Régime*. The society where enlightenment was born was ruled by an absolute monarchy

---

[*]   Adam Smith, *The Wealth of Nations* (New York: Bantam Classics, 2008).

and a feudal regime in which wealth and power was concentrated in the hands of the nobility and the clergy. For how long could this continue? Throughout the reign of Louis XVI it was increasingly evident that the system could not survive for both economic and social reasons. From the Thirty Years' War the French state accumulated a debt that plunged the country into deep crisis for the following three decades. While the nobility and the clergy were exempt from paying taxes, fiscal pressure on the rest of the population steadily increased, and in this way the conditions of the poor majority, especially the peasants, became unbearable.

The revolution that shook the world broke out with the assault on the Bastille by the Parisian masses on July 14, 1789. From that day many of the ideas and beliefs that sustained the European monarchies and political regimes started to crumble. Never in the history of Europe did the people's masses defy their rulers with so much strength and determination, nor were they ever as successful as a result of their revolt. The news of this event was going to frighten the rich and powerful and stimulate the poor and oppressed through all Europe. Revolutions break out when a majority of the population is so impoverished that they have nothing to lose by taking to the streets and fighting against the representatives of power. What happened in France in 1789 was going to repeat itself in the rest of Europe on several occasions over the two subsequent centuries, whenever the same conditions of poverty and despair existed in the population, accompanied by indifference and incompetence from government.

The second great episode of this revolution was the abolition of the feudal system by the new French National Assembly, which had kept the nobility and the clergy at the pinnacle of the social pyramid. Shortly after that, on August 26, 1789, the Declaration of the Rights of Man and of the Citizen was published. The letter constituted a genuinely revolutionary document. Inspired by the ideas of the Enlightenment, especially Rousseau's social contract and Montesquieu's separation of powers, it defined the principles on which the relationship between the government and its citizens should be based in a democratic society. Its author was the Marquis of Lafayette, an unruly member of the old nobility who had acquired substantial experience in the Revolutionary War, for he crossed the Atlantic in 1777 in order to join the American army in their fight for independence. After 1789 he was going to become one of the great figures of the revolution.

"Men are born and remain free and equal in rights," states the first article of the Declaration. "The aim of every political association is to preserve the natural and imprescriptible rights of man," states the second.

The document describes terms like popular sovereignty, freedom of expression, freedom of worship, and law-abiding state. Although it was never literally applied in revolutionary France, nor in any other revolution over the next decades, it was to be a key reference text for every movement that aspired to overthrow the old regime and advance toward a more democratic system. As a result of it, France evolved from being a country governed by the divine right of the kings to being governed by popular sovereignty, and at least theoretically by universal suffrage, according to what the 1793 constitution said.

The essence of the rights of man and of the citizen is summarized as "liberty, equality, and fraternity," a popular slogan that emerged in this revolution, and would later become the motto of the French republic.

The third episode of this revolution was the Reign of Terror. On June 24, 1793, the Convention passed a new constitution by which France became a republic and the government would be elected by universal suffrage. Such extraordinary changes took place amid an atmosphere of increasing confrontation between Jacobins, radical republicans, and the Girondins, the liberal monarchists. The Jacobins managed to impose themselves as a result of a wave of mass killings and violence, which according to some historians may have resulted in around forty thousand deaths. "Terror is only justice, prompt, severe and inflexible," stated Maximilien Robespierre, the chief proponent of this bloody period. The guillotine, the most efficient means ever invented to chop heads off, became an unforgettable symbol of this period.

On January 21, 1793, Louis XVI was guillotined at the Revolution Square in Paris, before thousands of citizens who witnessed how the Ancien Régime vanished with its king. His wife Marie Antoinette followed him in this tragic end, as did many French citizens—especially from the aristocracy and the clergy but also from many walks of life—who were accused of being against the revolution or were simply victims of the political purges that were taking place in those days. Robespierre himself died by the guillotine that he had so eagerly used against his enemies.

The Reign of Terror appalled the whole of Europe. The fact that revolution degenerated into such spiral of slaughter, violence, and political persecution constituted a great disappointment for many of those who had pinned their hopes on such a significant event. The most conservative observers interpreted the events in France as the proof that the revolution inevitably brings chaos, death, and ultimately a more unfair political system than the one that it aimed at substituting.

The revolutionary wars were the fourth major episode of the French Revolution. As a consequence of the revolution, many representatives of the old monarchy went into exile and put pressure on several European governments so that they would intervene against the French revolutionaries. Several monarchs, specially the Austrian emperor, contemplated the possibility of invading France with the aim of preventing the spread of the revolution across their countries. But France decided to take the initiative, and in April 1794 declared war on Austria. This constituted the beginning of a long era of war in Europe that was deeply to mark the future of the countries that were involved.

The most important consequence of this war was the rise of one of the most legendary leaders in the history of the world: Napoleon Bonaparte. Napoleon is simultaneously the product of war and revolution. He reached power thanks to military glory, and this same glory led to numerous historic victories, for let us not forget that Napoleon was above all a military genius despite his errors with the invasion of Russia and Spain. Revolutionary France lacked a genuine leader, and this power vacuum was filled by Napoleon.

General Bonaparte acquired great military prestige in the war by which France defeated Austria. After that, in 1798, he was put in charge of a complicated mission that he himself proposed in order to weaken Britain: occupy Egypt and make progress from there to Persia with the aim of intercepting the British route toward India. Occupying Egypt would also compensate France for the loss of the American colonies.

The Egyptian campaign had enormous influence on Napoleon's career. The very ambitious general who admired Alexander the Great so much dreamed of creating a new empire for France that would stretch from Egypt to the Far East. "Europe is a molehill, all great reputations come from Asia," he stated on one occasion.

After defeating the mamelukes, the Turkish-Egyptian militia that dominated the country, Napoleon focused on bringing the best of Western civilization to this part of the world, and also the principles of the Revolution. For this purpose he brought jurists, administrators, scientists, and artists with him, and they all helped in the task of founding a modern Egypt and leaving France's mark on the country.

Napoleon spread the message through the Egyptian people that he had come to liberate them from the tyranny of the mamelukes and allow them to live according to the rights of man that France had proclaimed. Loyal to the lay spirit of the Revolution, Napoleon's mission did not make any attempt to convert the local population to Christianity, as France and the rest of the European powers usually did in their colonial adventures. On the contrary, he scrupulously respected the Islamic culture and the beliefs of the Egyptians.

The general promptly launched a plan to invade Syria that would enable him to strengthen his position in the Middle East, and from there he could have marched over India or Constantinople, putting an end to the Ottoman Empire. Nevertheless, the plan proved to be far too ambitious. The British fleet in the Mediterranean, led by Admiral Horatio Nelson, isolated Napoleon in Egypt, and the Turkish troops managed to stop the French advance. In this way, Napoleon decided that his future was in Europe. He returned to Paris in 1799. Two years later, Cairo was conquered by British troops. Had Napoleon been successful with his plans in the Egyptian Empire, his country's destiny and that of the Middle East could have been very different. Even so, the Egyptian adventure left a deep mark in France, as in Europe. The Egyptian Institute, founded by Napoleon, constituted the beginning of the European passion for ancient Egypt and for archaeology of the ancient civilizations in that region. From then on, Western knowledge about early civilizations spread rapidly.

On returning to Paris, Napoleon experienced a meteoric rise that enabled him to consolidate a regime and an empire that would match his ambitions. Not satisfied with being appointed head of state for life, he decided that the pope, Pius VII, should crown him emperor of France in 1804. As his empire spread across Europe he chose several of his brothers to replace the dethroned royal families. Joseph Bonaparte was appointed king of Spain, Louis Bonaparte king of Holland, Jerome, king of Westphalia, and some generals were crowned in kingdoms like Naples or Sweden.

The fact that a Corsican soldier who spoke French with a foreign accent managed to sit on the throne that had been occupied by Louis XIV and his successors and transform his family into a ruling dynasty, shows how much progress the revolution had made in a few years. For many, Napoleon represented the principles of equality and meritocracy that replaced the divine right to rule, although for others the fact that he proclaimed himself emperor constituted a reversal of the principles of the republic established in 1793 and the spirit of Revolution. On the other hand, for all those affected by the Revolution Napoleon was seen as a devil, a usurper who threatened what they considered most sacred and their whole system of life. The fact that he accumulated so many enemies in his formidable expansion from the Iberian Peninsula to Russia made a great multinational coalition possible that would eventually overthrow him.

Napoleon led his *Grande Armée* with such success that he managed to conquer practically all of Europe, apart from the British Isles, in little more than ten years. He aimed at unifying the whole continent under French leadership and the same system of government based on the ideas of the Revolution, and his interpretation of liberty and equality. Nevertheless in his rapid expansion he was going to make several strategic errors. The Spanish guerrillas against French occupation and the Russian winter became invincible enemies. Nor did he assess the impact of a great coalition of enemy armies against France. On March 31, 1814, the troops of the Russian czar and the king of Prussia entered Paris, putting an end to Napoleon's empire. But he still enjoyed widespread support, which enabled him to regain power after escaping from the island of Elba where he had been imprisoned, and challenge the rest of Europe once again. But on this occasion, the European armies under the leadership of the British General Wellington led to his final defeat at the Battle of Waterloo in June 1815.

After Napoleon's defeat the Bourbons recovered the French throne, as did the rest of the royal families that had been overthrown by the Bonapartes. The monarchs and their governments that returned from exile aimed at setting the clock back to prerevolutionary times, but this was not possible any longer. The ideas that provoked the revolution had gone too far and the world on the whole had changed so much; it was not possible to reestablish the old regime, as Louis XVIII and several other kings were to experience.

Napoleon wrote in his memoirs from the isle of Saint Helena that he was going to be remembered not for the battles that he won but for his civil code.* The Napoleonic Code that was introduced in 1804 was a new civil code written in accordance with the ideas of the French Revolution, replacing a mélange of confusing and contradictory laws. But above all it was the clarity and simplicity with which it was written that set it apart from all other laws written before. It made law accessible to the average citizen and because of its success in administering law not only has it survived in France until the present, but it has been the most influential code in history. Because it was adopted by most countries occupied by Napoleon, subsequent civil codes were clearly inspired by it. Several nations in Latin America have used it as a model as well. In the Middle East the Napoleonic Code has been used as a reference by all those regimes wishing to modernize Islamic law. Despite his military genius it is after all Napoleon's civil code that makes him relevant in the contemporary world.

The revolution was not to have consequences over North Africa and Asia, as Napoleon would have liked, but it did have a great impact in America. The American Revolution was to play a very influential role on the evolution of the European empires in America, but it was the French Revolution that was to alter their destiny and precipitate their end.

The Caribbean colony of Saint-Domingue, in the Western half of Hispaniola, was to be the first place in America where the ideals of the French revolution succeeded.

Saint-Domingue was one of the best examples of how lucrative colonial plantations could be. It was the most profitable colony of the French Empire,

---

* Andrew Roberts, *Napoleon the Great* (London: Allen Lane, 2014).

and shortly before the revolution it produced sixty percent of the coffee and a forty percent of the sugar that was imported by France and Great Britain.[*] These extraordinary benefits were possible thanks to the work of over a million and a half African slaves who constituted eighty-five percent of the population in the colony. The rest was composed of black and mixed-race people who had obtained their freedom, and an elite of white landowners and administrators who constituted only three percent of the population. Being such a small minority the whites lived in constant fear of a racial revolt. As the Count of Mirabeau stated when he visited the colony: "The whites sleep at the foot of the Vesuvius."[**]

The news of the revolution was received with enthusiasm by the white elite in Saint-Domingue. Many of them thought that the opportunity for getting rid of the French taxes and mercantilist laws had finally arrived, and some even thought of independence. But they were not the only ones who decided to take advantage of the radical changes at the metropolis, the non-white population had similar aims.

The outbreak of the revolution surprised Vincent Ogé in Paris, a well-educated man of mixed race who came from a rich family, and he decided that this was his opportunity to claim equality for nonwhite free citizens like himself. On returning to Saint-Domingue he led a rebellion that culminated with his arrest and execution. But this was only the beginning of the black population's struggle for their rights. On August 21, 1791, the slaves rebelled and provoked a civil war in the colony. Paris decided to make concessions, and the Legislative Assembly granted that all free citizens would enjoy equal rights.

Nevertheless, French sovereignty in the colony was still in danger. After the outbreak of the war between France and Britain in 1793, the white elite negotiated a change of sovereignty. To combat the treason of the white minority, all the French government could do was to offer freedom to the African slaves in return for their help.

---

[*] Paul Butel, *Histoire des Antilles français, XVIIe–XXe siècle* (Paris: Parrin, 2002).

[**] C.L.R. James, *The Black Jacobins: Toussaint L'Ouverture and the San Domingo Revolution* (New York: Vintage, 1963).

In 1793 the National Convention, led by Robespierre, abolished slavery, and consequently France become the first European country where it was illegal to possess slaves. Although it gave the impression of being a desperate measure in order to maintain sovereignty over its possession, this was not quite the case. The antislavery cause already attracted a considerable number of supporters in prerevolutionary France. In 1788, the Society of Friends of the Blacks was founded in France, with the aim of abolishing first the slave trade, and eventually slavery. Among its members were outstanding thinkers of the Enlightenment like Nicolas de Condorcet, and leaders of the revolution like Lafayette. From 1789 the antislavery cause was increasingly popular despite the fact that this could affect French colonial interests. In fact Jacobins like Robespierre argued that if slavery was necessary in order to maintain the colonies the right thing was to abandon them.

After the abolition of slavery the leader of the slave uprising, François Toussaint Louverture, a former slave with outstanding gifts as a soldier and politician, offered the French his services in order to expel the British troops that cooperated with the whites in the invasion of Saint-Domingue. Once the aim had been achieved Toussaint Louverture proclaimed himself the new governor and managed to encourage a new nonwhite elite replace the white one. Not satisfied with these achievements, in 1801 he drafted a constitution that granted the colony full autonomy, and he named himself life governor.

The rise of Toussaint Louverture and his colony of free slaves constituted a threat for the stability of the French colonies and for the whole Caribbean. Also in the slave-owning South of the United States, the example of Saint-Domingue was feared. In Paris pressures on the governing elite for intervening were considerable; Napoleon himself was also eager to recover the prosperity that the sugar industry enjoyed before the Revolution. For all these reasons in 1802 French troops reconquered the colony, and Toussaint Louverture was arrested and deported to France, where he died shortly thereafter.

After reoccupying Saint-Domingue the aim of the French was to reintroduce slavery to exploit the plantations as they had traditionally done. Nevertheless, as Toussaint Louverture warned before leaving, this aim was not going to be possible, for the cause of liberty had gone too far among the population in the colony; the old slaves were prepared to die before submitting to the chains once more. Jean-Jacques Dessalines took over the leadership of the rebel Haitian army and eventually managed to defeat the French.

Having expelled the French, in 1804 Dessalines proclaimed Saint-Domingue's independence and renamed it Haiti, a name that came from the native Arawak tribe. On that same year when Napoleon was crowned emperor, Dessalines followed his example and proclaimed himself emperor of Haiti. But his imperial dream was short, for he was murdered in 1806. The country was then divided between an autocratic monarchy in the North and a republic in the South. The trajectory of Haiti as an independent nation was to be marked by political instability, confrontation, and deep poverty. Nevertheless, the first republic in the world led by an indigenous African was to remain a source of inspiration in the long march for independence in the American Empires, particularly for blacks and mixed-race peoples in their fight for equal rights.

The emergence of the United States of America, the French Revolution, and eventually Haiti contributed to make the French rethink their role in the world and the need to have colonies. Charles Maurice de Talleyrand, the cunning politician who shortly after the French Revolution began his long career as foreign minister, published a book in 1797 under the title of *Essay on the Advantages of Withdrawing from the Colonies*. It constituted a plea against any concept of colonization that implied transferring population and promoting settlements. According to Talleyrand, "individuals without industry, without leaders and without morals," had arrived in the thirteen colonies and the final rebellion was inevitable. On the other hand he admired the British experience in India, where the territory's wealth was being acquired by means of commerce and employing the local population that was "paid but not enslaved." This was the type of colonization for the future, as it created a relationship between the colonial power and the subject population based on cooperation, and it finally resulted in much more productivity.

Pierre-Victor Malouet had a similar opinion to Talleyrand's. Also reflecting on the consequences of the American Revolution he opined that in the long run colonies that were populated by members of the same culture could only be kept at the cost of perpetual war and oppression.

All of these opinions against colonial imperialism as it had been conceived until 1789, as well as the impact of Haiti's independence, contributed to Napoleon's disdain for the French Empire in America. The American colonies seemed far too problematic and unproductive, if compared to the political and economic benefits that he reaped from his European empire. For this reason, he decided to sell Louisiana to the United States in 1803. Nevertheless, despite the fact that the French Empire in America was diminished during his time in power, France was going to gain indirect control of the biggest empire in America as a result of the occupation of Spain.

Napoleon took advantage of the dynastic dispute in Spain between his ally, King Charles IV and his son Ferdinand, who was bluntly opposed to the Napoleonic order. He summoned the two of them to Bayonne in 1808. There he managed to make them abdicate and allow the throne of Spain to be occupied by his brother Joseph. In this way, the Bonapartes not only replaced the Bourbons on the throne of Spain but also as sovereigns of the Spanish Empire. At least this is how many inhabitants of Spanish America interpreted these events. The weakness of the government in Spain, political instability, and the fear of being governed by France—and last but not least, the ideas of the French Revolution—all contributed to provoke a wave of independence movements that was to spread across practically the whole Spanish Empire.

What was the situation of the Spanish Empire at the beginning of the nineteenth century? To what extent were independence movements making progress?

The Spanish Empire was in good shape at the end of the eighteenth century, which on the whole had been generally prosperous, particularly the second half. It proved to be remarkably resilient. Neither Spain's decline as a great power, nor the British, French, or Dutch attacks to snatch back some of their possessions from the Spaniards, nor the constant problems of the Spanish crown, not even the intrigues and power struggles that confronted the court in Madrid, nor the corruption in the higher echelons of the administration managed to dismember it.

The eighteenth century brought great changes in the administration of the American Empire. Spain underwent the so-called Bourbon reforms from the reign of Philip V with the aim of modernizing and improving the efficiency of the Spanish system of government and strengthening the cohesion of all territories of the Spanish crown.

As a result of these administrative reforms the vast viceroyalty of Peru, encompassing a territory that stretched from present-day Venezuela to Argentina, was divided. In 1717 the viceroyalty of New Granada was created and many years after, in 1767, that of Río de la Plata. Below the viceroyalties were the captain generalships of Venezuela, Guatemala, Cuba, Chile, and Puerto Rico. In this way power that was traditionally concentrated in Lima and Mexico, the capitals of the two great viceroyalties that originally formed the American Empire, was dispersed among various cities through Spanish America.

In 1717 the *Casa de Contratación* and the Council of the Indies, the two key institutions for the government and administration of the American Empire were moved to Cádiz, and in this way commercial exchange with the Americas was centered in this old seaport city. As a result of all these changes the kingdom of Spain managed to have a more direct control over the empire and also impose a more efficient administration. (Let us not forget that for the Spanish monarchy, the Indies were not considered a colony but as another kingdom, and for this reason the aim was to govern and administer America in a very similar way to Spain.)

The American Empire also managed to survive unscathed several disputes with other powers. In 1668 the Treaty of Lisbon sanctioned the separation of the Portuguese and Spanish Empires that had been unified since the reign of Philip II. As a result of Portuguese independence, several conflicts broke out over the frontiers with the Spanish Empire in America, and on several occasions they led to war.

A particularly conflictive point was the frontier between the viceroyalty of River Plate and Brazil. In 1688 the Portuguese founded Sacramento colony in present-day Uruguay. The Spaniards argued that this city was in their territory, and for this reason they decided to occupy it and rename it Rosario. Nevertheless, shortly afterward, the city was returned to Portugal. The city changed sovereignty on several occasions until finally the two powers decided to put an end to almost three centuries of territorial disputes with the Treaty of San Ildefonso in 1777. Sacramento was set to become Spanish in return for territorial cessions to Brazil.

Spain's most dangerous enemy was undoubtedly Great Britain, for the British were not only interested in several points of the Spanish Empire but their navy was superior to the Spanish. The war of Jenkins' Ear that broke out in 1739 could have brought very serious losses for the Spanish Empire, but it turned out to be the opposite. At the Battle of Cartagena de Indias in 1741, the Spanish troops under the efficient command of Blas de Lezo managed to repel a British invasion and inflict a humiliating defeat on Britain.

This victory was very important for Spain, for it proved that the Spaniards had a greater capacity to defend their empire than what the European rivals thought. Its status as an imperial power was considerably reinvigorated as a result of this war. For the rest of the eighteenth century, Spain continued to govern over the greatest empire in the world—only the Russian terrestrial empire could rival the Spanish in size.

Apart from consolidating an atmosphere in which peace and prosperity could prevail over their empire, Spain continued making important contributions to the exploration of the world and scientific discovery. Under the reign of Charles III, who eagerly promoted scientific research, important expeditions through the Spanish Empire were to take place. The most ambitious was that of the Spanish naval officer and explorer Alessandro Malaspina. In 1781, Malaspina and a crew of sailors and scientists embarked on a great journey across the world, and they also aimed at finding another of the great maritime dreams of that time, a northeastern path that would unify the Atlantic with the Pacific. Malaspina made very substantial contributions to the knowledge of world geography in those days, particularly of America.

In spite of all this progress, Spain had to face numerous internal problems that threatened the unity and continuity of its empire in the Americas. The claims of the Native Americans before the civilization that invaded their territory never ceased to be a source of problems for Spanish governors, particularly at the viceroyalty of Peru, where the majority of the population was nonwhite. In 1780 a descendant of Túpac Amaru, who called himself king of Peru, led an uprising against Spanish dominion that was mainly supported by the Incas. More worrying than the Indian revolts were those of the creole elites.

Just as it happened in the French and British Empires, mercantilism and the obsession of the metropolis to exploit commerce in America for its own benefit led to great resentment among the American settlers. The creoles considered the bureaucrats and the fiscal regulations that came from Spain a threat to their benefits and an obstacle for embarking on more ambitious projects that would have been allowed with free trade.

Another reason for discontent among the creoles was the feeling of being inferior to the elite that governed them from Spain and not being able to defend their interests or actively participate in the empire's government and administration. Just as it happened among the inhabitants of the British Empire in America toward the end of the eighteenth century, there was an increasing number of Spanish overseas subjects who thought that their interests would be much better served if they could govern themselves.

Increased political control and fiscal pressure from Spain provoked revolts in diverse places of the Spanish Empire, and in the second half of the eighteenth century these proved increasingly difficult to suppress. In 1765 a revolt took place in Quito due to an increase in taxes, which caused widespread indignation.

After the American and the French Revolutions, the leaders of the revolts against Spanish power no longer limited themselves to demanding more rights or less taxation; now they aimed directly at self-government. This was the case of the conspiracy of Gual and España that broke out in Venezuela in 1798, and it has often been described as the beginning of the Venezuelan struggle for independence.* Manuel Gual was an infantry officer and José María España a civil servant, and both of them led a revolt in Guaira and Caracas, which enjoyed considerable support among the population. Their aim was the expulsion of the Spanish authorities, the establishment of a system of free trade and production, and finally a political and administrative union of the cities of Caracas, Maracaibo, Cumaná, and Guayana.

In Spain the most acute observers of the evolution of the Spanish Empire were well aware of the flaws of the colonial system and of the increasing support for independence in some parts of the American possessions.

---

* Manuel Lucena Giraldo, *Naciones de Rebeldes* (Madrid: Taurus, 2010).

Very influential for the Spanish Empire were the decisions of the Count of Aranda, who was foreign secretary at the beginning of Charles IV's reign. A prominent statesman who was deeply influenced by the ideas of the Enlightenment, Aranda was mainly responsible for the decision to expel the Jesuit order from Spain. Ever since their arrival as missionaries the Jesuits had acquired much power in America. The Guarani Jesuit Missions were settlements founded by the Jesuits among the Guarani tribe and members of other local groups. Apart from propagating the Christian faith, the Jesuits also promoted the development of agriculture, cattle breeding, and artisan production, and they succeeded to the extent of creating genuine agricultural and industrial empires.

The enormous power of the Jesuits was seen as a potential threat by many governments in the eighteenth century. In the case of Spain it was feared that power accumulated in the Americas would lead them to declare independence in areas like present-day Paraguay, where they were particularly strong.

The expulsion of the Jesuits from Spain that took place in 1766 was one of the decisions that led Voltaire to comment that with half a dozen men like Aranda, Spain would be wholly regenerated.[*]

The Count of Aranda deserves to be remembered for having been capable of predicting the collapse of the Spanish Empire and recommending drastic measures to avoid a confrontation with the creole elites that would lead the Spanish American possessions to follow the same path as the British thirteen colonies. As ambassador in Paris he represented Spain in the negotiations of the Treaty of Paris that put an end to the American Revolution. Impressed by the rise of the new American nation, he feared that its influence would soon reach the Spanish Empire, and for this reason he wrote a famous report to King Charles III:

"Your Majesty must get rid of all his possessions in the continent of the Americas, keeping only the islands of Cuba and Puerto Rico, in the northern part and some other in the southern part that can serve as a base for Spanish trade. In order to carry out this great idea in a convenient way for Spain,

---

[*] Salvador de Madariaga, *España, Ensayo de Historia Contemporánea* (Madrid: Espasa-Calpé, 1979), p. 103.

three royal princes must be sent to America, one as king of Mexico, another as king of Peru and a third as King of the mainland, and Your Majesty must adopt the title of emperor."*

Had the advice of this statesman been followed in Spain, more than a decade of confrontation and wars against independence movements could have been avoided, its prestige as motherland of a community of Spanish-speaking nations would have been strengthened, and the Bourbons could have been pioneers in the creation of a new style of empire. But there were two main obstacles to implement it: in the first place, the king would have had to send his three sons to the Americas with the risky mission of creating new kingdoms, and on top of this he would have been left without succession in case the heir to the throne died. The second obstacle was that giving up inherited possessions was contrary to the principles of any king. In this way, the Bourbons preferred to face a similar fate to that of the British Hanovers in America rather than follow Aranda's wise advice.

Aranda was not the only one to warn the crown about the problems that were looming before the Spanish Empire after the revolutions in America and in France. Alessandro Malaspina presented a report in 1794 on returning from a tour around the world, which also included an analysis about the empire's political situation. After witnessing the increasing popularity of the independence cause, the explorer recommended the concession of a wide autonomy, especially in the possessions of the American mainland, and the creation of a confederation of nations that would be unified by commercial and economic links.** Far from following his advice, the government considered it inappropriate and dangerous in revolutionary times.

For those who wished to break away from the Spanish Empire the American Revolution served as the model on how to achieve independence, and the French Revolution constituted a source of ideas in the quest for the ideal society. But it was the Napoleonic invasion of Spain that triggered the outbreak of the armed struggle against the Spanish presence in America.

---

* Ricardo García Carcel, *La Herencia del Pasado, las Memorias Históricas de España* (Barcelona: Galaxia Gutenberg, 2011).
** Giraldo, *Naciones de Rebeldes.*

American viceroyalties owed obedience to the king of Spain but not to a usurper like Joseph Bonaparte, who had taken over the Spanish crown, and self-government was therefore justified. This is how many creoles interpreted the events that took place in Spain in 1808. The first autonomous junta of the Spanish Empire was formed in Mexico City with the aim of governing New Spain, and it was supported by the viceroy himself, José de Iturrigaray. At River Plate the Montevideo junta was formed and was followed by other juntas in La Paz and Quito. More than independence movements, they were uprisings against what was happening in Spain. In fact many of those who proclaimed rebellions did so in King Ferdinand VII's name, but as a result of it a staunch determination to run their own affairs was to emerge.

The rise of a liberal Spain that fought against Napoleonic troops but also aimed at establishing a new system of government could have been the solution for keeping the empire united. The Constituent Assembly established in Cádiz in 1810, where the 1812 constitution would be approved, inaugurated a new liberal regime that paid special attention to the demands of the citizens on the other side of the Atlantic. In fact it was in Spain at that time where the term "liberal" was born, and it gradually spread through Europe until it became one of the most influential political terms in the Western world.[*]

The Cádiz constitution stated that "the Spanish nation is the union of Spaniards from both hemispheres," and it granted "the Spanish kingdoms and provinces from America and Asia" the same rights as those of the metropolis. Both whites descending from Europeans, as well as the indigenous and mixed-race population, were defined as citizens with the right to elect deputies that would represent them in the new Spanish Cortes, the bicameral legislature. Thanks to this new liberal order, for the first time in the history of the Spanish Empire, and in fact of European imperialism, citizens throughout the empire had the historic opportunity of voting in joint elections in order to elect their representatives.

The constitution of Cádiz was to be very influential in Spanish America, but its liberal spirit and willingness to grant the Americans the same rights as the subjects of the Iberian regime did not go far enough. Only twenty-eight

---

[*] Raymond Carr, *Spain 1808-1975* (Oxford, England: Oxford University Press, 2000).

out of 104 deputies elected in the first Cortes were Americans despite the fact that American subjects exceeded the Europeans by more than five million.* This was one of many reasons for creole dissatisfaction, which led the American elites to persevere in their aim of marching toward independence.

On May 15, 1811, the Guarani Missions of River Plate declared independence of the territory that was later to form the Republic of Paraguay. Two months later the captain generalship of Venezuela declared its independence, and Cundinamarca and Cartagena were to follow suit. The wave of independence spread rapidly, and in a few years it was making good progress through the mainland of the Spanish American Empire.

What type of nation did the leaders of the independence movements aim at creating in the Spanish Empire? What were their ideological references and their models?

The independence leaders in Spanish America all shared the same social origins, for they all came from an elite that was well connected with Spain and Europe, and this enabled them to be in contact with the ideas of the Enlightenment and the revolutionary spirit that emerged in Europe toward the end of the eighteenth century.

One of the main precursors of the emancipation of Spanish America, Francisco de Miranda, was born in 1750. After a polished education he opted for a military career in Spain. As a member of the Spanish army he was sent to fight against Britain in the American War of Independence, and he lived in the United States in that historic moment when the new nation was formed. A few years later he participated in the French Revolution as general of the revolutionary army. Therefore, probably no one was better suited to carry the spirit of the revolutionary era to Spanish America than he. After serving the two great revolutions Miranda focused on the great project of his life: the independence of Spanish America. His aim was the creation of a great independent empire that would be known as Colombia and would stretch across all the Spanish territories of the Americas. Unlike other revolutionary leaders of his time, Miranda was no republican, for he aimed at unifying Colombia under a hereditary emperor that would receive the title

---

* Carr, *Spain 1808–1975.*

of Inca, in order to placate the indigenous peoples. The government would be elected by a bicameral parliament elected by representatives from all this new American Empire.

In 1806 Miranda reached Venezuela with British support, and he led a failed attempt at proclaiming its independence and fulfilling his great ambition. Four years later, he met another great Venezuelan independence leader in London: Simón Bolívar, who persuaded him to return to his homeland in order to fight for independence. In 1812 Miranda became the first president of Venezuela and was granted quasi-dictatorial powers, but the new republic still had to defeat the Spanish troops. As he led the struggle for independence against Spain the president was betrayed by Bolívar and handed over to the Spanish troops.* Miranda ended his days in a Spanish jail, and as a result of this ignominious end the leader of the Venezuelan independence was to become a martyr of the cause.

The elimination of Miranda allowed Bolívar to become the undisputed leader of the independence movement in Spanish America. Born into a patrician family in Caracas, Bolívar was educated in Madrid and briefly lived in Paris, where he was deeply influenced by the revolutionary ideals of that time. From 1812 he led a new revolution in order to consolidate Venezuela's independence, for which he was to be known as "the liberator."

Bolívar had a very similar dream to Miranda's, of unifying all territories of the Spanish Empire in America under a great confederation. With this aim he led the struggle for the liberation of the viceroyalty of New Granada from Spanish dominance. Once it was achieved, he was proclaimed president of Great Colombia, which included present Colombia, Venezuela, Ecuador, and Panama.

Shortly after this great achievement, Bolívar met the other prominent leader of Spanish American independence: José de San Martín. San Martín had a similar education to that of other Spanish American leaders. He followed a brilliant military career in Spain, which culminated in fighting against Napoleonic troops. He initiated the Spanish American independence

---

* Manuel Lucena Giraldo, *Francisco de Miranda La Aventura de la Política* (Madrid: Edaf, 1990).

movement from a Masonic lodge, for freemasonry was to accumulate much power in the revolutionary era. It was going to be very active in the promotion of US independence,* and was to promote the emancipation of Spanish America with the same enthusiasm. It constituted a very useful means of support for the independence leaders.

After returning to Buenos Aires in 1812, San Martín was to lead the movement that would culminate in the independence of the viceroyalty of River Plate. He also put together an army and crossed the Andes in 1817 to help the leading figure of the Chilean uprising, Bernardo O'Higgins, expel the royalist forces. As a result of this he would be known as the father of independence for Chile and Argentina.

The two so-called liberators met at Guayaquil in 1822, in the presence of Antonio José de Sucre, another prominent independence leader, with the aim of planning the liberation of Peru from Spanish power, but they clashed in their aims about the future of Spanish America. San Martín was in favor of appointing European princes to rule over the new independent nations, but this idea was incompatible with the plans of the Venezuelan leader. Nevertheless, San Martín decided to retire to Buenos Aires and later to Europe, where he died shortly afterward. In this way, Bolivar managed to emerge as the sole leader and later succeeded at making his ideas prevail in the final stage of the war of independence.

Simón Bolívar obtained his most important victory with the Battle of Ayacucho, in 1824, in which the last Spanish troops were defeated. As a result of this victory two new republics were created, that of Peru and Bolivia (the latter given its name in the Venezuelan leader's honor), and Bolívar was to occupy the presidency of the two.

However much Bolívar admired the North American republican system and the ideas of the French Revolution, he did not seem to consider them wholly suitable for South America. In 1815 he had written that Spanish America should "not adopt the best system of government, but the one that is most likely to succeed."** He believed in a compromise between authority

---

* Niall Ferguson, *The Square and the Tower* (London: Allen Lane, 2017).
** Salvador de Madariaga, *Bolivar* (London: Hollis and Carter, 1952).

and democracy, and ended up imposing what he described as the monocratic system, with a lifelong and hereditary president. He seemed to pursue the dream of unifying the old Spanish Empire by means of conquests, and in the Napoleonic style concentrate all power under his name. Nevertheless, his ambition was to fall victim of the Caesar-like politics and authoritarianism that he himself advocated, for in all conquered territories there were also influential oligarchies and leaders who were eager to defend their interests and reluctant to give up their power. In this way, the great Spanish American confederation was never to be realized, and in its place eighteen independent republics were later to emerge. "America is ungovernable, those who served the revolution ploughed the sea," lamented Bolívar toward the end of his life. Nevertheless, the authoritarian spirit of Bolívar was to have many followers—even up to the present day—who tried to press on the suffering masses what they understood to be a revolution.

The viceroyalty of New Spain was to follow slightly different paths from the rest of the Spanish Empire. The movement for independence took longer to take off. Rather than a rebellion orchestrated by the elite it was to be more a social revolution of the indigenous and the poor against the creole oligarchy. In these circumstances the Mexican creoles preferred to support the Spanish crown in spite of their wishes for independence. Mexican independence was to come through a more conservative path. A Mexican elite that was very much under the influence of the Catholic Church refused to accept the possibility of being governed by a liberal constitution from Spain. With the aim of preserving the traditional order they opted for an independence that would recognize Ferdinand VII as king. When this proposal was rejected by the Spanish Cortes, the creoles decided to proclaim their most prominent leader, Agustín de Iturbide, as emperor of Mexico on May 22, 1822. Nevertheless, the Mexican Empire was to be very brief, for a year later Agustín I was overthrown and the first Mexican Republic was proclaimed.

The loss of most of its empire had a devastating effect on the kingdom of Spain. Just as it happened with Britain after US independence, for many years Spaniards refused to accept the loss of the American Empire and treated its territories as fully independent nations. Reconciliation with the former subjects came gradually, mainly as a result of the increasing pressure to reestablish trade relations among the two sides of the Atlantic that was interrupted from 1824, and also due to the necessity to keep the remaining colonies of the American Empire.

Despite the fact that commercial exchange flourished again a few years after the final battle for independence, Spanish traders were to suffer the consequences of having to compete in the free market to sell their products in America, particularly due to the fact that the United States and Britain as well were to offer cheaper prices.

But the most enduring legacy of the Spanish in America was cultural. In fact the term *Hispanoamérica* was introduced by the independence leaders, acknowledging in this way the legacy of Spain in the new nations. Spanish was also proclaimed as the official language in all the new nations emerging from the Spanish Empire, and governments ensured that all educational institutions would teach in Spanish. These measures contributed to strengthen national cohesion, particularly in countries where there was a large indigenous population that had little contact with the creole elites and the population of European origin. It also allowed Spanish to become the lingua franca, spoken throughout vast territories that spanned from Argentina to New Mexico.

Once war wounds healed the common language and other aspects of the cultural links with Spanish America were to be particularly exploited by the Spanish government and its elites as a way of strengthening the role of Spain as the motherland of this new Hispanic world, and to a certain extent the American elites were receptive. But it was above all the constant influx of Spanish emigrants to the former colonies, particularly in the second half of the nineteenth century, that kept the transatlantic links between Spain and the old empire alive.

As regards the Portuguese Empire in America, its destiny in the revolutionary era was going to be the same as the Spanish, but only by a process that was to be less violent and traumatic.

The Portuguese royal family fled to Brazil after Napoleon's troops took over the Iberian Peninsula. As a result of King John VI's settlement in Rio de Janeiro, this city became the new capital of the united kingdom of Portugal, Brazil, and the Algarves, and Brazil was transformed into the center of the

Portuguese Empire. When John VI returned to Lisbon in 1821, the Brazilian elite, just like many Portuguese migrants who had settled in Brazil, refused to lose the status that they had acquired as the nucleus of the Portuguese Empire—or what was even worse, to go back to being a colony dependent on Lisbon. But on leaving for Portugal, John VI had left his son Pedro I as regent in Brazil, and the young prince saw the confrontation between Brazil and Portugal as his opportunity to create a new empire for himself.

The Portuguese prince, under the cry of "independence or death," bravely led the Brazilian nationalist movement, and in gratitude he was proclaimed emperor of Brazil on October 12, 1822.* In this way Brazil initiated its trajectory as an independent nation under the power of the same dynasty that had ruled over them as a colony. In spite of the important contributions to Brazil made by Emperor Pedro in his first years, the clashes with the creoles and their republican spirit did not allow him to consolidate his power. Pedro I abdicated in 1831 and his son Pedro II succeeded him as emperor of Brazil. Pedro II proved to be an efficient ruler and managed to consolidate a united Brazil in times of upheaval, but his popularity and that of the Braganza dynasty finally succumbed to the turbulence of Brazilian politics. A republic was finally proclaimed in 1889.

Europe was deeply transformed by the revolutionary era, for this reason it was not possible to go back to the old regime, as many monarchs and statesmen wished. The ideas of liberalism, equality, and democracy continued making progress in European societies. Another idea that was increasingly influential from the outbreak of the revolutionary era was nationalism, the desire to form nations among people who shared a history, a culture, and a language. Liberalism and nationalism were going to be the two great terms that inspired revolutions from the 1820s.

The revolutionary era was far from over after the Battle of Waterloo in 1815; the forces of change unleashed by it continued to shape politics in Europe and increasingly in the rest of the Western world. In 1830 a new revolution broke out in France against King Charles X, and it was to provoke a wave of revolutions that toppled several regimes and brought about

---

* E. Bradford Burns, *A History of Brazil* (New York: Columbia University Press, 1993).

major changes in the map of Europe. In France a constitutional monarchy was proclaimed under Louis Philippe Joseph d'Orleans.

A new nation was created, Belgium, also to be ruled by a constitutional monarchy. Greece obtained independence from the Ottoman Empire with the support of Britain, France, and Russia, and widespread sympathy throughout Europe, as it was commonly believed that such an important symbol of Western civilization and the cradle of democracy ought to break free from the oppressive Ottoman Empire.

Less than two decades later, a new wave of revolutions broke out. The 1848 revolutions provoked chaos in most of Europe and even some countries in South America for almost a year. In major cities from London to Warsaw the masses took to the streets to fight against the system of government. The aims of the revolts were diverse: national independence in some cases, and in others democracy or more rights were demanded, as well as an improvement in the conditions of the working class. That same year, two revolutionaries, Karl Marx and Friedrich Engels, published *The Communist Manifesto*: "A specter is haunting Europe: the specter of communism," could be read in the first line. Order was restored in most of Europe without great concessions to the insurgents, nevertheless this revolution constituted a warning for the governments and political elites about the consequences of ignoring peoples' demands.

Among the most important ideas bequeathed by the revolution, two of them were deeply to alter the concept of government in European nations, as well as their role in the world. The first is that the government must be the expression of the people's will. As a result of this, representative parliaments spread across Europe except in Russia, where the old regime's autocracy was to survive, with grave consequences, in the long run.

The way in which empires were governed was to change radically as a result of the principle of democratic representation, as well as the lessons learned from the wars of independence. The inhabitants of the colonies should be treated as citizens rather than as mere subjects. With the exception of colonies populated by indigenous groups that were considered primitive and uncivilized, the rest of the colonial population should have an active participation in the government and administration of its territory. Every empire that was kept together by means of force and oppression was doomed to disappear.

The second great idea bequeathed by the revolutionary era was that of equality of men as a human rights principle. As a result, the most shameful scourge of European imperialism was to disappear: slavery. France was the first European country to abolish it officially, although slavery lingered on in several parts of its empire. Britain came next. Thanks to the efforts of the politician and philanthropist William Wilberforce a law forbidding the slave trade was passed in the British Parliament in 1807; in 1833 slavery was finally abolished in the British Empire. Spain followed suit in 1811, except in Hispaniola, Puerto Rico, and Cuba, where slavery was not abolished until the 1880s. In the Dutch Empire slavery was also to continue until 1863, and Portugal was the last of the European countries to abolish slavery, in 1869—although it was not formally abolished in its empire until 1875.* The principle that it was unacceptable to possess slaves made progress in Europe over the first three decades of the nineteenth century—except in Russia, where serfdom continued until 1864.

Nevertheless, the antislavery cause was to take longer to reach the new nations in the Americas, especially in the regions where agricultural production depended on slave labor. In the United States, despite the enthusiasm with which the founding fathers proclaimed the equality of all citizens, it was inferred that this principle was only applicable to white men, and was not extended to the black population until 1865. Then, after a bloody civil war between the antislavery North against the slave-owning South the practice was finally abolished. In Brazil slavery was not abolished until 1888. Once slavery was abolished, the struggle against racial discrimination began: the legacy of over three hundred years of slavery was to be the most controversial of European imperialism.

With the emergence of independent nations throughout America, the relationship between the two sides of the Atlantic was to become increasingly cold and distant. The atmosphere of distrust, resentment, and desire for revenge that overshadowed the relationship between Americans and

---

* Thomas, *The Slave Trade.*

Europeans ever since the American Revolution was not going to disappear until the mid–nineteenth century.

In 1823 U.S. president James Monroe proclaimed the famous doctrine that would bear his name, under the slogan of "America for the Americans." It warned that the United States had no intention of meddling in European affairs, but it would consider any European attempt at colonizing America or interfering in American affairs as an aggression against the United States. It was inspired by the wave of independent revolutions that swept across Spanish and Portuguese America, and it aimed at avoiding other European powers taking advantage of the power vacuum in order to spread their influence through these territories after the fall of the Spanish and Portuguese Empires.

The Monroe Doctrine reveals the extent to which the United States' self-esteem had increased since the Declaration of Independence. It also shows the desire of United States to mark its zone of influence as an aspiring great power just as Europeans had traditionally done. But it is also a manifestation of a new feeling that was to predominate in America from the early nineteenth century: Americanism, an identity that considered itself the offspring of the American continent not the European, and standing up to any European power that dared to occupy the lands which American citizens legitimately considered their own.

Despite the fact that the United States and the rest of the new American nations were born under the spirit of anti–imperialism and a rejection of European expansionism, this did not imply that they were not willing to expand or even become empires themselves. In the case of the U.S. it soon became clear that the empire of liberty that Jefferson proclaimed was not merely a metaphorical term.

The desire for territorial expansion that could be perceived in the thirteen colonies increased considerably after the creation of the United States. Within a few decades after its birth the country's frontiers were to be broadened in a considerable way. Initially, the Americans gained territory at the French and Spanish Empires' expense with the purchase of Louisiana and Florida, and later at Mexican expense by the less orthodox method of conquest and submission. After war against Mexico broke out in 1846 over the possession of Texas, the United States not only kept this territory but all territories to the north of Rio Grande that had been Mexican until then. After this extraordinary southern expansion the U.S. focused on the conquest of the West that was to be crucial to the so-called frontier spirit that marked several generations of Americans. As a result of the western expansion the U.S. frontier reached the Pacific coast. Another substantial territorial acquisition was obtained in 1867 when Alaska was purchased from the Russians. In this way by the 1870s the United States became one of the largest countries on earth, with such vast dimensions that it had nothing to envy those of many European empires in history.

The expansionist spirit was also inherited from the Europeans by other American nations. Brazil, another new American nation of gigantic dimensions, had good reasons to proclaim itself an empire in 1822. As a consequence of Brazilian growth the Portuguese feared that it would seize their colonies in Africa and in the Atlantic. But Brazilians did not fall into the temptation of building an overseas empire because, as Pedro I stated, "Brazil is sufficiently big and productive for us."*

Brazilians also experienced a frontier spirit similar to that of the North Americans, although in their case the Amazonian jungle made expansion much more difficult than in the plains of the Wild West. The frontier spirit was also present among the Argentineans in the Pampas and Patagonia, among the Chileans in their internal colonization, and the Mexicans in their expansion through the Indian territories toward the north and south of their huge country. The conquest and expansion through the Americas that the Europeans started in 1492 was completed by their American descendants in the nineteenth and twentieth centuries.

While the cause of liberalism and democracy made its way in Europe with considerable difficulty against the forces of the old regime, in the United States it was to make a much smoother progress. Loyal to the principles of its Constitution, the United States consolidated the most advanced model of democracy in the early nineteenth century. It was based on a broad suffrage that included the majority of white adults, a system of checks and balances

---

* Roderick Barman, *Brazil: The Forging of a Nation, 1798–1852* (Stanford, Calif.: Stanford University Press, 1988).

that prevented many of the abuses of power that were experienced in the old world, and above all an enviable model of society based on cohabitation among citizens from very diverse origins and the promotion of prosperity.

In 1831 the French politician and historian Alexis de Tocqueville traveled to the United States in order to write a report commissioned by his government on the country's prison system. But it was only the pretext used by this French aristocrat in order to spend some time in the young American nation and analyze its politics and society that he found so fascinating. The product of this journey was a book published by de Tocqueville in 1835, under the title of *Democracy in America*, which apart from being widely read both in Europe and America was going to be very influential in Western political thought.

Alexis de Tocqueville explained how US democracy worked and why this country was achieving a much more advanced democratic system than any other European country. According to the French historian the key to the success of US democracy was in a society that combined egalitarianism, community spirit, and individualism. Tocqueville had the virtue of predicting the rise of the United States as a world power as well as that of Russia, for very different reasons. What fascinated the European readers about de Tocqueville's book was that it was like a journey to the future, as it not only warned the Europeans about the increasing importance of the United States but also that the type of democratic society that had emerged there would eventually reach old Europe. "The same democracy that reigns over American societies is rapidly advancing toward power in Europe,"* explained de Tocqueville.

On the other hand the Latin American experience with democracy and the values of the era of revolutions was going to be much more traumatic. Dictatorships, despotic regimes and exclusive oligarchies that emerged from wars and political upheaval were going to project an image from this part of the world that was radically different to the North American. Why did the European inheritance give worse results in Spanish and Portuguese America than in North America? A lot has been written about this topic, very often

---

* Alexis de Tocqueville, *Democracy in America* (New York: Penguin Classics, 2003).

under the influence of simplistic theories, stereotypes, or myths about the Anglo-Saxon people's inherent capacity to create democratic and stable societies, in stark contrast with the Hispanic world with its authoritarian tendencies and anarchic spirit. Yet there was a subtle difference. Latin American nations were born under the influence of one of the most advanced constitutions in the nineteenth century, the Spanish 1812 constitution. Liberalism and democracy were going to be aims proclaimed by the creole elites and they managed to make progress in some nations, although on the whole, the nineteenth century in the Latin American world, just as it happened in the Iberian Peninsula, was characterized by political instability.

The era of revolutions brought the end to a very substantial part of four great empires, the British, the French, the Spanish, and the Portuguese. Apart from losing sovereignty over most of the American continent, the Europeans were going to be confronted with a new American identity that rejected any sort of European hegemony on the other side of the Atlantic. Among the new nations, the United States, born under the determination to defend the principles of liberty and independence, was going to play the leading role in the defense of the American territory and sphere of influence.

Another major achievement of this era was the prohibition of the slave trade and the abolition of slavery in most of the European empires. New ideas about the citizens' rights, equality of men, or parliamentary representation—all of them seemed to be at odds with the predominant principles of conquest and submission of the colonized people by the colonizer. As a result, European powers were going to face increasing pressure from their political and intellectual elites to reconsider the way in which overseas possessions were governed.

Nevertheless, the era of revolutions did not speed up the decline of Europe despite the fact that so many overseas possessions were lost. On the contrary, political and social changes experienced in these days contributed to strengthen European societies, increasing their dynamism, their entrepreneurial spirit, and their capacity to solve internal conflicts in a peaceful way to find solutions to their citizens' problems. Freedom, social mobility, and meritocracy were to expand; equality of rights and opportunities became aspirations that would be worthy of any good society. In fact it is not a coincidence that the countries where parliamentary democracy made better progress in the nineteenth century ended up being the most powerful politically and economically. The era of revolutions gave way to a golden age in which Western civilization reached the highest summits of development in the economic, political, scientific, and cultural spheres, and in consequence, the gap between the West and the rest of the world was to be wider than ever.

While the Europeans assimilated the impact of the French Revolution another revolution was to start, one that was much more quiet, less violent and conflictive but no less consequential: the Industrial Revolution. The steam engine, the spinning jenny, the introduction of coal as the main biofuel, and extraordinary innovations in the iron production processes, all of these inventions and technological innovations took place between the late eighteenth and the early nineteenth centuries. They brought amazing changes in the economy and society that were going to affect individual lives more than ever before. Railways that revolutionized transport and massive emigration to the cities were two of the most significant products of this revolution. The country where the Industrial Revolution began, Great Britain, acquired an enormous advantage over rival powers, and this was going to play a crucial role in its rise to world hegemony. The Industrial Revolution provided much more wealth than the empire in America and gave a new meaning to its colonial empire as a source of essential commodities and an emerging market where the products of British factories could be exported.

The Industrial Revolution rapidly spread across Western Europe and the other side of the Atlantic starting with the United States, which was to emerge as one of the main industrial powers from the late nineteenth century. Industrialization was soon to become synonymous with economic development and prosperity, and any country that was not capable of industrializing was condemned to stagnation and backwardness. The Industrial Revolution compensated for many misunderstandings that emerged between Americans and Europeans as a consequence of the other revolutions that we have examined. America became an increasingly attractive market for European industrialists, whereas American entrepreneurs approached Europe and Britain in particular as a source of technological innovation, venture capital, and ideas for fostering industry and wealth creation.

Finally, a very important consequence of the revolutionary era for both Europeans and Americans was the rise of an Atlantic community. The origins of this Atlantic community can be traced back to the sixteenth century, when the first Europeans settled in America. But as long as there were European empires in America the colonial settlers were just an appendix of Europe, largely dependent on the metropolis that governed them. Nevertheless, with the formation of independent nations in most of the Americas from the early nineteenth century, a new relationship was to emerge based on mutual respect and increasing interdependence that could be described as an Atlantic community. Despite the US founding fathers' desire to create a very different society to that of old Europe, the philosophical and political principles that inspired them were European. As regards Latin America, there was a staunch determination for breaking away from the colonial powers. The legacy of pre-Columbian cultures and the presence of native Americans in some parts may have influenced the creation of a new identity, but even so, the model of society that inspired the new societies was European, and the culture and values cherished by the creole elites were always those of the former colonial powers.

After independence the American elites continued seeing Europe as a source of learning and improvement in many aspects, as a reference to their identity. Their trends of change in the political, economic, social, and cultural sphere continued being marked by Europe. On the other hand the Europeans persisted treating the American nations with airs of superiority, but they were also going to inspire much admiration. American democracy emerged as the great model that was particularly useful for regenerating old European politics. Brazil was for many decades an example of a new imperial power that both fascinated and worried the Portuguese. Argentina was in a similar way admired by the Spaniards.

Above all, the United States and almost all the American nations started to be seen by the Europeans as lands of great opportunity where dreams that seemed impossible in their countries of origin could become true. Trade between the two parts of the Atlantic and emigration to the Americas were going to strengthen the transatlantic community to the extent of becoming an essential aspect that accounts for the vigor of the European world in its hegemonic era.

The clash between revolutionary versus traditional reverberated through Europe ever since the start of this revolutionary era and the great imperial powers had to face the consequences of dramatic territorial losses or political upheaval provoked by the defeat of the old order. But far from weakening Europe it actually reinvigorated its civilization, allowing it to continue shaping the world in the most extraordinary ways.

Chapter 5

Eastern Dreams of Grandeur

How China, India, and the Rest of Asia Were Shaped
by European Expansion.

———————————————————

ong before European empires emerged it was in Asia where empires were built. From the Tigris and Euphrates, where the first civilizations took shape, the most extraordinary imperial feats were carried out first by the Persians in the Near East, while in the Far East China emerged as a colossus. The Silk Road, the first major trade route in history, connected these two civilizations as well as many other peoples of Asia. Silk, which was one of the main products exported from China and Japan, reached the Mediterranean world through the Silk Road, and it gradually became a network of trade and even cultural exchange between East and West.*

———————

* Peter Frankopan, *The Silk Roads: A New History of the World* (New York: Vintage, 2017).

Christopher Columbus had very good reasons for devoting many years of his life to discover a western route to Asia, for this continent was a symbol of wealth; whoever found a new route toward one of its lands could expect to be handsomely rewarded. The wealth in the Near East seemed inaccessible, as it was in the hands of empires that were hostile to the Christian world, but the Far East was, according to popular imagination, the place in the world where the greatest riches were stored.

The discovery of America and its subsequent colonization contributed to diminish European interest in the Asian continent. Nevertheless, Asia continued to exert great attraction, and the Europeans who traveled there starting in the sixteenth century were to find out that its wealth and trading possibilities matched the legends that the Europeans had believed about this faraway land. But extracting benefits from the Asian lands, settling there, and consolidating a hegemonic position over their peoples proved to be much more difficult, and even impossible in various cases.

The arrival of the Europeans in Asia provoked a clash of civilizations that, unlike in the rest of the world, did not always culminate with European predominance. In India, China, and Japan, Europeans discovered millenarian civilizations of great sophistication. The Chinese and the Japanese had science and technology, and ways of life that in some aspects seemed more advanced than those of the Europeans. These two nations were not only particularly proud of their civilizations, which they considered as the most advanced in the world, but they also had sufficient means to defend themselves from any foreign incursion. Nevertheless, the European presence in Asia ended up exerting a very powerful influence over them.

Portugal, a pioneer in the era of discoveries, was also the nation that deserves the credit for opening Asia for the European powers. Vasco da Gama's arrival on the western coast of India in 1499 was soon followed by the first Portuguese explorations through the Indian coast and eventually the first settlement with which European colonization began.

In 1505 King Manuel I of Portugal appointed Francisco de Almeida as viceroy of the new *Estado da India*, a company in charge of colonizing India and promoting trade in the Indian Ocean. Two years later, the sailor Alfonso de Albuquerque replaced Almeida. Albuquerque conquered the city of Goa, and he cunningly exploited rivalries between the neighboring kingdoms to impose Portuguese dominion and start promoting trade in the region. This constituted the beginning of a Portuguese presence in India that was to last for more than four centuries.

Shortly after consolidating Portuguese power in Goa, Albuquerque sent his fleet to the city of Malacca in 1511. Malacca, in present-day Malaysia, was one of the main crossroads of the Asian continent, and controlling this city implied gaining access to the markets in this part of the world. After occupying it, Albuquerque ordered the construction of a fort that was to bear the name of *A famosa* and he made Malacca the center of the Portuguese Empire in the Far East.*

The key to hegemony in Asia was to control the spice route, and for this purpose it was essential to have access to the Chinese Empire. For this reason, in 1513 Viceroy Albuquerque sent Rafael Perestrello to China with the aim of establishing trade relations between Portugal and the celestial kingdom, as it was known. A great paradox of history was that Perestrello was the cousin of Christopher Columbus's wife, and he had the honor of becoming the first European to fulfill Columbus's dream of reaching the Chinese coast.** His fellow countryman, Jorge Álvares reached the northern coast and present-day Hong Kong shortly after. After this initial contact with the Chinese civilization, in 1517 Fernão Pires de Andrade was sent with the mission of establishing formal relations between the two states that would give way to trade exchange. But he had to wait until 1521 to be granted an audience that would allow him to meet the all-powerful Chinese emperor in the Forbidden City in Beijing.

On top of the inconveniences of waiting for such a long time, the diplomatic mission had disastrous results. When Fernão Pires de Andrade was about to be received, a letter from the former sultan of Malacca reached the Emperor's court explaining how the Portuguese had expelled him from his kingdom. The scant sympathy felt by the Chinese mandarins toward the Portuguese totally vanished as a result, and all its members, including Fernão

---

*   Crowley, *Conquerors.*
** Ibid.

Pires de Andrade himself, were sent to prison and subsequently executed. After such a brutal elimination of the delegation, trade with the Portuguese was strictly prohibited in China. As other Europeans were going to discover over the next centuries, China was a most inaccessible civilization, and the great majority of the attempts to penetrate it were to culminate with humiliating rebuffs or forceful expulsions.

Prohibition did not manage to keep the Portuguese at bay, for many ships continued smuggling their products into China, and also managed to make some incursions into Japanese ports. In order to obtain benefits from both the Chinese and the Japanese market it was necessary to have a well-connected base in the region, and they finally found it in Macao. This was a peninsula in which the Chinese emperor had allowed the entrance of foreigners in order to trade with his subjects. But the Portuguese attempted to go much further, settling there permanently, and after much perseverance, in 1554, they were authorized to establish a settlement, though paying a high price for it. They had to pay tributes and always pay compulsory respect to the Ming dynasty. From 1573 the Chinese government demanded an annual amount from the Portuguese coffers and that the Chinese population in this settlement would be subject to Chinese law, even though the official administration there was Portuguese.

In Macao, the Portuguese traded European products like wool, golden linen, cotton, opium from India, species from the Moluccas, and even ivory from Africa. They bought from the Chinese silk, porcelain objects, gold, and copper. From there they also established commercial relations with Japan, a particularly closed market. The silver trade was to be especially lucrative for Macao.

Silver was the most demanded metal in China; it was twice as expensive there as in Europe or Japan. Traders from Macao were going to take advantage of the great shiploads of silver that arrived in Europe from Spanish America (especially from the discovery of the mines of Potosí in 1545), to do business with the Chinese. They also imported silver from Japan and from the Spanish Philippines, where shiploads of the precious metal arrived from America.

Within a decade after its foundation as a Portuguese settlement, Macao became a great trading center that attracted Portuguese, Chinese, and Asians from very diverse places. In 1565 the city had about one thousand Portuguese inhabitants, apart from several hundred who came from Malaysia, China, and India.* Many of the Portuguese had arrived from Malacca with their Malaysian wives, and others married Japanese women and brought them over to Macao. For this reason the city of Macao had, from its early stages, a large mixed-race population.

The Portuguese authorities promoted intermarriage as the only way of populating their Asian settlements. In the case of Goa, they offered land to the Portuguese settlers who would marry indigenous women—although marriage should be performed under Catholic authority, for promoting Christianity in Asia was one of the aims of the *Estado da India*.

Missionaries were among the first Portuguese settlers in Macao: Franciscans, Augustinians, Dominicans, and above all Jesuits, who were going to succeed in promoting Christianity in China more than any other order. In 1575 the pope made Macao an episcopal seat, with jurisdiction over China, Japan, and Korea, and the city became the gate through which Christianity was going to expand to these countries.

Macao was the last conquest with which Portugal consolidated its Asian empire, an empire that had managed to expand from India to China within a few decades, enabling the Portuguese to exploit the Asian market with practically no rivalry, for the only other European power that was present in Asia was Spain.

After the conquest of the Philippines by Miguel López de Legazpi in 1564, the Spanish Empire acquired a global dimension. Legazpi's achievement was another amazing adventure bequeathed by the era of conquistadors. He confronted several tribes in the Philippine archipelago, and Chinese and Japanese pirates, until he finally reached a Muslim enclave known as Maynilad, where he founded Manila, which was going to become the new capital of the Spanish Empire in the Far East. Legazpi remained in the territories he conquered, fighting against all kinds of adversity until his death in 1572. He never found out that shortly before his death the king of Spain had signed a decree appointing him governor and captain general of the Philippines.

---

*   Crowley, *Conquerors*.

After settling down in the Philippines, the Spanish conquistadors started to dream of a much more ambitious challenge: the conquest of China. From Manila, Legazpi wrote to Philip II proposing the construction of six galleys in order to "sail across the coast of China and reach the mainland." Over the next years, Spanish administrators and missionaries gathered plenty of information about the old civilization. Letters of the missionaries describe the Chinese as "people who are not warlike at all," and they also allude to the possibility of promoting intermarriage with the Chinese women, "normally of great beauty and discretion."* In the same way that the Caribbean islands had served as the base from which to conquer the mainland of the American Empire, the Philippine archipelago should lead into the last great frontier of the Spanish Empire: China and the other nations of the great Asian continent. Nevertheless, in those days the empire of Philip II already had too many problems to embark on an adventure of such vast dimensions, and as a result China and the Asian mainland were to be the great unfulfilled ambitions of Spanish expansion.

The captain-generalship of the Philippines was founded in 1574, dependent on the viceroyalty of New Spain, and it included Palau, Guam, the Mariana Islands, and the Caroline Islands, all of them conquered by the Spaniards in their Asian expansion.

In the early stages, the colonial regime in the Philippines was very similar to the one in the American settler colonies. The Spaniards acquired lands by means of the traditional system of encomiendas, and the local tribes worked the lands, paying tribute in return for receiving protection, as well as being prepared for baptism. Although Philip II had ordered Legazpi to carry out the colonization of the Philippines, "without violence nor injustices," the encomienda system as it happened in the Americas was prone to all sorts of abuses and even the enslavement of Philippine workers.

Nevertheless, the encomienda system declined toward the end of the sixteenth century, due to the bold intervention of the first Spanish missionaries in favor of Philippine workers. Ever since their arrival in Philippines, the

---

* Hugh Thomas, *World Without End: Spain, Philip II, and the First Global Empire* (London: Allen Lane, 2014).

Augustinians did not limit themselves to denouncing slavery before many local authorities that allowed it. Fray Juan de Alva went much further, and wrote a letter to the viceroy of New Spain in 1570, in which he described the destructive effects that slavery could have. Three years later, the Augustinians sent a letter to Philip II himself, recommending their liberation, and finally, a royal decree of November 7, 1574, expressly prohibited slavery in the Philippine archipelago. In 1581, on his arrival in the Philippines as the first bishop of this diocese, Fray Domingo de Salazar handed in a royal decree to the governor, which forced him to grant freedom to all Philippine slaves or members of any other community that were being enslaved.* Philip II's royal decree deserves a special mention, for as a result of it slavery was abolished in the Philippines almost three centuries before slavery was banned throughout the European empires. In this way Spain created an important precedent in the imperial world, although it did not have any impact not even within the Spanish empire.

Another reason why the encomienda system disappeared in the Philippines was due to the increasing number of Chinese immigrants. Chinese traders arrived in Manila with silk, porcelain, and other luxury items that the Spaniards could buy and export to New Spain. Trade with the Chinese became in this way a much more lucrative business than the cultivation of land. Furthermore, many Chinese were willing to work as farmers, artisans, or salesmen, or employ themselves in any service demanded by Spanish colonists. Taxes charged by Spanish authorities for all their working activities became one of the main sources of income for the colony.

In order to connect the Asian archipelago with New Spain, the Manila Galleon was founded in 1565, which sailed across the Pacific twice per year from Acapulco to Manila, stopping at Guam. Thanks to this galleon Columbus's old dream of opening a route that would allow Castile to benefit from trade with Asia was finally to come true. Among the products that were usually transported were silk from China and Japan, porcelain, shawls, and canes. Apart from typical products from the Far East, the galleon also transported cotton clothes from India and even Persian carpets, and obviously silver from

---

* Thomas, *World Without End.*

New Spain, for which there was great demand in the New World. Apart from the routes that connected America with Spain, this was the other great trading route from the Spanish Empire, and it constituted the main link of the Philippines with the external world over the following three centuries.

This trade route abruptly came to an end in 1814 due to the Mexican War of Independence. The disappearance of this commercial link with America constituted a hard blow for the Philippine economy. With the dramatic drop in benefits for commercial activities, the colony was forced to depend on the much less lucrative agricultural activity, which had been left aside in the sixteenth century.

The Philippines opened the doors of Asia for the Spanish Empire. It was a very attractive market but nevertheless too remote and unknown, which explains why very few people among the Spanish population ventured to travel there. Apart from those who were sent there to administer or defend this possession, very few Spaniards decided to make their fortune there. This is the main reason why the Spanish language did not manage to take root there as it did in America, for intermarriage was very limited. Families of mixed Spanish and Philippine blood were concentrated in Manila. Beyond the capital and the main urban centers the influence of the colonial community's culture was very limited. However, the colonial government's rule that all inhabitants should register with a name and surname that would be understandable in Spanish, led to the proliferation of Spanish names and surnames among the indigenous population.

A high percentage of the Spaniards who went to the Philippines in the first decades of the colony's existence went there as missionaries. Toward the end of the sixteenth century there were over three hundred members of the orders of Franciscans, Augustinians, Dominicans, and Jesuits, which propagated the Christian faith rapidly through the archipelago. Apart from building churches, the religious orders were also in charge of promoting education. In 1595 the Jesuits opened the College of San Ildefonso in order to educate the elite from Manila. Especially important was the founding of the University of Santo Tomas in 1611, the first university on the Asian continent. These initiatives contributed to make Spanish influence particularly perceptible among a Philippine elite that was going to mark the future of this part of the world. Personages like the writer José Rizal in the nineteenth century, who has been described as the tropical equivalent to the eminent Spanish nineteenth-century writer Benito Pérez Galdós, show the extent to which Spain was an essential cultural reference for the governing class and the learned minority from the Philippines.

The union of the crowns of Spain and Portugal did not imply important changes for their empires due to Philip II's intention to respect the existing autonomy among them. What was going to destabilize their position in the Asian continent was the irruption of a new European rival: Holland.

The States-General of the Netherlands were determined from their birth to promote the creation of an overseas empire that would propagate their trading interests throughout the world, and decided to make Asia their main base. They did not dominate the international order like Spain and Portugal, but they had very important assets to achieve their aims: the best financial system in Europe, a great entrepreneurial spirit, and a fervent desire to take revenge on the Spanish monarchy.

After the Dutch companies made the first incursions into Asian territory, their government decided that in order to consolidate an empire in this part of the world it was necessary to unify their commercial forces. In this way the Dutch East India Company was founded in 1602, from the outset counting on both economic and political support and sufficient military power to open its way in Asia and impose both on the indigenous people and the European rivals.

Penetrating the Asian empire implied ousting the Portuguese and the Spaniards. This is what the first Dutch ships did in Southeast Asia, attacking every Iberian ship that got in their way and inflicting particular damage on the Portuguese fleet—which after a few years of Dutch presence lost a great part of what it had built over a century. After managing to impose themselves by force, from 1609 Dutch ships started trading easily through routes that went from the Moluccas to Bantam and from Borneo to Japan.

Having succeeded at breaking into the Asian market, the next step for Holland was to create a base from which it could administer its new interests in Asia. Malacca, occupied until then by the Portuguese, was considered an attractive option, but in 1621 the governor of the East India Company, Jan Pieterszoon Coen, invaded Jakarta. After giving the place the Christian name Batavia, it was decided that the capital of the Dutch Empire in Asia would be there.*

Within a few years Holland managed to oust Portugal and marginalize Spain in the Asian market. On the other hand, England proved to be a more dangerous rival for its interests. The first English traders arrived in Asia at the same time as the Dutch and, as we have previously seen, by the same method, through a company chartered for trading in East India.

In the first trips of the English East India Company, the ships anchored at ports in the Red Sea and India, where they would supply themselves with cotton that was then exchanged for spices at Bantam and the Moluccas—for spices and pepper were the most profitable products to sell. The clash of interests between the English and the Dutch in Bantam almost provoked a war in 1618.

In order to prevent rivalry in Asia starting a war King James I of England and the Estates General of the Dutch United Provinces reached a cooperation agreement. The two countries agreed jointly to build a fleet of ten ships, with which they would attack Portuguese and Spanish ships and then share the benefits in the spice trade. But cooperation was not going to last for long. On one hand, the English soon started to think that the cost of the agreement was far higher than the benefits, and this, together with the fact that several Englishmen were killed by the Dutch in 1623, was to put a dramatic end to the period of cooperation. The Dutch achieved their aim of dominating the pepper and spice markets in the seventeenth century, but they could not neutralize their English rivals.

After consolidating their position in Southeast Asia from their base in Bantam, the Dutch also managed to make an incursion into India. In 1614 they accepted an invitation from the Mughal emperor, who was fighting against the Portuguese, to set up a factory in Surat, in the west of the Indian subcontinent. This enclave in India allowed them to thrive with the cotton market.

---

* Israel, *The Dutch Republic*.

The third great aspiration of the Dutch in Asia was to have a base in China just as Portugal, but paradoxically the superiority they had earned on the seas proved to be useless in this aspect. The Chinese authorities prohibited the Dutch from approaching their coasts, due to the reputation for brutality that they had acquired in their fights against the Portuguese and any Asian people that got in their way. In 1621 the governor of Caen sent a fleet to occupy Macao but the Portuguese aided by the Chinese managed to repel it. What the Dutch achieved was to take two fortresses originally built by the Spaniards at the island of Formosa. From there not only did they build a thriving business, trading in sugar, but they also managed to penetrate the Japanese market and expel the Portuguese.

Holland made good use of its economic prosperity and the strategic strength acquired in Asia to continue expanding at Portuguese cost. In 1637 the Dutch took advantage of an internal revolt at the Portuguese colony of Ceylon in order to invade it. Shortly after, they attacked the most precious Portuguese possession, Malacca. Despite the fact that King John IV of Portugal negotiated a ceasefire with the United Provinces in 1641, over the following decade the Dutch managed to definitively expel the Portuguese from those colonies, and as a result their empire was reduced to Goa and Macao.

The remarkable speed with which Holland consolidated an empire at Portuguese expense shows how far a European power could expand as long as its fleet was superior to the rest and it had sufficient economic capacity to finance the cost of colonial acquisitions. On the other hand, Portuguese colonies were going to constitute a classic example of the vulnerability of all territorial expansion that was not backed by a solid military force. In a few days a small but well-armed fleet could dramatically put an end to the progress made in several decades of colonization.

Holland was not only interested in creating a mercantile empire in Asia, but it also aimed at founding colonies where a Dutch population would settle permanently. Dutch settlement was promoted in Surat through generous offers of land, but lack of interest from the Dutch population to venture in India prevented the project from succeeding. Another important initiative was to allow a Dutch population to settle in the colonies and trade independently, but this ended up being a serious problem as independent traders proved to be dangerous competitors for the East India Company, and they even did business with rival European powers. The Dutch Empire was going to constitute another example of how difficult European colonization in Asia proved to be.

One aspect in which the Dutch Empire was going to be very different from other European powers in Asia was in its lack of Christian missionary zeal. Representatives of the Dutch Reformed Church arrived with the first ships from Holland but their main mission was going to be to look after the spiritual well-being of their fellow countrymen, and as employees of the East India Company they lacked the independence that Catholic missionaries had to promote their faith in the Iberian colonies. Far from contributing to the expansion of Christianity in Asia, the Dutch presence provoked the undesired effect of strengthening Islamic faith in Southeast Asia. The attacks against ships of Islamic merchants and against villages in the region of present-day Indonesia contributed to transform Islam into a symbol of resistance to European incursions.

The English East India Company was initially not as rich as its Dutch rival, nor did it have as much official support as the States-General, for at that time the English crown was much more interested in colonizing North America than faraway Asia. Nevertheless it managed to consolidate a position in the Asian continent that was going to have vital importance in the subsequent development of the British Empire.

The company's first expedition to Asia set sail from England in 1601, and after two years trading in Sumatra and Java it returned to England with great shipments of pepper that were to leave substantial benefits. The second journey was even more successful, bringing pepper, clove, and nutmeg. Problems with Holland that were to emerge due to clashes of interest were to be compensated by the progress made by the company in India.

In 1607, on the third journey to Asia, the company's fleet sailed to western India and stopped at Surat. Captain William Hawkins decided to request an audience with the Mughal emperor, Jahangir, who was in favor of giving facilities to trade with other people. He authorized the English to set up a commercial base in Surat.

In East India, the company started to trade with the city of Masulipatnam in 1611. After more than two decades of good trading relations, in 1639 company representative Francis Day requested permission from the local sovereign to settle in the coast. Once it was granted, Day ordered the construction of a fort, to be known as Fort St. George. Thus the English established the first permanent settlement in the Indian subcontinent. Further north, merchants opened trading bases in Balasore in 1633 and in Hugli, on the border of the Ganges River, in 1650.

In 1668 King Charles II married the Portuguese princess Catherine of Braganza. According to the marriage treaty Catherine gave the city of Bombay as a dowry to Charles, which had been under Portuguese dominion for several decades. Once it became a British possession the East India Company occupied Bombay, an insalubrious city with much less trading activity than what the English had in other parts of India, although eventually it was to become one of the great cities of the Asian continent.

The company's employees continued their expansion through India. First they built a fortification in Bengal and from there they expanded toward Calcutta where they built Fort William in 1697. Trade expanded rapidly in this city, to the point of becoming the most important possession in India.

The ships of the East India Company started to set up commercial bases in Surat, where the first fort was built in 1612. In 1634 the Mughal emperor cordially received its representatives and invited them to continue trading with his people. From then on the company's interests in India were going to intensify. In 1639 a commercial base was founded in Madras, and in Bombay in 1668 (which was Catherine of Portugal's dowry). A few years later, in 1690 the base in Calcutta was founded.

The East India Company always enjoyed the crown's support, especially during the reign of Charles II, when its powers were increased to include the right to acquire territories, mint money, command fortresses and troops, make war and peace, and exercise both civil and criminal jurisdiction over the acquired areas. The leading figure who was ultimately responsible was that of the governor.

The importation of cotton, silk, spices, and tea—among many other Indian products—to England was soon to give great benefit, and toward the end of the eighteenth century the company was giving a twenty-five percent dividend to its shareholders.* Comments on how rapidly the company's share-holders were making money could be heard in the circles of London's political and financial elite, and also in the harbors where the sailors disembarked on their return from India, with so many stories to tell about that faraway world. From then India became one of the most sought-after territories for those Englishmen who wished to make fortune.

As a result of trade with India, one of the most characteristic habits associated with British culture emerged at that time: drinking tea. Tea was one of the many products that the East India Company started importing to England, until it became the most popular. The introduction of the habit of drinking tea at the English court is attributed to Catherine of Portugal, for the Portuguese queen started to drink tea in England as she used to do in Portugal, where it had been introduced by traders coming from Asia. Initially tea was only drunk by the aristocracy and the most sophisticated elite, and doctors started recommending it due to its relaxing effect.

In 1660 Samuel Pepys wrote in his famous diaries: "I ordered a cup of tea, a Chinese drink that I had never drunk before."** Nevertheless, a few decades later, tea became so popular throughout the British Isles that it emerged as a national drink shared by all social classes. Tea was also to increase trading benefits in the West Indies ever since it became fashionable to drink it with sugar. In consequence, sugar plantations in the Caribbean colonies were to multiply their benefits. In this way, with every cup of tea, the British were to enjoy the benefits of colonization in two parts of the world: Asia and America.

European presence in Asia steadily increased in the eighteenth century. After the arrival of Spain and Portugal, Holland and England followed suit and even managed to oust the Iberians. While England started to consoli-date positions in India, Holland controlled Indonesian trade from Batavia to Malacca, as well as the maritime routes to Japan. Nevertheless the link of the Iberian powers with Asia was to be strong and long-lasting. In the case of Spain, its presence in the Philippines was going to be one of the longest in the history of colonization, and even more that of Portugal in Goa and

---

*   Lawrence James, *Raj: The Making and Unmaking of British India* (London: Abacus, 1997).
** Samuel Pepys, *The Diary of Samuel Pepys* (New York: Modern Library, 2003).

Macao. Moreover, through Portuguese and Spanish missionary activities, European influence also started to infiltrate into the inscrutable Chinese Empire as well as in Japan.

France in the seventeenth century was obviously also interested in having a presence in Asia. During the reign of Louis XIII the ambitious Cardinal Richelieu was well aware of the progress made by the companies of rival powers, and for this reason the French East India Company was created under his auspices in 1642, shortly before his death. After the first expeditions that were not particularly successful, in 1668 the French set up the first fort in Surat, in southeast India, but the Dutch managed to expel them from there. They were to be more successful in Chandannagar, where a trading post was established in 1673 after obtaining authorization from Ibrahim Khan, the Nawab of Bengal, and this was to become the first proper French colony in India. Shortly afterward, as a result of an agreement with the sultan of Bijapur, the representatives of the French company acquired some territories in this kingdom in the southeast of the Indian subcontinent. The colony of Pondicherry was founded there, which was destined to be one of the most enduring in the French Empire. Thanks to these two enclaves, France managed to consolidate a presence in Asia and obtain important benefits.

While all these European powers reached Asia through the sea another power was going to do it from northern lands until it managed to consolidate an enormous empire in this continent: Russia. We've already examined how the Russians expanded beyond the Urals from the sixteenth century. As a result of the conquest of Siberia, a good part of the Asian continent was going to be governed by Moscow, many people were to become subjects of a white-skinned Christian emperor, and the Russian language was to expand up to the frontier with Mongolia and China. In the case of Russia, colonization of Asian land was not simply limited to the development of trade links, for Russian emigrants settled there permanently and with them Russian culture was to get a foothold in the heart of Asia.

The Russians ran ahead of the Asian peoples and were pioneers in the colonization of that vast and scarcely populated stretch of land known as Siberia. In their southward expansion the Russians were to meet with another great Asian empire: Persia. After the conquest of Astrakhan in 1555, the

Russians managed to gain access to the Caspian Sea and consequently also to the Persian Empire. The Russians and the Persians had a common enemy: the Ottomans. This was initially to pave the way to an understanding between the Russian emperor and the Shah of Persia in order to promote commercial exchange. In this way a lucrative commercial route was to emerge in which Russian furs were exchanged for silk and other typical products of this ancient civilization, such as carpets. Persia and Russia consolidated a peaceful relationship based on trade toward the end of the sixteenth century but it was rapidly to deteriorate from the late eighteenth century due to Russian expansionist aims in the Caspian region, as we shall later see.

While Russia steadily made progress in its expansion toward the Caspian region, the enlargement of its empire toward the southeast proved to be much more challenging as it approached Chinese territory. In 1628 the Cossacks, under the leadership of the brave and daring Erofei Jabbarov, reached the valleys of the Yenisei River and the region of Tunguska. From there they continued advancing gradually until they reached the Amur River and finally the Pacific Ocean. The Amur could be considered the natural northern frontier of the Chinese Empire, but the Cossacks were to take advantage of the political instability in China after the fall of the Ming dynasty in order to cross that frontier and settle in these lands that were more fertile than Siberia. Jabarov proclaimed Russian sovereignty over the Amur region, and following orders from Moscow, imposed a tax on its population as new Russian subjects that was obviously going to cause much indignation.

But the presence of the Russians in Amur was not going to last for long. Some years later, the new Manchu dynasty that managed to restore political order in China also decided to recover the territory that had been occupied by the "Western devils." In 1685, the Chinese troops took the main fort that had been built by the Russians, forcing them to negotiate a new treaty. In 1695 the two nations signed the Treaty of Nerchinsk, by which the Russians withdrew from Amur and were granted in exchange the authorization to trade with China in the route that reached the country through the Selenga River. The treaty also established that the leaders of the Russian trading missions would have to show their respect to the Chinese emperor and prostrate themselves before him according to the ancestral protocol of the celestial kingdom.* In this way the Chinese managed to block the progress of another European power, demonstrating once more that their civilization would not yield to any other.

The European powers had very good motives for expanding their settlements in Asia. While in most of America, Africa, or Oceania, the Europeans only reached prosperity after a long process of colonization and creation of new markets, wealth in Asia seemed much more accessible for those who had just arrived. Apart from having the oldest trading routes and a great abundance of products that were to be increasingly demanded from the West, the largest economies of the world were there.

India was the largest economy in the world at the beginning of the eighteenth century. According to several historians, a fourth of the world's combined gross national products came from Mughal Empire's India.** The second economy in the world was China under the Manchu dynasty. India and China were also demographic giants, each one of them had over one hundred million inhabitants at that time.

The wealth of India and China was the product of two ancient civilizations that emerged on the border of the River Ganges and the Yellow River. From antiquity their inhabitants had developed the most sophisticated cultures and ways of life, their cities and customs had fascinated the Europeans, their palaces and treasures had dazzled them, and their armies had imposed much respect. From medieval times Europeans reaching these faraway lands were aware of encountering great civilizations that were superior to their own in some aspects. The "Asian estates have always had their own kings their own governments, their own laws and their own judicial system," wrote the Dutch jurist Hugo Grotius in his famous essay *Mare Liberum*, published in 1608. For this reason the Europeans who approached the Indian and Chinese civilization did so with much caution, and the methods that they used in order to attempt colonizing these lands were to be very different from the rest.

---

* Hosking, *Russia and the Russians*.
** David Landes, *The Wealth and Poverty of Nations: Why Some Are So Rich and Some So Poor* (London: Abacus, 1998).

The favorite place for the Europeans to promote their interests in Asia was undoubtedly India. Apart from the British, the French, and the Portuguese, the Swedish and the Dutch had also founded trading bases there, and in the case of the first two, their early settlements were soon transformed into important ports and urban enclaves. Chandannagar, under French dominion, grew to the extent of becoming the most important port in Bengal, and Pondicherry emerged as a prosperous city built according to the French architectural style. As regards the bases of the English East India Company, Bombay and Calcutta started to experiment the development that would eventually transform them into great megalopolises. Nevertheless, neither France nor Britain—initially the first European powers in the Indian subcontinent—had more than 15,000 people each in all their Indian possessions.* But despite the fact that European presence was very limited and their aims were strictly commercial, the decline of the Mughal Empire was going to leave a power vacuum that offered the powers great opportunities to strengthen their presence there.

The Mughal Empire had been founded by Babur in the sixteenth century. For two centuries the line of Muslim emperors that succeeded him expanded their possessions across India. But in the mid–eighteenth century an era of decadence began. The Persian shah took advantage of the situation to invade the northern part of the empire, while in central India the Maratha Confederacy of Hindu kingdoms rebelled and forced the Mughal forces to make a considerable retreat. The Maratha troops advanced toward Bengal and also threatened the cities of Bombay and Madras, making it very difficult for the Europeans to remain neutral if they wanted to keep their positions. Holland decided to abandon India, and Portuguese troops limited themselves to defend their settlement in Goa, but France and Britain on the contrary decided to take advantage of the predominant chaos in order to expand their power.

The governor of the French territories in India, Joseph François Dupleix, decided that the state of war that India had fallen into since his arrival in Chandannagar in 1720 was a golden opportunity for his country to replace the Mughals as the hegemonic power. With this aim in mind he negotiated

---

* James Mill, *The History of British India*, vol. 1 (London: Baldwin, Cradock & Joy, 1817).

agreements with several local sovereigns in order to expand French territories. The outbreak of the War of the Austrian Succession in Europe that confronted the French against the British gave Dupleix an excuse to get rid of the other obstacle for achieving his aim: Great Britain.

The French troops took Madras, and Fort St. David as well, in 1746. After signing the Treaty of Aix-la-Chapelle, France was forced to return these territories to Britain, but Dupleix refused. This decision led to confrontations with the British on several occasions over the subsequent years until finally the French government, embarrassed by the problems caused by the controversial and unruly Dupleix, decided to dismiss him and force him to leave India in 1754.

With the outbreak of the Seven Years' War, Anglo–French rivalry was going to lead to confrontation in India on one more occasion. On hearing about the war in Europe, the new sovereign of Bengal, Siraj Dowlah, decided to expel the British and the French. He initiated his offensive with the occupation of Calcutta in 1754. The French sought an alliance with the Bengali sovereign, considering that this was a golden opportunity to definitively expel the British from India. But the final result was to be the opposite of what the Bengalis and the French expected. Despite the fact that the British East India Company had few troops with which to defend its position, its governor, Robert Clive, made a very good use of his scarce resources, and with extraordinary strategic ability managed to recover Calcutta. He then expelled the French from Chandannagar and finally defeated Dowlah's troops in Plassey.

Plassey was to go down in history as the battle that decided which power was going to dominate India.[*] France was authorized to maintain its presence in Pondicherry at the peace treaty that put an end to the Seven Years' War, but from then on Great Britain imposed its hegemony on the Indian subcontinent and no other power had the will let alone the capacity to dispute it. At a time when the crisis of the British Empire in America began, the foundations of a new empire in Asia were laid.

With the victory at Plassey, Robert Clive's good fortune had only just begun: in 1764 the East India Company appointed him governor of Bengal.

---

[*]   James, *Raj.*

The fact that peace and prosperity prevailed in the territories administered by the British while the rest of India had sunk into chaos led the Mughal emperor to offer Clive an agreement so that the British would be in charge of the exploitation and administration of what was left of the empire, which was to include almost the whole of northern India. In this way, without pretending it, the British company ended up controlling a vast territory.

The scale of the East India Company's operations began to be so vast that it was no longer possible for the crown to consider them as mere trading activities, and there was increasing pressure in London for the British government to substitute the company in the administration of the Indian territories. As a result of this, in 1773 the Parliament decreed that the government should appoint a governor general who would represent it from the main headquarters in Calcutta. Warren Hastings was to be selected for this post, a prominent employee of the East India Company who became the first of a long line of administrators representing the British crown on the subcontinent. The way in which the British crown was suddenly to become responsible for ruling over India is a very good example of the historian John Robert Seeley's much-quoted statement that, "Britain acquired an empire in a fit of absence of mind."*

There was no preordained plan to govern India until the British political elite became aware of all that was at stake in this territory. As Clive himself stated in Parliament, "The directors of the India Company have acquired an empire that is larger than any European kingdom and have obtained an income of four million pounds."** The government could not afford to ignore such extraordinary achievements. It was essential that the British in India would cease to be merchants and become builders of a new empire.

Control over India gave Britain a great advantage over the rest of the European powers. From the mid–eighteenth century the spice trade started to decline mainly for two reasons: first because of the decline of spices as food preservatives and secondly due to the increasing popularity of sweet

---

* John Robert Seeley, *The Expansion of England: Two Courses of Lectures* (Sydney: Wentworth Press, 2016).
** James, *Raj.*

products. The Dutch Empire that was so dependent on the spice trade was seriously affected by this change in the market; Spain and Portugal were also to experience important losses. British trade on the other hand was to thrive as a result of India. India had been the world's main producer of cotton textiles from the seventeenth century, and the British were largely to benefit from these exports as well as silk, rice, and other agricultural products, and a rising demand for tea and even opium.

From the moment India officially became a colony, the interest of many British venture capitalists, speculators, and fortune-seekers was increasingly focused on it. Not only were employees from the East India Company rapidly enriching themselves but also members of the armed forces and crown representatives. Those who made a fortune in India were collectively to be known as Nabobs, deriving from the Indian *Nawab*. This aspiring, nouveau riche aristocracy was to acquire considerable influence in both India and Britain, and was also to be the cause of great controversies.

While Warren Hastings was governor general, corruption and misgovernment in India began to be a matter of great concern among the British administration, and the subject was frequently discussed among political circles in London. In fact, on his return to England in 1785 Hastings was accused by the prominent statesman and philosopher Edmund Burke of dishonoring the character of Britain and subverting the rights of Indians, and was brought to trial as a result of it. Although he was acquitted, the government decided that from then on the post of governor general of India should be occupied by prominent figures usually from the old aristocracy, who theoretically would not be driven by economic needs to accept it. They would also have the right education and sufficient social rank as to inspire respect from both the ruling elite and the poor masses in India. Charles, the 1st Marquess Cornwallis, was the first incumbent, and he was followed by a long line of great aristocrats, statesmen, and army commanders who would culminate their careers with the privilege of governing India.

How should this vast, enigmatic, and faraway territory be governed? Burke, who had been so appalled by rumors of serial plundering and abuses on the indigenous population, did not have any doubt: "India must be governed by the same laws that must be found in Europe, Africa, and Asia, and that are to be found throughout humanity, those principles of equity, humanity that are implanted in our heart."* But pretending to govern the inhabitants of the Indian subcontinent according to the principles of British democracy, the philosophy of the Enlightenment, and the ideas that prevailed in the Western world could entail serious problems.

India was a fascinating and enigmatic world within the Eastern universe. It was composed of a mosaic of ancient kingdoms and princely states, populated by diverse peoples who spoke more than three hundred dialects and worshipped thousands of deities. Societies ruled according to the caste system would seem unfairly fractured even to the eighteenth century visitor, and their customs and beliefs were often unintelligible to the European frame of mind. For this reason, all imposition from the Western world was doomed to fail and create more problems than they aimed to solve. In its place, the British initially utilized a much more subtle method of colonization based on cohabitation and minimum interference with the Indian people and its rulers.

British presence in India was based on an agreement with the Mughal emperor and the sovereigns of diverse kingdoms. The British governor general had the obligation of respecting the sovereignty of these territories as well as their customs, and could only interfere in matters of foreign policy and defense. His overall mission was to maintain law and order in India and ensure that prosperity would flourish as a result of commercial activities. In this way, the so-called *Pax Britannica* was to begin in India, whose aim was to allow the Indians and the British to cohabit peacefully and thrive. Nevertheless, the practical implications of this agreement were to be very complex, for they required that two worlds as different as the British and the Indian would respect each other. Maintaining law and order without interfering in the government of the Indian people was extremely difficult, as the successors of Warren Hastings were to find out.

Unlike India, where European presence was slowly but steadily to increase from the sixteenth century, in China the only power that managed to establish a permanent settlement from then was Portugal. Toward the end of the eighteenth century Britain decided to strengthen relations with the

---

* Jim McCue, *Edmund Burke and Our Present Discontents* (London: Claridge Press, 1997).

great eastern civilization but its aim proved to be very frustrating from the outset. The Chinese were happy to sell tea and authorize the representatives of the East India Company to trade, but allowing those whom they considered Western barbarians to infiltrate in their territory and civilization was another matter.

In September 1792 King George III sent a commercial envoy to China with the aim of finally opening its doors to British interests. It was formed by seven hundred people and it included diplomats, army men, traders, scientists, a clockmaker, a gardener, and five German musicians. The three ships that transported them were full of the most dazzling examples of Western progress: telescopes, watches, barometers, weapons, and even a hot-air balloon. This extraordinary display of human talent and technological innovation had the aim of convincing Emperor Qianlong that his people should trade with the West. Lord Macartney was put in charge of this mission, a wily diplomat whom the government had promised honors and a generous economic compensation if he managed to set up a permanent embassy in China.

In spite of the effort with which the British prepared this important mission, its result proved to be a spectacular failure. Apart from being received by the Chinese civil servants with little cordiality, Lord Macartney received an edict from the emperor indicating that "we do not need a single one of the artifacts that are built by your country."* To make matters worse, Lord Macartney refused to make the traditional kowtow as a sign of deference before the Chinese emperor unless a Chinese civil servant would equally show his respect before a picture of King George III. However, it is unlikely that a more submissive attitude would have made any difference, for a Dutch mission arrived shortly after the British and its members seemed willing to kowtow before the Emperor as many times as the protocol demanded, but they returned to their country as empty-handed and frustrated as the British. The Chinese continued to be convinced that they were the center of the civilized world and that the rest of the countries should kneel in obeisance before them. Neither the emperor nor any member of his court thought that trade with the West could bring benefits to them.

★ Alain Peyrefitte, *The Immobile Empire* (New York: Vintage, 2013).

The Chinese elite fervently believed that isolation was essential to maintain the splendor of their civilization and the Great Wall of China had been built with the aim of repelling any invasion from the North. The Western powers that approached their civilization through the coast were considered equally threatening regardless of the peaceful trading opportunities that they offered, and for this reason drastic measures were taken to prevent their population from being polluted by contacts with them. But China was eventually to pay a high price for isolation by lagging behind the West in trends of economic and scientific progress. Voltaire, a great admirer of Chinese culture and society, to which he devoted many hours of study, asked himself why scientific knowledge in China during the eighteenth century was not more advanced than that of Europe in the twelfth century. A century later the Chinese were to pay a much higher price for turning their backs on the West.

For Britain its trade deficit with China constituted a great problem. In return for the tea that British traders bought they did not manage to introduce any of their products in the Chinese market. Merchants from other European nations had the same feeling of frustration, for all of them were confined to Macao or Guangzhou Harbor, according to the rules established by the Chinese in order to control foreign presence. But the opium trade radically changed the situation.

Opium started to be exported to China by the Spaniards, together with other products from their empire, like tobacco and corn. The British East India Company began exporting opium from India, and Chinese smugglers sold it throughout their country until it became a product almost as popular among the Chinese as tea among the British.* But the effect of this addictive drug on the Chinese was soon to be resented. In 1838 Emperor Daoguang decided to take drastic measures and ensure that the prohibition that had been decreed long before would be drastically implemented. At Canton, British merchants were forced to hand over all their shiploads, and those who refused were imprisoned. Chinese troops also intercepted British ships in international waters and destroyed their opium cargos. The emperor did

---

* Julia Lovell, *The Opium War: Drugs, Dreams and the Making of Modern China* (New York: Picador, 2011).

not fear reprisals as he believed that the British had become too dependent on tea from China, but on this occasion the British did not hesitate to use their navy to teach the Chinese a lesson.

The British fleet reached the Chinese coast in 1840 and in an extraordinary demonstration of military superiority they took over Canton. After suffering a major defeat with important losses, the Chinese had no option but to sign the Treaty of Nanking in 1842, by which the island of Hong Kong was ceded and the harbors of Guangzhou, Shanghai, and several others were opened to trade without restrictions. In this way, the British finally managed to open the gates of the last great frontier of the Asian market. Their victory over the Chinese was also to benefit other Western powers two years later; the French and the Americans took advantage of this situation to sign treaties that would also allow them to trade with Chinese ports.

In spite of the victory the Opium War proved to be rather controversial. The eminent liberal statesman and future prime minister William E. Gladstone argued that the war could not be justified from the moral perspective, but the Conservatives insisted that it was a necessary war to put an end to the trade deficit and incorporate the Chinese into the world trade system. But as far as China was concerned this war was nothing but the pretext that the British had been seeking in order to break into its civilization. The Chinese did not take long to provoke a new conflict with the British.

In 1856 Chinese officers arrested the crew of a ship at Guangzhou under the accusation of smuggling and piracy. Britain demanded their immediate release arguing that the ship bore the British flag. This was the first of a series of incidents that were considered a violation of the Treaty of Nanking. A year later the elections in Britain gave the majority to the Conservatives, led by Lord Palmerston. The prime minister who had been responsible for sending the fleet that fought the Opium War did not hesitate to do the same again, with the purpose of defending his country's interest for a second time by force.

In the meantime the Chinese were to face a conflict with the French. A French missionary, Father Auguste Chapdelaine was executed by the Chinese at the Guangxi province. As a result, the French government decided to join the British fleet in a common punitive mission against China. Russia and the

United States also offered their support, and in fact a US ship intervened in one of the battles of this short war that was going to be known as the Second Opium War. The causes that provoked its outbreak were very similar to the previous one but on this occasion China had to confront a Western coalition that was determined to make their interests prevail before the Qing dynasty.

As could be expected the Western troops easily imposed themselves on the Chinese. A year after hostilities began, the Chinese emperor reluctantly signed the Treaty of Tientsin with the four interested parties: Britain, France, Russia, and the United States. According to this treaty, China opened eleven new ports to trade with the West and on top of this the four powers were given the right to open an embassy in Beijing, which had been a closed city until then.

Russia, which had been very active trying to strengthen its position in the Pacific, took advantage of the situation to force China to sign the Treaty of Aigun. By this treaty the frontier between Russia and China that had been agreed on in 1869 was altered to favor Russia on this occasion, and it gave them access to the southern border of the Amur River. Once this old territorial claim was acquired, the Russians were able to found the city of Vladivostok in 1860. This city was going to have great importance for Russian interests in the Pacific Ocean and it became a milestone in Western influence through the world. The construction of Vladivostok constituted the pinnacle of European land expansion. Four decades later, Moscow and Vladivostok were unified by the Trans-Siberian Railway. The old European dream of a fast and secure route to the Far East by land finally came true.

But the Chinese did not resign themselves to accept the terms of the treaties imposed on them by the West. New forces were sent to the ports to stop the Western advance and war broke out again, but on this occasion the Chinese defeat was going to be even more resounding. The Franco-British troops advanced on the Forbidden City, forcing Emperor Xianfeng to escape. His brother Prince Gong represented the Qing dynasty at the Beijing convention in 1860, with which peace was signed under terms that were even more detrimental than the previous ones. According to this convention, apart from ratifying concessions already made to the Western powers on previous treaties, China was forced to pay an economic compensation to Britain and France, hand over Hong Kong's Kowloon Peninsula, accept religious freedom, and also legalize the opium trade.

"Undoubtedly in 1860 the great civilization that China had been was totally defeated and humiliated by the West," wrote the Chinese historian Immanuel C. Y. Hsu.* This defeat could be considered the result of a long period of isolation from the trends of progress. When the emperor Qianlong despised the technological advances that Lord Macartney wanted to show during his visit to China, and refused to trade with a civilization that he considered inferior, he was condemning his country to stagnation. A few decades later the Chinese were to witness the weakness of their own civilization, which for many centuries had been considered as the most advanced by great industrial powers like France and Britain. But China continued to refuse to yield before Western influence. Its military and technological superiority, and the clash between the two civilizations, was to continue.

While Britain and other European major powers gained the upper hand over China, another great civilization on the other side of the Asian continent was also in retreat: Persia. From the mid–seventeenth century Persia had managed to defend its territory from Russian expansion in the North Caucasus, and even make new territorial conquests. In 1796 the troops of the Persian shah entered Georgia, which had become a Russian protectorate in the eighteenth century, and ravaged the city of Tbilisi. Emboldened by an alliance with Britain the new Persian shah, Fath-Ali Shah Qajar, decided to oust the Russians from the Caucasus, provoking the first full-scale Russian-Persian war in 1804. But on this occasion, the young Czar Alexander I, who had acceded to the throne three years before the outbreak of this war, was equally determined to expand Russia's frontiers at Persian cost. Eventually, Russia gained the upper hand, and in the Treaty of Gulistan in 1813, present-day Azerbaijan, Dagestan, and eastern Georgia were brought into the Russian Empire. The Persian shah sought revenge in a new war with Russia that broke out in 1828, but he was to face an even more humiliating defeat and the loss to Russia of more territories, including present-day Armenia.

---

* Immanuel C. Y. Hsu, *The Rise of Modern China* (Oxford, England: Oxford University Press, 2000).

European occupation of Asian land was also motivated by imperial rivalry, just as it happened in the Americas and other continents. The British invasion of Afghanistan was mainly carried out with the aim of preventing Russia from moving into this emirate and eventually threatening British India. In 1839 British troops marched into Afghanistan and replaced the amir, Dost Mohammad Khan who was suspicious of the alliance with Russia reached by his predecessor, the pro-British Shuja Shah Durrani. But the consolidation of this new pro-British emirate proved to be impossible. The presence of British troops in Afghanistan created great resentment, and two years later a violent rebellion exploded. Confronted with a jihad by the Afghan people Britain was not only forced to withdraw its troops but it had to face what has been described as the greatest disaster in its entire imperial history. As the British forces retreated, they were massacred by Afghan tribesmen. Out of an army of almost 20,000 who had initially invaded Afghanistan, only one person survived the humiliating retreat and reached British territory: Dr. William Brydon.*

Britain was to seek compensation for this disastrous military operation in Afghanistan by another invasion in 1878. This was also motivated by the fear that the emirate was falling under Russian influence. On this occasion the British managed to achieve most of their aims, imposing a treaty by which the Afghan ruler Sher Ali Khan ceded the country's foreign affairs to the British Empire. Nevertheless Afghanistan maintained its internal sovereignty, a wise decision, for the Afghans had proved in the first war against the British to be the most indomitable people. (And as other Western invasions in the twentieth and twenty-first century would corroborate, any attempt at occupying this barren land and interfering with the customs of its inhabitants was doomed to fail in the long run.)

As we have seen, one of the absolute priorities of Britain's imperial policy in Asia was to keep Russia or any other European power from approaching the frontiers of India. Nevertheless, the most serious challenge to the British presence in India was not posed by a foreign power but by the Indian

---

* William Dalrymple, *Return of a King: The Battle for Afghanistan, 1839–42* (London: Bloomsbury, 2013).

population. In 1857 an Indian rebellion broke out which seriously threatened British rule. The main cause of the rebellion was the discontent of the sepoys, the Indians serving in the British army.

Toward the mid–nineteenth century around 200,000 Indian soldiers served in the British army in India, while only 40,000 British soldiers were posted there.* Therefore law and order in India depended on the loyalty of the population that was being colonized. Despite the efforts made by the British to adapt military discipline to Indian habits, Indian soldiers were to accumulate many reasons for discontent. The soldiers who came from the higher castes refused to cohabit with their fellow countrymen from the lower social strata. Indians felt discriminated against by the British, who were more easily promoted. Worst of all was the indignation caused both Muslims and Hindus for being asked to bite off paper cartridges for their rifles—which were rumored to be greased with animal fat obtained from pigs and cows, their sacred animals.

This was much more serious than an army rebellion, for in several regions Indian sovereigns, supported by their people, decided to take this opportunity to free themselves from British dominance. The agreement reached with the British about their government responsibilities was not always respected by the latter. The British had assumed the compromise of not interfering with Indian customs, but they decided to forbid traditions that were considered uncivilized, like childhood marriage or the suttee, the traditional burning of a widow after her husband's death.

Last but not least there were also economic reasons for rebellion, for in order to balance the budget of the East India Company and finance the cost of the army, taxes were levied on the Indians that caused much discontent and also interfered with the fiscal systems of the Indian kingdoms. Therefore it was a rebellion among several princely states, along with Indians from diverse social backgrounds, and it was so extended that several Indian historians have referred to it as the first Indian War of Independence.

After much violence and atrocities from both sides, the British managed to gain the upper hand and suppress the rebellion. One of the first measures

---

* James, *Raj.*

that was taken to reestablish order was to send into exile the last Mughal emperor, Bahadur Shah Zafar, who had hoped to recover his dynasty's lost wealth and power after expelling Britain.

Above all, the British decided to introduce changes that would allow them to continue with their presence in India without further upheaval. In 1858 the East India Company was officially dissolved and its power was transferred to the British crown. From then on the crown was to appoint a viceroy, who would represent it before 562 princely states that existed in India and whose independence the British government had vowed to respect. The princely states represented forty percent of the Indian territory and twenty-five percent of its population, so a good part of the Indian subcontinent was not under British control except in the spheres of defense and foreign affairs.* In the rest, governors represented the viceroy and a new institution, the India Office, was to take charge of administration. In this new system of administration the crown also pledged not to meddle in moral or religious issues, particularly in all that could be interpreted by the Indians as a westernization attempt.

The 1857 rebellion gave way to the birth of the British Raj, and from then on India was to be commonly described as the jewel in the crown of the British Empire. The frontiers of the Raj went well beyond those of present-day India and Pakistan, for it also included Burma (present-day Myanmar), Ceylon, and even Singapore, which officially became a colony toward the mid–nineteenth century. It was therefore a formidable empire governed from Calcutta, its administrative capital.

The following decades constituted a golden age for British in India. Great changes took place that allowed the Indian civilization to start industrializing and experiencing rapid technological innovation. In the 1860s the British started the construction of railways across the Raj making such good progress that by the early twentieth century India had the fourth-largest railway network in the world.** They also built roads and bridges, and introduced the

---

* Dominique Lapierre and Larry Collins, *Freedom at Midnight: How England Gave Away an Empire* (New York: Simon & Schuster, 1975).
** James, *Raj.*

telegraph. Toward the end of the nineteenth century India was to consolidate what was arguably the best postal system in Asia. All these changes greatly increased mobility among Indian peoples that had traditionally been deeply divided by geography as well as by religion, language, and culture.

The British Raj was also instrumental in the emergence of a new Indian civil society in the urban centers, where the middle classes were to play a very important role. Universities were founded under British inspiration, mainly in Bombay, Calcutta, and Madras, there the new urban elites were not only educated but were also to learn about the new Western political and philosophical trends, from utilitarianism to socialism. Schools modeled on the British public school system proliferated around the Raj for the children of the landowning classes. Among the wealthiest members of the Indian elite, and especially among aristocratic and princely families, it became a tradition to send their children to be educated in the top English public schools, and some of them even finished their studies at Oxford or Cambridge universities. After completing their education they would return to India and devote themselves to dynastic obligations, in the case of the hereditary princes, while those who came from the bourgeoisie would embark on liberal professions, business, or administrative careers. In those days, social mobility and economic progress for Indians implied studying or working at an institution created by the British, and above all, knowledge of the English language.

English became the language of communication not only at an official level but also in the realms of business, politics, and culture. It was to be implemented not only because it was the language of the colonizing power but also because it was soon consolidated as the only common language spoken by the high echelons of society from north to south of the Indian subcontinent.

In 1877, as a result of a proposal by Prime Minister Benjamin Disraeli, who was so fascinated by the eastern world, Queen Victoria was officially made empress of India. Judging by the enthusiasm with which Indian maharajas and representatives of princely states participated in British royal ceremonies over the next decades, the degree of satisfaction with this new European empress who never visited her Asian empire was very high.

Nevertheless, the golden days of the British Raj also had their dark side, particularly for the Indian subjects. Despite the fact that according to the official discourse all subjects of the empire were equal, in the case of the Raj some were more equal than others (as George Orwell famously wrote), and the differences between the British and the Indians were considerable. Promotion in the Raj's administration and the army was much more difficult for Indians, and the highest posts were always in the hands of the British. For example in 1909, only 65 out of a total of 1244 members of the Indian Civil Service were Indian. Even in the railway service, which was less attractive for the British, only ten percent of the leading posts were occupied by Indians.*

Racial discrimination always raised controversy in British India. The existence of clubs with exclusive access for the whites, where the British used to socialize, provoked much indignation among Indians. Most controversial of all was discrimination in the judiciary. In 1883 Viceroy Lord Ripon proposed changing the law so that Indian judges could prosecute British citizens, and a compromise was reached in order to increase the number of Indian judges.**

India became the most coveted posting not only for soldiers and civil servants but also for politicians with a penchant for exotic experiences. Being governor of an Indian province was a particularly prestigious post, and obviously becoming viceroy of India was a dream for the most ambitious and adventurous in high politics, for the viceroy not only exercised an extraordinary amount of power but would enjoy symbols of luxury and wealth that were only accessible to European royalty. Apart from providing better salaries and living standards, India offered a fascinating life full of enjoyment, from tiger hunting parties on elephants to polo matches and carefree summer holidays at the city of Shimla. As James Mill, author of a monumental history of British India in the nineteenth century, wrote "India was a vast system of open air entertainment for the British upper classes." And obviously, among so many privileges and perks that surrounded the British it was difficult to remember Queen Victoria's mandate that all subjects were equal in India. Much more appealing seemed Rudyard Kipling's statement that, "the responsibility of

---

* James, *Raj*.
** Ibid.

governing India has been placed by the inscrutable design of providence upon the shoulders of the British race."[*]

Britain was certainly not the only European power that consolidated an Asian empire in the nineteenth century. Despite the fact that France lost practically all its power in Asia in the eighteenth century, a century later it recovered a very influential position by the creation of French Indochina.

French presence in present-day Vietnam goes back to the seventeenth century, but it did not start as a result of trading or military incursions but of missionaries. The first Jesuit mission was established in Hanoi in 1615, and there the Frenchman Alexandre de Rhodes played a role that was going to be particularly influential. He contributed to the creation of the Paris Foreign Missions Society, a missionary organization that was going to be especially active in Southeast Asia over the subsequent two centuries. And it was the protection of this Christian mission, rather than any wish for territorial expansion, that caused French military intervention in the mid–nineteenth century.

In 1857 two Spanish missionaries were executed under the orders of the Vietnamese emperor Tu Duc. As a result of this incident a Franco-Spanish punitive expedition was sent under the command of French general Charles Rigault de Genouilly, which culminated with the occupation of Saigon.

Despite the fact that Rigault de Genouilly's mission was exclusively to guarantee the protection of the missionaries and not to colonize, the French policy toward Asia changed radically after 1862. Emperor Napoleon III, determined to expand the power of France throughout the world, decided to take advantage of the army's presence in Saigon to create a new Asian empire. With this purpose in mind the French authorities put pressure on the Vietnamese emperor so that he would grant access to the ports of Annam, Tonkin, and he would cede Cochinchina.

As it happened so often to the European powers in the world, the French expanded in this territory as a result of the rivalries between kingdoms in southeast Asia. King Norodom of Cambodia had been struggling for a long time to prevent his more powerful enemies, Vietnam and Siam (later known as Thailand) from distributing his small kingdom among themselves. French

---

[*] Lapierre and Collins, *Freedom at Midnight.*

incursion into the region provided the solution, and the Cambodian king invited the French emperor to establish a protectorate over his kingdom. Many Cambodians supported this drastic decision, arguing that it was better to live under the control of a European power than to see their kingdom dismantled by their neighbors. But in return for accepting the Cambodian proposal, the French demanded to have control of the kingdom's finances.

The next territorial aspiration for the French was going to be more conflictive, for the region of Tonkin to the north of present-day Vietnam was under Chinese influence, and the great Asian power warned that it would not tolerate European presence in this territory. This gave way to the outbreak of the Franco-Chinese war in 1885. The French army finally imposed itself on the Chinese but with great difficulty, and the losses suffered by the French in this war provoked the resignation of Premier Jules Ferry. The overall costs of this war were so unexpectedly high that a withdrawal was proposed at the French National Assembly. Had this proposal succeeded, the history of Vietnam would undoubtedly have been very different.

What started as a timid incursion into Asia ended up provoking a bitter colonial war, but in consequence, the French were to consolidate their Asian empire. In 1887 French Indochina was born, which included Vietnam and Cambodia, and in spite of the traumatic memories left by the war with China, expansion through the region did not cease. The desire to annex the territories of Laos in 1893 provoked a new war against another dominant power in the region: the kingdom of Siam. Siam hoped to stop the French advance over Laos with British help, for Burma was part of the British Empire and it shared a frontier with both Laos and Siam. But the British were not willing to confront France over an Asian kingdom, although at least they promised that they would demand respect for the kingdom's independence. In this way, after winning an unequal war against Siam, France consolidated all the territory that was going to be known as French Indochina, and becoming the second most important Western power in Asia.

Toward the end of the nineteenth century, Europe had consolidated a notable presence in Asia. Through colonies, protectorates, commercial bases, or religious missions, the Europeans managed to infiltrate the enigmatic and faraway Asian world. The civilization that for a long time proved to be more resistant to Western penetration was Japan, although it finally ended up being the most Westernized.

For several centuries Japan maintained a strict independence from Western influence with great success. Despite the fact that the Jesuits managed to start their missionary activities in Japan in the sixteenth century, a century later they were expelled, and those whom they had converted to Christianity were persecuted. The European merchants who tried to set up commercial relations with Japan were to face even more difficulties than with China, for the shoguns who governed the country on behalf of the emperor did not trust them, and feared that these apparently peaceful merchants would pave the way for an armed conquest. Only the Dutch merchants managed to establish trading relations at the port of Nagasaki, but with much difficulty.

Japan's opening to Western trade finally took place in the nineteenth century, but it was not as a result of European pressure but that of the United States. In 1855 Commodore Matthew Perry, commanding several frigates, arrived in a Japanese port and threatened to use his fleet's force unless Japan acceded to accept his demands for establishing trade and diplomatic relations with the United States. A year later, the Kanagawa Convention was signed, by which the Japanese granted all that the bold Perry had demanded. After this display of what critics have described as classic gunboat diplomacy, Great Britain, France, and Russia signed similar agreements.

The Japanese reaction to the arrival of the West in their country was very different from that of the Chinese. After the 1868 restoration of Emperor Meiji, who put an end to the feudal power of the shoguns, the Japanese elite reached the conclusion that far from rejecting Western culture, which was exerting increasing influence, the best they could do was to adopt it and make it part of their own. This extraordinary pragmatism was also motivated by self-defense, for they were aware that only by Westernization would they be able to narrow the gap with powers like the United States or Russia, which were militarily and technologically superior.

After an intensive campaign of Westernization, industrialization, and rearmament, Japan emerged as an imposing power with a fervent desire for expansion, to the point of becoming the most powerful rival of the Western powers in Asia. The first important step in the construction of the new empire was in the armed conflict against China over the possession of Korea in 1894. After overpowering China and neutralizing it, Russia became the next obstacle to deal with in the Japanese expansion.

Japan toward the end of the nineteenth century decided to join the league of great imperial powers, which until then had been exclusively formed by European countries. With this aim in mind the Japanese did not set any limits to their expansion in Asia and the Pacific. Their decision was to have serious consequences for the Western world, as discussed in Chapter 9.

The climax of four centuries of European expansion in Asia was marked by the Boxer Rebellion. The Chinese never resigned themselves to accept the terms of the treaties signed with the Europeans in the mid–nineteenth century, and for this reason, hostility toward any European presence could be felt throughout the country. The society of "righteous and harmonious fists," a nationalist group specializing in martial arts, launched a rebellion against Western influence in 1900. The Boxers, as the members of this society were to be known by the West, made several attacks against European presence. The Chinese empress used these incidents to declare war on the Western powers. As a result of this all foreign embassies were under siege by the imperial army and the Boxers for fifty-five days.

This Chinese rebellion against Western presence led to the formation of the greatest coalition of Western forces that was seen until then in Asia. Britain, France, Holland, Russia, Austria-Hungary, Italy, the United States, and Japan joined their forces in order to defend their embassies and their citizens in Beijing. As a result an international force of 20,000 soldiers took the imperial city by force and defeated the Chinese once more. The Boxer Protocol, with which the rebellion officially ended in 1901, condemned China to pay reparations to the eight nations affected by the siege. Consequently, the Chinese were not only deeply humiliated but considerably impoverished by this war.

The Boxer Rebellion came to demonstrate on one more occasion the power of the West in the world, not even the old and mighty Chinese civilization could stand up to it, at least by military means. The fact that Japan was included in the Western coalition confirmed that the only way of matching the power of the West was to follow the same trends of development in its cultural and economic sphere.

Four centuries after the first attempts at settling in Asia the continent finally became an essential part of the European empires and their trading networks, and it allowed some of them to be described as global empires. Asia was a dream for European navigators and fortune seekers, with its combination of old and densely populated civilizations, fertile lands, and thriving markets where a good part of the world's wealth was concentrated. To a large extent Asia was the solution sought by the critics of colonization who demanded the creation of mercantile empires that did not require exporting large numbers of their populations. Nevertheless, in Asia as in the rest of the world, mercantile empires could not really be dissociated from colonization, for in order to extract wealth it was necessary to create settlements in that part of the world.

Europeans always opted for territorial expansion when the opportunity arose, and this was certainly the case in Asia where small trading posts were eventually transformed into large colonial territories. Their presence there not only had a deep impact on the European economy but also on their diet, their social habits, and their culture.

The most intense clash of civilizations in the history of colonization took place in Asia. The encounter between the West and the East had very diverse results. In India a peaceful cohabitation emerged although not exempt from frequent conflicts, and this was going to leave an indelible mark on both the Indians and the British. This type of cohabitation also emerged in the Philippines under Spanish rule and in Southeast Asia with the Dutch. On the other hand the experience with China was going to be very different, where all Western influence was constantly rejected and Europeans only managed to overcome Chinese isolation by means of force. Even then European influence was going to be marginal except in the colonies of Macao and Hong Kong, and it also created great resentment among the Chinese, which was going to have deep consequences in the twentieth and twenty-first centuries. The case of Japan was rather different from the rest of Asia, for the Japanese did not lose power or sovereignty as a result of the encounter with the West. On the contrary, thanks to the West and the self-imposed Westernization program that was going to be imposed from then on, Japan became a great power. And finally, there were also parts of Asia that managed to keep strict independence before European colonization like Persia, Mongolia, or Thailand.

"We are what we think, what we are emerges from our thoughts, with our thoughts we make the world", stated the Buddha, the founder of one of the great religions. This thought seems to have played an influential role in the attitude of many Asian peoples before the West. They did not give up their identity or their interpretation of the world, although the Europeans modified their way of thinking in some cases. What sometimes provoked a dramatic clash of civilizations was also to lead to a dialogue between East and West that was to become particularly intensive in the twenty-first century.

Chapter 6

In Search of a Better World

How European Culture and Values Were Propagated by the Great Migratory Waves.

———————————————
———————————————

O ne of the reasons why the Europeans succeeded at building the greatest empires in history was because they were also the most committed emigrants. While sailors, merchants, and soldiers opened up the frontiers of many territories in the world, it was the migrants who were really to determine their fate and leave an indelible mark on them. Without massive emigration of their peoples, European powers would not have been capable of accumulating so much influence, and the legacy of their cultures and Western civilization on the world would never have been so enduring. From the sixteenth century European migration increased progressively, most of it settling in the Americas but also in Africa, Oceania, and to a lesser degree in Asia. As a result many territories throughout the world and even continents were to have a majority white population; the culture of the white settlers was to take root, and in some cases replace the one that had previously existed. Their religion was to expand throughout the planet, as well as their systems of government, and their economies and laws. Cities were to be known with names that already existed in Europe, or in reference to symbols of their culture: New Spain, New England, New France, New Caledonia, New Amsterdam—all of these colonial territories were to be to a large extent copies of the countries where the settlers came from.

The greatest migratory waves in history were those carried out by Europeans between the sixteenth and the twentieth centuries. The motives that led so many inhabitants of the European continent to abandon their land where they were born are very diverse: poverty, famine, political and religious persecution, the desire to make a fortune, or simply the wish for a better life—essentially the same motives as emigrants from other races and peoples. It must also be stressed that not everyone migrated voluntarily, for the Europeans also experienced forced emigration and exile.

In an opulent society full of opportunities that the Western world has enjoyed over the last decades, the idea of spending one's entire fortune on a single ticket, without a return date, that would take us to an unknown country may seem foolhardy or even a sign of utter madness. Nevertheless, for many generations the Europeans, particularly those living on the Atlantic coast, were to place all their bets on the migration card. They considered that their future was in the ships traveling toward the West, and for this reason they often risked even more than what they possessed in order to set sail to a distant land. In the majority of cases emigrants were so poor that they did not even have the means to pay for their own journey. But the fates of emigrants were to be very diverse, as we shall later see. However, the advantage that Europeans enjoyed over other emigrants is that they migrated to territories that in most cases belonged to their countries of origin, or had been previously occupied by them, and they were also migrating at a time when the power of Europe was steadily increasing.

The settlement in America took some time to be backed by a substantial number of emigrants from the discovering countries. Among Iberian colonizing pioneers, overseas possessions were initially seen as places that could provide both wealth and influence but certainly not as ideal destinations for great contingents of their population (among other reasons because Spain and Portugal did not have much population to spare in those days). The New World was a place for conquistadors with a spirit of adventure, as well as zealous missionaries, but not for ordinary men. This is the reason Columbus had great difficulty recruiting a crew for his Atlantic crossings. Nevertheless, as the first proofs of wealth in the Indies were provided and the myth of El Dorado spread, an increasing number of people dreamed of starting a new life on the other side of the Atlantic.

Another reason why emigrants were initially not so numerous was the very selective criteria established by the authorities for who could emigrate to the New World. Initially only citizens from the kingdom of Castile could travel to the Indies, and on top of this they were expected to be good Catholics. Another barrier was the cost of the journey; the over twenty ducats that crossing the Atlantic would cost prevented those who belonged to the humblest social strata from traveling.

The *Casa de Contratación* (which literally means House of Trade) was set up in Seville in order to keep track of emigration. Every traveler to the New World had to be registered in it, and according to its archives, around 56,000 people emigrated throughout the sixteenth century.* However, this figure is probably no more than a fifth of all those who arrived in America, for many managed to cross the Atlantic without submitting to this system of control. According to the most recent estimates, between 1500 and 1650 around 437,000 Spaniards arrived in the New World, as did 100,000 Portuguese between 1500 and 1700.** Not only did people from most parts of the Iberian Peninsula begin to emigrate, but also from other places in Western Europe—in particular from Italy, France, and several major cities of the Holy Roman Empire.

Spain had eight million inhabitants toward the end of the eighteenth century, and Portugal only one million, so the Iberian Peninsula was far less populated than the rest of Western Europe. If demographic pressures

---

* John Elliott, *Empires of the Atlantic World: Britain and Spain in America, 1492–1830* (New Haven, Conn; Yale University Press, 2006), p 175.
** Kamen, *Empire*.

were generally an incentive throughout history to promote the expansion of peoples, it certainly was not in the case of these two kingdoms. It was not possible to promote large-scale emigration, neither from Spain nor from Portugal, nor from other European countries in those days. The cost of the journey and the risks and the dangers of the New World were the main factors that put people off. For the poorest sector of society it was hard to earn a living in the cities of Seville or Salamanca, as the literature of Francisco de Quevedo, Lope de Vega, or other authors of Spain's golden age shows, but even so the great majority preferred to endure poverty in their homeland than expose themselves to the perils of the Indies.

Although the figures that are shown above are considerable, they are very modest if we take into account that their aim was to populate territories of enormous dimensions. Another problem was the lack of married couples and emigrants who went to America with their families, for generally those who took the risk of embarking on the adventure of the Indies tended to do it on their own and hoped to return to their homeland. This is one of the reasons why intermarriage was going to make progress in the majority of the Spanish settlements, especially in the viceroyalty of New Spain and in Peru. The example of Cortés and Pizarro, who left mixed-race descendants, was going to be followed by many men, some of them married as good Christians like Pizarro. Others maintained sporadic relations with the indigenous women, as did Cortés. In the cities of New Spain and other settlements where white settlers cohabited with local peoples, there would emerge an increasingly mixed-race population that was brought up between their traditional customs and the Western culture of the conquistadors.

For the inhabitants of the British Isles, the incentives to emigrate were far greater than in the Iberian Peninsula. The living conditions in England toward the sixteenth century constitute a good explanation of the reasons why colonizing America seemed increasingly attractive for the poorest sector of the population. Due to the hardship of the rural world and the lack of work, the cities were increasingly populated, and a great part of their inhabitants were crammed in slum areas with insalubrious living conditions. With such poor prospects for a better life in England, emigration to America seemed the best option, however dangerous and uncertain the journey could be. The 105 people who founded the settlement of Jamestown in 1607, after being transported by the Virginia Company, played a vital role in the history of migration to North America. Only sixty-one of them were still alive three years later, but their survival was going to pave the way for the settlers who arrived after them.

Apart from poverty another reason for emigrating to America was religious persecution. The storied *Mayflower* that carried 102 members of the Puritan community in 1620 was the first of many ships boarded by citizens who were persecuted or marginalized for reasons of faith. After the colony of Plymouth, founded by the so-called Pilgrim Fathers, others like Maryland and Pennsylvania were founded for religious reasons, and consequently faith was to be an essential part of those who arrived in America in search of fortune.

The Mayflower Society is nowadays a very prestigious and exclusive historical society in the United States. Membership is only open to those who prove to be descendants of the Pilgrims. Its members are proud of being the living link with the first European settlers who, according to the country's official history, brought with them the principles of civil and religious liberty that became symbols of US identity.

The first English settlements on the shores of North America were not only scarcely populated but were also threatened by a very high mortality rate. Apart from the feared Native Americans, the hardship of the long journey, as well as the North American weather, was going to find many victims. Out of the 15,000 emigrants who arrived in Virginia between 1607 and 1622 only 2,000 survived.* For this reasons their continuity initially depended on a constant influx of immigrants.

The main obstacle for migration to America was the cost of the journey, which must have been as expensive for the English as for the Spanish and Portuguese. In the early seventeenth century crossing the Atlantic took a minimum of eight weeks, and it would cost £5 plus the cost of the necessary provisions to reach America.** For the majority this implied selling all

---

*   John Elliott, *Empires of the Atlantic World.*
**   Ibid.

their belongings in order to pay for the journey, and very often this was not enough, and they would need some sort of external aid in order to be able to go on board.

Due to the prohibitive cost of the journey the most likely method to go to America was the indentured servitude, by which the emigrant would repay the cost of his voyage with several years' work in his posting. Until the introduction of African slaves, the work of the white emigrants plowing the land and performing all sorts of necessary tasks allowed the economy to start taking off in the early days of colonization. Up to sixty percent of the immigrants to the British colonies in North America and the Caribbean during the seventeenth century arrived with some sort of indentured servitude contract.* Their conditions varied, but the most common was a four- or five-year contract of hard labor. For the majority indentured servitude constituted an agreement to be slaves for several years with the aim of eventually becoming free workers.

A great incentive for emigration was undoubtedly the potential ownership of such fertile lands as those in the eastern coast of North America. From 1618 the so-called headright system of land grants was introduced, by which forty hectares of land were offered to each settler and another hundred for every person brought by him. Despite the fact that becoming a landowner in New England was a very attractive life plan, fear of the dangers of the New World explains why emigration was initially so scarce. Even promotional pamphlets were produced, like New England's *Plantation*, published in 1630. "Here wants as yet the good company of honest Christians to bring with them horses, cows and sheep to make good use of this fruitful land . . ." one of them urged.** Initiatives like this largely contributed to the Great Migration in the 1630s, during which 69,000 Britons crossed the Atlantic to settle in North America. Out of this figure only 21,000 went to New England,*** but nevertheless the proportion of women and men who brought their families with them increased considerably, and as a result of it, from the mid–seventeenth

---

*   Elliott, *Empires of the Atlantic World*.
**   Ibid.
***   Ibid.

century onward there were sufficient women as to guarantee that population numbers would be maintained.

The settlements that were founded by the first colonists on the eastern coast of North America bore a great resemblance to England in their customs, institutions, and organization. The predominantly rural atmosphere of great farms and plantations was interrupted by small urban centers like Boston, Newport, or Charlestown. The architecture in these cities was very similar to the English, except for the important innovation of streets that were designed in perfect parallel and perpendicular alignment.

As we have previously seen, the main way of earning a living for the early settlers was through the acquisition and cultivation of land. The desire to acquire and accumulate lands that settlers in the eastern coast had in common accounts for the enormous pressure to expand toward the west that existed from an early stage. North America was not a place for making a fortune overnight, settlers only reached prosperity after many years of hard work and sacrifice.

A more lucrative alternative to North America for English emigrants was the Caribbean. Sugar, the most profitable commodity in the British Empire, was cultivated in the colonies of the West Indies. Demand for sugar grew steadily until it accounted for a fifth of the British imports in the eighteenth century.* It was much more in demand and considerably more expensive than tobacco, the main export of the North American colonies. Exports to Britain from the small Caribbean colony of Saint Christopher and Nieves were three times larger than those from New York between 1714 and 1773.** This explains why the Caribbean was much more attractive for the first emigrants, but what is less well known is that the majority of English immigrants in the seventeenth century, more than sixty percent, went to the West Indies. Nevertheless, emigration to the Caribbean dramatically declined in the eighteenth century, the fact that African slavery substituted for white labor, and also a high mortality rate caused by the tropical climate, ended up discouraging emigrants.

---

* Sidney W. Mintz, *Sweetness and Power: The Place of Sugar in Modern History* (New York: Penguin, 1986).
** Ibid.

Unlike the kingdom of Castile, the English authorities did not attempt to restrict emigration to their own people, nor did they make strict selections on who should be allowed to travel in their ships. For this reason emigration was soon to extend to Scotland, Ireland, and to a certain extent Wales, where living conditions were often even harsher than in England. In the eighteenth century, the majority of emigrants to America from the British Isles were Scottish or Irish. Among the Irish, those from Northern Ireland predominated those who were of Scottish origin, but southerners were soon to proliferate as well. Two fifths of British emigrants between 1701 and 1780 were Irish.*

In Scotland living conditions were much harder than in England, especially in the rural areas and the Highlands. This contributed to the development of a struggling and entrepreneurial character among the Scots that made them very good emigrants. *Per mare et per terras* (By sea and land) can be read in the motto of the MacDonald clan, one of the largest of Scottish clans, which seems to take inspiration from the Scottish diaspora throughout the world. Many Scots emigrated to Northern Ireland in the sixteenth century, and when the opportunity of emigration to America arose, it became so popular that according to the most critics it was to be considered like an infectious fever.

Destruction of forests, land evictions in the Highlands, and above all the elimination of the clan system after the Battle of Culloden in 1746—all of these factors contributed to a dramatic rise in emigration from the mid–eighteenth century. As Samuel Johnson described in his book *A Journey to the Western Islands of Scotland*, published in 1775, living conditions for most of the Scottish people were so bad that it was quite understandable that such high numbers considered that their only future was in the boat to America. Throughout the nineteenth century Scottish migration steadily increased, particularly to Canada, to such an extent that in the Canadian province of Nova Scotia, fifty-nine percent of British settlers were Scottish in the first half of the nineteenth century. In the United States Scottish migrants were increasingly visible, and by 1890 over 250,000 of those who had recently

---

* Niall Ferguson, *Empire: How Britain Made the Modern World* (New York: Penguin, 2004).

arrived had been born in Scotland.* The experience of emigrating left important traces in Scottish literature. The great Scottish writer Robert Louis Stevenson wrote *The Amateur Emigrant* in 1880, a travel memoir based on his journey from Scotland to California, which constituted a vivid and detailed description of the migrating experience in the nineteenth century.

For those who were used to the adversity of the Scottish rural world, living conditions in North America constituted a major improvement, and this accounts for their rapid integration in American society. The seventh U.S. president, Andrew Jackson, was the son of Scots–Irish colonists who had emigrated to America.

President William McKinley was also of Scottish ancestry, although much more remote. Not only were there many Scottish surnames in high-level US politics but also in industry. An extraordinary case of success in America was that of the famous tycoon Andrew Carnegie, who was born in Scotland in 1835 and arrived in Pittsburgh when he was only twelve years old. Carnegie led the expansion of the steel industry in the late nineteenth century, with such success that by the end of his career he was identified as the richest man in the world. His career as a philanthropist was no less influential. Three thousand public libraries were founded throughout the English-speaking world with his funds; he also donated large sums to educational, cultural, and scientific institutions that are still influential.

Among the Celtic world, the emigrants par excellence were undoubtedly the Irish. No people in Europe have had stronger motives for emigrating than the Irish. Apart from being as affected by poverty and barren lands as the Scots, the Irish had strong religious and political reasons to abandon their homeland, for they were oppressed by the English. In fact, as they were colonized by England, they considered themselves to be the first victims of its imperial expansion. In the seventeenth and eighteenth century British laws forbade Irish Catholics from owning land and occupying public office. Marginalized in their own homeland they could not have had better reasons for emigrating. If the Irish often lamented that their country was too near England, on the other hand they had the good fortune of being

---

*   Ferguson, *Empire.*

geographically the closest European country to the eastern coast of North America. From the eighteenth century the number of Irish emigrants who settled on the other side of the Atlantic steadily grew. It was increasingly difficult to find an Irish family that did not have relatives in America, and family networks contributed to a constant inflow of migrants, particularly to the city of Boston. For very good reasons Irish president Mary Robinson stated in 2001 that spiritually Ireland was nearer Boston than Berlin. This has certainly been the case for the last three centuries.

From the eighteenth century on, not only did population from Ireland and the British Isles arrive in North America but also from other places in Europe. News about the opportunities that could be found on the other side of the Atlantic spread rapidly through continental Europe, where an increasing number of people decided that their future was in America. The frontiers of the first British colonies in America were open to all European migrants willing to settle and work there, and for all those who were not British or Irish there was no barrier that prevented them from succeeding in America, apart from the initial disadvantage of not speaking English.

In the case of the Dutch their presence in North America is as old as the British. After the foundation of Fort Orange by Dutch settlers in 1614, thirty families traveled in order to settle in the colony of New Amsterdam. Over the following decades the Dutch West India Company offered their fellow countrymen free land on the banks of the Hudson River, and as a result of this a thriving community of Dutch settlers was to emerge. Among the families that arrived in those days were the Van Burens, from whom U.S. president Martin Van Buren descended. The Roosevelts as well, who apart from making a fortune two centuries later, became one of the most outstanding American political families with two great presidents, Theodore and Franklin D. Roosevelt.

Toward the mid–seventeenth century, New Amsterdam had eight thousand Dutch inhabitants. In Delaware the Swedish founded a small colony where around fifty families settled, but this was to be annexed by Holland. After the English conquest of New Amsterdam in 1664, renaming the city New York, the population tacitly accepted a change of sovereignty. In this way the first substantial injection of population from continental Europe to the British thirteen colonies was to take place.

As regards the French contribution, France was the most populous nation in Europe when the colonization of North America began, but as we have seen before, French emigration to its colonies on the other side of the Atlantic was very scarce in spite of all attempts made by the crown to promote it. In the case of France in the sixteenth and seventeenth centuries, colonizing was more appropriate for adventurers and missionaries than for families that wished to improve their lives. This explains why in the early eighteenth century the population of New France was not even a tenth of the population of the thirteen colonies. Nevertheless the French did emigrate to America for religious reasons. The Huguenot community was persecuted in France for practicing their Protestant faith, and for the same reasons they were not allowed to settle in New France. As a result of this they opted to migrate to the English-speaking east coast, particularly to the colony of Pennsylvania.

The largest contingent of population from continental Europe that was to arrive in North America was German. The German princely states had similar problems to the British, which made emigration very attractive for many of their inhabitants, but they did not have overseas colonies. This situation changed toward the end of the seventeenth century: the German lawyer, Franz Daniel Pastorius arrived in Pennsylvania in 1683 to buy 15,000 acres of land on behalf of a group of Quaker countrymen who were eager to leave Europe. Germantown was founded in these lands where German customs prevailed despite the fact that they were in British America, and Pastorius was to be the *burgermeister* until the end of his life. The first German families arriving there transformed this settlement into a prosperous city that was very similar to the German towns in Europe, and its economy was based on the textile industry.

From 1714 when the first member of the German house of Hanover, George I, ascended the British throne, German emigration to the American colonies was eagerly promoted from the crown. About 14,000 Germans arrived in America from England.[*] Throughout the eighteenth century companies proliferated in America specializing in financing trips to America for German emigrants. According to the British parliament,

---

[*] Burk, *Old World, New World.*

in 1716 a third of the population of Pennsylvania was German. Many also settled in the lands of New York, founding the cities of Manheim, Oppenheim, and Herkimer. In Virginia they were to settle in Germanna, which specialized in iron mongering, while Maryland attracted many German Catholics.

Due to all this migration German became the second most commonly spoken language in the thirteen colonies. German communities rapidly thrived and made very substantial contributions to the economic development of British America and later the United States. The most outstanding example of success among German immigrants was undoubtedly that of John Jacob Astor, who arrived in New York in 1784. The ambitious and smart German businessman specialized in trading with hides, but also invested in other lucrative businesses as real estate speculation in New York. He made his companies so profitable that he became the first multimillionaire in the history of the United States, and on his death in 1848 he was the wealthiest man in the country. He was followed by an influential dynasty in business and politics in the Atlantic world. One of its most famous members in Britain was Nancy Astor, the American-born socialite who married Viscount Astor and eventually became the first woman member of parliament to sit in the House of Commons.

It has been assumed that as the colonization of America made progress and the migration of Europeans increased, European culture was inexorably imposed. Nevertheless, it was not the case initially due to the fact that the majority of those who crossed the Atlantic between the sixteenth and eighteenth centuries did not come from Europe but from Africa.

From the sixteenth century the importation of African slaves expanded rapidly across America. Initially, the slaves started to be used in the Spanish colonies of Cuba and Hispaniola. Later they were employed in great numbers in the plantations of Brazil, and from there the habit of owning African slaves spread across the European colonies in the Caribbean and finally to North America. The fact that the development of the plantations, and consequently of the colonial economy, depended on African labor contributed to the rapid increase of its demand. The white man in America was increasingly dependent on the black man.

One and a half million Europeans had emigrated to America toward the end of the eighteenth century, but four times more Africans were transferred there to serve them.* More than seventy percent of the passengers in the ships who crossed the Atlantic between 1589 and 1820 were African. It has been calculated that from 1600 to the end of the nineteenth century, over twelve million African slaves were brought to America.** The reason why the figure of black population is so high is not only due to the increasing demand but also to the fact that mortality rate among them was very high and reproduction very low. Shipments of slaves were constantly needed in order to maintain a stable black population.

The fact that the black population was more numerous than the white in America from the sixteenth to the eighteenth century contributed to the expansion of the culture of the African people—and not just the European—in the New World. Blacks were forced to live in a world that was dominated by whites, they lost their native African languages, eventually replaced their religious beliefs with Christianity, and were also to be known by the names and surnames given by their owners. In spite of all this, African culture was initially clearly visible in any plantation or any place where black population concentrated. In music, gastronomy, and also their beliefs and way of speaking the African legacy was clearly perceptible. After slaves were set free African culture was increasingly visible in some colonies. In the case of Brazil, the black population was to have much influence in its popular culture and folklore. In the coasts of present-day Venezuela, Colombia, Suriname, or Guyana, and especially in the Caribbean islands where black population constituted a majority, the culture and customs of Africa were particularly visible, as they still are.

Had the same distribution between black and white populations in America been maintained, the Atlantic civilization would have had a strong African presence. Nevertheless, as a result of demographic changes in the nineteenth century the presence of black people was to be more marginal. The importation of an African population to America came to an end after

---

*   Fernández-Armesto, *Civilizations.*
**   Thomas, *The Slave Trade.*

the prohibition of the slave trade in 1807. On the other hand, in the nineteenth century the biggest wave of white emigration from the other side of the Atlantic was to take place. From then black Americans ceased to be a majority in many places, and were even to become an ethnic minority, especially in the United States. As a result of this, the Atlantic civilization became a Western civilization, which, as according to the historian Felipe Fernández-Armesto, is another name for a white civilization of Western origin.*

In 1798 the English cleric Thomas Malthus published his *Essay on the Principle of Population*, which was going to become one of the most influential books that have been written in the Western world about population. In this essay, Reverend Malthus analyzes the consequences that the increase in population could have on society and warned that contrary to what was thought in those days, the constant rise in population would have devastating effects on Britain and on any other country. One obvious consequence of the rise in population was the increase in workforce which leads to the reduction of salaries, explained the cleric. A much more devastating impact of demographic growth was the shortage of food, for Malthus explained in his work that a critical moment would be reached in which agricultural and livestock production would not be sufficiently high as to feed the entire population.

Thomas Malthus's apocalyptic theory about the consequences of population growth had a great impact on Britain in his day. As a result of it, in 1800 the first population census was commissioned, according to which the population of Great Britain was approximately ten million. Although Malthus's prediction never came true—so far—it did contribute to raise social awareness about the dangers of population growth in his time. The natural formulae that traditionally prevented the increase in population were wars, plagues, and famines, as Malthus explained in his book, and the less painful alternatives were through birth control, which in those days could only be implemented through celibacy or delaying the marriage age. One third option to prevent the undesired increase in population was emigration. This is the reason why both Great Britain and many other European governments promoted emigration, especially those with overseas colonies where the spare

---

* Fernández-Armesto, *Civilizations.*

population could be sent. The fact that it was the poorer sector of society that was forced by circumstances to emigrate constituted a relief for the governments, for the problems associated with widespread poverty were reduced and the Malthusian nightmare was in this way scared away.

Without reading Malthus a high percentage of Europeans were well aware of the problems created by overpopulation. Shortages of jobs and food in rural areas provoked emigration to the cities, and in many of these the situation was not much better. Although prospects for the future were bleak for many workers in old Europe, the advantage that those who were born in the nineteenth century enjoyed over their ancestors was that opportunities for emigrating were far greater.

The favorite destination for European migrants was the United States of America. The fact that several European countries already had communities of emigrants settled in this country intensified emigration throughout the nineteenth century. To be the first independent nation in the Americas was also an incentive for many emigrants who did not belong to any colonial power. Above all, the United States needed emigrants to stimulate its economy and populate the territories that it was acquiring, and the possibilities of making a fortune there were greater than in any other place in the world.

British emigration continued throughout the nineteenth century, particularly from Scotland and Ireland as we have seen, although the fact that emigrants from Great Britain had opportunities for migrating to so many places of its vast empire contributed to their expansion throughout the planet.

Irish emigration to the United States steadily increased throughout the nineteenth century. The rebellious Irish were naturally attracted to the United States as a country that had managed to break away from British sovereignty. From the 1840s it became not only a land of opportunity but also the country that allowed them to recover from the most traumatic experience in their history: the potato famine. The famine caused by the potato blight of 1845 provoked the loss of almost a fourth of Ireland's population and plunged the island into an economic crisis that was to last for several decades. Out of almost two million Irish who abandoned their country in the decade of the potato famine, the majority went to the United States.

Toward 1850 the Irish constituted one fourth of the population in the cities of Boston, New York, Philadelphia, and Baltimore.* Earning a living in the United States did not seem easy for them, facing prejudices of the English against the Irish, the Protestants against the Catholics, and the rich against the poor, which explain why the Irish community was initially so marginal. Despite the fact that equality of all citizens before the law was proclaimed by the U.S. Constitution, and the political establishment took pride in the country's egalitarian ethos, not all emigrants were equal, the legacy of the struggle among European people was going to be present in the great American nation. Nevertheless the Irish managed to make progress and gradually overcome all obstacles until they managed to reach the economic and political pinnacle of American society. One of the Irish emigrants who left their island during the decade of the potato famine was Patrick Kennedy, who emigrated from the county of Wexford and settled in Boston in 1849, where he earned a living as a tanner. From such humble origins his son Patrick Kennedy managed to become an influential politician in Massachusetts, but this was only the beginning of the political rise of the Kennedy family in the United States.

The other great contingent of European emigrants was German. The crisis of the 1840s and the 1848 revolution provoked a massive exodus of Germans from many of its kingdoms and princely states. Around one million settled in the United States over the following decade. Not only did they settle in cities that had been founded by their ancestors but they expanded throughout the country. In New York the German community was substantial. The influence of revolutionary exiles could be felt with the founding in 1867 of the first American Socialist party. In the following years German emigration intensified, and toward the 1880s another million entered the United States. Milwaukee and Cincinnati became the two main centers of German culture in that country. Thanks to the entrepreneurial and industrial spirit that characterized the Germans, several of them followed the path of John Jacob Astor and joined the country's business elite.

Another country that played an active role populating North America was Sweden, from whence more than a million emigrants left in the

---

* Thomas J. Archdeacon, *Becoming American: An Ethnic History* (New York: Free Press, 1983).

nineteenth century. From Norway around 750,000 people emigrated between 1820 and 1900, the equivalent to four-fifths of its population, and in Holland around 350,000 people left.* Generally, apart from the English, the Scottish, and the Welsh, emigration from northern Europe and the Protestant countries in Europe was more welcome by the political elite and the government of the United States. In fact apart from Britain the three countries where the U.S. opened agencies to promote emigration were Germany, Sweden, and Norway.

Prejudices against the Catholics provoked pressures especially from the Republican Party to restrict the arrival of Irish and German Catholics, and in this way preserve the culture with which the majority of the people from the U.S. were identified.

Despite the fact that the French Empire offered many attractive options for the French who wished to emigrate, the opportunities in the United States attracted many of them, some also arrived there through Canada. In total around 700,000 Frenchmen settled in the United States in the nineteenth century.**

From the 1870s onward, emigrants from Eastern and Southern Europe began to proliferate. In Italy, the demographic explosion and the decline in living conditions in both the urban and rural centers provoked a wave of emigration toward the end of that century, and the United States was going to be the main recipient. Over the last decade of the nineteenth century more than 700,000 Italians entered the country. The Greeks also started to emigrate to North America in those days, and even the Portuguese, who were usually more attracted by Brazil. Austrians, Hungarians, Poles, Czechs, Serbians, and other nationalities in Eastern Europe also went in search of a better life to the United States—and finally Russians.

Despite the fact that the Russians had many opportunities for emigration within their huge terrestrial empire, this did not allow them to escape poverty or political oppression. This is the reason why emigration to the United States became popular, to such an extent that according to the data of the frontier controls, over three million Russians reached this country

---

*   Archdeacon, *Becoming American.*
** Ibid.

between the nineteenth century and the first decades of the twentieth century.[*] Among the Russian emigrant population Jews proliferated, especially from 1881, when persecution against this community dramatically increased. Two million Jews emigrated to the United States between 1881 and 1914, and the majority came from Russia.[**]

Crossing the Atlantic was an expensive and risky adventure for the Irish, the Scots, or any other people in Western Europe. It was particularly the case for the Poles or the Russians, who lived so far away from the main ports that were connected with America. It took almost two months to cross the Atlantic, and much longer if one was traveling to South America. The ships crammed with emigrants who were forced to travel in very poor hygienic conditions required very good health and a capacity to endure adversity. In 1710 a typhoid epidemic broke out in a ship with 2,810 German passengers, causing the death of 446 of them. Death and sickness were inseparable companions of the transoceanic crews, and those who arrived at their destination were always fewer than those who left.

Fortunately for the emigrants in the first decades of the nineteenth century, traveling conditions started to improve. Technological innovations of the Industrial Revolution were soon to be applied to maritime transport. Steamships with metallic hulls, pushed by propellers, replaced the traditional sailing boats. They also increased in size and comfort, and were specially designed by the naval companies to board hundreds of passengers for the long journeys across the sea. As a consequence of these changes the era of great ocean liners was going to start. From the mid–nineteenth century great liners started to proliferate that managed to make transoceanic journeys considerably shorter as well as much more comfortable, and last but not least, they became much cheaper.

The great nineteenth century transatlantic ships constituted an essential contribution to the power of Europe in the world, almost as important as the caravels in the fifteenth century. If these made the discovery of America possible, the former made mass emigration possible to America and other

---

[*] Stephen Birmingham, *"The Rest of Us": The Rise of America's Eastern European Jews* (Boston: Little, Brown, 1984).
[**] Ibid.

points in the planet, without them Western civilization would not have been so predominant.

The era of the great transatlantic liners contributed to improve the relationship between Europe and America in general, particularly between the United States and Britain. It was then that the relationship between the two countries started to be really special. The ships that sailed across the ocean with increasing frequency not only contributed to make more emigrants travel but also businessmen in search of opportunities. Among the many business opportunities offered by the United States, the railway played a very important role, as it was growing so rapidly that in the decade of the 1840s it had more miles of railway track than the whole of Europe, and a considerable amount of British capital was invested in it, as well as Dutch and German. The relationship between the British aristocracy and the American elite was progressively strengthened since then. Marriages between members of their families, which until then would have scandalized the British upper classes, became increasingly frequent. Particularly famous was the marriage of the rich heiress Consuelo Vanderbilt with the Duke of Marlborough or the one between Randolph Churchill with Jennie Jerome, the daughter of a New York stockbroker, whose eldest son was destined to become one of the greatest symbols of the Anglo-American relationship: Winston Churchill.

Literature was going to reflect very well how the transatlantic relationship evolved through the century of great migrations. Charles Dickens traveled to the United States on two occasions, where his books were nationally popular. He left written records of his impressions that were often not positive in his *American Diary*, and also in his famous novel *Martin Chuzzlewit*.

But the most detailed and subtle descriptions of the Anglo-American world in the nineteenth century were those of the Boston writer Henry James, who reflects in his works their mutual admiration as well as the grudges and historic prejudices. James lived between the two countries for most of his life and eventually became a British citizen.

The extraordinary territorial expansion experienced by the United States through the nineteenth century would not have been sustainable in the long run if it had not been backed by a very considerable increase in population.

In this aspect the great waves of European emigrants were essential. From the major cities on the east coast to the most remote places, Europeans from very diverse origins gradually settled in this great country and made it their home. European migration was also a very important element contributing to the spectacular growth of the American economy from the mid–nineteenth century and the transformation of the United States into the largest economy in the world from the early twentieth century.

The other major North American destination for emigration was Canada. Canada in the early nineteenth century was, as it continues to be today, one of the less populated areas in the world, but it was also one of the richest in fertile lands and mineral resources. Britain promoted emigration to its most extensive colony with much success throughout the nineteenth century. In another period of intense emigration that was to be known as the Great Migration, from 1815 to 1850, 80,000 Britons reached Canada.* The cultural impact of this migration wave was considerable for the population of French origin, which until then had been the largest contingent, was transformed into a minority. The emigration of French-speaking inhabitants from Quebec to the United States that took place at that time was mainly the result of resentment against the British.

In 1851 gold was discovered on the west coast, provoking the arrival of a great influx of emigrants from both Europe and the United States. One year later, Britain declared British Columbia officially to be a colony, with the aim of ensuring that this region would remain under British sovereignty due to the increasing interest of the United States to annex the territory. Although the gold rush did not last for long, it helped attract population to this remote region and transform it into a very attractive destination for emigrants.

The great migration contributed to unify this huge North American territory under British dominion, although with a high level of independence. In 1838 the governor of British North America, the earl of Durham, presented a report that was going to be very influential in the history of the British Empire. In this report he recommended that all territories in Canada should

---

* Archdeacon, *Becoming American*.

be represented in a great autonomous parliament, in this way the loyalty of the colonials to the motherland would be guaranteed by granting them the maximum level of independence. Durham seemed to have learned the lessons of history and he made a very important contribution with this report to prevent an armed conflict similar to the one in the thirteen colonies, which would have led Canadians to break away from Britain.

Despite the essential role played by the Great Migration in the early development of Canada, its population was still insignificant for such a vast territory. In 1871 the population of Canada was about three and a half million. For this reason, in the 1870s its government started to promote emigration in Scandinavia, Germany, and central Europe, announcing itself as "the last and best West," which led many Europeans to consider this colony as a better alternative to the United States. This publicity campaign was responsible for an increasing number of emigrants from diverse European countries who were to join the English-and French-speaking settlers in Canada.

While emigration contributed to strengthen links between North America and Europe, other parts of the American continent were to experiment with a similar process. The American dream that was so deeply associated with the United States was also to take place in several other parts of the Americas. The dismemberment of the Iberian empires in America did not constitute the end of the Spanish and Portuguese influence on the other side of the Atlantic. The great migratory movements of Spain and Portugal were still to come after the emergence of the Latin American nations.

Spain did not have an excess of population to send to America as Britain or Germany did, nevertheless the economic need for emigration was constant for many Spaniards in the nineteenth century. In an agricultural economy like Spain's, a big percentage of the population was exposed to the problems of the rural world. Except for the aristocracy and the small bourgeoisie, emigration for the rest of the population constituted the only opportunity for acquiring wealth and climbing the social ladder.

After the 1820s the only remaining colonies where the Spaniards could emigrate were Cuba, Puerto Rico, and the Philippines. Cuba became by far the most important, and it was going to attract the largest percentage of

Spaniards who left their homeland in search of a better life. The most out-standing of these emigrants who thrived on the Caribbean island was the marquis of Comillas, Antonio Lopez.

Antonio Lopez started working in Cuba as a teenager. Once he had saved enough he founded a transport company that steadily expanded until it became the Transatlantic Company, which controlled a large part of the transport between Spain and Latin America. He also used his fortune to promote diverse business ventures with the Spanish colonial world. He founded a colonial bank and also made incursions in the tobacco trade, founding the General Tobacco Company of the Philippines, which was going to expand to the point of becoming the first Spanish multinational company. Lopez was rewarded by King Alfonso XVIII, for his prominent role in the business world with the title of marquis of Comillas, his home-town in northern Spain where he also founded a university.

The marquis of Comillas was the most outstanding example of the so-called *Indianos,* as those who made a fortune in America were known, and they played a very important role in the economic development of Spain in the nineteenth and twentieth century. The legacy of the Indianos can be perceived in many places throughout northern Spain. Apart from great man-sions of colonial style that they used to build on returning to their homeland, those who were wealthy enough would make donations for important social works. Their example was going to inspire many young Spanish workers in search of a better life. The Indianos became a great symbol of success in the colonial era and afterward as well, as several great modern Spanish novelists show from Benito Pérez Galdós to Pío Baroja.

In one of the streets of the northern town of Santander, an old plaque from the Transatlantic Company founded by Comillas announces monthly journeys to Havana, Vera Cruz, Montevideo, and Buenos Aires. From the last decades of the nineteenth century to the mid–twentieth century, many inhabitants of this province boarded one of these ships with the hope of finding a better life, for hope was the main fuel for emigrants. In other ports of northern Spain and also in Barcelona, Cádiz, or the Canary Islands, ships full of workers setting out to "do the Americas," as it was popularly said in those days, was for many decades a very common scene.

Spanish emigration intensified in the last decades of the nineteenth century and was to continue in the twentieth century. Between 1882 and 1935 around four million Spaniards left their country.* Cuba was the main source of attraction until it ceased to be a colony in 1898. The second most attractive posting was Argentina, then Mexico, Chile, and Uruguay—and Brazil was also included among the options for Spaniards.

Only fifteen percent of Spanish emigrants opted for non-American destinations. Most of them went to the Philippines and the less adventurous opted for Morocco and Algeria.

Unlike migrants from northern Europe, many Spaniards did not consider emigration as something permanent, and they hoped to return to their homeland as soon as they could. In fact, fifty-seven percent of those who left between 1882 and 1935 returned to Spain. There was a lot of temporary emigration, particularly to the rural zones in Cuba or Brazil, where many Spanish peasants traveled to work for only the harvest months and return thereafter.

As regards Portugal, its population was to show an extraordinary migratory spirit, particularly to Brazil, the pearl of its empire. Until the early eighteenth century, few Portuguese were attracted by Brazil. Nevertheless, with the discovery of gold during that century emigration rapidly increased. It was then that Portuguese was imposed as the official language in the huge colony, as more and more people from Portugal settled in Rio de Janeiro, São Paolo, Salvador de Bahia, and many other smaller settlements that they would found throughout the Brazilian coast. But mass migration did not take place until the second half of the nineteenth century, as in the rest of America.

The recent independence of Brazil did not constitute an obstacle for the young nation to be filled with Portuguese immigrants. On the contrary, the political break did not affect its economic and cultural ties with Portugal. After large contingents of migrants arrived in the major cities, migration to the rural areas ensued, for as a result of the abolition of slavery the demand for labor intensified, and many peasants were to start the American adventure working in the plantations. In total more than 300,000 Portuguese emigrated to Brazil in the last decades of the nineteenth century.

---

*   Raymond Carr, *Spain 1808–1975* (Oxford, England: Clarendon Press, 1982).

Brazil was also to attract much German emigration. In 1820 New Fribourg was founded by several families of German and Swiss settlers. After independence, Emperor Pedro I, who had married a Habsburg princess, welcomed German emigration, especially to populate the region of Rio Grande do Sul, and German population progressively increased over the rest of the century. Just as it happened with its North American equivalents, Nova Friburgh and other small settlements were to be perfect copies of German towns on the banks of the Amazon.

However, toward the end of the nineteenth century the most numerous contingent of Europeans in Brazil was the Italians. After United States and Argentina, Brazil was the favorite destination for the huge wave of Italian migration that took place in the late nineteenth and early twentieth century. The total number of Italians who entered Brazil between 1876 and 1920 was around 2,200,000. Integration in their country of adoption was easy for the Italians, and the second generation already considered themselves Brazilians, but this did not prevent Italian influence from being considerable in this vast country. Around a third of the white population in Brazil nowadays claims to have Italian ancestry.

Apart from Portuguese, Italians, Germans, and Spaniards, Brazil was going to attract emigrants from other European nationalities, especially Poland, Austria, Ukraine, and Russia. Due to this emigration, São Paolo and the main cities of this great country became a mosaic of European cultures that cohabited more or less peacefully along with African and Amerindian cultures.

A very special destination for European migration was Argentina. The country that emerged from the old viceroyalty of the River Plate was going to become one of the largest in the American continent. From the city of Buenos Aires the successors of the founding leader Jose San Martín were going to face the great challenge of conquering, populating, and governing over great tracts of land. The frontier spirit that was so characteristic in the United States was reproduced in several South American countries, particularly in Argentina.

In the 1830s, Argentine president Juan Manuel de Rosas promoted what was to be known as the Patagonia campaign, with the aim of occupying land in Patagonia and the Pampas, devote them to agriculture and livestock, and also expel the indigenous tribes that inhabited them. Four decades later the so-called conquest of the desert took place with the aim of taking possession of Patagonia and preventing Chile from taking the lead. Another consequence of this conquest was the expulsion and elimination of the Indians who lived there by Argentine troops.

Argentina emerged from the mid–nineteenth century as one of the most attractive countries for European emigrants. Moreover, the Argentine government promoted European migration very actively, to the point of including this intention in the 1853 constitution, which stated that, "the government will promote European emigration." Juan Bautista Alberti, who largely influenced the content of this constitution, published a book at that time on the organization of the Argentine Republic, in which he explained that "populating is a civilizing act when it is done with civilized people, which means with people from civilized Europe."* In several of his works Alberdi not only argued that Argentina should be open to European settlers but he also discriminated between Europeans who were more civilized than others, and for this reason he insisted on the need to attract emigrants from Anglo-Saxon and Germanic countries. Although British, Irish, and German migration was going to be intensive, from the decade of the 1870s emigrants from all over Europe were going to reach Argentina, both the civilized and educated as Alberdi wished, as well as those who were backward and illiterate. Even emigrants from the Ottoman Empire were going to reach Argentine ports.

The Argentine government was probably the most active in all the Americas in the promotion of European migration. Apart from opening agencies in the most important European cities and subsidizing the journey to Argentina for the poorest emigrants, it actively promoted the colonization of the remotest territories. The results were extraordinary. In 1869 Argentina had a population of 1,800,000 inhabitants, of which 160,000 were Europeans who had recently arrived. In 1895 it had increased to 3,954,911 inhabitants.

---

* Maria Saenz Quesada, *La Argentina: Historia del País y de su Gente* (Buenos Aires: Sudamericana, 2001).

Over the following decades the emigrant population grew to such an extent that in 1930 there were 6,330,000 emigrants, of which over three million were permanent settlers, and the rest was a floating population that remained in the country for a certain period.*

Apart from those who descended from the original Spanish settlers, the British were the oldest community among those who settled in the country from the mid–nineteenth century. British investment in Argentina was going to be very important, especially in the most vital sectors of its economy like the railways. Apart from being the wealthiest of all recent settlers the British community earned much respect among the Argentines, and consequently their customs were to take root in the country—particularly sports like polo and soccer, as well as their social habits. The Irish were also to proliferate, particularly after the potato famine. Another large community in Argentina was that of the French, due to the fact that they were the second most important European investor in the country. Nevertheless over the last three decades of the nineteenth century great waves of emigrants were to arrive from south, central, and eastern Europe.

The most important migrant contingent was clearly the Italian. When the first population census was carried out in Argentina in 1869, the Italians constituted thirty-three percent of the foreign population. This was only the beginning, for in 1895 they were almost half a million inhabitants and they represented forty-eight percent of the total foreign population.** Although the majority were poor emigrants from the South, soon Italian surnames were to proliferate in the world of business, politics, and culture. From the humblest districts to the most exclusive circles of Buenos Aires and other important cities, Italian influence was to be very visible, leaving a deep mark on the formation of the Argentine identity.

The Spaniards were also to be very numerous, with 1,400,000 settling in Argentina between 1880 and 1914. The great majority came from Galicia, which explains why Spaniards were popularly known as *Gallegos* in Argentina. Another contribution to the mosaic of European cultures in this country was that of the Russians. The first ones to arrive were the German Russians

---

*   Saenz Quesada, *La Argentina*.
**   Ibid.

from the Volga region, in order to colonize the lands of the Pampas, but soon the presence of Russians was to increase dramatically toward the end of the nineteenth century. Ukrainians, Poles, Romanians, and representatives of other central European nationalities were also to arrive.

Among the Russian citizens there was a high percentage of Jews, as had happened with those who arrived in the United States. Many arrived thanks to Baron Maurice de Hirsch, a Jewish entrepreneur and philanthropist of German ancestry who founded a Jewish community in Buenos Aires and other Jewish settlements in rural Argentina.

The internal colonization of Argentina is full of extraordinary tales of adventure, endurance, delusions of grandeur, and even madness. A very good example was that of the Julius Popper, a modern conquistador who went to colonize Tierra del Fuego, where there were abundant gold deposits. Popper aimed at founding a settlement under the name of Atlanta, patented a gold harvester that could have been a great business, and consolidated a small empire in this remote land that was controlled by his own private army. But he was also to go down in history as the person responsible for the destruction of the indigenous tribes that inhabited this remote region. There were also stories of people who made fortunes in a very short time, like the Italian Antonio Devoto, founder of the Bank of Italy and River Plate, and who also founded the district in Buenos Aires that bears his name.

Perhaps what gave Argentina such a strong European character was not only the fact that its emigration was overwhelmingly European, but also that other races did not have as much presence as in other countries of the Americas. The majority of the indigenous population in the Pampas, Patagonia, and the northern part of the country was expelled or exterminated with the arrival of the white settlers. As regards the population of Africans, the viceroyalty of the River Plate had a large population of slaves until the eighteenth century, but a good part of them had vanished or were killed, and those who remained was too small in number to have a visible presence. The great Argentine writer Jorge Luis Borges explained very well the difference between the Argentine identity and that of the rest of Latin America: "The Peruvians descend from the Incas, the Mexicans descend from the Aztecs, and the Argentines descend from the ships."

The city of Buenos Aires is the most evident proof of the European influence that was predominant in the construction of Argentina. That beautiful Argentine city seems like the capital of an empire that never existed, as André Malraux defined it. It reminds the visitor of Paris, Madrid, Milan, or other cities of the old continent, and it is one of the best reproductions of the urban European atmosphere that has been made in the Americas.

Toward the end of the nineteenth century all nations of Europe seemed to be represented in Argentina. Its constant influx of European population contributed to keep very strong links with the old continent, yet despite the fact that the recently arrived emigrants had their hearts on the other side of the Atlantic, they were to be quickly assimilated by their country of adoption. A plan of compulsory national education in Spanish and the opportunities that the vast country offered for all those who had recently arrived contributed to make the second generation of emigrants become Argentines loyal to their new homeland. As the senator of Irish origin Eduardo Casey stated, "Europe is nothing compared to our country, the richest and the greatest in the world."* Argentina was one of the best destinations in the world for those Europeans who, frustrated in their countries of origin, went there in search of opportunities. This explains the pride showed by first-and second-generation Argentines.

Despite the fact that America was the favorite destination for European emigration, a considerable number of alternatives emerged as empires expanded. One of the farthest and most enigmatic places for migration was Australia.

On January 19, 1788 a fleet with 737 convicts arrived in Botany Bay, near present-day Sidney. This crew of convicts was the first group of European settlers in the British colonization of Australia. Between 1788 and 1853 about 123,000 men and 25,000 women were sentenced to exile in Australia.** The crimes for which one could be condemned to Australian ostracism were very diverse: crimes against property proliferated and there were also many

---

*   Saenz Quesada, *La Argentina*.

**   Winston Churchill, *A History of the English-Speaking Peoples: The Great Democracies*, vol. IV (London: Cassell, 1982).

political prisoners. A fourth part of those who were deported to Australia were Irish. Nevertheless, although it was a nation founded by convicts, what seems extraordinary was that it was soon to become a colony where the majority of its inhabitants were loyal subjects of the crown and where one could prosper and live peacefully.

The person who was primarily responsible for this transformation was Lachlan Macquarie, who was governor of Australia from 1809 to 1821.*

Macquarie decided that Australia should be a land for atonement rather than punishment. In order to achieve this he decided to employ the prisoners in the construction of the city of Sidney, and he managed to transform it into a model colonial city during his mandate. The elegant buildings built by the prisoners constituted the introduction of Western classic architecture in Oceania. But above all, Macquarie gave the convicts great incentives to become good citizens, even offering twelve hectares of land to those who finished their sentence. Apart from settling down as farmers or stockbreeders, many ex-convicts that were not allowed to return to Britain opened up businesses in Sidney. The most outstanding example was probably that of Samuel Terry, a thief from Manchester who went into the hostelry business and also became a pawnbroker, managing to consolidate a fortune in the decade of the 1820s that made him the richest man in the colony. Nowhere else in the world were ex-convicts given better opportunities for reentering society. As a result, deportation to Australia evolved from being feared to becoming the ideal destination for many of those who were sentenced to prison.

Despite the fact that there were more free citizens than prisoners after 1823, Australia attracted very little emigration, mainly due to the distance, as the United States and Canada seemed better and cheaper alternatives for British migrants. Nevertheless, the discovery of gold in Victoria, to the southwest of Sidney, in 1851 provoked a rapid influx. In those days Australia had around 400,000 inhabitants; one decade later the population had increased to 1,150,000. Victoria evolved from having only eighteen percent of the settlers to forty-seven percent.** As it had been demonstrated

---

*   Churchill, *A History of the English-Speaking Peoples.*
**   Ibid.

from the times when Columbus reached America, no land was too distant for Europeans at the prospect of acquiring gold. But apart from the lucky few who managed to discover gold, the main business for the settlers in this island was stockbreeding, especially with sheep. As regards the aboriginals, the impact of the arrival of the British settlers was equally harmful as it had been for the indigenous peoples in the Americas. The British brought diseases that were lethal for them, and the aboriginal population declined to the point of becoming a very small minority in their own land. The land occupied by the settlers for livestock and agriculture was also going to reduce their natural habitat.

The colonization of New Zealand, the other great colony in Oceania, was to follow different paths. Its main promoter was Edward Gibbon Wakefield, a wealthy British entrepreneur who wished to create a new system of colonization. Wakefield was deeply influenced by the Malthusian theories that were fashionable in his time and which considered colonization to be the solution to the problems of overpopulation and poverty that affected the main cities in Britain. His plan was to set up a company that would occupy land and exploit it, founding colonies by means of agreements with entrepreneurs, artisans, and workers. The New Zealand Company was created with this aim, and the first ships were sent in 1839 to start the colonization of these islands.

Nevertheless, Edward Wakefield never enjoyed the support of the government circles, and for this reason the crown eventually decided to formally occupy New Zealand. This was mainly to avoid the problems that this company could create, and also to protect British interests against the French and American whaling ships that roamed around the coasts. Another reason why the crown took this island was in order to prevent confrontations with the Maori people, whose warlike spirit was well known by all those who approached these islands.

In 1840 the British crown signed the Treaty of Waitangi with the Maori, by which a governor was sent to New Zealand, the land was recognized as property of the Maori, and they were to have the same rights as the British citizens. Despite the fact that the treaty seemed to leave the relationship between the two parties very clear, the Maori interpretation of the treaty was different, as they expected to obtain the protection of the British government and were going to be outraged by the arrival of an increasing number of European settlers who occupied their lands.

After neutralizing the power of the New Zealand Company by means of economic compensation, from then on the government supervised the arrival of British settlers who were initially only 37,000 in 1871, but this figure trebled by the early twentieth century.* A big percentage of them were Scottish, but not all immigrants were British, for New Zealand was also to attract emigrants from central Europe, especially from the Austro-Hungarian Empire. Two decades after it was officially established as a colony, the majority of the population of New Zealand was white.

Another increasingly attractive destination for European migration from the nineteenth century was South Africa. In spite of the huge distance South Africa was a place of great strategic value, its vast unpopulated territories offered many opportunities for the settler with an entrepreneurial spirit, and from there the possibilities of expansion toward the north seemed to have no limits where a whole continent was still to be discovered. The 20,000 Boer settlers who lived in South Africa in the early nineteenth century were well aware of the privilege of being the first European settlers in this part of the world, which they had transformed into their homeland. Sharing this paradise with British settlers proved to be a major challenge for them, and led to several conflicts.

After Cape Town was ceded by Holland in 1815, the British government considered this territory as another ideal destination for its migrant population. In 1820 the first British contingent reached South Africa. Five thousand settlers reached Cape Town determined to prosper there. The clashes between the British and Boer community was going to be the cause of the first major European incursion into the interior of the African continent. Between 1835 and 1843 the so-called Great Trek took place. Around fifteen thousand Boer families set out on a journey to the north of Cape Town with the aim of founding new settlements where they could govern themselves and decide their own future.

---

*   Churchill, *A History of the English-Speaking Peoples.*

The idea of traveling so far in order to earn a living farming or cattle breeding did not seem particularly appealing for either the British or emigrants from any other place in Europe. What really attracted them was the search for gold or precious metals. For this reason the discovery of gold and diamonds in South Africa changed its fate. The news of the first discoveries of gold and diamonds north of Cape Colony attracted thousands of emigrants from Britain. The city of Kimberley, where the largest deposits of diamonds and gold were found, experienced an extraordinary increase in population through the 1870s. By 1873 it had 40,000 inhabitants, becoming in this way the second most densely populated city in South Africa.* Diamonds made the businessman Cecil Rhodes and his business partners from the De Beers company immensely rich, and contributed to make of South Africa one of the most prosperous colonies in the British Empire.

Apart from South Africa, the African continent was generally seen by Europeans as a territory that was far too hostile for emigration. From the Portuguese pioneers in Angola to the rest of the powers that participated in the scramble for Africa, colonizing did not necessarily imply populating. Algeria, and to a certain extent Tunisia and Morocco, constituted the exception. With French colonization of Algeria, the relationship between Southern Europe and North Africa that was practically lost since Roman times was to be recovered again. Algeria became a very attractive place for agricultural colonization, and by the early twentieth century there were 150,000 European settlers, not only French but also Italian and Spanish, and the figure was going to continue increasing throughout the first half of the twentieth century. Tunisia attracted a small percentage of the massive Italian emigration toward the end of the nineteenth century, and some Spaniards opted for nearby Morocco to settle down.

More impenetrable than Africa for the masses of European migrants was the Asian continent. Except for the Russians, who colonized the Eurasian steppes and Siberia, no other power showed genuine interest, let alone capacity, to send large contingents of subjects to settle indefinitely in Asia.

British India was never seen as a posting where migrant population could be sent. On the contrary, despite the fact that it was the jewel in the crown

---

* Churchill, *A History of the English-Speaking Peoples*.

of the empire, the British Raj was seen as a world that was far too different and complicated for a British family to settle there indefinitely. The British considered that their mission was to govern, administer, and generate wealth, but not to populate a land that was already well populated by diverse indigenous people. According to an 1861 census India had a British population of 125,945 people, of whom 84,083 belonged to the armed forces.* The rest worked in diverse colonial departments and a small percentage was associated with the world of business or some liberal profession. For the great majority their presence in India was linked to the colonial administration.

Nevertheless, after two centuries of colonization, an Anglo-Indian community emerged. It was formed by British people who were born in India or had spent a great part of their lives there, and therefore felt that their identity was not exclusively British. General George Roberts, the first Earl Roberts, belonged to this community. He was born in Cawnpore in 1832, the son of an army officer serving in India, and it was there where he spent the most important part of his outstanding military career. The most famous member of the Anglo-Indian community was undoubtedly Rudyard Kipling. Kipling was born in Bombay in 1865 into a middle-class family that had emigrated to India for professional reasons. Although he also lived in England for a substantial part of his life and traveled extensively through the British Empire, it was his native India and Bombay where he spent an idyllic childhood that was to inspire his most famous works.

For some British soldiers, civil servants, or diplomats, Asia became the place where they spent most of their lives as a result of their professional postings. People from these professions could be sent not only to India, but also to Burma, Ceylon, Singapore, or Hong Kong and many of them rotated between different postings until they became great experts on the Asian world. As Benjamin Disraeli, who was always fascinated by the eastern world, wrote in his novel *Tancred*: "The East is a career," and many of them made of Asia a lifelong professional posting.

One of the pioneers in making a career out of the East was Stamford Raffles, known as the founding father of Singapore, for the greatest feat in

---

* James, *Raj*.

his life was to found this city in 1819. After arriving in Malaysia as assistant to the governor of Penang, in 1805 Raffles was going to devote the rest of his professional life to expanding the British dominion over this part of Asia. He also devoted much time to the study of its people and their culture, which culminated with an influential history of Java.*

The history of colonial Hong Kong was to be linked to an exclusive community of crown representatives like Harry Parkes. Parkes arrived in China in 1841 and spent the rest of his life in this part of the world. After more than twenty years of distinguished diplomatic service in China he was also posted in Japan and Korea. (Parkes Street in Hong Kong is the living testimony of his legacy.)

In the case of neighboring Macao, the result of a Portuguese presence since the mid–sixteenth century was the emergence of a Macanese community, formed mainly by those were posted there by the Portuguese crown. Their descendants, very often mixed-race Portuguese citizens, cherished their Portuguese identity although very often they spent their whole lives in Asia.

In the Spanish Philippines, the Spanish community of emigrants was always very small, as very few Spaniards ventured to travel so far, apart from those who were posted there on official duty. Nevertheless the economic history of the Philippine archipelago was deeply marked by the feats of outstanding Spanish emigrants like Antonio de Ayala. Ayala launched business ventures in the 1830s in partnership with the German industrialist Andreas Zóbel. As a result of it the Ayala Corporation was to emerge, which up to the present has been one of the most powerful business groups in this part of the world and their descendants the Zóbel de Ayala family are very influential.

Emigration was the inseparable companion of European empires in their process of expansion. In consequence, colonization became synonymous with populating, and this colonizing population and its descendants were going to make it possible for Western culture to occupy such a predominant place in the world. Overseas empires gave European powers the opportunity to propagate their influence through all continents, particularly through the

---

* Victoria Glendinning, *Raffles and the Golden Opportunity* (London: Profile Books, 2012).

Americas and Oceania, which were scarcely populated until the arrival of the Europeans. Despite the fact that European imperial powers had managed to spread their culture through a substantial part of the world between the sixteenth and the eighteenth centuries, they lacked sufficient population to send over to all occupied territories, and in this way consolidate their influence in the world. Nevertheless, this situation radically changed in the nineteenth century. Throughout this century a great part of Europe experienced a demographic explosion; technological innovations brought by the Industrial Revolution improved the conditions for traveling and settling in increasingly remote areas of the planet.

The great waves of European migration that started in the nineteenth century and continued until well into the twentieth century were to give the imperial expansion a special meaning, and managed to propagate European influence well beyond the colonial world. The fact that the great majority of emigrants settled in America had a crucial importance in the development of this continent, from Canada to Argentina. Without the constant injection of European migration, the territorial expansion of the United States would not have been so successful, nor would it have had the spectacular growth that transformed this country into the largest economy in the world after 1900. Its values and signs of identity as a superpower would not have been the same without the contribution of the Europeans. European migration also contributed to strengthen the identity of the nations that emerged from the Iberian empires as Western nations, especially Argentina, Brazil, Mexico, Chile, and Uruguay. European emigration to North and South America made the emergence of a new Atlantic civilization possible; in consequence the world economy was to become increasingly dependent on the activities between the two sides of the Atlantic Ocean.

Chapter 7

The Power and the Glory

The Golden Era of European Hegemony.

T he nineteenth century was the European century par excellence, a time when European civilization was at the height of its powers and Europe was the center of the world, projecting its influence to the remotest parts of the planet. At that time Europe experienced the most remarkable scientific and technological progress, making the Industrial Revolution possible. Great powers continued expanding until they consolidated global colonial empires. Against this backdrop of industrial and imperial expansion the peoples of Europe experienced great social and economic changes. The continent also became the world's intellectual hub, from which political ideas emerged that have transformed the entire world. Rising living standards and increasing leisure contributed to the birth of culture as an industry that has been entertaining and cultivating minds, and influencing people's thoughts since then.

The ultimate consequence of this age of improvement and progress was the emergence of what became identified as a European way of life. This was synonymous with progress, excellence, and the highest forms of civilization. It attracted Americans and other members of the Western world who reproduced it in their own countries. Even some members of elites in other civilizations followed the European way of life and attempted to incorporate it into their own culture, as they considered that Europeanization was the key to success.

The term European progress must be used with caution. Evidently there were substantial differences between the great powers and the rest of the European nations, and between industrial nations and those that remained agricultural. But even so, there was an ethos of progress and an aura of superiority that the peoples of Europe had in common. Europeans grew increasingly aware of the magnitude of their achievements and leading role in the world. This was not only the case with those who lived in the European continent but particularly among those who emigrated or were posted abroad.

What can justly be described as the European golden era began in 1815, with the end of the Napoleonic wars, and was to last until 1914. Peace was one of the crucial factors that made it possible. Between 1814 and 1815 the coalition of powers that defeated Napoleon met at the Congress of Vienna with the overall aim of ensuring a lasting peace and putting an end to this era of upheaval that had kept the continent at war for over twenty years. This gave way to what was called the Concert of Europe, a system of dispute resolution primarily based on keeping balance of power between the four main powers that had won the war: Britain, Austria, Prussia, and Russia. Its main proponent was Prince Metternich, who represented Austria and acted as host in the Vienna congress. His aim was to maintain the balance of power among Austria and other major powers by holding regular conferences where disputes would be amicably solved. He was also determined to oppose revolutionary movements and keep the rising ideologies of nationalism and liberalism under control. The Concert of Europe has been criticized as a reactionary agreement that ultimately failed to prevent nationalism and liberalism from making progress. Nevertheless, it did achieve its main aim of keeping peace in Europe for over a century. It is true however that there were revolutions and wars between several countries, but on the whole peace prevailed until 1914. More than ever this was a time when the philosopher Immanuel Kant's dream of perpetual peace in Europe—where nations would peacefully trade with each other—seemed to come true. As a result of this Prince Metternich became the most influential statesman in the nineteenth century, after Napoleon. He was a source of inspiration for several statesmen, particularly the U.S. Secretary of State Henry Kissinger who wrote his doctoral thesis at Harvard University on the Austrian prince and the Congress system and was to apply his principles of balance of power during the Cold War.*

The international order established at the Congress of Vienna was the closest that Europe has come to universal governance since the collapse of Charlemagne's empire. It produced a consensus that peaceful evolutions within the existing order were preferable to any other alternative; that the preservation of the system was more important than any single dispute that might arise within it; and that differences should be settled by consultation rather than by war.

The second factor determining the golden age was the Industrial Revolution, which led to one of the most profound changes in human history. As a consequence a transition to new manufacturing processes was made possible by new technology, and societies where it took place were rapidly transformed from rural to industrial and urban. The main beneficiary in its initial stages was obviously Britain, where the revolution began. This greatly consolidated its position as the leading world power. But soon several countries in Western Europe were going to join this revolution, as well as the United States and Canada. Industrial nations not only enjoyed technological superiority and an extraordinary improvement in living standards but above all they became fabulously rich in comparison to all other countries. The gap in terms of economic development and quality of life separating them from the rest of the world was progressively increasing throughout the nineteenth century. From 1870 to 1913 Western Europe came to represent thirty-three

---

* Henry Kissinger, *Diplomacy* (London: Simon & Shuster, 1994).

percent of the world's gross domestic product. European industrialization largely contributed to the Industrial Revolution in the United States by exporting the capital, technology, and labor that made it possible.

Last but not least, expansion throughout the globe continued strengthening Europe's position in the world. The process of discovery and exploration that Europeans had begun in the fifteenth century speeded up in the nineteenth. Technology and scientific improvements allowed Europeans to reach the last confines of the earth and penetrate the remotest territories that until then seemed impossible. Africa, which had remained virtually unexplored, was finally opened up. Once the heart of Africa was explored, a rapid process of partition of the continent between the great powers ensued. In the meantime colonial empires continued to grow in other continents. While the British reached the Pacific coast of Canada, the French reached Southeast Asia, and the Russians made remarkable progress with the colonization of Siberia. Trade networks expanded more than ever to include China and Japan, and the new principle of free trade started to make steady progress, considerably strengthening the market economy. In this process Europeans acquired a larger capacity to shape the world according to their interests as well as their values.

If the nineteenth century was a golden era for Europe on the whole, this was particularly the case for Britain as this was the British century par excellence. Europe's impact on the world was to a large extent the result of Britain's extraordinary performance.

From the Battle of Waterloo to the Boer War in 1901, Britain took advantage of a series of favorable circumstances that allowed it to consolidate the largest empire the world had ever seen and consolidate a model of society that was universally admired.

In 1825 the engineer George Stephenson invented the locomotive, perhaps the most important invention of the nineteenth century, as it made railways possible, radically changing human transport. A few years later, Isambard Brunel, one of the most ingenious figures in the history of engineering, designed the first railway system and founded the Great Western Railway that connected London with Wales. Railways soon rapidly spread not only across the whole of the British Isles but also a substantial part of the British Empire.

India was soon to have the best railway system in Asia. British railway companies proliferated from southern Europe to Latin America. British banking and its increasingly sophisticated financial system funded this remarkable expansion throughout the world, including the United States, until the early twentieth century. Britain also exported much of the material that was used by other nations in order to build railways. From the mid–nineteenth century a system that allowed the population to be transported by train was an essential element in any nation in the world that aspired to be modern and prosperous. Britain for a long time enjoyed the benefits of this great invention. It was the main exporter not only of steam engines but of all sorts of tools essential in the industrial era, incuding textile equipment, as initially Britain was also a pioneer in textiles and heavy industry.

Britain implemented one of the most important economic principles, which was to have a deep impact on its economy and eventually on the whole world: free trade. In the 1840s mercantilism was abandoned and replaced by free trade. The critical moment came in 1846 with the repeal of the Corn Laws, which had imposed stiff tariffs on imported grain. From then on the British market was opened to unfettered competition, grain prices fell and food became more abundant. A wide range of products experienced the same process, leading to a reduction of prices and an expansion of wealth. Two great British classical economists had contributed to the idea of free trade: Adam Smith extolled the advantages of the division of labor, while David Ricardo explained the theory of trade.

But it was thanks to the manufacturer and Liberal politician Richard Cobden that free trade was finally put into practice. Cobden had cofounded the Anti–Corn Law League in 1838 with the aim of abolishing the Corn Laws, which mainly protected landowners' interests. Cobden campaigned for free trade not only in Britain but also in Europe and America. He considered that free trade would be the greatest revolution of all time: "It would draw men together and make the whole world become one country and it would be the best way of bringing universal and permanent peace."

Lord Palmerston espoused this idea of free trade when he argued that commerce is "the best pioneer of civilization, making mankind happier, wiser, and better." This justified the Opium Wars (by which China was forced to open its ports to free trade), arguing that no regime had the right to deny its benefits to its own people.

In 1860 the Cobden-Chevalier Treaty was signed, by which Britain and France agreed to eliminate trade duties between the two countries. The idea that constituted the essence of liberal economics had finally triumphed. From 1860 until the Great Depression in 1930s, free trade spread rapidly through the world with great benefits for the economy. British benefits from the export of industrial products and technology steadily increased, and this also contributed to their expansion thoughout the world. Food became considerably cheaper, as well as manufacturing goods, all of which had a very positive impact on British living standards.

In 1851 the Great Exhibition was inaugurated by Queen Victoria at the Crystal Palace, itself a symbol of industrial prowess, made out of prefabricated iron and glass. Britain was the leading industrial power, producing half its own iron, coal, and cotton cloth.* From then it became known as the workshop of the world. As manufactured goods dominated world trade this had a substantial impact on British wealth. Between 1870 and 1900 economic output per head of population in Britain and Ireland rose by a staggering five hundred percent.**

No less extraordinary was the transformation of British politics and society in those decades. Dickensian Britain is associated with the grinding poverty, social injustices, and the hardship of life endured by the majority of the British population, as described by Charles Dickens in his popular novels that became world classics. Britain's population rose from eight million in 1801 to over fifteen million in 1851. A large percentage migrated to the burgeoning industrial towns in search of work and a better life than they had in their rural birthplaces. The populations of Manchester and Sheffield quadrupled in this period. That of Glasgow and Bradford grew eightfold. In 1851 Britain became the world's first urban nation. These drastic social changes and the problems suffered by the emerging proletariat was to inspire a whole generation of thinkers, social reformers, and politicians whose ideas

---

*   Landes, *The Wealth and Poverty of Nations*.
**   Ibid.

and proposals on how to improve society not only transformed Britain but eventually the rest of the world.

This was the time of Jeremy Bentham, founder of modern utilitarianism, describing utility as the sum of all pleasure that results from an action, minus the suffering of anyone involved in the action. He also advocated the greatest happiness of the greatest number to be the foundation of morals and legislation. Philanthropic businessman Robert Owen aimed to change human society and campaigned for cooperative societies, factory regulation, and trade unions. William Cobbett, the pamphleteer and farmer, campaigned for reforming parliament and against the Corn Laws because they contributed to rural poverty.

The idea of Britain in the Golden Era is synonymous with Victorian Britain. Strictly speaking this was the reign of Queen Victoria, from 1837 to 1901. Throughout her long reign Victoria made the monarchy reach the highest levels of popularity. She contributed to consolidate constitutional monarchy as a political system that provided stability. The fact that she became the matriarch of a Europe-wide royal clan played an important role spreading this model of government, but it was above all the prestige that the crown acquired in her lifetime that was to make constitutional monarchy popular both in Europe and in many parts of the world. Queen Victoria ruled strictly according to how the editor of the *Economist*, Walter Bagehot, defined a constitutional monarchy: "independent of private interests and above party politics, in which the rights and duties of the monarch were to be consulted, to encourage and to warn."

Victorian was a very powerful word in modern history, as it defined most of what had made Britain great. Victorian values on the whole could be considered somewhat contradictory, but all of them together seem to give the explanation for such an extraordinary age. Victorians believed in progress, for otherwise rapid industrialization would never have taken place. They also believed in tradition, allowing old customs to survive in spite of all the sweeping changes that took place in those decades. For example the National Trust for Places of Historic Interest was created in 1894, to preserve country houses and the heritage that was threatened by property development and industrialization. In the twentieth century it evolved as the largest heritage organization in the world.

Freedom was another sign of identity for the Victorians. They saw them-selves as a traditionally free, having never been victims of tyranny like so many European nations. This explains why Britain developed the smallest central government machinery ever found in an industrial society. This also contrib-uted to the respect for crown and parliament as symbols of the country's ancient liberties. Respectability was another sign of Victorian identity, as the British struggled for self-respect and at the same time to promote a respectable civil society. While Samuel Smiles's book *Self-Help* became a bestseller, charities proliferated more than ever. Finally, the Victorians were religious, and those who were not at least believed in the ethics of Protestantism, puritanism, self-restraint, and finally thrift.

As regards the system of government it was during the Victorian era that the House of Commons and the House of Lords at Westminster became a universally admired bastion of democracy. Although by our contemporary standards the British parliamentary system left a lot to be desired, it provided a stable government that proved capable of avoiding revolutionary upheavals while introducing important progressive reforms and defending Britain's interests in the world. This was achieved by consolidating a two-party system, alternating in power. The Tories stood for tradition and the Liberals for change. The two most well-known party leaders were Gladstone and Disraeli. They had great differences in personality and background but they both had solid Victorian values in common: Gladstone was deeply religious and believed in social progress; Disraeli craved tradition and individual freedom. The fact that Disraeli made such a remarkable political career despite the fact that he was born into a Jewish family is in itself an indication of how open British society was, as this would have been inconceivable in most of Europe at that time.

British foreign policy in the post-Napoleonic era can be summarized by Lord Palmerston's famous maxim: "We have no eternal allies and we have no perpetual enemies. Our interests are eternal and perpetual and those interests it is our duty to follow." In a career that spanned over four decades, Palmerston, who served both as foreign minister and prime minister, was to put his words into practice with considerable success. The Crimean War was a good example. This brief war was caused by British opposition to Russia, a former ally, expanding into the Crimea.

The government also showed determination to defend the private interests of individual citizens wherever they would be, as the David Pacifico
affair in 1850 showed. David Pacifico was a Jew working in Athens as a
Portuguese consul, whose house was vandalized in anti-Semitic demonstrations. The Greek government refused to compensate him, and Pacifico, who
was a naturalized British citizen, turned to the British government for help.
Palmerston reacted by sending a squadron of the Royal Navy and imposing
a blockade over Athens's port of Piraeus. The Greek government budged and
promptly agreed to settle Pacifico's claim. Palmerston justified his actions in
Parliament with one of his most brilliant speeches, which was to be known
as *Civis Romanus Sum*, in which he explained that the interests of British
citizens were to be defended at all costs throughout the world, with the same
determination as those of Roman citizens in imperial Rome. Not long after
similar principles of defending British interests led the British to send the
Royal Navy to China, leading to the Opium War.

British foreign policy from the 1860s was inspired by what was later
going to be defined as splendid isolation, based on the principle that the best
way of serving the country's interest was by avoiding any entanglement in
European alliances or conflicts, and focusing on expanding British interests
in the world. It very much contributed to the strengthening and expansion of the British Empire, which reached its apogee toward the last three
decades of the nineteenth century.

The empire, which was acquired, according to Seeley, in a fit of absence
of mind, occupied a central place in the British government from the 1870s.
The first prime minister to focus on the expansion of its frontiers was Benjamin Disraeli. He was responsible for the purchase of Suez Canal shares that
ultimately turned Egypt into a British protectorate. He reached an agreement
with the Ottoman Empire to occupy Cyprus, preventing the Russians from
doing so. He also ordered British troops to march into Afghanistan before
Russia was tempted to take over.

Disraeli was convinced that the British Empire was a force of good,
and he was determined to make it popular among the British public. His
initiative of granting Queen Victoria the title of Empress of India provoked
considerable controversy in Britain, as many people brought up under austere

Victorian morality considered it an unnecessary extravagance inspired by exotic myths. But the British prime minister justified it in this way: the Empress-Queen who governed over the greatest empire on earth would have the same imperial rank as the Russian czar, the German kaiser or the emperor of Austria. Disraeli, for whom the queen felt great affection, succeeded with this aim, as from then the British monarchy became fully aware of its imperial duties. To visit India and the main possessions of the empire became an obligation for Victoria's heirs.

Imperialism became an increasingly popular cause, as Disraeli could appreciate, but it was also a risky one, for the difficulties in the South African war and in Afghanistan led the Conservatives to electoral defeat in 1880. But if territorial conquests could have a high price from the electoral point of view, retreats were even worse, as Prime Minister Gladstone was to see. The Liberal prime minister, who was always a reluctant imperialist, was not willing to continue with his rivals' expansionist policy on returning to power. But his decision to withdraw from the Sudan in 1885 when it was attacked by the khedive of Egypt, and abandon General Charles Gordon to his fate, was considered by British public opinion an insult to national pride, and it precipitated the end of Gladstone's government.

The organization and administration of such a large and diverse empire occupied a central place in British politics. It acquired a solid and well-coordinated administrative structure by which a small elite of specially trained civil servants kept law and order in colonies throughout the world. Several generations of British professional elites educated in the top public schools were imbibed the imperial ethos and then developed a passion for it. Officers from Sandhurst Academy, from Gordon to Churchill, were well aware that postings in colonial regiments offered the opportunity for quick promotion and adventure. Oxford and Cambridge graduates often joined the India Office or other colonial departments with the aim of being posted in an empire that was full of attractive places that offered British functionaries more money, comfort, and above all a much more interesting life. The most important post in each colony was that of governor, to which the empire's most ambitious servants aspired. Especially relevant was the post of viceroy of India, created in 1858 to replace that of the governor general. It was given a grandiose name in order to confer it the rank of crown's representative to the person who would have to deal with the sovereigns of the Indian states.

The British government was well aware of the differences between ruling over territories that were inhabited by peoples who were considered backward and those populated by a majority of European settlers. The latter became more conflictive, for they demanded the same right as white settlers to govern themselves. This led to the creation of the dominion status, which allowed self-government in everything except foreign and defense policy. The first colony to become a dominion was Canada in 1867, followed by Australia, New Zealand, and South Africa in the early twentieth century. In a visit to Australia in 1884 Lord Rosebery described the empire as a Commonwealth of Nations. Shortly afterward, in an imperial congress in 1887, the term began to be used mainly in reference to the so-called white dominions. This formula by which several territories of the empire became practically independent nations allowed the life of the British Empire to retain its popularity among many subjects, and it prolonged its life considerably. It allowed the governing elites to spread democracy, the rule of law, the market economy, and all that they considered positive from the motherland.

In 1885 the radical liberal politician Joseph Chamberlain acceded to join the conservative government, and requested a post that had been generally neglected until then: that of colonial secretary, as he believed that nothing was more important in British politics than the administration of the largest empire in the world. He was well aware that he was living in an era of imperialism. "The day of small nations has passed away; the day of empires has come," he stated on one occasion, and of course he was absolutely convinced that the British Empire had a very special role to play among all other empires as a force of good: "It is not enough to occupy great spaces of the world unless you can make the best of them."* For this reason he believed that the empire should be remodeled as a federation of Anglo-Saxon nations, peacefully trading with each other under British principles. But Chamberlain never lost an opportunity to expand this empire into Africa.

---

*   Churchill, *History of the English-Speaking Peoples.*

Toward the end of the nineteenth century, the empire became a very popular cause, and this explains why it continued expanding. Lord Salisbury, the most influential statesman in the last fifteen years of the Victorian era, defined himself as a reluctant imperialist. But even so, on the three occasions in which he was prime minister Britain consolidated a new colonial empire in Africa. As Salisbury commented to the French ambassador in relation to his African policy: "l'appetit vient en mangeant" (appetite comes from eating). Defending the British Empire implied on most occasions expanding it. Lord Salisbury complained that his advisers would have liked to annex the Moon in order to prevent its being appropriated by the planet Mars. This led Britain to rule over a quarter of the earth and around 450 million people—a fifth of the world's population was under British sovereignty. Never had an empire ruled over so many people.

As all first-world powers in history, Britain in its golden era was both envied and admired. Because of its transport and communication technology, and the global nature of its empire, it enjoyed more external influence than any other empire in history. It was seen as a leader in this European civilization that dominated the world.

The British were also seen as a kind of aristocracy of the world, which explains why the British way of life was admired and imitated beyond the confines of its empire. The British gentleman, with his sartorial habits and his code of conduct according to the highest standards, inspired educated men in the whole of the Western world and beyond it. The middle and upper classes throughout the world adopted habits like drinking tea and practicing British sports, while the splendor of stately English homes was reproduced by the lucky few who were rich enough to imitate it.

All this had a great impact on how the British perceived themselves, and largely contributed to the development of a sense of superiority. "To be English is to win the first ticket in the lottery of life," stated the imperialist businessman Cecil Rhodes. "I believe that the British race is the greatest of the governing races that the world has ever seen," said Joseph Chamberlain. Self-confidence and pride in their civilization contributed to make the British propagate their interests more than ever at this time.

Another great protagonist in this era of European splendor was undoubtedly France. In spite of its defeat in 1815 and all the subsequent political turbulence, the French in the nineteenth century were also at the height of their powers and played a significant contribution propagating European influence through the world.

The French Revolution bequeathed a very important political legacy that has shaped politics in Europe, the West, and eventually the rest of the world: the notion of "right" and "left" as a way of classifying ideologies in politics was invented in France. After 1789 the members of the National Assembly were divided into two groups, those who supported the revolution, known as "the party of movement" sat on the left and those supporting the king, known as "the party of order," sat on the right. From then to be on the left implied believing in the principles of the Enlightenment that inspired the French Revolution, and the subsequent revolutions that broke out in Europe.

Left-wingers believed that all men were equal and it should be the role of the government to ensure that this equality of opportunities or equality before the law was strictly applied. They also believed that the eradication of poverty and oppression was implicit in a society where wealth and power was in the hands of a privileged minority, and in order to do this it was the right of the state to distribute wealth by means of taxation, or even expropriation of private property. The left considered that science and technology were useful weapons for achieving progress, and that neither religious beliefs nor ancient traditions should stand in the way of bringing about genuine progress in society.

Right-wingers on the other hand did not believe in equality, as nature and society made human beings very different. For this reason maintaining the hierarchical structure of society, with the crown and the nobility at the top, and the church as representative of God and repository of ancient wisdom, ought to be preserved. Law, order, and tradition ought to be upheld before any change. Private property should also be respected. Poverty could be alleviated in a compassionate society.

The monarchy of Louis Philippe, from 1830 to 1848, constituted a brave attempt to incorporate ideas of the left into an institution that was conservative by nature. The regime that replaced it, that of Napoleon III, claimed to be loyal to the legacy of the French Revolution. The Third Republic, the most successful and lasting French regime of the nineteenth century, consolidated the republic in France by transforming the president of the republic into an elected president, who retained all the pomp and grandeur of the old monarchy. It was a model of a republic that was to inspire many republican regimes in the world.

What all nineteenth-century regimes had in common was their determination to expand French influence throughout the world. The colonization of Algeria, which began in 1830, was followed by more daring conquests.

In 1848 Napoleon's nephew, Louis Napoleon Bonaparte, was elected president of the French republic and four years later he proclaimed himself emperor under the title of Napoleon III. As a good Bonaparte he was convinced that France represented the highest level of civilization and ought to be expanded, and since it was no longer possible to do it within the frontiers of Europe, as his uncle had done, his aim was to do it overseas.

While he was in power, from 1848 to 1870, French overseas territories increased in three continents: Asia, with the occupation of Indochina; Oceania, with the acquisition of Polynesia; and Madagascar in Africa. Napoleon even attempted to build a new empire in Mexico and fill the vacuum left by Spain. In 1861 Mexican president Benito Juárez failed to continue paying a loan given by France, and Napoleon III used this affront to French interests as an excuse to invade Mexico. He then chose a member of the Habsburg family, Maximilian I, to be proclaimed emperor of Mexico. The French Mexican adventure was brief, and Emperor Maximilian paid the highest price by being executed by Mexican rebels in 1870. It was in this decade that the term Latin America was introduced by the French on refereeing to the group of nations that had been colonized by the Spanish and the Portuguese, instead of Iberian America or Spanish America. The term eventually started to be used by all Americans and was gradually adopted in the rest of the world.

Another international symbol of French prestige was the Suez Canal. This prodigious work of engineering by which the Mediterranean was linked to the Red Sea was built by the French engineer Ferdinand de Lesseps and inaugurated in 1869. He also attempted to repeat this feat by connecting the Pacific and Atlantic Oceans through the Panama Canal, which began construction in 1879.

The French Second Empire collapsed in 1870 when German troops defeated France in a dispute over the possession of the Alsace-Lorraine region.

It was replaced by the French Third Republic, which officially had less expansionist zeal. Paradoxically, it was under this new regime when French power in the world experienced the most dramatic growth.

Between 1871 and 1900 over 3.5 million square miles were added to the French Empire.* Apart from possessing great expanses of land, the French republic built naval bases from Saigon to Dakar. It made the empire an essential aspect of the French economy. The colonies became a new market for exports and also provided raw materials for the expanding industries. In Algeria, arable land cultivated by farmers increased three-fold from 1830 to the late nineteenth century, and a similar process of agricultural growth took place in Tunisia and Morocco. Loans granted by Parisian banks to French settlers in North Africa contributed to the modernization of agricultural techniques and the improvement of their efficiency. As a result of this from the early twentieth century, this helped make this area emerge from the twentieth century as one of the main providers of agricultural products. Exports also grew steadily. French settlers in Indochina transformed this colony into one of the main producers of rice and rubber.

Apart from the wealth created by the colonial empire, France also benefitted from the business networks created by its companies. During the last decades of the nineteenth century, French banks and financial institutions rapidly expanded, and after London, Paris emerged as the second financial center in Europe, with the largest volume of international businesses.

During the time of Napoleon III a colonial administration was set up, which increased its responsibilities as the empire expanded. In 1858 the Colonies Ministry was set up as well as the Algeria Ministry, which received special treatment. During his visit to Algeria in 1860 Napoleon III declared that he was as much emperor of the Arabs in Algeria as of the French. During this time the French state also granted the right of every citizen in the colonies to obtain French nationality, as long as he spoke French and gave up customs that were illegal in France, like polygamy. The right to trade with third countries was also recognized, clearly contradicting the predominant

---

* Denise Bouche, *Histoire de la Colonisation Française* (Paris: Fayard, 1991).

idea in the colonial era that colonies could only export their products to other territories of the empire to which they belonged.*

French colonization from the time of the Second Republic was very much influenced by the ideology of the philosopher Henri de Saint-Simon, which was to be known as utopian socialism. Saint-Simon advocated industrialization based on social needs and a larger fraternity by which the richer would subsidize the rest. In this sense Saint-Simonian thought justified colonization with the aim of helping the most backward people. Inspired by Saint-Simon, and also out of sympathy toward the Arab world, some personages promoted important projects in Algeria and North Africa, like entrepreneur Prosper Enfantin, who proposed the idea of building the Suez Canal.

The colonies and the colonial administration were to be one of the most enduring legacies of both the French Empire and the Third Republic. In the early stages of the French republic colonization was an unpopular cause, particularly among the most conservative sectors for whom the priority should be to recover from the defeat against Germany and get ready for future revenge. For this reason they considered that economic growth and modernization of the army should be the priority, and colonization was seen as a useless distraction that would impoverish the French state. As the right-wing senator the Duke of Broglie stated in 1884, "colonies weaken the nations that found them, far from strengthening them, they absorb their forces."**

On the other hand, colonialism was popular among liberal and left-wing politicians who believed that the most noble causes could be promoted by acquiring colonies. Republican politician Jules Ferry was an enthusiastic supporter of colonial expansion. On becoming prime minister in 1880, he embarked on a new colonial policy with the conquest of Tunisia, which laid the foundations of the vast empire in Africa. In 1885 Jules Ferry explained in the French Assembly the reasons for promoting colonization. "It must be openly said that the superior races have a right before the inferior ones. There

---

*   Bouche, *Histoire de la Colonisation Française*
**   Ibid.

is a right for the superior races because there is also a duty toward them. They have the right to civilize inferior races."[*]

The Colonial Party, a group of prominent figures created in the early 1870s to promote colonization argued that France, as the country of the rights of men, had the opportunity to promote these through their colonies. According to them French presence in other continents could contribute to the emancipation of oppressed peoples, combat primitivism, and allow them to live under the principles of liberty, equality, and fraternity, like the French.

France enjoyed a golden era from the cultural point of view in the last decades of the nineteenth century and early twentieth century. For very good reasons this era was to be known as the Belle Epoque. The greatest symbol of those years of grandeur and refinement in France was Paris. The city that inspired the works of nineteenth-century authors like Victor Hugo or Émile Zola, was transformed during the regime of Napoleon III. The famous builder Baron Haussmann designed new districts with luxurious buildings and great avenues. Its modernist style was to be imitated by many cities in the world.

Paris as the City of Light was showcased by the great international exhibitions of 1889 and 1900. The 1889 exhibition had been timed to coincide with the centenary of the French Revolution. It aimed to epitomize progress in science and technology, and for this reason the high point was the Eiffel Tower, an extraordinary structure built with the most advanced engineering techniques, which became a singular French icon. Quite appropriately it was compared with Denis Diderot's *Encyclopédie*—based on intellectual rigor, manual labor, and mobilized energies.

The 1900 exhibition aimed at showing Paris as the capital of the civilized world, the leading edge of modern civilization, and highlighting its civilizing mission in the world. "Paris is the world, the rest of the earth is nothing but its suburbs," wrote Pierre de Marivaux in the eighteenth century. This seemed particularly the case as the City of Light entered the twentieth century. Paris during the Belle Epoque was consolidated as the capital of the world, a title that no other city has enjoyed.

---

[*]   Bouche, *Histoire de la Colonisation Française.*

The most imposing rival to these two European imperial nations emerged in 1871: Germany. It had merely been a geographic expression until it culminated its process of unification in 1871. This was a turning point in the era of imperialism for its new sovereign Kaiser Wilhelm I, who did not just proclaim Germany as a new unified nation but rather as a new empire, the First Reich.

The proclamation of the German First Reich was like the appearance of a giant who, due to his size alone, intimidated those around him. Germany was huge in many aspects. In 1871 it had a population of forty million that would reach sixty-eight million in 1914, becoming the most populous country in Europe, after Russia. Its citizens also had a high level of education, an essential aspect to explain the speed with which the country's economy grew and its influence in the world expanded. Its economic power was mainly based on the fact that it had been rapidly industrializing. Its metal production multiplied twelve times from 1870 to 1914, to the point of overtaking Britain, France, and Russia combined. Coal production increased five times in thirty years, its fabrication of manufactures was multiplied by four, and its exports tripled.* Krupp, the famous family business that specialized in metal and weapons production, emerged in the early twentieth century as the biggest firm in Europe. Other great German firms like Siemens and AEG were also created at that time. With these extraordinary figures, Germany managed in 1914 to become the leading industrial power in Europe.

German chancellor Otto von Bismarck, who governed a unified Germany for the first twenty years of its existence, was the most influential statesman of his time. In a famous speech in 1851 he had proclaimed that Germany would be unified by blood and iron, and after achieving his aim he became a symbol of nationalism, a major driving force in the nineteenth century. Despite the fact that Bismack had successfully waged war against all powers that opposed unification, once this was achieved, to the relief of his European counterparts, he declared Germany a satiated power.

---

* Paul Kennedy, *The Rise and Fall of the Great Powers: Economic Change and Military Conflict from 1500 to 2000* (New York: Fontana Press, 1989).

Many Germans did not share Bismarck's views and thought that Germany had the historic opportunity to emerge as the first world power and should therefore not let the opportunity pass to expand its power and impose it over the rest of Europe and the world. The problem for the Germans was that this strategy would lead to war, and expanding into other continents was not so easy, as a good part of them had already been colonized by the great powers.

The pressure exerted by the German colonial lobby, and the part of the public that demanded that Germany have a larger presence in the world, made Bismarck—until then reluctant to acquire colonies—radically alter his policy. For this reason, in 1885 he ordered the founding of colonies in Africa, and later some enclaves in the Pacific. But this colonial empire, modest for a country as powerful as Germany, did not at all satisfy Germany's wish for power. One of Kaiser Wilhelm II's constant laments was that Germany had arrived late in colonization and that the most desirable territories were already occupied.

Kaiser Wilhelm II was much more ambitious than Wilhelm I, and also much less prudent. He thought that Germany had a great mission to perform beyond the narrow limits of old Europe. In 1898, an intensive naval construction plan was launched, by which the German navy, which was the sixth-largest in the world, was going to be transformed within a few years into the second in the world. The person responsible for it, Admiral Alfred von Tirpitz, had argued that overseas conquests were as irresistible as natural law. The foreign minister Bernhard von Bülow declared in 1899 that "we cannot allow any foreign power tell us that the world was already distributed."

Expansionism and the desire for world supremacy that could be felt in the upper echelons of power was not only the result of Germany's economic and industrial might. German currents of thought also seemed to have been encouraging it for some time.

In 1832 the Prussian general and military theorist Carl von Clausewitz published his magnum opus, *On War*. In this work he reflected on the art of war and its relation to politics, and his general thesis was summarized in the aphorism that war is not simply a political act but also a political instrument, a continuation of the same act by other means. This book was generally interpreted as an apology for war without ethical questioning of whether it was right to wage it, nor a moral criticism of the price to be paid for it in terms of suffering or loss of human lives. *On War* was critically acclaimed not only in Germany but in many other countries for over a century. Both Vladimir Lenin and Mao Zedong admired Clausewitz's work, as it provided guidance on how to promote political aims through war. Prussian militarism, so influential in the rise of Germany as the most powerful nation in Europe, was very much influenced by Clausewitz's theories.

German thought in the nineteenth century produced great figures who were going to exert a very influential role throughout Europe. Especially influential was the philosopher Friederich Nietzsche, whose work leads to an understanding of the mentality that prevailed not only in Germany but throughout Europe, in order to justify imperialism. In one of his great works, *Thus Spoke Zarathustra*, Nietsche explains that humanity is divided into slaves and masters, with different moral attitudes. Masters have great faith in themselves and admire all superior forces; everything that leads to strength and dominance. Slaves, on the contrary, have virtues that are typical of those who are weak and oppressed, like meekness and obedience. Nietzsche, who also opined that God is dead, advocated the need to replace traditional Christian values that are appropriate for slaves by new ones that will allow the emergence of what he described as an "Übermensch"—a superman.

Many of those who sought supremacy and the right to govern over weak peoples would be identified with Nietzsche's theory of the superhuman. But it would be unfair to summarize German thought at a time when it rose to world supremacy with theories about war or superhumans. Traces of German genius can be perceived in most manifestations of European thought and culture. German philosophy in the nineteenth century also produced other influential philosophers like Hegel and Schopenhauer.

Romanticism, one of the most important cultural movements in the early nineteenth century, taught us how to appreciate the beauty of nature and exalted the value of emotion over reason. It would not have been the same without the literary genius of Wolfgang von Goethe. The leading composers of classical music, which had been Austrian in the eighteenth century thanks to Mozart, became German in the next with Beethoven, Brahms, and Wagner.

Italy emerged as a united nation after undergoing a similar process of unification as Germany. In 1871 Italy proclaimed itself unified under Rome. The Risorgimento movement, aiming for a rebirth of Italy, was one of the great romantic causes of the nineteenth century. It brought together very diverse Italian personalities. Guiseppe Garibaldi, a romantic figure who believed in revolutionary nationalism, and Guiseppe Mazzini, who aimed to transform Italy into a democratic republic. But it was a more Machiavellian figure, the prime minister of Piedmont Sardinia, Count Cavour, who led the final stages of unification. Cavour, as the father of modern Italy, defined it as a constitutional monarchy under King Victor Emmanuel II of Savoy.

The main victim of both the German and the Italian unification was Austria. A substantial part of the Habsburg Empire both on the north and the south was lost to the new German and Italian nations. Austrian authority in Europe was also considerably diminished as Prince Metternich had ultimately failed to prevent the expansion of nationalism and liberalism that posed such a challenge to the interests of this old empire. On the other hand while it lost power to these two new nations, Austria benefitted from the decline of the Ottoman Empire, and managed to expand into the frontiers of present-day Greece. In this way it consolidated an empire at the heart of Europe, which constituted a mosaic of nations and cultures, and despite the difficulties of governing it, the Habsburgs managed to keep it united until 1918. Austria was thus a pretty unique case among the European empires as it was the only one that did not have territorial aspirations beyond the old continent.

From the end of the Napoleonic wars Russia emerged as another great European power. The dream of Peter the Great finally came true. After four centuries of expansion the huge Russian Empire also emerged as a demographic giant, which in 1890 reached 116,000,000 inhabitants. It had the largest army, of over one million soldiers, and it also had five million people in the reserves. As long as size and population were determining factors in international relations Russia was to play an important role.

As a result of its decisive contribution to the defeat against Napoleon, Russia's position toward the rest of the powers was going to be strengthened. For good reasons Czar Alexander I was described in 1815 as Europe's savior. The czar took advantage of his strong position in the Congress of Vienna to consolidate Russian power in Poland. Despite the fact that he already ruled over a sixth of the earth, his successors made several attempts to expand their frontiers even further.

Russia put special emphasis on dominating an empire in decline, like the Ottoman. In 1853 a conflict broke out between France and Russia about which of the two should be the guardian of the sacred places in Jerusalem that were part of the Ottoman Empire. Czar Nicholas I decided to back this claim by mobilizing its troops over Ottoman territory. France and Britain as well refused to allow this, and the Crimean War broke out, in which Russia suffered a humiliating defeat. Nevertheless, friction from Russia's territorial aspirations continued.

The Russian Empire benefitted more than any other from two of the great inventions of the nineteenth century: the train and the telegraph, which improved communication in the vast empire and allowed much closer control from Moscow. Nevertheless, these were the only two major advances of the Industrial Revolution that reached Russia, for the industrialization of czarist Russia was practically nonexistent, and unlike the other great European powers it remained an agricultural and underdeveloped nation.

The Russian elite led by the czar considered themselves an essential part of the European world, and Russians made great contributions to Western culture in the nineteenth century. Tchaikovsky's music and the literary works of Tolstoy, Dostoyevsky, and Turgenev, among other talents, impressed the entire Western world. In spite of this Russia proved incapable of introducing the ideas that made Europe evolve in the nineteenth century. Russian thought was divided into two factions: Westerners defended the idea of opening the country to European ideas, while Slavophiles who defended the authenticity of the Russian without foreign imitations. While the Westerners dominated the world of culture, their power in the political sphere was scarce. Despite the fact that some czars, like Alexander II, had a more liberal attitude, generally all of them stubbornly defended the principle of autocracy, with disastrous consequences for the country.

While in the rest of Europe imperialism was justified as synonymous with prosperity and more efficient ways of governing, it did not happen the same way with Russia, whose main signs of identity were autocracy and stagnation.

While emerging powers focused on expanding and acquiring new possessions, declining powers like Holland, Portugal, and Spain strived to keep what was left of their great glorious past. Holland still benefitted from trading, which had brought it so much wealth since the sixteenth century. In the late nineteenth century it also joined the Industrial Revolution, with success. On the other hand Spain and Portugal in particular missed the Industrial Revolution that was spreading across Western Europe. No country lived with such an intense struggle between the forces of liberalism and traditionalism as Spain in the nineteenth century, which on the whole was a disastrous century for its interests. Nevertheless, both Spain and Portugal kept considerable influence over former possessions, and both clung to what remained of their empires, which allowed them to be described as imperial powers.

The nineteenth century clearly had its winners and losers, its great and declining powers, and those nations that gained power at the cost of others. But there are several factors that explain why this extraordinary age took place in Europe and why the peoples of Europe on the whole made it possible and enjoyed its benefits.

Finance played a very important role in this golden era. Without it the Industrial Revolution would not have made so much progress, nor would Europeans have been able to project their influence so far.

Bankers and entrepreneurs were aware that without money, imperialism in its economic, political, and military dimension could not take place. Financial institutions built networks throughout the world and, backed by European laws and regulations, established the rules by which they were to operate. Consequently, the market economy experienced an unprecedented expansion, and by the end of the nineteenth century the whole planet was unified under a single commercial system.

The best example of the extraordinary capacity acquired by European banks to enrich themselves by business ventures throughout the world was that of the Rothschild family. The Rothschilds first rose to prominence due to their pan-European vision. In the mid–eighteenth century a Jewish pawnbroker known as Mayer Rothschild decided to expand his banking business in Frankfurt, and he sent each of his four sons to a major European city: Vienna, London, Paris, and Naples. The family gained preeminence in the bullion trade by relying on a network of agents and couriers that allowed them to receive information in all these cities well ahead of their peers.* One of the most famous anecdotes of the Rothschilds, was that on June 19, 1814, Nathan Rothschild made a record killing in the stock market after hiring a special yacht that brought him news of Waterloo several hours in advance of his rivals.

The Rothschilds then expanded their business interests into a wide range of fields, from financial services to real estate and mining. Most important of all, toward the end of the eighteenth century governments in several European countries were increasingly asking the Rothschilds for loans in order to finance their peacetime ventures, as well as their wars. As a result not only did they possess the largest private fortune in the world in the early nineteenth century, but they became powerful to the extent of determining whether there would be war or peace in Europe. No one has described the Rothschild power better than Lord Byron in his poem "Don Juan," in which he referred to the banker as "the real owner of Europe," who controls the balance of power and whose loans could create nations or topple thrones.

Having created a model of international banking, the Rothschilds were then in an ideal position to foster their most ambitious projects, mainly from London, but also from their other bases in Europe. The Rothschilds financed the construction of the Suez Canal and the most ambitious adventures of the British magnate in South Africa, Cecil Rhodes, from the creation of De Beers Company to the founding of Rhodesia.**

London emerged as the world's financial center in the early nineteenth century, or even more importantly what the great French scholar Fernand Braudel defined as a globally hegemonic city—a status that no other city enjoyed until New York took over in the 1920s. Being the capital of the largest empire and the first industrial nation were certainly very important assets. The fact that the most important banks had their main headquarters at that square mile that became known as the City of London, as well as one

---

* Niall Ferguson, *The House of Rothschild, Money Prophets, 1798–1848* (London: Penguin, 1999).
** Ibid.

of the oldest stock exchanges, played an important role in its unprecedented expansion and explains why British capital went everywhere from the mid–nineteenth century. In 1860 Britain ranked as the largest trading nation. British foreign trade tripled between 1870 and 1914.*

Although London's financial hegemony could not be challenged, cities like Paris, Frankfurt, Amsterdam, or Milan also played an important role in the internationalization of the European economy. European capital was not only financing projects within continental Europe and in the imperial world but far beyond it. The United States was one of the main beneficiaries in the first half of the century. It also helped many emerging economies. The best example is Argentina, where European investment increased tenfold between 1870 and 1900, helping transform this country into one of the richest in the world.** Other nations, like Brazil or Mexico, also reaped great benefits. At the other end of the world Japan was another example of a country transformed by European capital. The rebirth of Mediterranean trade propelled by European capital explains the meteoric rise of a city like Beirut. The export of capital implied the creation of modern institutions such as banks, insurance companies, and the stock exchanges all around the world. In this way European entrepreneurs and financial institutions managed to make the market economy expand throughout the entire world.

As a result of European promotion of the market economy, between 1840 and 1913 the value of world trade increased tenfold. Such an extraordinary figure would only be exceeded in the postwar years, from 1948 to 1971. It is also worth noticing that intercontinental trade between North and South constituted a higher proportion of global trade in this era than in the late twentieth century when globalization was at its highest point.

The second factor, perhaps the most important to explain European hegemonic power in this era was technology. The steamship and the railway are the two major symbols of the Industrial Revolution. One of the reasons why the Industrial Revolution had such extraordinary impact was because it

---

* James Foreman-Peck, *A History of the World Economy: International Economic Relations Since 1850* (New York: Barnes & Noble, 1983).
** Ibid.

led to a transport revolution. Until the invention of the locomotive and the emergence of the railway line the key to create global empires was maritime transport, but the train offered great possibilities of terrestrial expansion and control over vast territories that could not be reached by sea. As we have seen, Britain not only built railway lines through its empire but it also obtained great profits exporting railway technology to diverse countries, from the United States to Egypt.

A terrestrial empire like Russia particularly benefitted from the railway as it gained an internal cohesion inconceivable until then. The Trans-Caspian Railway, inaugurated in 1881, put an end to isolation in this remote and conflictive area. In 1891 Russia embarked on an even more difficult undertaking, that of the famous Trans-Siberian Railway, which was not finished until 1904. This constituted one of the most ambitious works in the history of railroads; in consequence Moscow was connected with Vladivostok, Europe, and Asia, which had been separated by geography throughout history, but were finally connected by a means of transport. From then it was possible to travel from Moscow to the Pacific coast in seven days, and the commercial and population exchanges between the European and Asian part of Russia steadily increased.

In the case of the French Empire in Africa, the train helped control such vast territories. Germany also used the railway to foster its interests abroad. The Berlin-Baghdad railway project was launched in 1903, a vast undertaking by which the Germans hoped to have a direct link with Bagdad, where they planned to establish a port. This railway, which was to go across a substantial part of the Ottoman Empire, was also to serve Turkish interests. This project very much worried Britain and other imperial rivals, but it was so ambitious that it would not be finished until 1940.

The train transformed European society and gradually the rest of the world. Connecting cities by a fast and relatively secure means of transport changed the way nations were organized, altering people's lives in both urban and rural settings. Trains made a very important contribution to the chronometric standardization of society. They functioned according to a strict timetable, and their efficiency was judged by their ability to depart and reach their destination on time. For this reason, punctuality became an essential requirement for all those using trains, and this was mainly made possible by another great nineteenth-century European invention: the pocket watch. The mechanical clock had been organizing communities in Europe since the fifteenth century, but it was the pocket watch that was to order and discipline daily lives by constantly reminding them how time was passing. The main pocket watch producer was initially Switzerland, followed by France and Britain. It was initially a symbol of social status, but it became progressively democratized through the nineteenth century. By the early twentieth century any person of certain means that claimed to be organized would carry one. The United States, another main producer, also contributed to its propagation throughout the Americas. It became an emblem of Western civilization and one of its most successful exports, and by the end of the nineteenth century it had been adopted by other cultures.

The telegraph constituted the first form of telecommunications, allowing people to transmit messages that were received almost instantly. Several European scientists from Alessandro Volta to Hans Christian Ørsted contributed to this invention until its emergence in the nineteenth century. The first commercial electrical telegraph was patented by William Cooke and Charles Wheatstone in 1837, and installed between Euston and Camden Town in London. Electrical overland telegraphy came into use in 1844 and the first underwater cable was laid across the English Channel in 1851. The major breakthrough came in 1866 when the first transatlantic telegraph line was established. Three decades later the whole world was connected by the telegraph.

This invention has been described as the Internet of the Victorian era, an exaggerated remark, as it did not change the life of ordinary citizens in the way that the Internet did in the twenty-first century. But it was certainly a very important milestone in the history of global communications. International relations and political administration were greatly affected by it. The power and autonomy of an army general commanding troops overseas, or an ambassador representing a state, was significantly diminished as a result of this new technology that allowed them to transmit news to their government instantly and also receive orders. But the capacity of European governments to control overseas possessions greatly increased as a result of the telegraph, and European expansion in all its dimensions was significantly benefitted by it.

The expansion of the telegraph implied the titanic undertaking of cabling the world. The total length of submarine cables grew from 4,400 kilometers in 1865 to 406,300 kilometers in 1903. This telegraph age lasted until the emergence of long distance telephony. The telegraph laid the foundations of two life-changing inventions. The telephone was patented in 1876 by the Scottish inventor Alexander Graham Bell. The electric incandescent bulb was also patented at that time but this time by an American, Thomas Edison, who was originally a telegraph employee. Edison also developed a method of recording sound: the phonograph.

The telegraph made it possible to be instantly informed about what was happening at another point of the world. This first person to become aware of the business potential of this invention was Paul Julius Reuter, a German entrepreneur. Reuter opened the first news agency in London in 1851, selling last-minute news provided by the telegraph. Initially it simply covered commercial news and served the banks and brokerage firms that profited from it. But soon newspapers subscribed to its services and Reuters started providing all sorts of news. As the telegraph expanded through the world Reuters opened new branches. Reuters was the first to report Abraham Lincoln's assassination and by the 1860s it had become the most important news agency in the world, radically changing the press. From then on newspapers started competing against each other in order to publish on a daily basis the most recent news throughout the world, and every good newspaper felt that it had the responsibility to print news not only about what was happening locally and nationally, but also internationally. This also implied relying not only on news agencies like Reuters but also sending journalists abroad wherever the news was taking place. This led to the birth of the foreign correspondent. The era of the global news had begun.

A great contemporary invention of the telegraph was photography. The age of photography dawned in 1838 when the French artist Louis Daguerre invented the daguerreotype, the first photographic process. Few inventions have had such an impact on the history of private lives and people's feelings as photography. Individual or family portraits had been a privilege of the wealthy minority, but the photograph made them affordable to the average citizen. Photography made people acquire a much better perception of the reality surrounding them. Until then they had seen it through the artists' subjective perception of what they were painting, whether it was a person or a landscape, but a camera objectively reflected what it had in front of it. Photography broadened peoples' knowledge of the world in an extraordinary way, which is why it became an essential component of journalism or publishing. Photographs allowed people to see what other countries looked like and become familiar with great cities or traditional exotic customs without traveling. Apart from being a great eye-opener photography also allowed people to have a better perception of the injustices surrounding them, whether these were living conditions in a slum area or children begging on the streets. The horrors of war had been traditionally transmitted to civilians through surviving ex-combatants, but the photograph allowed them to perceive their crude reality. The first great conflict for which there was photographic evidence was the American Civil War.

Few decades after the photograph came its corollary, cinema. In 1895 two French inventors, the brothers Auguste and Louis Lumière patented the cinematograph, a motion picture film camera. Shortly after the first motion picture, *Sortie de l'usine* (*Exit from the factory*) was shown in Paris. In this way the seventh art was born, an entertainment that would fascinate and enrich people's lives to an extraordinary degree. It was in the United States in the 1920s that film was transformed into an industry that reached the masses throughout the world, but long before that several nations in Europe discovered the potential by the end of the nineteenth century. The first major event to be filmed was Queen Victoria's Diamond Jubilee.

Another European nineteenth-century invention, without which our contemporary world cannot be understood, is the internal combustion engine. From the eighteenth century several European scientists made contributions to this invention, but it is Germany that deserves the credit for putting it to practical use. In 1885 Gottlieb Daimler patented a precursor of the modern gasoline engine, and Karl Benz patented the *motorwagen*, the first commercial automobile. Soon they worked on the creation of two major brands, Mercedes and Daimler. Shortly thereafter French industrialists became attracted by the prospects of this new industry. In the early twentieth century Schneider, Peugeot, Michelin, and Renault were market leaders in the automobile industry. Until the appearance of American entrepreneur Henry Ford in the 1920s France was the largest producer in the world. In the early twentieth century Britain emerged as a major competitor with brands like Rolls-Royce, Bentley, Austin, and Rover.

Scientific and technological advance was also going to have an impact on the weapons industry, helping increase European military superiority even more. The machine gun, which allowed high rate of fire and mechanical loading, constituted the most significant advance in lethality. The first model, the Maxim gun, was patented by the British-born American inventor Hiram Maxim in 1883. It could fire as many as six hundred shots per minute.

The Maxim gun was going to be most associated with the British imperial expansion, particularly in Africa. It was first used by colonial forces in the first Matabele War in Rhodesia. In the battle of Shangari, seven hundred British soldiers managed to fight off a surprise attack of over five thousand Matabele warriors. With just four Maxim guns, the British killed over 1,500 enemy fighters while suffering only four casualties. Such massacres of indigenous forces were going to be repeated in several colonial wars wherever native peoples decided to openly confront Europeans. The Maxim gun came to demonstrate that in Africa or anywhere else in the colonial world, if there was a need to use military force, Europe would always have a winning hand. As Anglo-French poet Hilaire Belloc wrote some years later:

Whatever happens, we have got the Maxim gun, and they have not.

In 1896 an improved version of the Maxim gun was launched after the British Vickers Company bought Maxim: the Vickers machine gun. This was only the beginning of the increasingly destructive capacity of modern weaponry. Initially it benefitted European hegemony but not in the long run, as we shall later see.

Politics played a very important role in this golden era. Europe was shaping the world according to its political priorities, political systems were exported with considerable success, and the ideas and political beliefs that marked the nineteenth century exerted universal appeal. It was then that democracy began to be regarded in the Western world as the best system of government, or at least according to Winston Churchill's dictum, the worst form of government except for all others.

Britain became the best exporter of democracy. Its two-party bicameral system had already inspired the United States, which emerged after its civil war as a bastion of democracy in the world. From the 1870s Britain spread democracy to the white dominions of its empire. Canada, Australia, and New Zealand became solid democracies from the moment they were given quasi-independent status within the British Empire. South Africa also became a democracy, although only for the whites, and its controversial segregation of its nonwhite population prevented its proper development. The myth that democracy worked better in English-speaking countries, or those originally populated by Anglo-Saxons, was going to propagate in the twentieth century partly due to the political stability that countries like Canada, Australia, or New Zealand enjoyed, as well as the United States.

British politics and its political institutions were also a source of inspiration for many countries throughout Europe. Carefully planned marriages among Queen Victoria's numerous offspring contributed to the spread of constitutional monarchy in Europe, from Belgium to Bulgaria and Greece. The fact that the British model of democracy provided such stability and success partly explains why constitutional monarchy was adopted by both Germany and Italy after their unification. It also explains why this was also the model for Spain and Portugal after so much political turbulence. On the other hand, after several frustrated attempts at consolidating a constitutional monarchy, France emerged as an ideal example of a democratic republic. The only European nation where democracy made virtually no progress was in Russia, where the czars stubbornly insisted on ruling as autocrats, and in this way condemning themselves to a tragic end.

But what kind of democracy did Europeans enjoy? Behind the façade of a bicameral party system legislating according to a constitution, and elections taking place to choose a government, it was the extent to which citizens had a vote that determined whether democracy was genuine or not.

The principle of universal male suffrage was proclaimed during the French Revolution but it was not implemented. It was also included in the U.S. Constitution, although it did not specify who had the vote, and until the American Civil War it was restricted to white citizens.

Greece, the cradle of democracy, was the first European nation to recognize full male suffrage in 1830. After the 1848 revolutions France and Switzerland adopted universal male suffrage. In Spain it was introduced in 1869 and shortly after that in Germany. By the early twentieth century the principle that universal male suffrage was the sine qua non condition for a true democracy was widely accepted throughout Europe, except in Russia. Britain had been lagging behind in extending the franchise after the 1867 reform, by which two thirds of the electorate could vote, but in 1918 it introduced genuine universal suffrage, which included women. British women in the suffragette movement had been pioneers in the fight for women's votes, although paradoxically New Zealand and Australia introduced it before Britain. Finland became the first country to introduce the vote to all male and female citizens in 1906.

Giving all citizens the right to vote did not really make sense unless they had the minimum education to acquire information and think for themselves. This is why literacy became such an important aspect in the development of a modern society.

Prussian King Frederick William I was the pioneer introducing compulsory free education in 1717. The Austro-Hungarian Empire adopted this model in 1778. It then inspired the United States and was introduced in Massachusetts in 1852. Spain and Italy came next in the 1850s. In Britain, free education became compulsory for children between the age of five and ten in 1870. France followed suit in 1881. By the late nineteenth century lack of free compulsory education was considered a sign of underdevelopment throughout Europe. More challenging was the implementation of the law of compulsory free education, which explains why in the early twentieth century illiteracy was scandalously high in most of southern and eastern Europe. The gap in literacy between the industrial powers and rural nations in Europe was wide. But above all Europe had successfully introduced the principle that no society could call itself advanced without a literate population.

Traditional society was based on three "Estates of the Realm": the nobility, the clergy, and the commoners. The first two were represented in the House of Lords and the latter in the House of Commons, in the English case. Similar hierarchical distribution between an upper and a lower chamber took place in several European nations, which gave birth to the bicameral system on which Western democracy is based. But in 1787 Edmund Burke, looking up at the Press Gallery of the House of Commons said, "Yonder sits the Fourth Estate, and they are more important than them all."

The press had existed in Europe since the seventeenth century when the first periodicals appeared, and it became increasingly influential in the eighteenth century through newspapers, which became the main channel of communication by which news was delivered. But it was in the nineteenth century when the press was consolidated as a pillar of democracy.

The nineteenth century was the golden era of the newspaper. Technology contributed to improve printing and distribution techniques as well as the capacity to publish news as quickly as possible. As illiteracy declined the number of readers steadily increased. The extension of the franchise in some countries implied that a larger number of citizens who had the right to vote needed to be informed. Political parties and pressure groups also strived to launch newspapers that would represent their views of reality and defend their interests in society.

Newspapers became so powerful that they could cause the outbreak of a war or topple a government. In Britain the *Times* was so influential that it was seen as an integral part of the political structure. It was so successful that soon papers in many parts of the world appeared bearing its name: the *India Times*, the *New York Times*, the *Cape Times*, *Le Temps* in Switzerland, the *Manila Times*, *El Tiempo* in Colombia, etc.

The rise of the newspapers consolidated journalism as a respectable and very influential profession. How far should journalists be allowed freely to express their opinions? The struggle for press freedom was a long one, as it implied defying the interests of the government, the church, and the establishment in general. "The individual has the right of expressing himself so long as he does not harm other individuals," wrote John Stuart Mill in *On Liberty*, one of the most influential books in the history of liberalism. This idea was broadly accepted by countries that called themselves democratic, and press freedom was consolidated as an essential ingredient of a democratic society.

The press made an important contribution to the emergence of the intellectual as a prominent figure in society. This became a very singular characteristic of European society that later expanded to other parts of the Western world. The term intellectual could be applied to a person dedicated to critical thinking of society's reality and the proposition of ideas to change it. Europe from the early nineteenth century became increasingly open to allow any person with ideas to publish and propagate them. From reformers to the so-called utopians, intellectuals became very influential figures, to the extent that they could be described as a new aristocracy or as Henri de Saint-Simon, a leading intellectual himself, described them: a new clergy that was replacing the influence that representatives of the Church had enjoyed in Europe until the Enlightenment.* In Russia the intelligentsia, which laid the foundations of the revolutionary movement, saw themselves as critics of the world in which they had no place and prophets of a world that had not yet come into being.

During the post-Napoleonic era Europe emerged as an ideological breeding ground. The ideologies that have shaped politics and inspired the formation of most political parties across the world until the present were born in the old continent at that time. Whoever wants to understand contemporary politics in all its complexity needs to refer to the intellectual history of Europe. One of the explanations for this proliferation of ideologies is the quest for freedom that characterized Europeans at that time. Europeans were constantly struggling to set themselves free from whatever they felt was oppressing them: a nation, a state, a ruler, a landlord, a social class system, or poverty itself. Unlike their ancestors, at that time they felt that freedom was within their reach and that it was possible to bring about changes that would allow them to live in a truly free society.

The most prominent of nineteenth-century ideas was liberalism. Liberalism as a political philosophy, based on the concept of individual liberty and equality, can trace its roots to the Enlightenment. Liberals as a political group emerged in Spain. The *Liberales* wrote a constitution in 1812, which even though it ended in failure in Spain, it became a source of inspiration for liberal movements both in continental Europe and Latin America.** Another

---

* Paul Johnson, *Intellectuals, From Marx and Tolstoy to Sartre and Chomsky* (London: Harper Perennial, 2007).
** Carr, *Spain 1808–1975*.

branch of liberalism advocating economic freedom and civil liberty spread from Britain, and it appealed to a wide range of intellectuals, from economists like Adam Smith to philosophers like John Stuart Mill.

The abysmal differences between the rich and poor, and the appalling living conditions of the working class in the early days of the Industrial Revolution were going to inspire a wide array of revolutionary ideas on the left. The first person to coin the term socialism was Count Henri de Saint-Simon. French philosopher Charles Fourier and the English social reformer Robert Owen advocated similar ideas of state ownership, public administration of the means of production, and more equitable distribution of income that would ultimately improve the conditions of the working class.

In 1848 two revolutionary thinkers Karl Marx and Friedrich Engels published *The Communist Manifesto*, which marks the beginning of the most revolutionary of ideas: communism. Marx's posthumous work *Das Kapital* (*Capital*), published by Engels, was initially read by only a minority of intellectuals and revolutionaries. Who could then predict that it was going to become one of the most influential books of all time and inspire the political system that would govern over a third of the world's population?

Anarchism, a political philosophy that aimed at creating self-governed societies under no state or official authority, was initially inspired by the philosophy of Pierre Joseph Proudhon. Another prominent anarchist, Russian revolutionary Mikhail Bakunin founded collective anarchism, advocating the abolition of ownership of all kinds.

In spite of their differences all of these left-wing ideologies shared the wish to deeply change society in order to improve the conditions of the working class. This led them to form the International Workingmen's Association in London in 1864. The first congress of what was most commonly known as the First International took place in Geneva two years later. From then working-class movements steadily expanded throughout the world.

Another ideology making progress among Europeans was pacifism. From the times of the early Christians many European thinkers have manifested themselves against war. In the nineteenth century they started to organize themselves. British philanthropist William Allen founded the Society for the Promotion of Permanent and Universal Peace in 1816, and the first international Peace Congress was convened in London in 1843 by Reverend Henry Richard. Much more influential on an international scale was the First Congress of Peace and Freedom hosted in Geneva. Pacifism gradually became an influential transnational lobby, and in 1889 the first Universal Peace Congress attracted 310 activists. Pacifism was supported by great intellectuals like Leo Tolstoy. In 1894 Tolstoy published *The Kingdom of God Is Within You*, in which he explained his pacifist beliefs. The book greatly influenced Mahatma Gandhi and his strategy of nonviolent resistance was mainly inspired by it.

If it was not realistic to eradicate war, at least the suffering of those taking part in it should be alleviated. This was the idea behind the first international humanitarian organization that was created in Europe: the Red Cross. This organization was founded by the Swiss businessman Henri Dunant, who witnessed the battle of Solferino in 1859, where thousands of wounded soldiers were abandoned to perish on the battlefields. In 1863 the International Committee of the Red Cross was created, with the aim of protecting the victims of conflicts, whether they were war wounded, prisoners, or refugees. Shortly after the first international conference was convened in Geneva, where delegates of thirty-six countries agreed to abide by a set of rules by which the wounded would be assisted by medical personnel with an armlet bearing a red cross. From then they would be present in most armed conflicts.

Science in Europe played a very important role in changing people's frame of mind and leading to revolutionary ideas. It laid the foundations of many of the beliefs that have shaped politics and society until the present. In 1859 British scientist Charles Darwin published *On the Origin of Species*, the most revolutionary book in the history of science, which founded evolutionary biology. According to this book all species, including the human being, evolved over generations through a process of natural selection. It constituted a scientific refutation of the Bible's explanation about the origins of human beings and the appearance of all species on earth.

Darwin's theory constituted a major challenge to Christian religion and all religions that attributed a divine origin to human beings. Not surprisingly Darwin was declared persona non grata in Christian circles. He also had significant influence on several currents of thought that became very influential from the late nineteenth century, although he did not show any sympathy toward any of the theories that derived from his theory.

British scientist Sir Francis Galton, who was actually Darwin's half cousin, concluded after reading *On the Origin of Species* that there was a genetic element that made some humans flourish while others decay. He first coined the term eugenics, which aimed at improving the genetic composition of human population. Its practical application implied encouraging marriage and reproduction of those people who are deemed healthy and genetically fit, and the prohibition or even sterilization for those who are considered genetically unfit or undesirable. Eugenics appealed to many legislators in Europe who considered it a solution to the crime and debauchery that was rife in many working-class areas. It then became particularly popular in the United States in the early twentieth century.

British sociologist Herbert Spencer famously coined the term "survival of the fittest," after reading *On the Origin of Species*. All species strive for survival, but only those that are fit enough and capable to adapt to changes in the environment survive and become stronger. Those that fail degenerate or even become extinct. This law of nature could also explain human behavior in society, and it became known as Social Darwinism. According to Social Darwinists the reason why some people became wealthy and flourished in society was because they developed a greater capacity to respond to changes in society and benefit from them; they proved to be the fittest and became a privileged elite. According to this current of thought, legislating in favor the weak and poor or redistributing the money of the wealthy minority was not in a country's interest, as it would interfere with natural law.

The Social Darwinist theory of the survival of the fittest was particularly suited to explain international relations. Some nations were capable of accumulating wealth and power to the extent of becoming great powers whereas others incapable of dominating the environment declined and were ruled by the strongest, or simply disintegrated as nations. This theory was very appropriate to explain and justify imperialism. European powers had been expanding and creating great empires because they had proven to be stronger and more capable than any other civilizations. The law of nature had determined that the Europeans would rule over the rest of the world. Social

Darwinism also explained the struggle for supremacy in Europe: Britain and France had become great powers at the cost of Spain and Portugal which had declined because of their lack of capacity to adapt to changes, and moreover, the last decades of the century Germany experienced a meteoric rise because it proved to be fitter than any other rival.

Social Darwinists bolstered a racial interpretation of history that had been popular among Europeans and people of European stock almost since the early stages of European colonization. It was to play a very important role in Western politics until the mid–twentieth century and even further.

French diplomat and writer Arthur de Gobineau published *An Essay on the Inequality of Human Races* in 1853. This book analyzed the history of what he considered three races: the European, the African, and the Asian. He reached the conclusion that "history springs from contact with the white races." Within the white race, according to Gobineau, the Aryans had reached the pinnacle of development. He also attributed the decline of some nations and civilizations to intermarriage.

Gobineau's book was critically acclaimed in both European and American intellectual circles as an important contribution to social science. To say that the white race was superior was not controversial, as it would be in today's world. *"Pick up white man's burden, send forth the best you breed,"* wrote Rudyard Kipling in a poem in 1898, urging the Americans to take up the burden of empire as had Britain and other European powers—as if it were the responsibility of the white race to rule over others. For many people in Europe and other continents the idea that the white race was superior seemed to be the conclusion that explained the abysmal differences in economic development and living standards between societies formed by white people versus other people. Moreover, belief in the superiority of the white race was not seen as a contradiction with the idea that all men were equal, as the principle of equality was not applied to other races. Karl Marx, who sent a copy of his unfinished *Das Kapital* to Darwin, expressed great admiration for the theory of evolution. He considered it natural and desirable that white Europeans would rule over other races in order to promote progress and development among them. "All is race. There is no other truth," said Benjamin Disraeli.

Culture played a very important role in the global projection of European civilization. All participants previously mentioned, as well as some exceptionally talented personalities, contributed to the splendor of European culture at that time. All this contributed to the prestige and the great attraction that culture enjoyed throughout the world. What was particularly extraordinary was that European culture not only penetrated societies that were colonized by Europeans but even those beyond the confines of European empires, where many people voluntarily adopted it.

In the post-Napoleonic era Europeans on the whole became particularly proud of their heritage and history. This explains the effort carried out by most nations to organize their collective history. National archives and most national libraries were founded then. The museum, dedicated to the preservation and display of diverse aspects of a nation's history and culture, was very much a European nineteenth-century invention. Encyclopedias, a major product of the Enlightenment era, flourished a century later, and from then on most European nations, as well as the United States, had a multivolume encyclopedia that claimed to condense universal knowledge. World exhibitions also proliferated, as an attempt to display not only the scientific and technological progress but also the culture that made it possible.

The modern university was to emerge in Europe in the nineteenth century. It was then that it became a basic institution in the development of civil society and the preparation of professional elites. Above all it played an essential role in making knowledge a hallmark of progress.

There was nothing special about the European creation of universities, for other great civilizations like that of China or the Islamic world had developed similar institutions to educate young people, transmit knowledge, and hold intellectual debates at the highest level. But the way European universities evolved in the nineteenth century determined what we conceive as a university in the contemporary world and transformed it into a pillar of a developed society. Strictly speaking it was defined as an institution of higher learning, providing facilities for teaching and research, and authorized to grant academic degrees.

What made European universities very unique was, first of all their independence. Whereas in China they were controlled by the state and in the

Islamic world by the religious hierarchy, in Europe they emerged as independent. This was absolutely essential, as it became an institution where freedom of thought was practiced and research was carried out without interference or external pressures. This made possible the rise of the academic in society. The Oxford and Cambridge don in Britain or the university professor in many European countries became a very influential figure, transmitting knowledge at the highest level and adopting a critical attitude toward society from a strictly independent position.*

The second factor determining the rise of the European university was wealth. Universities became particularly well endowed either by private or public means, as civil society became aware of their importance. The third factor was specialization. It underwent a process of increasing specialization in all fields of knowledge. Geography became a scientific discipline studied at the university in the 1830s under the influence of Alexander von Humboldt and Carl Ritter. Humboldt, a man of encyclopedic knowledge, also made very important contributions to botany, geology, and other more specialized branches of science like climatology, oceanography, and ornithology.** He justly became known as the father of universal geography.

Many other academic disciplines emerged. Economics faculties first appeared in Britain under the influence of classical economists. Anthropology, archaeology, and sociology were other important social sciences. Physics, chemistry, and biology faculties were created as independent branches of experimental sciences. All of this had a very positive effect on scientific progress. Scientists ceased to be self-educated amateurs as they had traditionally been and became salaried professionals.

The university became an institution for intellectual training as well as socialization, character formation, and self-discovery, where the young people would spend a few years between school and the beginning of their professional life. University students became a new social group generally characterized by its rebellious spirit, its wish to experiment with new ideas

---

* Jurgen Osterhammel, *The Transformation of the World: A Global History of the Nineteenth Century* (Princeton, N.J.: Princeton University Press, 2009).
** Ibid.

in search of a better world, and its tendency to question inherited wisdom. Revolutions and revolutionary movements, as well as many political changes taking place in the world from the nineteenth century would have been inconceivable without university students.

The European model of the university was exported with success. The oldest universities in the United States and Canada, beginning with Harvard and Yale, had used Oxford and Cambridge as the models to imitate, and those founded in the nineteenth century continued using them for reference. In Latin America new universities were inspired by the Spanish medieval university of Salamanca, with which academic links were kept by the cultural elites in the new independent nations. The French university and its *grandes écoles* provided a very attractive model for educating a well-prepared elite of civil servants and statesmen. German universities like Berlin became examples of meritocratic modern institutions for forming professional elites, particularly in Asia and the Middle East. Tokyo University and the Chinese Imperial University, founded in 1898, were inspired by French and German universities.*

The expansion of knowledge and the professionalization of those devoted to the acquisition of knowledge had a positive effect on European societies, which became much more educated and prepared. Knowledge began to be seen as the cornerstone of modern society. As knowledge expanded, and those in charge of its promotion became proper professionals, it also became popular to reward those who made the most important contributions.

In 1901 the first Nobel Prizes were awarded in Stockholm for chemistry, physics, medicine, literature, and some years later for economics and peace. This prize was created by Alfred Nobel, a Swedish chemist who had amassed a fortune by inventing dynamite. Toward the end of his life he thought that he did not want to be remembered for his contribution to the armament industry and decided to bequeath his fortune for the creation of an international prize that would reward notable people for the "greatest benefit to mankind." The Nobel Prize was soon to be internationally recognized as the most prestigious for its different disciplines. All over the world the most

---

★   Osterhammel, *The Transformation of the World.*

distinguished scientists, academics, and writers aspired to be Nobel laureates. Soon many other European nations followed suit, granting prestigious awards for excellence in arts and sciences.

While European societies paid more attention to the cultivation of the mind they also started to cultivate their bodies. Sports began to proliferate and an increasing number of Europeans would practice sports or watch sports in their free time.

The inventor of sports par excellence was Britain. Prosperity and social progress played an important role in this, as they allowed an increasing number of people to afford to take time off to practice or watch sports. The British exported their sports to the rest of Europe, their empire, and a substantial part of the world with extraordinary success. The universal admiration that British society and culture inspired in the Victorian era very much contributed to the expansion of its sports. Cricket soon became a passion in India and the West Indies. Rugby, which emerged as the main public school sport toward the mid–nineteenth century was successfully introduced in all dominions of the empire as well as in top US schools and universities, plus Argentina, Uruguay, and Chile. Polo became a national sport in India, Argentina, and Iran. Tennis, which had been played in the royal court in England from the fifteenth century, was reinvented as lawn tennis in the nineteenth century. By the end of the century it became popular among elites in different continents. The Wimbledon championship, founded by the All England Club in 1877, was shortly afterward opened to international competition, thus becoming the first major international sporting event.

No sport had as much international projection as football (renamed soccer in the U.S.), which emerged with its present rules in the mid–nineteenth century. As it gained popularity throughout Europe the English Football Association planned to set up an international body in coordination with other European national associations. FIFA, the *Fédération Internationale de Football Association* was founded in Paris in 1904. From then it steadily grew until it became the most popular team sport in the world.

At a time when all these sports expanded internationally, the idea of an international sporting competition became popular in England. In the meantime the Greeks had begun a modest revival of the Olympic Games that took place in ancient Greece. After attending these games, French educator Pierre de Coubertin founded the International Olympic Committee with the aim of organizing an Olympic Games that would take place in a different country every four years. The first Olympic Games took place in Athens in 1896, in which athletes of fourteen nations participated. The world's foremost sports competition had been born.

Increasing affluence and availability of time to spend money led to the emergence of new European products that were to be exported with great success. One obvious one was the restaurant. Restaurants as we conceive of them today originated in Paris in the eighteenth century, as a more sophisticated version of the eating houses, inns, and taverns that existed everywhere until then. Essential ingredients of every restaurant were a chef in charge of a good menu and certain rules of etiquette in order to book a table and socialize on its premises. Another one was the department store, where everything that the average consumer needed would be elegantly presented within a single edifice and in great quantities. Department stores revolutionized commerce. Their history can be traced back to Harding Howell & Co., which opened in London in 1796. But department stores relied heavily on mass production of most of the goods on offer and were therefore an offspring of industrialization. The first modern department stores opened in Paris in the 1850s. In the 1880s Charles Digby Harrod opened a store that was a hybrid between a business where the best quality products were sold and a club. Harrods was soon to find a competitor in Selfridges. Thousands of stores across the world attempted to reproduce this model of Western-style consumerism.

Europe set the trends that were to determine how people dressed not only in the Western world, but also in a substantial part of the world where European sartorial habits were regarded by many as a symbol of civilization and progress. Britain was largely responsible for this. British gentlemen acquired an aura of elegance and sophistication that was universally admired. Those who had the opportunity would be dressed by a London tailor or otherwise try to imitate the Savile Row suits. As far as women's fashion was concerned it was Paris that dominated. On the whole the tie, white collar, frock coat, or dark suit of the European bourgeoisie became internationalized to the extent that it became the clothing of the civilized people throughout the world.

In Latin America creole elites dressed according to the standards of the former metropolis and the dark, closely-fit suits became a way of demarcating oneself from the backward indigenous population and the peasantry. From Mexico to Chile dressing like the indigenous people became a symbol of backwardness, particularly in urban areas. This explains why dark suits would be worn even in tropical climates.

The Western style of dress made remarkable progress among the indigenous populations in many parts of the world, particularly in the case of all those making a career in any European administration or in the liberal professions. In India, one prominent example was a young lawyer known as Mahatma Gandhi, who proudly wore dark pinstriped suits, with a tie and golden chain watch, long before he decided famously to wear homespun khadi cloth. In Egypt, the Khedive Isma'il Pasha dressed like a Victorian gentleman, while in African colonies like Lagos, local Africans elites, particularly those who were Christian, would go to church following the strictest laws of European etiquette.

Many other aspects of European daily life that had become basic Western features were internationalized as the emergent bourgeoisie in many countries attempted to imitate Europe. The habit of eating on tables with metal cutlery is one of the most obvious. It did not succeed when it clashed with habits of great ancient civilizations like the Chinese, where the knife and fork never reached domestic life, nor the Japanese, where the chair was rejected. But on the whole this became another example of Western habits that were globalized as a result of European ascendancy.

While the train, the ocean liner, and the telegraph speeded up international connections, it became urgent to reach an agreement that would establish uniformity of time measurement. The person who can claim to have invented the worldwide standard time was Sandford Fleming, a Scottish engineer who emigrated to Canada. On one occasion in 1876 he missed a train in Ireland because the departure time on the schedule printed P.M. instead of A.M. He therefore proposed the establishment of a single twenty-four-hour clock for the entire world, and once this was achieved he has justly been described as the most successful globalizer.

In 1884 an international conference took place Washington, D.C., in which representatives from twenty-five countries approved a single world time, which is still in use today. The world was divided into twenty-four time zones. The most contentious issue in this conference was where should time be measured from. The Royal Observatory at Greenwich had been used by sailors as the prime meridian. New Zealand had become the first country to use Greenwich Meridian Time as official in 1868, and shortly afterward, Canada and the U.S. had also set their clocks in accordance with the GMT. Despite the opposition from France and other countries that refused to acknowledge British hegemony in such an important sphere, it was internationally accepted as the prime meridian.

Europeans also determined how to keep track of the days in the year. The Gregorian calendar, a technological improvement over Julius Caesar's calendar, spread through Europe toward the end of the sixteenth century. Imperial powers contributed to spread it to other continents, and by the nineteenth century it became the most widely used calendar. Others adopted it not because of any imperial pressures but because of its precision. Japan for example introduced the Gregorian calendar almost half a century before Russia, which kept the Julian calendar until 1916. Turkey adopted it in 1927.

Europeans had been the pioneers exploring the world; they had named continents, oceans, seas, and many territories, and also produced the first world maps that became commonly used. Several regions of the world were also named after European terms. Latin America became to be used by French intellectuals in the 1860s in what was until then known as Hispanic America or Iberoamerica, with the aim of replacing pan-Hispanism with pan-Latinism. The term gradually became accepted. Territories toward the east of the Bosphorus became to collectively known as the Orient. Turks, Arabs, and Persians were included in this "Oriental" world. The vast part of the world described as the East was divided into the Near East, the Middle East, and the Far East, the last including China, Japan, and the countries that are farthest from Europe. Slowly but steadily from then on, these terms became common throughout the world.

The most successful transmitters of their language had initially been the Portuguese and the Spanish. From the 1880s creole elites in new independent nations of Latin America were determined to consolidate Spanish and Portuguese as official languages and ensure that the indigenous peoples would speak it. This led to an extraordinary expansion of these two languages through America.

From the eighteenth century French was known as the language of diplomacy, the main foreign language learned by educated elites in the Western world. But as a result of French colonial expansion in the nineteenth century, it became a global language. The French language was taught in all colonies, and the fact that command of the French language was required to acquire French nationality became an important incentive that contributed to its expansion. In the early nineteenth century French was only spoken in Quebec and three small Caribbean islands. A century later, it was the most widely spoken European language in Africa, and as a result of colonization there were French-speaking communities on five continents.

French culture enjoyed so much prestige that even the Russian nobility spoke it among themselves. But Russian also experienced an extraordinary growth that has been underestimated, for it was in the nineteenth century that Russian was consolidated as the official language in the vast Russian Empire that spanned Eurasia.

But no other language experienced such an amazing expansion at this time as English, which became the first truly global language. As the British consolidated their colonial administrative structure in India in the second half of the nineteenth century, English became the official language in the British Raj. Not only was it adopted by the Indian middle classes who wished to work in the Indian civil service, but also by the social elites and intellectuals as a language that would allow communication with the outer world. Many other regions of the world became English-speaking territories as a result of British colonial expansion. In Egypt the Arab-speaking elite enthusiastically learned English as the language of progress and modernity, whereas at the other end of the African continent, in Cape Colony, English imposed itself over Afrikaans, the original European language spoken in the colony. English not only benefitted from British colonial expansion but also from the legacy of the first British Empire. Mass migration to the United States from the mid–nineteenth century, transformed this country into the most rapidly expanding English-speaking community.

Beyond the colonial world, there was an increasing awareness and pressure to learn a European foreign language or at least to translate the most important works written in Europe. This was particularly the case of Japan. In China they had never felt the need to learn a foreign language apart from the three official languages of the Chinese state during the Qing period: Chinese, Manchu, and Mongolian. But this gradually changed from 1862 when the Tongwen Guan translation school was founded, the first Western-style educational institution founded in Beijing. In the Ottoman Empire elites had traditionally learned French but from the 1990s German became the main foreign language as Turkish-German relations strengthened.

The city was certainly not a European invention. While the Greek polis emerged, other civilizations provided similar forms of urban life. But Europe in the nineteenth century consolidated an urban civilization that was to set the trends of urban development and expansion until the present. From the seventeenth century European empires had founded colonial cities that became pillars of their economic power. Many of these cities were later transformed into great trading and economic centers once they left their colonial past behind. In the Americas, this was certainly the case of New York, Toronto, Mexico City, São Paolo, and Buenos Aires, all of them founded by Europeans. They all became the largest cities as well as the main trading and economic centers of the nations to which they belonged. Similar trends of development were followed by other cities, which evolved as great ports and trading hubs while they were still colonies. In the British Empire there is a long list of cities like Calcutta, Bombay, Melbourne, and Hong Kong. France transformed cities of its empire like Casablanca and Saigon into great ports. Jakarta in the Dutch Empire experienced the same process. As global trade accelerated all of these benefitted and increased their trading and exporting activities.

Europe at this time also created a model of the modern megalopolis that was to be later reproduced in other continents. It was in Britain, the first predominantly urban nation, where this model of new city emerged. Massive emigration to the cities not only transformed London into a megalopolis but also made cities like Manchester and Birmingham emerge as great urban centers of industry in the mid–nineteenth century. As we have seen before, the problems created by the new dwellers of these cities were phenomenal, as the influx of labor ran well ahead of urban planning. The slum areas, with improvised dwellings to accommodate masses of poor emigrants, were only one of the major problems. Dirt provided a sanitary problem and the risk of epidemics spreading. The smells and the noise made many areas uninhabitable, and the lack of any proper architectural planning produced a sense of chaos and ugliness that depressed its inhabitants. While writers like Charles Dickens described the horrors of life in new urban civilization, and reformers like Friedrich Engels denounced its injustices, Alexis de Tocqueville summarized this model of urban life as the transformation of civilization into barbarism.

On the other hand it was remarkable how the combination of legislation, science, and technology tackled many of the problems associated with this new model of urban life and steadily improved it.

A major technological innovation that drastically altered life in the cities and constituted a revolutionary change in urban public transport was underground transport. The first underground train system opened in London in 1863, and was hailed by the *Times* as "the great engineering triumph of our day." It was mainly the result of Charles Pearson's extraordinary vision, and it implied engineering works of epic proportions, combining a railroad system with tunneling techniques. In 1890 electric traction replaced steam engines, which made underground trains much faster and cleaner. The possibility of traveling securely and at great speed through tunnels allowed the inhabitants of a city like London not only to move quickly through the urban areas but also to reach the center from the outskirts. This invention offered great possibilities of urban expansion into rural surroundings; it also opened the prospects of commuting on a daily basis between the rural and the urban world.

This revolutionary transport technology soon spread to other cities in Europe and America. In 1896 Budapest inaugurated its underground. Four years later Paris inaugurated its metropolitan train that was to be known as the Metro, and this would be the standard name all over the world. While it continued spreading through other European cities, it soon crossed the Atlantic. The New York subway opened in 1904; Buenos Aires came next in 1913.

Underground transport is only one of the major aspects of the urban revolution that started in the mid–nineteenth century. A new model of a modern civilized city emerged in Europe that included paved streets as well as lighting in the main areas, potable water available on taps, drains and a sewer system, a fire brigade, a police force, and a professional municipal administration. This urban model that emerged in Europe spread across America and certain cities of the colonial world. But what was extraordinary was that several countries beyond the Western and the colonial world voluntarily adopted it as the model that would determine their urban development. This was not only the case with Tokyo, which became the main gateway for Western influences, but also Seoul. It also happened within the Ottoman Empire in Istanbul and Beirut. Old imperial cities like Beijing, Cairo, and Teheran adopted certain aspects of this Western model in the process of modernization and reinvention that they underwent from the late nineteenth century.

In the sphere of exploration the advances of the era of imperialism were going to be outstanding, partly due to the scientific and technological advances that were to allow explorers reach the remotest areas of the planet. With the expeditions through the heart of Africa carried out by Dr. David Livingstone and other explorers from the 1850s, Europeans managed to penetrate the interior of the last continent that had resisted their curiosity from the outset of the era of great geographic discoveries.

What was still to be explored? What secrets did the remotest areas of the world hide that could quench human thirst for scientific knowledge and contribute to the understanding of the natural habitat? What opportunities for further exploration did technological innovation offer? These were the questions asked by scientists, navigators, and explorers at a time when Europe was at the height of its powers and when they felt that it was their duty to complete the task initiated by their predecessors four centuries before, when the era of great discoveries began.

Literature played an important role stimulating European zest for adventure and the exploratory ethos. From the 1870s French writer Jules Verne became famous for his science fiction and adventure novels. In *Around the World in Eighty Days* he described a fascinating journey around the world in only eighty days, carried out by a British gentleman Phileas Fogg. This extraordinary tale became credible thanks to a major engineering achievement like the Suez Canal and faster means of transport. *20,000 Leagues Under the Sea* was another highly acclaimed novel in which Verne imagined a submarine, the *Nautilus*, led by Captain Nemo, roaming the seas free from any government supervision and familiarizing himself with the bottom of the oceans, about which so little was known. It was amazing how Verne described submarine technology that was well ahead of his time, for Captain Nemo's submarine was electrically powered and was capable of performing advanced marine biological research. Verne allowed his imagination to travel even further with his *Journey to the Center of the Earth*. This was a much more sinister journey carried out by a scientist from the interior of a volcano into the center of the earth, and the author speculates on what could be found in the interior of our planet if it were possible to travel all the way to the center.

British author H. G. Wells, who wrote novels like *The Time Machine*, *The Invisible Man*, and *The War of the Worlds*, also made significant contributions to the popularity of science fiction at that time. The literary success of authors like Jules Verne or H. G. Wells reflected the widespread interest in learning about the new horizons that scientific and technological progress offered.

In late nineteenth century Europe became the focus of international efforts that resulted in intensive scientific and geographical expeditions.

This culture set the tone to the heroic age of polar exploration. The aim was to reach the North and South Poles and explore Antarctica, a continent that is uninhabitable due to its low temperatures that seemed impenetrable, with its interior permanently covered in snow. This era became known as heroic because those who ventured into such risky journeys, and were willing to endure so much suffering, could only be described as heroes. Being the first to reach the North and South Poles was the main aim that inspired these extraordinary journeys but there were also diverse scientific aims. The whole coastline of Antarctica was explored and mapped as a result of it.

"Men wanted for hazardous journey. Low wages, bitter cold, long hours of complete darkness. Safe return doubtful. Honor and recognition in event of success."

Despite such a discouraging advertisement more than five thousand people replied, which says a lot about the bravery, abnegation, and adventurous spirit that prevailed in Europe at that time.

Captain Robert Scott set a record in his first expedition in 1901 by reaching the southernmost point on earth. He was one of the main contenders in the race to reach the South Pole, and in 1911 he led an expedition with this aim but he was finally beaten by the Norwegian Roald Amundsen. Judging by his achievements Amundsen can be described as the best polar explorer of his time, as he was the first person to reach both poles. Scott and his crew died of hypothermia as they attempted to return from this expedition.

Another of the great polar explorers was the Irishman Ernest Shackleton, who led an expedition in 1914 to cross Antarctica from sea to sea through the South Pole. These three great explorers characterized the last episode in the history of great geographic expeditions. With them the epoch began by Portuguese and Spanish navigators in the fifteenth century was brought to an end.

The race to reach the North and South Poles that took place in the early twentieth century constituted the epilogue to the era of great discoveries. Once human beings had reached the North and South Poles there remained no large territory in the world to discover. The Europeans had completed the process of discovery and exploration of the world, which they had begun in the fifteenth century.

After decades witnessing the most extraordinary changes and enjoying the benefits of what has been described as an age of improvement, Europeans toward the end of the nineteenth century felt that they were living in the crest of a civilization that was greater than any other. The modern world that Europe began creating during the Renaissance had now reached maturity and was expanding universally. The network of peoples connected by trade, migratory waves, and exchange of knowledge had spread through most of the planet, and European capitals were leading it. The three factors that made it possible were imperialism, the expansion of the market economy, and finally technology. European technological inventions not only improved human mobility but they speeded up all forms of human connections.

What historians have described as the Great Divergence was clearly perceptible by the end of the nineteenth century. Industrialization and economic growth had made most of Western Europe fabulously wealthy. Links with North America allowed the United States and Canada to follow the same trends of industrialization that allowed them to join this exclusive club. Beyond the Western world Japan was incorporated into this industrial elite as a result of its contacts with Europe. The gap in wealth and living standards between this group of countries and the rest of the world became abysmal. From then on this group of leading industrial nations in three different continents was going to set the trends of global economic growth, and their examples were to inspire all other nations in their quest for wealth and prosperity.

Chapter 8

The First and Last Great Frontier of Civilization

The Scramble for Africa on Behalf of Civilization, Christianity, and Imperial Interests.

Africa was the first great frontier traversed by Europeans in the era of the great discoveries. From antiquity North Africa had been the natural area of expansion for Mediterranean civilizations, attracting fortune-seekers, merchant-adventurers, and conquerors. From the time when part of North Africa was incorporated into the Roman Empire, news about this vast and exotic continent began to circulate among the peoples of Europe. "Out of Africa always something new" wrote Pliny in ancient Rome. In the early modern era the continent continued to evoke the thrill of discovering a new land permanently under the sun. "I speak of Africa and of golden joys," wrote Shakespeare. This spirit has persisted until the present.

It is therefore not surprising that the first territories occupied by Europeans in the era of discoveries were African. Yet, apart from South Africa and a few enclaves in the north and northwestern coast, this continent remained unexplored until the late nineteenth century. It was often described as the "Dark Continent," as it was a totally unknown world that evoked great mysteries and perils. Due to its gigantic size, with endless rainforests and the dangers of its fauna and flora, the interior of Africa seemed to be forbidden to the European. Nevertheless, the curiosity of the Europeans, their eagerness to acquire wealth, and also to propagate their civilization had led them to explore other continents; regions that were apparently as dangerous and inhospitable as Africa. For this reason by the early nineteenth century the expansion of Europeans into this continent seemed imminent, although initially nothing indicated that it would end up playing such an important role for Europe in the era of imperialism.

Long before Europeans occupied virtually the whole African continent in an extraordinarily rapid process, some of its inhabitants had been affected by Europe through one of the most notorious aspects of its expansion: the slave trade. Slavery was well known throughout Africa, as the Arabs had been capturing slaves from the south of their frontiers for centuries. Also, weak tribes had also been enslaved by dominant ones. But as we have previously seen, from the sixteenth century, when Europeans decided that Africans were ideally suited to work in the plantations in America, the peoples of the West African coast were dragged into the Atlantic triangle. This brought a triple round of profits to European merchants: on the outward journey to Africa they brought linen, cloth, metalware, beads, brandy, wine, and firearms, then they picked up slaves that they sold in the Caribbean or Brazil, taking back cargoes of tobacco, sugar, and rum.

The slave trade was initially controlled by Portugal from its enclaves on the coast of West Africa, but by the late seventeenth century the English, Danes, and Swedes had built forts along the Gold Coast in order to benefit from it. Initially the most important slaving port was Luanda. It has been calculated that during the three and a half centuries of the transatlantic slave trade, some 2.8 million slaves were dispatched from Luanda.* In the meantime rival slave traders established themselves along the coast of Benin, where the supply of slaves was so prolific that it became known as the Slave Coast. (A fourth region that was to deliver a huge number of slaves from the eighteenth century was the Gold Coast.) "The trade in slaves is the business of kings, rich men, and prime merchants," wrote an English slaver at the time. But not only Europeans were benefitting from the slave trade. African tribes were also making great profits selling people of their own race, and they were also to express their regrets when the slave trade was banned and posed all kinds of obstacles to ending it.

Several decades after the end of the slave trade European powers were to focus their attention on Africa, initially with the aim of exploring its interior, but soon this led to much higher aims of opening the continent to trade and incorporating it into civilization. Europe's sudden interest in the unexplored African interior owes a lot to a Scottish missionary who became famous for his explorations and became one of the great figures of Victorian Britain: Dr. David Livingstone.** Born in Scotland in 1818 into a poor and deeply religious family, Livingstone studied medicine but it was his missionary vocation that determined his destiny. After graduation he was sent by the London Missionary Society to South Africa. Young Livingstone was convinced that Christianity and commerce would be the twin solutions to Africa's evils, as they would eradicate the slave trade that was so deeply entrenched and allow Africans to escape poverty and backwardness. He first settled in a small village with his wife and children, but frustrated by the missionary's sedentary life he decided to explore the unchartered terrain further north. He became the first European to see what he named Victoria Falls in honor of Queen Victoria, and above all he managed to open the path to the heart of tropical Africa.

On returning to England in 1857, Livingstone published a critically acclaimed book about his explorations, which managed to awaken the general public's interest in Africa, and with the support of the Royal Geographical

---

* Thomas, *The Slave Trade.*

** Ronald Robinson, J. Gallagher, and A. Denny, *Africa and the Victorians* (London: I.B. Tauris, 1965).

Society, he obtained financial backing from the government to lead an expedition with the main aim of finding a navigable route to the interior. Unfortunately, this was not achieved. After five years exploring the area around the Zambezi River, the search was abandoned after great adversity. In 1866 Livingstone set out from Zanzibar with several experts on a mission to discover the source of the Nile. He failed, but in compensation he found another great African river, the Congo. Shortly thereafter, abandoned by all members of the expedition, he lost contact with civilization, and many believed that he was dead. By then there was so much public interest in the Scottish explorer that the *New York Herald* commissioned a journalist named Henry Morton Stanley to travel to Africa in search of Livingstone and write about his adventure for the newspaper. Stanley miraculously found Livingstone in a village near Lake Tanganyika, on October 26, 1871. The article under the famous headline: "Dr. Livingstone, I Presume," which described the encounter, spread the fascination with Africa throughout the entire Western world, and would inspire several generations of explorers who ventured into the heart of Africa.

Livingstone refused to return to England with Stanley, and lived up to the legend he had created for himself by continuing to search for the source of the Nile until he died of malaria in 1874. He was buried with the highest honors in Westminster Abbey.

Livingstone devoted his life to open Africa to Christianity, commerce, and civilization. These three words summarized his mission, as the monument dedicated to him in Victoria Falls reminds us today. Judging by his popularity he undoubtedly managed to fascinate the general public about Africa. After his death several of his admirers continued with his exploratory missions, among them the most famous of all, Stanley.

Stanley was sponsored by the *New York Herald* and the *Daily Telegraph* to find a route from the Congo River to the sea. In 1874 he led the expedition with over three hundred men, most of them local porters.* Unlike Livingstone, who inspired kindness and admiration among the African tribes, Stanley was a strict expeditionary leader who did not hesitate to inflict

---

* Stanley, Henry. *How I Found Livingstone: Travels, Adventures, and Discoveries in Central Africa* (London: Wordsworth, 2010).

the harshest punishment on those who disobeyed him and eliminate those who posed difficulties for him. On one occasion he took reprisals against a tribe that refused to assist his expeditionary group, and he admitted in his newspaper reports to have killed thirty-five men. Many of his readers were outraged by this and sent protests to the Royal Geographical Society and the Foreign Office, arguing that such brutality was incompatible with Britain's civilizing mission. But Stanley never expressed any repentance as he believed that survival in the African jungle required a domineering character that went beyond civilizing rhetoric and Christian principles. He finally achieved the aim of the expedition but it took him more than two years, and he lost two thirds of his men on the way. On returning to London he focused on highlighting the merits of his expedition and describing the wealth that was hidden in Africa's interior, insisting that just as Livingstone had wished, Britain should take up the responsibility of opening the continent to trade and Christianity. But to his disappointment the government seemed reluctant to listen to him.

Until the mid–nineteenth century, Britain did not have more than one strategic aim in Africa, to safeguard the route to India, but circumstances rapidly changed. In 1867 the discovery of gold and diamonds in Kimberley transformed South Africa into a very attractive destination for European emigration. From then on, British fortune-seekers reached Cape Town in rapidly increasing numbers and as they marched toward the north they inevitably provoked clashes not only with the locals but also with the Boers, who had been there since the seventeenth century. In 1874 Sir Henry Bartle Frere was sent to South Africa as high commissioner in order to introduce a federal model of government that would incorporate both the locals and the Boers, just as Lord Carnarvon had successfully done in Canada. But this was only possible at the cost of two wars: the first one against the native Zulu. Frere, without British approval, sent the troops into Zululand after the Zulus' King Cetshwayo refused the ultimatum to accept the proposed federation.

The first major war against African people that was fought as a result of European incursion into this continent was closely followed by the great powers. An initial Zulu victory caused much commotion, particularly in France, as one of its fatal casualties was the heir to the Bonaparte dynasty who had joined the British army. But this was compensated by the Battle of Rorke's Drift, in which no more than 150 British soldiers managed to repel the attack of over 4,000 Zulu. This battle became legendary in the history of the British Empire, and was later immortalized in a 1960s film which made the actor Michael Caine famous. It came to prove that a few disciplined and well-coordinated men with the help of modern technology could conquer and govern Africans regardless of how numerous they would be.

On the other hand, the Boers successfully rebelled against the British annexation of their Transvaal Republic. Prime Minister Gladstone, always reluctant to get the government entangled in colonial affairs, signed a peace treaty 1879 accepting Boer autonomy within the British Empire. But this was only the beginning of the conflict with the Boers, who proved to be more defiant toward the British Empire than any other African people.

Strategic and economic interests linked to the route to India also led Britain to increase its presence in Egypt. The Suez Canal, which provided access from the Mediterranean to the Indian Ocean, was vital for British interests, and for this reason the British government showed great enthusiasm for this great project, although in the end France gained the upper hand when their engineer Ferdinand de Lesseps was commissioned to build it. Nevertheless, Sultan Ismail's regime had built the canal by obtaining a huge loan from European banks which he could not repay, even after a huge increase in taxes, which made him extremely unpopular among the Egyptian population. Shortly after the canal's inauguration in 1869 the Sultan had no option but to sell the Egyptian shares of the canal, and the British government took this golden opportunity to buy the shares. As a result Britain jointly owned the canal with France. From that point British intervention in Egypt steadily increased, first to control the country's political situation which was very convulsive, and secondly to avoid France once more taking the lead. After a nationalist revolt in 1882, Britain and France sent troops to Egypt and ended up bombarding Alexandria. From that moment, the country formally became a British protectorate.

Africa not only offered expansion opportunities for the great European powers but also for small ones like Belgium. King Leopold II of Belgium followed the news of the expeditions through Africa with more interest than any other monarch. Ever since his accession to the throne in 1865 he had set himself the aim of increasing the prestige of this small kingdom that was surrounded by much more powerful states. He decided that the acquisition of a colony in Africa seemed the best way of achieving it. Neither his government nor Belgian society in general shared his colonial ambition, for Belgium had become a rich country as a result of its industrial development, and they suspected that an African colony would only be a source of worries and expenditure rather than extra wealth. For this reason Leopold II decided to embark on his colonial ambition with his own money. After all he was one of the wealthiest men in Europe and he had recently managed to multiply his fortune by speculating with Suez Canal shares.

The king of Belgium decided to use his prestige as a sovereign to open the heart of Africa to European colonization. For this purpose he convened a conference at his palace in Brussels in 1876, to which leading European geographers and explorers were invited. In his welcoming speech he took special care to highlight Europe's philanthropic duty to take civilization to the African continent, and he spoke of the need for an international crusade, worthy of that century of progress. This conference led to the formation of the International African Association, presided by the king of Belgium. Major European powers were invited to contribute with national committees. It was not clear how the areas of influence in Africa would be divided among them at a time of increasing imperial rivalry, but above all the conference served the purpose of promoting the cause of Africa among European elites, which Ferdinand de Lesseps described as the most important task of our time.

King Leopold managed to be associated with the noble cause of opening Africa to civilization, to such an extent that in British circles he was considered the person who could carry out Livingstone's mission. But despite the fact that the king took special care to avoid showing the minimum imperial ambition, it was clear that his ultimate aim was to ensure that Belgium would receive a substantial part of the benefits of colonization in Africa. As he wrote to the Belgian ambassador in London: "I do not want to miss the good opportunity of obtaining a share of this magnificent African cake."[*]

---

[*] Martin Meredith, *The Fortunes of Africa* (New York: Simon & Schuster, 2014).

In order to fulfill the colonial aims for which he had money but no official support Leopold II needed an explorer capable of reaching the heart of Africa and taking possession of those territories on his behalf. This was to be none other than Henry Stanley. The Belgian king had been thrilled by the news that the British government was not interested in establishing a protectorate over the lands that had been explored by Stanley. This was his opportunity. If Britain was not interested in the privilege of becoming the nation that would open the heart of Africa to Western civilization then Belgium would do it. After the British government's rebuff Stanley happily signed a five-year contract in 1878 to serve the king of Belgium with the mission of opening hospitals and scientific stations, and building roads that would connect the Congolese population, but soon more material aims would become evident.

While the king of Belgium initiated his colonial adventure France, which was already a veteran in North Africa, expanded its interests much faster than it probably would have wished. From 1830 the colony of Algeria had steadily grown due to French migration, to the point of becoming the most important colony in the French Empire. Once established in Algeria the temptation to expand through North Africa was going to increase. In 1881 the French government used a Tunisian incursion into Algerian territory as a pretext to send troops to Tunisia and establish a protectorate over the neighboring country.

In the meantime a young adventurer and explorer known as Pierre Savorgnan de Brazza was going to promote French expansion through Central Africa with so much success that he ended up becoming one of the great figures of French colonization. De Brazza was a good example of a transnational European upbringing. Born in Italy into an aristocratic Italian family he had been educated in France and made an extraordinary career serving the French Republic. Thanks to good family connections, which included politicians like Jules Ferry and Léon Gambetta he managed to raise 10,000 francs from the French colonial department to finance his first expedition through Africa.

After initiating the first expedition through the coast of present-day Gabon, de Brazza met King Makoto, sovereign of the lands and the great lake that gave access to the whole region. He persuaded the king to reach an agreement by which he would cede sovereignty to France and allow the establishment of a French settlement in return for trade benefits for his people. As a result of this de Brazza, who opened Congo for French colonization, became Stanley's worst rival. Rivalry between the two explorers to take possession of Congo was so intense that it almost provoked a diplomatic conflict between France and Belgium.

On returning to Paris in 1882, de Brazza tried to persuade the French government about the need to establish its sovereignty over the lands of King Makoto, for humanitarian as well as economic and political reasons. His request had huge popular support, for it was backed by the popularity that he had earned with the African adventure. The young Italian aristocrat came to represent the romantic cause of colonialism in contrast with Stanley's more materialistic and crude vision. The French press described him as the "peaceful conqueror" and "freedom's apostle," as he had managed to establish a friendly dialogue with Africans and convince them of the benefits that they would obtain from Western civilization.

In 1883 de Brazza returned to Gabon as colonial governor, with the mission of establishing a French colony there. From there, French dominion gradually expanded until it eventually became the largest colonial empire in Africa. But Stanley had not really lost the race; Leopold II decided to create the International Congo Society with the aim of founding the Congo Free State in the areas that Stanley had taken on his behalf. Abiding by his philanthropic aims, the king promised to promote business among European firms in order to develop this remote land, also warning that he himself would abstain from any economic activity there. He also promised to grant independence to the new state as soon as its population proved capable of supporting itself. It only remained for the king to convince the skeptical European powers about the sincerity of his promises.

Initially Germany seemed no rival for European powers in Africa, for Chancellor Otto von Bismarck, who had unified Germany and transformed it into one of the most powerful nations in the world, considered colonies a useless distraction.

Nevertheless, the ideas about acquiring colonies that Bismarck expressed in the 1870s seemed to have become obsolete in 1880s. The race for Africa was gathering momentum, European powers were occupying territory, and German citizens asked themselves why their nation, which aimed to be the most powerful in Europe, was staying on the sidelines, giving up all potential benefits of the African continent. It was felt that Germany should embark on the conquest of Africa before it was too late. For this reason, in May 1884 the German chancellor ordered the German flag to be hoisted over Cameroon, Togo, and Agra Pequena, in southeast Africa. With the occupation of these territories Germany began to build an overseas empire that was going to be five times the size of the German Reich.

Germany joined the race to colonize Africa at a time when this was starting to cause disputes among European powers. In order to avoid further tensions provoked by the German incursion into Africa, the chancellor organized a conference in Berlin in 1885 to discuss the future of Africa. The overall aim of the conference was very much along the lines of the one hosted by the king of Belgium: to promote civilization among the Africans and open the continent's interior to trade, but in order to avoid future disputes three important decisions were agreed to: Congo should be a free-trade area; the Niger River should be open to free navigation, and any future annexation of territory should be carried out under acceptable terms for all other European parties.

The Berlin Conference, also known as the West Africa Conference has often been described as the starting point of what was later to be known as the scramble for Africa, but this process had already started, and would have gathered momentum with or without this event. What this conference managed to do was lay down a series of rules among the powers that had decided to colonize the African continent. One very important contribution was to make the statesmen in attendance agree to colonize Africa in accordance with Livingstone's ideals of introducing trade, Christianity, and civilization there. The Scottish missionary would have been pleased to witness how European governments took up his ideals even though they were mainly motivated by nationalist aspirations and economic ambitions.

Initially, the great winner of the Berlin congress seemed to be King Leopold II, for there his grandiose plan of creating the Congo Free State was sanctioned by all other powers. Shortly afterward, a territory that was initially 500,000 square kilometers expanded to 2,300,000 square kilometers and the Belgian sovereign acquired a colony that was going to be 75 times the size of Belgium.* No one could say any longer that he ruled over a small kingdom. The Belgian king had finally managed to lead the way into central Africa and place his country among the leading colonial powers. Nevertheless, opening Africa to civilization was far from the benign civilizing crusade promised by Leopold II.

Germany also made remarkable progress expanding its African empire. A few days after the Berlin Conference on March 3, 1885, an imperial charter was granted to the Society for German Colonization created by the explorer Carl Peters to establish a protectorate in East Africa. This news was particularly worrying for the British government as it confirmed the fears that Bismarck was starting to give free rein to his expansionist zeal in Africa, while Britain seemed to be losing influence there. Three months earlier, on January 3, 1885, the British suffered a humiliating defeat at Khartoum, where the famous General Charles Gordon was killed.

General Gordon, most commonly known as Gordon of Khartoum, was one of the legendary figures produced by the colonial world. Gordon, who was the epitome of Victorian virtues, had a lot in common with Dr. Livingstone: both were deeply religious, believing fervently that Britain should fulfill its civilizing mission by expanding through Africa. They also shared an abhorrence of slavery and became major symbols in the fight against the slave trade in Africa.

After making his reputation in China, the prestigious General Gordon arrived in Cairo in 1874, commissioned by the khedive—always eager to attract European talent—to lead the Egyptian troops in their advance toward the Sudan. Once this mission was accomplished Gordon was appointed governor general of the Sudan with British acquiescence, and throughout the years he occupied this post not only did he manage to put an end to the rebellions against the Egyptian troops but he established his ascendancy over this vast territory in a very significant way. He made a considerable contribution to stamp out the slave trade, despite the fact that it played a very important

---

* Thomas Pakenham, *The Scramble for Africa* (London: Abacus, 1991).

role in the Sudanese economy. He also made notable improvements in the Sudanese administration by combating corruption, and abolishing torture and public flogging. Exhausted by the thankless task of fighting with local elites and changing backward mentalities, he resigned in 1880 and went back to England. By then he was considered both in Egypt and in Britain as a saintly figure who had established a close rapport with the Sudanese population and made remarkable progress fighting against all odds to bring European modernity and civilization into Sudan.

Nevertheless, the effects of Gordon's civilizing mission were not long-lasting. Shortly after his departure, Sudan fell under the spell of the self-proclaimed Mahdi, Muhammad Ahmad, who hated the khedive and his entourage of what he considered Europeanist infidels, and he led an Islamic revolt against British influence. The press in England stoked public clamor that Gordon should be sent back to the Sudan. Prime Minister Gladstone eventually agreed to send Gordon but with a limited mandate of evacuating Khartoum. On arriving in Khartoum Gordon evacuated the civilian popu-lation, protecting them from an imminent attack from the Mahdi, but he decided to stay with his troops to face the enemy. He ordered reinforcements to defend Khartoum, and the government reluctantly agreed to send some, but they arrived too late. Gordon died heroically fighting the Mahdist troops. The Mahdi, as the ultimate symbol of revenge, ordered the general's head to be hung from a tree before the Sudanese people.

The news of Gordon's tragic end and the defeat of his troops caused widespread indignation in Britain. Queen Victoria herself expressed her disappointment to Prime Minister Gladstone for having left such a national hero in the lurch. The crisis came to demonstrate that it was not totally true that citizens were not willing to support risky military campaigns in Africa. On the contrary, when they considered that their interests and their civiliza-tion had to be defended, the British demanded more intervention. In a crisis, Prime Minister Gladstone failed to understand this, which brought his long career to a dramatic end. But his successors clearly did, judging by British expansion in Africa over the following two decades.

After the defeat at Khartoum, the British government was going to pay much more attention to fortune-seekers or settlers in Africa who recommended the establishment of areas of influence. This was the case with the veteran businessman Sir George Taubman Goldie, who formed a company to obtain benefits from the territories around the Niger River, which both the French and the Germans strove to control. In 1886, the Royal Niger Company formally began the British presence in West Africa.*

Much more decisive was the British occupation of East Africa. For a long time the port of Mombasa had been a point of strategic interest on the route to India. From the mid–nineteenth century both fortune-seekers and explorers who ventured into the fertile lands around Mount Kilimanjaro were deeply impressed by them. The Scottish businessman William Mackinnon, who had made a fortune by creating trade routes around the Indian Ocean, reached an agreement with the king of Zanzibar to do business in his kingdom. This led the British government to grant a license in 1888 to create the Imperial British East Africa Company. The government's decision to back Mackinnon was not so much motivated by his initiative but by that of his German rival Carl Peters, whose influence was rapidly expanding in the area. It became evident that unless the British government took action, Germany would take over that region.

As it had previously happened in European colonial history, particularly British history, trade preceded the flag. Setting up trading companies was a good way of promoting economic interests but they inevitably led to an official takeover. This was the case with the Royal Niger Company, which was officially bought by the government in 1900, thus establishing a protectorate over the area and transforming Nigeria into the main base for British Empire in West Africa.

On other occasions there was government intervention to solve problems caused by a trading company. This was the case of the British East Africa Company. The explorer and colonial administrator Frederick Lugard attempted to spread the company's interest through Uganda, but only after great economic losses and several conflicts with the local tribes. As a result of this, in 1894 the government intervened and declared a protectorate over Uganda and neighboring territories, which formally became known as British East Africa. A few years later, in 1905, the capital was set up in Nairobi and

---

* Pakenham, *The Scramble for Africa.*

Colonel James Sadler was sent as governor. From then on, present-day Kenya became one of the favorite colonial postings for the British.

British policy in Africa and expansionism in that era is above all associated with Cecil Rhodes. No European fortune-seeker was as successful in the African continent as this businessman, mining industry magnate, and imperialist politician. From his childhood Rhodes had delusions of grandeur and was convinced that he was destined for greatness. His works would give testimony to his vocation, and not for nothing was he popularly known as "the colossus."

Cecil Rhodes's business career came to prove the extent to which South Africa had become the new El Dorado for European expansion in the 1870s. The son of a Hertfordshire vicar, Rhodes was sent by his family to South Africa as a teenager in the 1860s to help his brother in a farm in Natal. In 1871 the Rhodes brothers abandoned farming for diamond trading in Kimberley, which was soon to become one of the most lucrative businesses in the colonial world. A great negotiator and workaholic to the extent that he never married because he said that he did not have time for it, Rhodes obtained financial support from Rothschild and Sons, and devoted seventeen years to buying small exporting businesses from the diamond mines. His ultimate aim was to consolidate a diamond exporting monopoly which he finally achieved in 1888, when the company De Beers was created. As a result of this he became fabulously rich.

While he made his fortune, Rhodes also decided to become the main promoter of the British Empire in South Africa. "It there be a God he would like me to paint Africa British—red as possible,'" he once stated with his characteristic messianic mentality. Shortly after becoming the prime minister of Cape Colony in 1883, he proposed a plan to annex territories in the North so that the frontiers of the British Empire would almost reach Central Africa. The magnate explained that by means of territorial expansion Cape Colony would become the most powerful state in Africa, which would allow it to propagate civilization through the heart of Africa. The main obstacle for his expansionist plans was that the colony did not have the means to subsidize

---

*   Anthony Thomas, *Rhodes: The Race for Africa* (New York: Thomas Dunne Books, 1997).

such an ambitious scheme, but this posed no obstacle for someone who had never been stopped by lack of money. He proposed the creation of a new company that would obtain the support of London's government. In this way the British South Africa Company was born. Another problem was to obtain the authorization of the indigenous peoples that inhabited the region, but once more, they were easily coerced to accept the advance of the European.

Shortly after Rhodes became Cape Colony's prime minister in 1890 a group of two hundred European men set out from Cape Town to Mashonaland, where each one of them was granted three thousand acres of land to begin a new life. Rhodes had ensured that the colonists of the new lands would be carefully selected, and among them were farmers, engineers, miners, hunters, and some missionaries as well. Contrary to the Great Trek organized by the Boers fifty years before, this mission did not include women and children. The families arrived later, once the pioneers had settled in the lands. The new colony was baptized Rhodesia, after its promoter, and it occupied the lands of present-day Zimbabwe.

Rhodes also aimed at definitively putting an end to the Boer opposition to their full integration into the British Empire. For this he embarked on a risky plan, the Jameson Raid, by which British workers from the Transvaal were encouraged to rebel against the Boers and use this as a pretext for sending troops under the colonial administrator Leander Jameson, with the aim of taking over. Nevertheless, the rebellion that broke out in December 1895 failed a month later, and Rhodes, as its main promoter, was forced to resign.

The failure of the Jameson Raid haunted him until the end of his days. He died of a heart attack in 1902, during the Second Boer War. "So many things to do and so little achieved," he lamented shortly before this death.[*] Quite an ironic comment for a person with such remarkable achievements, despite his short life. Few Europeans have left such a deep mark on Africa, although much of his legacy is quite controversial, and he is associated with the most negative aspects of colonialism and for creating problems that have plagued South Africa until today. He aggravated the confrontation between

---

[*]   Thomas, *Rhodes*.

the Boers and the British. His views on the indigenous peoples, considering them as children who should be denied a franchise, contributed to the racial segregation that laid the foundation of the apartheid system. He founded a company that still exists, De Beers, which dominates what is also a controversial industry in Africa. On the other hand, Rhodes used part of his money to launch the first international scholarship program. Students from all ethnic origins in Africa and many other parts of the world have been able to study at Oxford University as a result of this, letting Rhodes's fortune have a positive impact on many professional lives.

Italy was another of the great players in the scramble for Africa. As Italians began to enjoy their golden era as a unified nation in the 1870s Africa emerged as a unique opportunity to create an empire that they had not enjoyed since the time of ancient Rome. Just like Bismarck, the Italian leader the count of Cavour was led into the African colonial adventure not by mere ambition but by realpolitik. He realized that in order to be granted the desired status as a great European power, it was imperative to acquire colonies.

The Italian colonial adventure began shortly after French annexed Tunisia, which had a substantial population of Italian settlers. As a result of this the Roman colonial lobby put pressure on the government to occupy another territory. After engaging in secret negotiations with the British government in order to avoid clashes of interests in Africa, the first Italian colonies were acquired: the Eritrean port of Massawa in the Red Sea and present-day Somalia. Not satisfied with these acquisitions the government set its eyes on Ethiopia. In 1887, Prime Minister Francesco Crispi, one of the most enthusiastic supporters of colonization, decided to expand his country's power by means of peaceful persuasion. In 1889 the Treaty of Wuchale was negotiated with the Ethiopian emperor Menelik II, by which Italy ceded to Ethiopia territory on the Red Sea in return for the emperor acceding to convert his country into an Italian protectorate. At least this is what the Italian version of this treaty explained, but the translated version for the Ethiopians did not seem to say the same. Certainly the emperor and his entourage never thought that as a result of this treaty they had become subjects of the Italian Empire. Frustrated by this, the Italian government opted for armed intervention, a decision they were soon to regret.

This conflict was to show that there was a great difference between colonizing sub-Saharan Africa, inhabited by backward peoples, and the old Christian kingdom of Ethiopia. The Ethiopian troops were not only much more numerous than the Italians but they had also imported modern weapons from Europe. As a result, they managed to repel the attack and forced the Italian troops to withdraw to their bases in Eritrea.

The defeat in the war against what was once Abyssinia had a devastating effect over Italy. As a result of it Francesco Crispi resigned, putting an ignominious end to his career as the architect of the Italian Empire in the Horn of Africa. On the other hand, Emperor Menelik II had good reasons to feel euphoric. With this victory Ethiopia was to be known in the world as the African country that had defeated a European power, avoiding submission to colonial status.

"I have no intention of being an indifferent looker-on if the distant powers have the idea of dividing up Africa, for Ethiopia has been for more than fourteen centuries an island of Christians in the middle of the sea of pagans," said Emperor Menelik II in 1891.[*]

This war caused considerable commotion both in Europe and in Africa. It contradicted the theories that were popular then about the racial supremacy of whites, as on this occasion they had been defeated by Africans. Some African historians and politicians have suggested that this war constituted the beginning of an African movement for independence. This interpretation is exaggerated, as the case of Ethiopia cannot be extrapolated to such a diverse continent as Africa, and the independence movement was virtually nonexistent toward the end of the nineteenth century, but there is no doubt that the Italian defeat constituted a warning to the Europeans about the risks of colonizing Africa. It was very easy to build empires and distribute territories from the European capitals, but as the explorers, missionaries, and traders who ventured into the African continent knew, in most cases their inhabitants were not going to give in to the conquerors' civilization, however many advantages it could have.

If experience in Africa would have counted in the distribution of its territories among European powers, Portugal was the pioneer that would

---

[*] Pakenham, *The Scramble for Africa.*

have taken the lion's share. Nevertheless, toward the end of the nineteenth century European expansion was determined by political and economic power, and Portugal, as a declining power, was found lacking. This is the reason why the Portuguese, rather than benefitting from the scramble for Africa, simply focused on holding on to its old and considerable possessions of Mozambique and Angola.

At a time when Europeans decided to explore the heart of Africa, the Portuguese, loyal to their old tradition as explorers, were going to make an outstanding contribution. This was particularly the case with Alexandre de Serpa Pinto who became the fourth explorer to cross Africa from east to west. He was rewarded by his country with the appointment of governor of Mozambique. From the second most important colony of the Portuguese Empire he advocated an ambitious plan to annex the territories separating it from Angola. Nevertheless, the desire to unify Portuguese Africa clashed with an even more ambitious plan of unifying the British Empire from Cape Town to Cairo, and its main supporter was none other than Cecil Rhodes. Despite the fact that the British government did not show any interest in the plan, Rhodes was determined to stop Portugal from expanding at British cost, and in January 1890 Portugal received an ultimatum to withdraw from territories where Rhodesia was to be founded. Shortly after that the two powers signed the Treaty of London, by which the limits of the Portuguese colonies were fixed, corresponding to present-day Angola and Mozambique.

The British ultimatum was a clear example of one power imposing its will over a weaker one. It caused such political upheaval in Portugal that it made the government fall, and the monarchy that symbolized the greatness of the Portuguese Empire entered into terminal decline.

The sixth European country to occupy a part of Africa was Spain, although its share was a modest one. Just like Portugal, Spain had had a presence in Africa from the fifteenth century, when the two North African enclaves of Ceuta and Melilla were occupied, and have remained Spanish until the present. The nineteenth century was a disastrous era for Spain in which it lost its vast American Empire. This explains the eagerness of some Spaniards to acquire a new empire in Africa in spite of the country's internal problems.

In the eighteenth century Spain had built a fortress in the island of Fernando Po, off the central West African coast. From there it expanded into the mainland in the 1860s, creating the small colony of Spanish Guinea. Later, in 1884, it established a trading post in the much larger coastal area between Cape Blanc and Cape Bojador that was officially recognized at the Berlin conference as the Spanish Sahara. Finally there was the Spanish protectorate in northern Morocco. On the whole it was quite modest compared to the Spanish Americas, but sufficient to allow the country to continue describing itself as an imperial power.

The scramble for African territory became particularly acute toward the end of the nineteenth century, as all European powers with territory in Africa hastened to take their share of that magnificent cake (as King Leopold II described it) before there was nothing left. At that time, Britain decided to embark on the reconquest of the Sudan, both for strategic and security reasons, as the Mahdist Islamic regime was threatening the whole of Egypt and jeopardizing British interests in this country. The wish for revenge could also be perceived in this decision, as Gordon's beheading in Khartoum in 1885 left a deep scar on Victorian Britain.

As a result of this, in 1896 the veteran General Herbert Kitchener was commissioned to lead the Anglo-Egyptian troops to the Sudan. The mission culminated with the Battle of Omdurman, an extraordinary exhibition of European military superiority and modern weaponry. The crucial factor in this war was the Maxim machine gun, the great military invention which explains why the Mahdist troops suffered as many as 12,000 dead while the British had only forty-seven. From the moment the British took this weapon with them to Africa their success was guaranteed, as tribesmen who decided to confront the British in open battle did not have a ghost of a chance of winning. Fear of this weapon also helped keep the peace in many colonies as the news of its lethality spread across Africa.

After this historic victory by which great part of the Sudan was finally under British influence, the temptation to continue expanding toward the south was to increase in order to make the dream of an empire from Cape Town to Cairo come true. The problem was that while the colonial lobby in London planned to have the Union Jack flying over territories from north to south, the French also aimed to hoist their tricolor from Senegal to the Red Sea, and in this way consolidate an equally imposing empire. This would inevitably lead to a critical moment in which the two empires would collide and only one empire would be able to grow at the expense of the other. This moment arrived in 1898 at the city of Fashoda, where the two empires intersected. The French government sent an expedition from Brazzaville under Colonel Jean-Baptiste Marchand with the aim of occupying Fashoda and preventing Britain from annexing the whole of the Sudan. But after the French troops took Fashoda, the British government ordered General Kitchener to advance toward this town with the aim of sending a clear message that its annexation by France would not be tolerated.

Despite public indignation caused by the British warning, the French government decided that this barren town did not deserve a war. French troops were ordered to withdraw from Fashoda, and an agreement was reached between the two powers by which this town and the River Nile would be the frontier between their two vast empires. The French foreign minister Théophile Delcassé was determined to use this conflict to put an end to Franco-British rivalry.* This was eventually achieved with the signing of the Entente Cordiale in 1904, by which France gave Britain freedom of action in Egypt and in return it was granted the same over Morocco. But this provoked an official protest from their most dangerous rival, Germany. An international conference was convened at Algeciras, in southern Spain. Spain then took advantage of German opposition to France and occupied a substantial part of north Morocco and eventually, with the sultan of Morocco's acquiescence, his kingdom was divided between France and Spain. But unfortunately it was not the last time that European powers squabbled over the control of Morocco.

In 1911 a revolt broke out against the sultan of Morocco and the French government sent troops to restore order. But Germany reacted by sending a gunboat to the Port of Agadir, a deliberate provocation with which Kaiser Wilhelm II aimed to show his discomfort with French influence in Morocco and at the same time test the strength of the relationship between Britain

---

* Eugene Rogan, *The Arabs* (New York: Penguin, 2012), p. 165.

and France.* To a certain extent he obtained what he wanted, for neither the French nor the British government was willing to go to war against Germany because of Morocco, and the crisis was solved by France making a territorial compensation to Germany in Central Africa.

Although all of these conflicts were amicably solved among European powers, they show the extent to which, within a few decades, Africa had become the new setting of imperial expansion and a new cause of confrontation between the great powers. By the late nineteenth century Europe had not only introduced its civilization into Africa, with all its positive and negative connotations for the African people, but also the rivalries and diplomatic tensions of its main powers. Only a few years after the Berlin conference that marks the beginning of the scramble for Africa, the continent had become an integral part of the globalized world that Europe had been creating through its trade and colonial networks since 1492.

Africa was going to inspire plenty of literature in Europe from the mid–nineteenth century. The image of this continent in the rest of the world, and many of the myths and legends associated with it, are largely the result of the literature published in Europe at that time. The long tradition of European travel literature that played such an important role in its expansion through the world was very much enriched by Africa.

The first great chronicler of Africa in the modern era that had a Europe-wide impact was David Livingstone. In 1857 he published his first book, *Missionary Travels and Researches in South Africa*. Among the many impressions of Africa transmitted by Livingstone was its beauty, that exuberant beauty of lush green vegetation that had been immaculately preserved. On discovering Victoria Falls, known by the locals as "the smoke that thunders" waterfall, he wrote that "scenes so lovely must have been gazed upon by angels in their flight." Livingstone transmitted the thrill of discovering natural paradises like no other explorer. He also described the way Africans lived in harmony with nature. On the other hand his works are also an invaluable testimony to African horrors, like his description of how around four hundred Africans were massacred by slavers on the banks of the Lualaba River and

---

*   Rogan, *The Arabs.*

how corpses of dead slaves thrown into the river constantly obstructed the steamboat on which he traveled. He used his works to denounce what was degrading Africa, particularly the slave trade, and warn against the dangers of penetrating tropical jungles, with deadly diseases like malaria, which eventually killed him.

The famous explorer did not live to enjoy the success of most of his works, travel diaries, and correspondence. The great beneficiary was Henry Stanley, but he certainly deserved it, for after all it was thanks to his chronicles in the British and American press that Livingstone became an international celebrity. Later, his book *How I Found Livingstone* was a bestseller on both sides of the Atlantic. His own extraordinary experiences as an explorer inspired books like *Through the Dark Continent*. Stanley offered a much cruder image of Africa than Livingstone and was even accused by his contemporaries of brutality, as he wrote that "the savage only respects force, power, boldness, and decision." On the other hand he praised the superior beauty of Africans, something that was very unusual among Europeans in those days.

In 1885 Henry Rider Haggard published *King Solomon's Mines*, the first adventure novel based in Africa. Haggard had served as secretary of Natal's colonial governor, and he drew on these experiences as well as his fertile imagination to write this famous novel that describes the journey of a group of Englishmen in search of the fabled mines at the heart of Africa. It had all the essential topics for a successful adventure novel: expedition through the African jungle under the spell of a legendary king, rivalry in search of a hidden treasure, hostile native tribes, and even a romantic affair with a local. Its publication constituted an enormous success to the extent that it gave birth to a new literary genre: fiction based on exotic and unknown lands, which would inspire many authors at that time: from Rudyard Kipling to Thomas Hardy in English literature, and many other authors in other European languages.

The first wars between Europeans and Africans were soon to inspire plenty of literature. A classic in this genre was Winston Churchill's *The River War*, which describes the war against the Mahdi, in which he himself fought as a cavalry officer. The book was critically acclaimed from its publication, and because of Churchill's subsequent fame as a statesman it was to have numerous editions. It not only contains the most vivid and dazzling descriptions of the Battle of Omdurman but it also reveals Churchill's imperial creed that was later to be so influential. It describes the British Empire as a dynamic force for the improvement of mankind, which by expanding through Africa was not only bringing peace and stability but also allowing backward peoples to enrich themselves by joining the modern world. As regards the enemy's culture and religion, Islam, the future statesman wrote that "no stronger retrograde force existed in the world as Islam," and warned that it was a militant and proselytizing faith. On the other hand the young soldier was appalled by the crudeness of war, which clashed with his more humanitarian view of imperial expansion. He severely criticized the inhuman slaughter of the enemy's wounded troops and General Kitchener's cruelty.

By the late nineteenth century Africa had become a Europe-wide genre. The famous French sailor and writer Pierre Loti, fascinated by Turkey and the Eastern world, also wrote a travel book about Morocco, *Au Maroc*, published in 1890, shortly after a journey he made through the country. In the German-speaking world, *Timbuktu* constituted a great success, a chronicle of the geologist Oskar Lenz, who together with the Spaniard Cristóbal Benítez, became the first Europeans to visit the city of Timbuktu. In Portugal, Alexandre de Serpa Pinto narrated his experiences in the book *How I Crossed Africa*.

The press also made an important contribution to turning tales of journeys through Africa into a new literary genre, awakening interest in the enigmatic continent for European and American readers. Editors of the great newspapers discovered that publishing chronicles about their expeditions would boost their sales. The example of the *New York Herald,* which published Henry Stanley's chronicles, was going to be imitated by many other European newspapers, well aware that Africa was an endless source of news and chronicles that deserved their headlines. Africa fascinated all types of readers, from the rich and powerful who read newspapers on a daily basis in their clubs or in their mansions, to the most humble workers who would browse through newspapers in pubs and public transport. Some would look in the African chronicles for ideas and opportunities to make a fortune, others for a place where they could migrate in search of a better life. There were also those who were eager to acquire knowledge about such exotic lands and unknown ways of life, but the great majority simply looked for entertainment with which they could forget the monotony of their lives.

How far was the European conception of Africa shaped by late nineteenth-century European literature? The image of Africa that could be generally perceived by chronicles and newspaper articles was that of an immense and extraordinarily diverse continent with climates that were often not appropriate for the European, inhabited by primitive peoples who were generally indifferent and often hostile to the so-called civilized world. All of those who wrote about Africa then were firmly convinced that European civilization was superior and could improve African lives by bringing intellectual and scientific enlightenment. They never posed the essential question of whether they really had the right to rule over such foreign lands, alter their way of life, or transform their habitat. None of the colonial powers produced a nineteenth-century equivalent of Father Bartolomé de las Casas in Spain. Nevertheless conceptions of African tribes are very diverse. Livingstone transmitted the idea of the noble savage, that Africans were good-hearted people, affable, and humble, and that by means of the right education they could become good Christians and adapt themselves to superior ways of life. Henry Rider Haggard also did this in his famous novel, attributing to the African man important virtues like bravery, loyalty, and sensibility. He liked African women so much that he even dared to describe a love story between an Englishman who wished to marry a young woman from a local tribe, in this way defying the code of conduct imposed by colonial powers that banned sexual relations with Africans. But these positive visions belonged to a minority.

The majority of the chroniclers, like Henry Stanley, insisted on using epithets like "barbarians," "savages," and "ignorant" to describe Africans and justify violence as the only way of disciplining them and earning their respect.

Generally, all those who wrote about Africa in that era seemed to be firmly convinced of Europe's civilizing mission in that continent and that the three C's, Christianity, commerce, and civilization were the keys to justify their presence there. They were clearly the product of an era of imperialism, although soon the most sensible observers were going to feel scandalized by the methods generally used by the Europeans to introduce these three key words. This would lead them to rebel against their culture, giving birth to a literature critical of the phenomenon of civilization.

If all European powers agreed in the belief that their aim was to open the African continent to Christianity, commerce, and civilization, the methods that they used to introduce them varied considerably, as did their results.

Christianity had been present in Africa from the time of its birth. The Copts and other Christian communities had spread from Egypt to Ethiopia and managed to survive despite the overwhelming presence of Islam from the eighth century. European colonization gave Christians a golden opportunity to spread through the rest of the continent. Despite the fact that Islam was firmly entrenched in North Africa, it had considerable difficulty winning followers beyond its sub-Saharan stronghold. Christianity was much more successful, and one of the most enduring legacies of the Europeans in Africa was that from South Africa to Congo and from Angola to Kenya, countries with a Christian majority were to emerge.

The lives of Christian missionaries were full of dangers and sacrifices, and unlike that of fortune-seekers, had no material rewards. But it did have a spiritual reward, that of witnessing how their faith was accepted by people who had never heard of the Gospel, who willingly replaced their beliefs and superstitions with a Christian life. But why were Christian missionaries more successful than the Muslims? The main reason was because Christian missionaries offered solutions to improve their daily lives and even solve existential problems, particularly slavery.[*] The slave trade had been a lucrative business in the Islamic world from time immemorial. Arab traders organized expeditions through the African interior in order to capture and enslave local tribesmen. As a result of this, Arab traders were both feared and abhorred in the African interior. On the other hand the Europeans promised to abolish slavery, and this explains why Pierre Savorgnan de Brazza was received as a liberator and why General Gordon, who launched a crusade against the slave trade, became so popular with the population of Khartoum. While the Arabs had promoted slavery, the Europeans (after promoting and benefitting from

---

[*] Adrian Hastings, *The Church in Africa, 1450–1950* (Oxford, England: Oxford University Press, 1994).

it for over three centuries), finally aimed at abolishing it. This was to have a positive impact over Christian religion in Africa.

Wherever there was a European settlement or protectorate, Catholic and Protestant missions would follow. Missionaries established close relations with African peoples, and at the same time as they preached the Gospel they also worked as teachers or brought in doctors to improve their living conditions. This is the reason why they managed to be trusted by many African people who were converted into Christianity despite the fact that Christian morality was not always compatible with their customs.

As regards commerce, the first settlements that were established by the Portuguese in the fifteenth century were motivated by commercial concerns. This was also going to be the reason why they became protectorates and colonies, as the fortune-seekers persuaded their governments that the African continent had great wealth to search. For commercial reasons, many African monarchs and leaders allowed Europeans to settle in their lands, as they promised to create wealth, although this did not always reach their hands. On occasion they were simply swindled.

Africa, as well as America and Asia, was an endless source of wealth for fortune-seekers. The products that could be exported from their lands were endless, from spices to timber, from food products to exotic animals, and all types of commodities, minerals, and precious stones. Due to the fact that Africa was more backward than America and Asia, the Europeans penetrated the interior of the continent with the same passion with which the mythic El Dorado had been searched in America.

The lands of South Africa were particularly good for agriculture and livestock, but the discovery of gold and diamonds in this region transformed it into the favorite posting for European fortune-seekers, whose wealth was to multiply in a spectacular way. In Congo and in other areas of Central Africa the exploitation of wood, minerals, and rubber were soon to be established. In North Africa, mineral deposits constituted great sources of wealth, and with the arrival of the Europeans agriculture the spice trade was to flourish. As a consequence of the opening of Africa to world trade, many of its ports like Cape Town, Mombasa, Dar es Salaam, Dakar, Casablanca, Tangier, Tripoli, and Alexandria were transformed into great cities with an extraordinary commercial activity.

On the other hand opening Africa to world trade as Europeans from Livingstone to King Leopold II wished did not always bring benefits to the native population. Exploiting Africa's enormous sources of wealth and incorporating them into the trends of the market economy required a labor force that was provided by the Africans, in most cases in degrading conditions. Despite the fact that slavery was strictly forbidden in Europe, and several of the great powers set the aim of abolishing it in Africa, many European settlers forced local tribes to work in conditions that were no better than slavery. The eagerness of the Europeans to acquire wealth in Africa, and the fact that they were not controlled by any official authority in those remote territories let them to submit Africans to all types of abuses. The most scandalous case was that of the Congo Free State, to which ironically King Leopold II had given the motto of "work and progress." In order to satisfy the increasing demand for the rubber that had become Congo's main export, the local population was not only forced to work in conditions of slave labor, but they were punished in the most inhuman way. Those who failed to meet the rubber collection quotas would be punished by death or often their hands and those of their direct relatives would be cut off. The discovery by missionaries and government officials of villages where most of its inhabitants had been mutilated led to protests, and this eventually inspired the report published by British diplomat Roger Casement in 1904, which caused great upheaval in Europe and transformed the Congo Free State into the most shameful case of colonization in Africa.* If this was the most extreme case, there were many other abuses committed on behalf of trade, which explains why many Africans were to be so skeptical of the theoretical benefits of opening their continent to world trade.

If the introduction of commerce was not initially going to be beneficial for most of the Africa's indigenous people it was certainly much less for its fauna and flora. The ivory trade had existed in Africa long before the first European settlers, but as a result of the scramble for Africa it rapidly expanded, reaching a peak toward the end of the nineteenth century. Ivory became an essential product in the luxury industry that spread through affluent areas

---

* Mario Vargas Llosa, *The Feast of the Celt* (London: Faber & Faber, 2012).

in the world. Ivory was used for piano keys, billiard balls, and diverse decorative objects associated with exotic wealth. Europeans were not the first exterminators, as elephants had already been wiped out of North Africa long before the colonization era, but they did exterminate them in South Africa and parts of West Africa. Other emblematic African animals were affected in a similar way: rhinoceros, hunted for its horn became an endangered species by the early twentieth century. Europeans created a market for ostrich feathers, hides, skins, horns, or specimen animals, and consequently a new profession emerged, that of the professional hunter, which would replace the hunter-gatherers who had lived in perfect harmony with the ecosystem for so many centuries. With the help of infallible rifles hunting became both a safe and lucrative profession. M. J. Koekemoer, a South African hunter, claimed to have killed 108 lions in a single year in the 1870s. Hunting parties were another increasingly popular activity in most European colonies, which had a particularly devastating effect on wildlife.

Hunting expeditions with local porters carrying elephant tusks and corpses of great African animals behind proud white hunters became one of the most frequent images associated with European colonization. South Africa acquired a reputation for having the best game-hunting grounds on the continent. Hunting parties organized there often included guests, from European dignitaries and even members of royal houses, all of whom were attracted by the pleasure of killing animals. As a result of this by the early twentieth century the abundance of wildlife roaming around the vast open grasslands of South Africa had ended. Further north and particularly in the African rainforests, wildlife seemed to be safe from rifles in the hands of European intruders, but it would only be a matter of time before it faced a similar danger. Once Africa had been opened to commerce there was a market for all it had to offer.

Occupying Africa on behalf of civilization also implied opening the continent to emigration. Although Africa never seemed as attractive for European emigration as the Americas, colonization certainly contributed to the emergence of European communities there. In the north Algeria became a very interesting option not only for the French but also for Italians and Spaniards. By the 1879s there were about 250,000 European settlers in French Algeria, mainly devoted to farming.* But undoubtedly the most attractive destination for European emigration was South Africa, particularly after the discovery of diamonds in Kimberley. Within less than a decade after this discovery was announced over 50,000 new settlers had arrived. On the whole, according to a census in 1904, the white population in Cape Colony was 579,741.** Rhodesia soon became a country with a substantial European population of around 200,000. Portugal had great difficulty encouraging settlers to move to their African colonies, which hardly reached 100,000. Germany had similar problems promoting migration to its German colonies, which peaked in 1913 with a modest figure of 19,679. Unlike Spaniards and Portuguese in Latin America, Europeans did not contemplate promoting population growth by intermarriage. The German government banned marriage with locals in 1905. Although other colonial powers did not pass legislation which explicitly forbade mixed marriages, prevailing codes of conduct in all European colonies prevented the emergence of mixed-race populations.

Although Europeans were convinced of the superiority of their civilization, the method of introducing it in Africa varied, depending on the region as well as their guiding principles and strategies. In the North, Europeans had to learn to cohabit with Arab civilization, well aware that interfering with Islamic customs could easily lead to a revolt. For this reason European influence did not go beyond the application of minimum rules to promote trade links and keep law and order in those territories. A remarkable example of cultural cohabitation achieved by the Europeans was the Moroccan city of Tangier, which in the early twentieth century had a population of 40,000, of whom 20,000 were Muslims, 10,000 Jews, and 9,000 Europeans. The three communities contributed to its substantial wealth and cosmopolitan atmosphere. Another major port in North Africa that experienced an extraordinary development as a result of European presence was Alexandria. After bombing it in 1882 the British promoted it as a major trading hub, attracting migration from Greeks, Armenians, and Jews from nearby regions. Consequently, its urban culture reflected more European than Islamic influence. As a result

---

*   Meredith, *The Fortunes of Africa.*
**   Ibid.

the number of foreigners soared from 90,000 in the 1880s to 1.5 million in the 1930s.* But these cities were exceptional, generally speaking; segregation between the European settlers and the local peoples was the rule in all colonies. One important difference that set the French Empire apart from the rest was the idea that colonial subjects should become French citizens with the same rights as those in France.** French nationality was offered to every African subject capable of speaking French and adopting French customs.

Very often throughout colonial Africa, particularly in the sub-Saharan regions, local tribes were considered too primitive to be brought into the civilized world. In the most extreme cases this led to the belief that they could only be used as a labor force, or even exterminated. The most notorious case was that of the Congo Free State, where according to Robert Casement's report, depopulation had four main causes: indiscriminate war, starvation, reduction of births, and disease. It is impossible to quantify the number of deaths accurately, but it has been calculated that as many as ten million may have died due to the living conditions imposed by the colonizers. As Joseph Conrad described it, this was the vilest scramble for loot that ever disfigured the history of human conscience.***

The other major example of brutal racial extermination was that of German West Africa. In 1904 the Herero and Nama tribes rebelled against the German settlers, causing numerous deaths. Kaiser Wilhelm reacted so virulently that the punishing measures were to be described as "the kaiser's first war." General Lothar von Trotha was appointed commander in chief of the colony, with the order that the punishment should be so severe that the tribes would never forget. The German troops trapped the Herero tribe in a desert where many were to die of thirst and starvation, and those who surrendered were interned in concentration camps. According to a survey that was carried out in 1911, less than half of the Nama survived and only a fourth of the Herero population were still alive after the German repression. It was

---

*   Meredith, *The Fortunes of Africa.*

**   Christopher Harrison, *France and Islam in West Africa, 1860–1960* (Cambridge, England: Cambridge University Press, 1988).

***   Ibid.

later to be described as one of the first genocides of the twentieth century, and in this way Germany introduced in Africa the strategy of genocide with which it was sadly to be associated in the twentieth century.

On the other hand two of the major symbols of European civilization that the Europeans were to introduce in Africa were science and medicine. The first hospitals and public health infrastructures were built in order to protect settlers and make colonization possible by combating the tropical diseases that had prevented Europeans from penetrating sub-Saharan Africa. Nevertheless Africans were also gradually to benefit, as the colonial settlers spread the benefits as an integral part of their civilizing mission. Modern medicine not only saved Africans from cholera, smallpox, leprosy, tuberculosis, and many other illnesses that had been frequent in Europe, but also tropical diseases like yellow fever or malaria. All colonial powers introduced vaccination programs, more or less efficiently. In 1904 French laws about compulsory smallpox vaccination were applied in the colonial empire, although obviously they were difficult to implement in rural Africa. All other European colonial powers followed suit in their African colonies. Although it is difficult to evaluate their efficiency, the introduction of modern medicine was going to be one of the most enduring positive legacies for the native population, and eventually allowed it to grow more than ever in the twentieth century.

Education was another important introduction made by the Europeans that was eventually going to have a substantial impact on the Africans. There was no such thing as a civilizing mission without education, and it also offered the best way of promoting language and the values of the metropolis. The French relied on the state to introduce the same educational system in the colonies as in France, and they were particularly proud of the fact that by the early twentieth century lycées were open in all African colonies. Britain and the rest of the colonial powers left education in the hands of the missionaries. Nevertheless the percentage of Africans who benefitted from school education was to remain very low, particularly in sub-Saharan Africa. One of the reasons for this was that European colonial elites were often reticent to extend education to Africans, and also the latter were sometimes reluctant to give their children what they considered the white men's education.

The Moroccan University of Al Quaraouiyine in Fez and the University of Timbuktu claim to be the oldest universities in the world. But the university in the modern sense was to be introduced by Europe. The University of Cape Town was the first European-style university to be created in South Africa, in 1829. Also at that time the University of Sierra Leone was the pioneer of education in West Africa. The University of Algiers, founded in 1909, stemmed from several educational institutions created in the nineteenth century.

If only a very small percentage of Africans were to benefit from educational systems introduced by the Europeans, they were to be influenced by European education and culture through a very powerful channel of communication: language. French spread with particular efficiency in its African empire to the extent that by the early twentieth century it was the lingua franca in all its territories, except in Algeria and the Arab-speaking colonies, where it cohabited with Arabic. English also made substantial progress in both East and West African colonies. In South Africa, it shared official status with the Dutch-derived Afrikaans, which had initially been the most widely spoken European language. Portuguese proved equally resilient in the Portuguese colonies, and even Spanish had an impact on the population of Equatorial Guinea. The Germans and the Italians also achieved a modest presence for their languages in their African empires.

The other major element of European civilization that was to leave an indelible mark on the African continent was the transport system, as without this European colonization would not have been possible. Of all the systems of transport, the train, the great symbol of the Industrial Revolution, was undoubtedly the most important.

The first train line in Africa was built in Egypt in 1854 by Emir Pasha, who aimed at modernizing his country by importing European technology. Over the subsequent decades the railway networks gradually expanded as Europeans made progress occupying the continent. Cape was the most advanced colony in railway construction. Its first railway line was built in 1860, and by the end of the nineteenth century not only all major cities in South Africa were communicated by railway but also Rhodesia. The imperialist aspiration of connecting Cape Town with Cairo by rail was to be an impossible dream, among other reasons because German East Africa interfered with it, but the train reached Khartoum in 1897. Four years later Mombasa and Lake Victoria were joined by rail. In the meantime France made substantial progress with similarly ambitious projects like the train line from Dakar to Niger, which due to very difficult geography it was not to be completed until 1924. The steamboats introduced by Europeans from the mid–nineteenth century also played an important role as they allowed the great rivers like the Nile and the Congo to be transformed into highways through which European progress penetrated the heart of Africa.

Last but not least, Europeans were to shape the African continent by laying the foundations of an urban civilization in several areas. In South Africa the three main cities, Cape Town, Johannesburg, and Pretoria, were founded by Europeans and designed with the inspiration of Western cities. Cape Town together with Durban and Kimberley became the largest cities south of the Sahara toward the end of the nineteenth century. Nairobi was a swampy area that began to be developed by British settlers as a logistical center for the construction of the Uganda railroad until it became the capital of British East Africa, and eventually it would emerge as the most significant urban center in East Africa. In Central Africa, Brazzaville became a key city in the French expansion through the interior of the continent, and it was going to rival Leopoldville, the capital of the Congo Free State. (That name was not going to survive the decolonization process, due to the notoriety of the Belgian king, but after renaming itself Kinshasa it was transformed into one of the main megalopolises in Africa.) Many other ancient African cities like Cairo, Tripoli, Rabat, or Casablanca were going to grow and see their structure modified by investors, architects, and European builders. An urban civilization is one in which the values of the city prevail over those of the rural world. From the late nineteenth centuries these values started to make steady progress on a continent where they had been virtually absent.

Africa was the last great frontier of European exploration, the last continent (with the exception of Antarctica) to be incorporated into Europe's sphere of influence. Once this frontier had been crossed Europeans were capable of spreading the trends of progress and modernization throughout the world. Four decades after Livingstone first traveled to Africa, practically the whole continent was controlled by European powers. Only Ethiopia and Liberia were going to keep their independence; the rest were colonies or protector-ates under European control. Never in the history of humanity had so much territory been occupied in such a short timescale.

Becoming Europe's backyard had deep implications for the African con-tinent. It joined the global economy that European powers had been building since 1492, as well as the imperial system that they had been spreading. It was also increasingly exposed to all that European culture had to offer. From that point on there were British Africans, French Africans, German Africans, etc., all of them steadily influenced by a new civilization that the imperial power to which they belonged were introducing.

From the 1890s the struggle for supremacy that was taking place in Europe and the rest of the imperial world was also fought in Africa, and this continent became a clear reflection of the European balance of power. Judging by the size of their African empires Britain and France were the main beneficiaries of the scramble for Africa, followed by Germany and Italy, two aspiring powers. Portugal and Spain managed to hold onto imperial status as a result of their possessions in this continent while Belgium, a small industrial nation, could call itself an imperial power as a result of its Congolese adventure.

Why did Europeans decide to occupy practically the whole of Africa? Was it because they were eager to spread their civilization, as Livingstone had urged them to do, or were they motivated by economic ambitions or by nationalist aspirations? It seems clear that unlike individual Europeans, governments were guided by national interests more than any other consid-eration on deciding to take up colonies in Africa. In fact as we have seen very often they occupied territory in order to avoid a rival power from doing so.

Civilizing rhetoric played a very important role justifying European colonization, but the problem was that often colonial powers did not live up to those expectations. This not only ended up turning indigenous peoples against them, but even European public opinion, which was increasingly disappointed by the effects of imposing a civilization that was often rejected by the natives. But Europe had introduced forces of change and moderniza-tion into Africa by the early twentieth century, and from that point onward Africans had to learn to live with them and make them compatible with their own heritage and customs.

Chapter 9

The Wars that Shook the World

How the Two World Wars Precipitated a New Post-European Era.

E urope in the year 1900 was at the apex of its civilization. Its inhabitants on the whole were basking in the glory of achievements in all spheres of knowledge, enjoying the benefits of economic growth and rising living standards. Europeans lived in a golden age of security as Stefan Zweig described it in his memoir *The World of Yesterday*. He also described this time as an age of reason, in which no one thought of wars, revolutions, or revolts, and all that was radical and violent seemed impossible. Throughout the world, Europe inspired admiration and envy, even among those who considered themselves enemies or victims of European expansion.

Yet only fourteen years later Europeans started the First World War, the most destructive of all wars fought until then, which undermined much of what European civilization had achieved. It also led to an era of unprecedented political extremism, nationalist exaltation, and collective anger that culminated with the even more barbaric Second World War. Between 1914 and 1945 Europe and the world were plunged into an age of total war, when human destructive capacity reached the highest peak.

How could this be possible on a continent that seemed so peaceful and civilized in the early twentieth century? How could Europeans accede to fight, on two occasions, wars that brought so much suffering and were so self-destructive?

A lot has been written about the causes of the First World War that initiated this dark age in Europe, which lasted for over three decades. It can be considered as the culmination of the age of new imperialism. From 1870 the great powers embarked on an unprecedented quest for overseas possessions, mainly in Africa and the Pacific. Germany and Italy as well as the United States and Japan joined this imperial race. As a result of this, the atmosphere of rivalry, mistrust, and envy prevailed in the international sphere.

The world's international order in the early twentieth century could be summarized as follows: Britain was at the zenith of world supremacy. It had consolidated the largest empire in history and its model of civilization enjoyed extraordinary projection. With such a privileged position its aim was to maintain the balance of power and prevent any European rival from expanding at its cost. France had also built a huge colonial empire and was therefore also interested in keeping the balance of power, but at the same time it subtly looked for opportunities to expand its influence at British cost. Germany was a new colossus; it had overtaken Britain as the top industrial nation but on the other hand it had a small colonial empire. For these reasons Germany was eager to shake the international order to place itself above Britain and France. Russia on the other side ceased to consider Britain as its worst enemy and feared the consequences of German ambitions on its frontiers. Austria-Hungary was desperately trying, with great difficulty, to hold on to its empire in times of growing nationalism, and Italy resented the obstacles posed by France to its wishes for imperial expansion. In the meantime the United States had also acquired great-power status after taking over Spain's last colonies, and Japan was eagerly looking for opportunities to expand into Asia and the Pacific.

By the early twentieth century there were no longer unoccupied territories in the world available to quench the thirst for imperial expansion. The international order became a zero-sum game. Amid growing tensions and an atmosphere of mutual resentment, leaders of the European powers created a series of alliances that were mainly guided by the old principle that my rival's foe is my friend.

The first pillar of this complex system of alliances was laid by Germany. Chancellor Bismarck wanted to strengthen Germany's position in Europe by means of a new defensive alliance with Austria-Hungary. They were interested in an alliance with Germany that would protect it against Russia, its great rival in the Balkans. The two countries signed a defensive alliance in 1879. Three years later a new country joined this alliance, Italy. Having given in to France over the possession of Tunisia, Italy decided to seek the protection of Germany and Austria-Hungary in retaliation. In this way the Triple Alliance was born, to the satisfaction of the cunning statesman Bismarck.

The countries that felt most seriously threatened by the Triple Alliance were France and Russia. Despite the fact that the French republic and the Russian autocracy had nothing in common from a political point of view, their governments soon decided that it was in their mutual interest to reach an alliance. For this reason, in 1894 the czar of Russia and the president of the French republic signed the Dual Alliance, by which they agreed to support each other in case of being attacked by one of the members of the Triple Alliance.

The power that was then most seriously affected by the alliance system was Britain, as it had been left dangerously isolated. For this reason, in 1902 the British government decided to sign a defensive alliance with an Asian power that shared a rivalry with Russia: Japan. But soon Britain was going to look for allies in Europe to defend itself from Germany, which had become its most dangerous rival. In 1904 Britain signed the Entente Cordiale with France, officially putting an end to several centuries of rivalry. The motives that led these two nations to overcome their differences and agree to help each other in case of being attacked was their shared fear of Germany.

Moreover, the desire to defend themselves from Germany also led Britain and Russia to overcome their historic rivalries. In 1907 the Treaty of Friendship and Cooperation was signed between Britain and Russia. With this treaty the Triple Entente was born, by which Britain, Russia, and France assumed the compromise of helping each other in case of an external aggression.

Alliances had traditionally been the formula by which diplomacy prevailed over war and the balance of power was kept in Europe and the rest of the world. Alliance agreements between powers served to warn a third power about the dire consequences of an aggression. But in the early twentieth century the great powers were so focused on the struggle for supremacy in Europe that it transformed the alliance system from deterrent to a trigger that could lead to war on a much larger scale.

As we have previously seen, confrontations over colonial issues and particularly the scramble for Africa always ended with a peaceful resolution, as all countries seemed to agree that a territory in the colonial world, however important, was not worth a war against another great power. But this was not the case with territorial disputes in Europe.

In 1912 Greece, Bulgaria, Montenegro, and Serbia created the Balkan League and declared war on the Ottoman Empire with the aim of making it withdraw from its ancestral lands. The Balkan League easily defeated the Turkish army and in May 1913 a peace treaty was signed by which the Ottoman Empire gave up practically all its territory west of Constantinople. Nevertheless, the lack of consensus among the countries of the Balkan League over how to distribute the gained territory provoked a new war. Bulgaria declared a war on its Balkan allies, but ultimately Serbia and Greece were the winners.

What was the attitude of the great powers before this grave conflict in the heart of Europe? Russia considered this conflict as an opportunity to overthrow the Ottoman Empire once and for all, and gave Serbia all its support. Then the Serbs felt increasingly supported to make claims against the Austro-Hungarian Empire. Britain and France sympathized with Greece. Germany on the other hand was increasingly worried to see how its old ally the Ottoman Empire was defeated, and it compensated Bulgaria, defeated in the second war by transforming it into a new ally. In this way imperial tensions of the great powers were dangerously concentrated in Eastern Europe.

Another factor that deepened the crisis of European imperialism was the rivalry between ruling dynasties. From the end of the nineteenth century there was the happy coincidence that the majority of the ruling monarchs in Europe were relatives. Kaiser Wilhelm II and King George V were grandsons of Queen Victoria, and Czar Nicholas II was married to her granddaughter. King Alfonso XIII of Spain was also married to another of Queen Victoria's granddaughters. Queen Victoria was very appropriately known as Europe's grandmother. For a long time William II, George V, and Nicholas II, the three cousins, as they used to call each other in their correspondence, kept a cordial relationship. The fact that rivalries between empires and European nations could be solved as a family dispute should have been another way of guaranteeing peace in Europe. This was another advantage of provided by Europe's ruling monarchies. Nevertheless reality proved to be very different.

Few men in history have had as much access to wealth and power as Kaiser Wilhelm II of Germany. When he was crowned kaiser, he inherited not only a magnificent official residence in Potsdam but also almost thirty castles and mansions around Germany, which he used to visit in his own train. He also had his own yacht, the *Hohenzollern*, with a crew of around three hundred men, and the best country estates, where on one occasion in the hunting season, he killed one thousand animals in one week. But nothing of this seemed to compensate for the bitterness produced by the feeling that he was ruling over an empire that was smaller and less powerful than the one his cousin the Prince of Wales was going to inherit.

Throughout his reign Kaiser Wilhelm II focused on the aim of over-taking Britain and transforming his country into the leading world power. After deciding that the future was in the sea, he decided that Germany should have a larger navy than Britain. This provoked an arms race that led the British leaders and George V himself to the conclusion that only a war would stop his cousin Kaiser Wilhelm.

Nationalism promoted via terrorism ranks highly among the causes of this war. On June 28, 1914 in Sarajevo, a Serbian-Bosnian nationalist named Gavrilo Princip murdered the heir to the Austro-Hungarian throne, Arch-duke Franz Ferdinand of Austria and his wife. With this murder Princip aimed to put an end Austrian rule over his homeland. But he achieved much more than that—he provoked a war that precipitated the end of the Austro-Hungarian Empire and the era of European imperialism. Never had a terrorist act had such far-reaching consequences.

In the atmosphere of jingoism and resentment that was predominant in 1914, the European system of alliances not only failed to prevent a war, but actually contributed to its outbreak. On June 29, Austria-Hungary invaded Serbia in reprisal for the murder to Archduke Franz Ferdinand. Germany, in solidarity with its ally, ordered the mobilization of its army. France, fearing a new German invasion, also mobilized its army. On August 1 Germany declared war on Russia. Britain demanded Germany guarantee Belgium's neutrality, but Germany refused. As a result Britain declared war on August 4, dragging its ally Japan into the fray.

After almost a century of peace, great European powers found themselves in a war. This was a war caused by rivalries between European powers, but on this occasion it was not only going to be fought exclusively on the European continent. From the moment European nations were at war, so were their empires, which implied that a substantial part of the planet was going to suffer the effects of this war. Also as a consequence of its British alliance, Japan was dragged in making the Far East another war scenario. War had been a natural phenomenon among human beings from the beginning of time, all civilizations had benefited or suffered from it, but only Europeans had the capacity to transform an armed conflict into a global phenomenon that would affect the entire world.

One of the reasons why the era of imperialism culminated with the outbreak of the First World War is the fact that none of the powers feared the consequences of war and hoped to obtain great benefits from it. Those who declared war in 1914 had been brought up in a culture in which, just as Clausewitz had explained in his famous theory, war was seen as the continuation of politics by other means. It was considered as a natural phenomenon that occurred frequently in the human race, and it allowed countries to solve their differences when it was no longer possible to do it by peaceful means.

This explains why the atmosphere that prevailed in the main capitals of Europe when war broke out in August 1914 was one of optimism and even euphoria. In all countries involved in the war, young men from all social strata and very diverse backgrounds dutifully obeyed the order to enlist in the army, and they generally did so with enthusiasm, for they had been educated under the principle that serving one's country in war was a duty as well as an honor. There was the general feeling that this would be a short war, and for this reason many soldiers went to the front with the idea that they were embarking on an exciting adventure with which to break the monotony of their lives, and hoping to be back before Christmas.

Military strategists, especially in Germany, made optimistic predictions that the war could easily be won, even within a few weeks. The German strategy was based on the Schlieffen Plan. In order to avoid a two-front war General Alfred von Schlieffen had planned that Germany should carry out a swift offensive against France while fighting on the defensive in Russia. But the plan failed, producing a stalemate between opposing forces that took years to overcome.

Strategists not only failed to predict the length of the war but also the impact of modern military technology, which multiplied the weapons' destructive capacity to an extraordinary degree. Rifles, machine guns, and the new tanks gave armies in the battlefield unprecedented power to kill enemy troops in great numbers. Airplanes introduced a new dimension in modern warfare. For the first time, air bombardments made war a much more devastating phenomenon, and as a result the battlefronts were not the only theatres of war but the cities as well. German zeppelins bombed cities in southern England. War was also to be waged from under the sea with submarines, or U-boats. Chemical warfare was introduced in this war. Chlorine gas was first used by the Germans. The deadlier phosgene and mustard gases, which blinded people, were used by both sides of the war.

The First World War was initially known as the Great War, for obvious reasons. It could also have been known as the war of the empires, as all great empires were confronted in this conflict. Some fought in order to expand their empires, others to prevent it or to stop rival powers from expanding at their cost. Until then European imperial powers had fought in wars without necessarily involving all their subjects. But on this occasion all subjects of the empires, European or not, were going to be involved.

Out of approximately sixty-two million troops that were mobilized during the First World War, non-European troops were going to play a very important role. The outburst of patriotism provoked by the war could also be felt across the colonial empires, and it generally contributed to strengthen their unity. Despite the tensions that existed within the empires, solidarity and loyalty to the metropolis prevailed in the colonial world, even in those colonies where pro-independence movements had emerged. Mobilization contributed to instill in young soldiers the feeling that they had a great mission to perform and pride in contributing to a worthy cause by serving their empire.[*]

Africa, like the rest of the colonial world, was led into the fray. The order for mobilization was dutifully obeyed by colonial settlers with discipline despite the fact that many of them considered that the causes of the conflicts had nothing to do with them. Not more than a decade after the race for Africa was over and the colonial powers had divided practically the entire continent among themselves, once the war broke out they were going to try to occupy their rivals' territory, and Africans were going to be recruited for this purpose. More than two million Africans were conscripted by the colonial powers as soldiers, porters, or laborers.[**]

Although war in Africa was on a much smaller scale, for the first time practically the whole continent was at war. German colonial Africa was clearly in the minority against the Franco-British forces, nevertheless under the military leadership of General Paul von Lettow-Vorbeck, German forces kept the enemy at bay until the end of the war. Both sides used scorched-earth tactics, by which villages and crops were destroyed, bringing devastation to the rural areas. As a result of this, toward the end of the war many European colonial settlers felt that the original high aims of opening Africa to trade and civilization that had brought them there could no longer be justified.

"Behind us we leave destroyed fields, ransacked magazines, and for the immediate future, starvation," wrote Ludwig Deppe, a German doctor. "We

---

[*]   Max Hastings, *Catastrophe 1914: Europe Goes to War* (New York: William Collins, 1914).
[**]   Meredith, *Fortunes of Africa*, p. 495.

are no longer the agents of culture: our track is marked by death, plundering, and evacuated villages.[*]

Africans not only served in their homeland but also in the Middle East and Europe. There were 150,000 Africans serving on the Western Front in France and Belgium.[**] One regiment from Morocco became the most highly decorated regiment in the whole of the French army.

In the British Raj, the war was supported not only by the Indian sovereigns but contrary to what the British government feared, also by many of those who advocated the end of colonial rule. The Indian National Congress, which at that time was simply aiming at home rule, showed support for the British war effort, hoping that they would be rewarded after the war with a higher level of autonomy. More Indian men than British were mobilized during the war. Over one million Indian troops served in different war theatres, from German East Africa to the Middle East and the Western front.

The India Gate, one of the great architectural symbols of British colonial rule in India, was built in 1931 in honor of the approximately 74,187 soldiers who lost their lives fighting for the British Empire.[***]

As regards Britain's white dominions, they dutifully contributed to the war effort. Canada recruited a total of 630,000 men and women, many of whom served on the Western Front. Shortly after the war broke out troops from New Zealand took German Samoa while Australian forces attacked German New Guinea.

Asia and the Pacific gave this war a truly global dimension. For Japan, the First World War constituted a golden opportunity to assert its power over this part of the world. On August 27, the Japanese imperial navy, supported by the British, violated Chinese neutrality and blocked the waters of Kiautschou Bay in Shantung. It then took possession of the port city of Tsingtao, where the Germans had established a base since 1897. Japan then presented China what they called the 21 Demands, which included not only

---

[*]   Meredith, *The Fortunes of Africa*.
[**]   Ibid.
[***]   James, *Raj*.

control over Shantung and an island in South Pacific controlled by Germany, but also southern Manchuria and Eastern Inner Mongolia.

Such high demands came at one of the worst times in the history of modern China. A rebellion in 1911 had provoked the fall of the Qing dynasty, which had ruled China since the seventeenth century. The young Chinese republic, in a chaotic situation, had no option but to accept the humiliating Japanese demands. Chinese public indignation at this helped allow the new president, Sun Yat-sen, the founder of the nationalist party Kuomintang, to justify his bid for a monarchy, although he failed. The one-year empire was proclaimed by Yuan Shikai, who declared himself emperor. Then the republic returned amid political chaos. There was a strong pro–Allied faction led by Duan Qirui. Germany secretly supported Zhang Xun in a monarchist coup that took place in 1917 to prevent the pro–Allied forces from winning power. Once the coup failed Duan used this incident as a pretext to declare war on Germany on April 1917. Apart from revenge on the Germans Duan's strategy was also motivated by the aim of earning a place for China at the postwar bargaining table and rejecting the terms of the Japanese incursion.

Some 140,000 Chinese men served in the Labor Corps supporting British and the French forces on the Western Front during and after the war.[*]

The global effects of this war, caused by Europeans, culminated with the intervention of the United States. On April 6, 1917, a declaration of war was passed by the U.S. Congress. This was mainly caused by the German sinking of the British ocean liner RMS *Lusitania*. But American intervention in this war had ultimately much higher aims than retaliation against Germany. As President Woodrow Wilson argued in his first war speech, his country's sole purpose was "to make the world safe for democracy." Winning this argument with American public opinion was considerably difficult as there was a large community of citizens of German ancestry. Above all there was widespread support for the principle, established by Washington and the founding fathers, of staying away from European entanglements, which had become the cornerstone of US foreign policy.

---

[*] Alex Calvo and Bao Qiaoni, "Forgotten Voices from the Great War: The Chinese Labour Corps," *The Asia-Pacific Journal*, 13(49).

On the other hand the U.S. had already abandoned its traditional isolation when it declared war on Spain in 1898, with the aim of expelling the old European power from Cuba, Puerto Rico, and the Philippine colonies. After this war the U.S. officially annexed Puerto Rico and occupied the Philippines. Despite the fact that the U.S. rejected the policy of acquiring colonies as the European powers did, this occupation was justified in order to bring progress and democracy to these territories. This was also in line with the Atlanticist foreign policy establishment, an increasingly influential elite led by personalities like ex-president Theodore Roosevelt, who believed that cooperation with nations on the other side of the Atlantic should be strengthened in defense of common interests and culture. This contributed to an Anglophile interventionism that eventually prevailed toward the end of the First World War.

The United States mobilized four million military personnel, of whom two million fought on French soil,* and its intervention constituted a turning point in contemporary history. Although officially the U.S. did not join the Allied forces but simply fought against Germany, it provided Britain, France, and other members of the Allied coalition with the decisive aid to win the war. Once it had determined the fate of Europe in such a decisive way the United States could not afford to return to its isolationist policy. As a victorious power the U.S. consolidated a new role as a great power and earned a major position in the postwar era.

What did they fight for in this terrible war? Apart from defending their own national interests the leaders of each nation involved in this war explained that the most sacred values were at stake. The "Great War for Civilization" could be read in the Victoria Cross, the highest award granted by the British government to the bravest soldiers. In France and in Belgium, they also talked about the war as preserving civilization. But Germans and Austro-Hungarians also considered themselves to be defending civilization. Nevertheless many of those who witnessed the atrocities in the war, and how the lives of so many young men were sacrificed, asked themselves about the meaning of a civilization that was capable of provoking such a destructive

---

* Winston S. Churchill, *The World Crisis, 1911–1918* (New York: Penguin, 2005), p. 691.

war and causing so much suffering. Others sought consolation in the fact that however destructive and barbaric this war seemed it would be the last one. "The war to end all wars," as British author E. H. Carr described it in 1914. The term became a popular catchphrase among combatants to justify their suffering, and some years later it was referred to sardonically when it became evident that the First World War had failed to put an end to warfare.

A great part of the literature that was produced during this war described the disappointment and indignation felt by those who suffered it and condemned the society that had caused it. One of the first writers to describe the horrors of war in a novel was the Spanish novelist Vicente Blasco Ibáñez, who published *The Four Horsemen of the Apocalypse* in 1916, which soon became an international bestseller. The novel tells the tragedy of a prosperous Franco-German family of international connections that ends up fighting on opposite sides, and it shows the devastating effects of this war on European society.

One of the best poets of the war generation, Wilfred Owen, who actually died at the front, broke with the European poetic tradition of extolling the patriotism and the bravery of the soldiers, focusing instead on the horror of life in the trenches and the traumatic experience that this war constituted for his generation. Some years after that, other great novels of this conflict like *A Farewell to Arms* by Ernest Hemingway or *All Quiet on the Western Front* by the German author Erich Maria Remarque, transmit the same feelings of horror, distress, and the emptiness felt by those who survived the ordeal. On the German side, there was however an influential current of thought which glorified war and described it as an edifying experience for the human character. The war memoirs of German officer Ernst Junger, *Storm of Steel* is the best example.

Long before the outbreak of this war, socialists and trade union movements, as well as all branches of the left in general, had described war as a product of capitalism and imperialism in which members of the working class were sent to fight against working class brothers in other countries to defend the interests of their bosses and those of capitalism in general. In August 1914 some of them demonstrated against conscription, hoping that if they were followed by the working-class masses war would not take place, but they failed. Workers throughout Europe joined the military, driven by a sense of duty and even enthusiasm. Nevertheless, opposition to the war, as well as desertions, progressively increased during the conflict, particularly among the countries that were ill-prepared for such a war, like Russia.

The first major casualty of the First World War was czarist Russia. Czar Nicholas II committed many mistakes in his unfortunate reign, but undoubtedly the most serious of all was to lead Russia into a war for which the country was neither technologically nor economically prepared. By 1917 the situation was unsustainable, with an ill-prepared army facing defeats on the front and widespread scarcity and hunger in the cities. Nicholas II was forced to abdicate in February 1917, putting an ignominious end to the dynasty that had ruled for over three hundred years and transformed it into an empire. The provisional government that took over, led by social democrat Alexander Kerensky, insisted on the need for Russia to continue fighting the war. As a result, general discontent did not cease.

Revolutions take place when the majority of the population has nothing to lose by taking to the streets and overthrowing the established order. This was very much the situation in Russia during the summer of 1917. Well aware of this, the German authorities made special arrangements for the Bolshevik leader Vladimir Ilyich Lenin, who was exiled in Switzerland, to be allowed to travel through Germany in a sealed train all the way to the Russian frontier. Once in Russia Lenin and the Bolsheviks embarked on a plan to win the support of the population under a popular slogan: All power to the Soviets (workers councils), all land to the peasants, end of war.

In October 1917 one of the great turning points in contemporary history was to take place: the Russian Bolshevik revolution. Strictly speaking, more than a revolution, it was a well-planned coup in which Bolsheviks allied with a rebel branch of the army easily overthrew a weak and unpopular government. Shortly after attaining power the commissar for external relations, Leon Trotsky, signed the Treaty of Brest-Litovsk with Germany. Under this treaty Russia gave up Finland, Poland, Ukraine, Lithuania, Latvia, Estonia, and some territories to the Austro-Hungarian and Ottoman Empires. The terms of peace were humiliating and the territorial concessions were considerable, but it was the only way of putting an end to this unpopular war and focus on the Bolshevik priority, which was to bring about the revolution. For the first time in history a communist utopia was going to become a reality.

The First World War finished with the defeat of Germany and its allies in April 1918. The Great War had a devastating effect on the whole of Europe. It brought the golden era to a dramatic end. "The lights are going out all over Europe, we shall not see them lit again in our lifetime," commented the British foreign secretary Edward Grey when war broke out in 1914. From 1918 onward Europeans were to witness the sad truth behind this famous melancholic quote. Then from 1918 onward many aspects of the old European world were quickly to vanish.

This was the most deadly of all wars that had ever taken place. From the outset it became evident that new military technology was going to increase the number of deaths by an extraordinary amount. In the 1916 Battle of Verdun, 976,000 French and German soldiers died. In the Somme, where the British confronted the Germans that same year, the total number of casualties reached 1,219,200. By the end of the war the total number of casualties reached a staggering thirty-eight million: seventeen million dead and twenty million wounded. Approximately seven million out of the seventeen million dead were civilians.

Shortly after the armistice, Kaiser Wilhelm II abdicated and went into exile, and the Austro-Hungarian emperor Charles followed the same path. In this way, three great European dynasties, the Hohenzollerns, the Habsburgs, and the Romanovs lost the throne as a result of the war. Ottoman sultan Mehmed V also abdicated after being defeated. This was the great irony of the First World War. Several of the empires that that fought in this fray with the aim of expanding and increasing their power achieved nothing but their own extinction.

Above all the First World War brought a new world order. In January 1919 a conference was convened in Paris by the victorious powers in order to discuss the terms of the peace treaties to be signed with the defeated powers and ensure that the conditions for a lasting peace would be created. Thirty-two countries in total were invited to participate, as well as representatives of several nationalities. Among them four powers were going to be primarily responsible for its result: Britain, France, Italy, and the United States. They were represented by "the big four" as they came to be known: British prime minister David Lloyd George, French president Georges Clemenceau, Italian prime minister Vittorio Orlando, and U.S. president Woodrow Wilson.

Many peace conferences had taken place in Europe but no one was organized on such a scale. The last antecedent was the Congress of Vienna, but on that occasion only European representatives discussed issues that that mainly affected the European continent. But in 1919, the Paris peacemakers were going to make decisions that would have an impact on the entire world, and that shaped international relations until the present day. During six months a diverse representation of statesmen, diplomats, lawyers, and economists made plans for the creation of a new world order. Empires were officially wiped out while others expanded, borders were redrawn, new nations were created, very often at the cost of others, and peoples and races saw their ancestral rights finally recognized. Not only was politics discussed in these conferences but also very important social issues like women's rights, labor relations, race relations, or minority rights. As historian Margaret MacMillan wrote, in 1919 Paris was the capital of the world and the peacemakers were the world's most powerful people.*

This peace conference marked the beginning of the end of the European era while the U.S. entered the world stage as a great power determined to shape international relations. Japan was also given a decisive role in this conference, as a member of the coalition of allies that had defeated Germany. European powers not only had to sit at the negotiating table with the nations that had allowed them gain the upper hand in this war, but also with a series of new nations that from then on were to assert their independence and their right to influence the new world order. This was the case of the British white dominions Canada, Australia, New Zealand, and South Africa, which were granted the right to have their own representative, independent from Britain. Even India was allowed this, despite the fact that it obtained no self-government after this conference. China also sent a delegation, in this way putting an end to its traditional isolation from international affairs. Brazil and several

---

* Margaret MacMillan, *Paris 1919: Six Months That Changed the World* (New York: Random House, 2001).

Latin American nations were also present in an international conference for the first time in their history. Aspiring nations also sent delegates, from the Irish and the Armenians to the Zionists and the Vietnamese.

In December 1918 President Wilson embarked on a journey that was to make history for several reasons. He became the first U.S. president to travel to Europe while holding office.* What was more important was that for the first time in history a non-European power was going to determine the terms of a war waged by European powers. From then on the United States was internationally recognized as one of the main power brokers in the world. Before leaving office, President Wilson gave a speech in the U.S. Congress in which he spelled out the famous Fourteen Points, which should be the basis for making peace. Some of these points were to have particular influence in international relations: prohibition of secret diplomacy, freedom of seas, removal of economic barriers in order to promote free trade, and adjustment of all colonial claims taking into consideration, "the interests of the population concerned." Last but not least, point fourteen proposed the creation of a general assembly of nations, which would ultimately be in charge of maintaining world peace and guaranteeing the independence of all nations.

The European allies tacitly accepted Wilson's Fourteen Points, as well as his leading role in the conference, without dispute. Not only in recognition of the US war effort that had given them the final victory, but also because they acknowledged the fact that after this war they no longer had the capacity nor the moral strength to dominate the world. After the butchery that had taken place in the Western Front Europeans could no longer talk about their civilizing mission in the world with the same confidence. The time had come to share this mission with the United States, which was after all an offshoot of Europe.

The Treaty of Versailles, which the Paris peace conference produced, marked the death sentence of the old world order. Three empires were liquidated, the German, the Austro-Hungarian, and the Ottoman. Britain, France, and Japan were to benefit from it. Germany, as the aggressor, was to pay high reparations that were never fully paid. In this way the treaty, in

---

* MacMillan, *Paris 1919.*

Henry Kissinger's words, was too punitive for conciliation and too lenient to keep Germany from recovering.[*]

The British Empire was the main beneficiary in terms of territorial gains from the demise of the German Empire. Both German East and West Africa were incorporated into the British Empire as protectorates. In this way the dream of a British Empire from Cape Town to Cairo came true.

Britain and France were also to benefit from the dismemberment of the Ottoman Empire. Both Britain and France were determined to expand at the cost of what had for long been described as the "Sick Man of Europe," but without allowing this to revive old imperial rivalries among themselves. In 1916 they had signed the Sykes-Picot Agreement, by which they divided important parts of the Ottoman Empire in case they won the war. In 1919 the time had come to implement it.

Britain aimed at having control over Palestine, which was next to the Suez Canal, and also the oil-rich region of Mosul, as oil had by then acquired vital importance. France on the other hand had set its gaze on Lebanon and Syria.

A conversation between Lloyd George and Clemenceau that has often been reproduced by the critics of European involvement in the Middle East shows how easily and amicably they distributed territories from the Ottoman Empire.

"Well," said Clemenceau, "what are we to discuss?"

"Mesopotamia and Palestine," replied Lloyd George.

Clemenceau: "Tell me what you want."

Lloyd George: "I want Mosul."

Clemenceau: "You shall have it. Anything else?"

Lloyd George: "Yes, I want Jerusalem too."

Lloyd George then promised to support France in its demand for control over the Lebanese coast and the interior of Syria, and that France would have a share of whatever oil was found in Mosul.

A source of major dispute during the Paris peace talks was the emancipation of the Arab world. On June 8, 1916, Sharif Hussein of Mecca, head of the

---

[*] David Fromkin, *A Peace to End All Peace: Creating the Modern Middle East, 1914–1922* (New York: Henry Holt, 1989).

Hashemite dynasty, led an Arab revolt against the Ottoman Empire with the aim emancipating the Arabs from Turkish rule and proclaiming himself king of the Arab countries. The Oxford archaeologist T. E. Lawrence, who became internationally known as Lawrence of Arabia, played a very special role in this revolt. Lawrence, who was fluent in Arabic and had worked in the Middle East as an archaeologist, was recruited by the British intelligence service in 1914 to liaise with the leaders of the Arab revolt, which Britain was determined to support. He then played a quasi-heroic role in several military engagements and enthusiastically espoused the cause of Arab nationalism to the extent of becoming a legendary figure both in the Arab world and the West.[*] He was not only the best friend of the Arab world ever to be born in Europe, but also its most loyal ambassador.

Lawrence of Arabia contributed to the capture of Damascus, where the Arab revolt culminated in 1918. He envisioned this city as the capital of a new great Arab nation, which he had promised the Arab leaders. But he was disappointed and embarrassed by the fact that Britain and France had other plans. Sharif Hussein's son Faisal was proclaimed king of Syria in March 1920, only a month after he was expelled by the French troops taking over their new mandate. The Republic of Syria was proclaimed shortly thereafter, under French supervision. Another republic that was created by the French was Lebanon. Britain on the other hand was more inclined to create constitutional monarchies in its new colonial mandates.

Sharif Hussein's pan-Arab imperial dreams were shattered after the end of the war when the Allies were only willing to recognize him as king of the Hejaz. But in compensation, the British government proved willing to support the Hashemite dynastic interest in the region, making his sons Abdullah king of Transjordan and Faisal king of Iraq.

The British had divided Transjordan into three local administrative districts at the end of the war. These were to be unified as the Emirate of Transjordan, to be ruled by Emir Abdullah I. Traditional but much more forward-looking and pragmatic than his father, Abdullah became the first Arab leader to adopt the system of a constitutional monarchy.

---

[*]   T. E. Lawrence, *The Seven Pillars of Wisdom* (Radford, Va.: Wilder, 2011).

The kingdom of Iraq was a British invention; an attempt to simultaneously satisfy Arab nationalism, the ambitions of the Hashemite dynasty, and at the same time safeguard Britain's interests. Peoples who had been separated by geography and history were unified into a single state. Half of the population was Arab, the rest Kurds and Assyrians. The majority of them, around fifty percent, were Shia Muslims, but the country's elite was to be formed by Sunni Muslims. Above all of them, Emir Faisal, who had proved his charismatic leadership qualities in the Arab revolt, was to rule as king of Iraq. Shortly after its creation, this nation was blessed with wealth when huge oil fields were discovered. Despite the King Faisal's efforts to unify all Iraqi people in a constitutional monarchy, this system was not to survive internal turbulences, and it finally succumbed to a coup in 1958. This was only the beginning of Iraq's troubles.

Palestine proved to be by far the most conflictive territory of all those acquired by Britain in the Middle East. In 1917 Foreign Secretary Arthur Balfour made a historic declaration promising British support for the establishment of a national home for the Jews in Palestine. The Balfour Declaration was celebrated by Jews throughout the world, well aware that with British support the Jewish state would eventually become a reality. On the other hand, the Arabs regarded this as an affront to their interests: a European power proposing the creation of a state without taking into account the wishes of the majority living in the territory. King Hussein of the Hejaz refused to ratify the Treaty of Versailles in protest. In this way the seeds of what was to be described as the world's most intractable conflict were sown.

The dismantling of the European part of the Ottoman Empire proved particularly rancorous. Greek Prime Minister Eleftherios Venizelos was determined to expand his country's frontiers beyond Constantinople and the whole of Asia Minor, recovering all coastal lands that Greece had occupied around almost three thousand years before. France and Britain, driven by pro-Hellenic sympathies, were willing to support this. It would also be a way of taking revenge on a historic humiliation for Europe and the Christian world, which was the fall of Constantinople to Muslim invaders. The Treaty of Sèvres, signed in 1920 between the Allies and Turkey, sanctioned the pan-Hellenic dream as well as other historic decisions like the creation of an Armenian state and an autonomous Kurdistan, all at the expense of Turkey, which was reduced to a small state in Anatolia. But the terms of this treaty were to be thwarted by the Turkish War of Independence. The Turkish National Movement was born with the determination to resist the Allied decision to liquidate Turkey. General Mustafa Kemal led the Turkish forces with such extraordinary military talent that they managed to defeat the combined French, Greek, and Armenian forces. In this way the international community was left with no option but to accept the re-conquest of Turkish territory as a *fait accompli* as well as the fact that Constantinople was to remain Turkish. Nevertheless, the new Turkish republic that was founded in 1923 was not going to attempt to revive the old Ottoman Empire but to transform itself into a modern European nation. Turkey was no longer shaped by the East and Islamism but by Europe and Western culture. The maker of this extraordinary change was Mustafa Kemal, later to be known as Atatürk (Father of the Turks). Atatürk, with his piercing blue eyes and elegant Western-style suits, not only became the utmost symbol of modern secular Turkey, but also a reference to all those nations wishing to implement European culture and modernity.

The Kemalist revolution started in 1922, when the Sultan Mehmed VI was deposed. Five centuries of Ottoman rule were brought to an end and replaced by a Western-style republic. The first reforms aimed at eradicating the influence of Islamic religion, which Atatürk considered as an obstacle to Turkish progress. The Caliphate was abolished in 1924, shortly after Islamic courts were closed and a new Turkish civil code was introduced, modeled on the Swiss civil code.[*]

Atatürk also decided that Turks should replace the sartorial traditions of the Islamic world with modern European attire. A Hat Law was introduced in 1925 with the aim of replacing the traditional fez with Western-style hats, which Atatürk described as the headgear of civilized nations. Women were also encouraged to give up the veil and dress like Europeans. The eradication of Islamic culture went as far as introducing a new alphabet for the written Turkish language, based on the Latin alphabet instead of Arabic script. From

---

[*]   Patrick Kinross, *Ataturk: The Rebirth of a Nation* (London: Phoenix, 1993).

then on children would learn to write in the Latin alphabet not the Arabic.[*] By the time of Atatürk's death in 1938, the Europeanization of Turkish culture and society had made remarkable progress. New urban middles classes were emerging that had been educated under Kemalist principles. The army, eager to defend Atatürk's legacy, ensured that the Turkish republic would remain secular and European.

Asia and the Pacific were also to experience important changes as a result of the Treaty of Versailles. Here the great winner was undoubtedly Japan, despite its disappointment with the final outcome of the negotiations. Japan, represented by Prince Saionji Kinmochi, was the fifth most powerful nation at the Paris peace conference. Well aware of their contribution to the Allied cause in Asia, the Japanese were determined to consolidate their position as the leading power in the Far East. For this reason, the delegation at Versailles demanded sovereignty over the German colonies in the Pacific islands as well as the Shantung Peninsula in China.

The Chinese also considered themselves major contributors to the Allied victory in the war. In Shanghai and all major Chinese cities the armistice had been celebrated with widespread joy. The Chinese delegation, led by Premier Lou Tseng-Tsiang, traveled to Paris hoping that as an ally of the great powers its territorial independence would be recognized. Tseng-Tsiang not only demanded the end of European imperial incursions and lease agreements of Chinese territory but he resolutely opposed the Japanese claim over Shantung, based on the principle of self-determination, which was mentioned in Wilson's Fourteen Points.

Choosing between rewarding China or rewarding Japan, the great powers in Paris clearly opted for the latter. Japan was seen as a loyal ally from the outbreak of the war, and above all it had clearly earned its great power status. For this reason it was duly granted the right to expand its empire at the expense of Germany and China, that latter of which was then seen as a weak and divided nation.

The Japanese delegation also took to Paris a racial-equality clause. It demanded that a clause declaring that all races are equal should be included

---

[*] Kinross, *Ataturk*.

in the League of Nations Covenant. Such a well-meaning proposal, which would particularly benefit the colonial world, was motivated by self-interest, hoping that with this clause the Japanese would finally be treated as equals to the European powers and the United States.

But to talk about racial equality in 1919 was rather controversial, particularly because many people, including the Big Four, would not agree with it. The proposal was also resolutely opposed by Australia and New Zealand, fearing that it would be used by Japan as an excuse to expand into their area of influence and justify Japanese migration to their countries. Therefore the clause was ultimately not included. The Japanese delegation was dismayed by this result. They immediately left Paris as a sign of protest with the feeling that despite their efforts to contribute to the new international order they were still treated as inferiors by the great powers. The resentment created by this rebuff contributed to the rise of nationalism in Japan in the postwar years and led its government to turn away from cooperation with the West.

China on the other hand was outraged by the outcome of the Paris conference. "To allow Shantung to remain under foreign control would be to leave a dagger pointed at the heart of China," stated the Chinese delegation.* But after 1919 the German presence on the Shantung Peninsula was replaced by the Japanese. As a result of this the Chinese delegation left without signing the Treaty of Versailles. Disappointment with the government and collective indignation at the way China had been humiliated by the West led a group of Chinese nationalists to form the Chinese Communist Party under the leadership of Mao Zedong.

The victims of interethnic hatred were also very numerous, and some countries were accused of having promoted ethnic cleansing and genocide. In the Ottoman Empire, over one million Armenians lost their lives as a consequence of the Turkish policy of expelling Armenian people from their frontiers.** Jews were persecuted and killed in Russia, as well as members of several nationalities in the Austro-Hungarian Empire.

---

* Margaret MacMillan, *Peacemakers: The Paris Conference of 1919 and its Attempt to End War,* (London: John Murray, 2009).
** Taner Akçam, *A Shameful Act: The Armenian Genocide and the Question of Turkish Responsibility* (New York: Metropolitan, 2007).

To make matters worse, violence did not cease in Europe after the armistice. After the war, conflicts continued in several places throughout the European continent. The bloodiest were undoubtedly in Russia. The revolution provoked a terrible civil war between the "reds" and the "whites" in favor of the old regime, which was to last for five years. The chaos that ruled over the country during this period has not allowed consensus on the number of deaths, but it is calculated that over three million people died at the front, by execution, or from the famines that spread around the country, as well as a large number of missing people. Last but not least, around seven million orphan children roamed around the streets after the conflict.

Until 1914 the great majority of Europeans were identified with the civilizations that represented European nations. On the whole, they felt proud of their nations and believed in the values that Europe represented in the world. Nevertheless, from then on, many were going to lose confidence in a civilization that was capable of causing such destructive wars, and give the impression of living in permanent conflict. In 1918 the return of the soldiers to their homes in order to resume their lives as civilians was going to be a very traumatic process, especially for those who returned to defeated nations. The economic crisis provoked by the war was to give way to a political crisis. It was caused by a citizenry that had generally ceased to believe in their leaders and their political system, and questioned the values of the society to which it belonged. This was the ideal breeding ground for new political mass movements promising a new society. Apart from communism, another movement that was going to exert great attraction from the masses in the 1920s was fascism.

Fascism emerged as a political movement that aimed at capitalizing on the general discontent that European society experienced after the First World War, and offered an alternative to communism, revolutionary ideologies, and liberal democracy. In 1919 an ex-combatant named Benito Mussolini, who had originally been a member of the Italian Socialist Party created the *Fasci Italiani di Combattimento* (Fascist Combat Squad), an armed group to fight against the revolutionary movement and denounce the social chaos they provoked. Encouraged by the widespread support, particularly among industrialists and landowners, a year later he created the National Fascist Party.

The Fascist party was primarily defined by strong right-wing nationalism. It believed that the communist threat was the consequence of liberal democracy, a weak and obsolete ideology that was blamed for Europe's decline. Instead it advocated a single-party government, with the Fascist party exclusively in charge of defining national interests. Its economic policy was that of state capitalism and the replacement of free trade by autarchy in order to promote the nation's self-sufficiency. In foreign policy it defined itself as imperialist and proposed to create a new Roman Empire that would transform Italy into a dominant power in the Mediterranean.

On October 28, 1922, Mussolini led his army of notorious Blackshirts into a march through Rome. This triumphal entry in the Roman capital allowed him to take power without the need to stand for elections. The king of Italy decided that in view of Mussolini's strength and popularity the best option was formally to invite him to form a government. The first Fascist government in Europe steadily made progress toward the consolidation of a totalitarian regime under Mussolini's leadership. The pillars of his government were absolute power of the state over society, strict government control of the media and press censorship, illegalization of all political parties, and persecution and elimination of all dissenting voices.

Fascism, with its formidable ability to impose law and order by means of repression, strengthen national pride, and restore faith in the future, emerged as an attractive model for many Europeans in the postwar years. In the 1920s replicas of the Italian Fascist party were to appear in several countries while admirers of Benito Mussolini and his methods proliferated.

In 1919 an Austrian ex-combatant named Adolf Hitler joined a modest German Workers' Party, which in spite of its name was fervently anti-Marxist, deeply nationalistic, and also anti-Semitic. The young Hitler did not have a brilliant CV that would herald a promising career in politics. After eking out a life as a mediocre artist during the war, he served in the German army where he became a corporal and considered war the greatest of all his experiences. Nevertheless, he was a good orator with a special ability to attract an audience, equally capable of provoking indignation with his criticism of those he considered Germany's enemies as showing enthusiasm for his proposals to transform the country.

In 1920 Hitler's party was renamed as the National Socialist Party, better known as the Nazi Party. Shortly after, he became party leader and his criticism of politicians he considered guilty for Germany's defeat—the Communists and the Jews—attracted a very diverse public, from members of the working class and the armed forces to rich industrialists. In 1923 Hitler felt strong enough to plan a coup d'etat in Munich that would then lead to a march through Berlin, as his admired Mussolini had done in Rome. However, the coup failed and Hitler was sentenced to five years in prison. But this was only the beginning of his political career.

Another country where the fascist model enjoyed considerable support was Spain. The constitutional monarchy under Alfonso XIII confronted a serious crisis with an increasingly aggressive working-class movement and a corrupt and inefficient parliamentary system. The demand for an "iron surgeon" who could set the country to rights became increasingly widespread. This prompted General Miguel Primo de Rivera to seize power by means of a coup d'etat in 1923. Primo de Rivera's dictatorship simply aimed at ruling for a brief period in order to reestablish order and ensure that the country would be governed again by a constitutional monarchy. Primo de Rivera's ideology was that of a conservative army officer, but he nevertheless admired Benito Mussolini and many of his government's policies, such as the state's planning of the economy, corporatism, and press censorship. Portugal followed the same path. In 1926 a coup d'etat put an end to sixteen years of political instability under the weak democracy of the First Republic in Portugal. A powerful branch of the Portuguese army established a new authoritarian regime under the name of Ditadura Nacional.

The Wall Street crash of 1929 further benefitted fascism's expansion. On October 24, 1929, the New York Stock Exchange experienced a devastating collapse. As share prices plummeted European stock markets suffered phenomenal losses. The prosperity of the merry twenties dramatically came to an end and the world was plunged into the Great Depression—over ten years of crisis in which most Western countries lived under the twin evils of massive unemployment and a dramatic reduction in industrial output.

The 1929 crash showed the extent to which the center of the world economy had shifted from Europe to the United States. Count Metternich had stated that "when Paris sneezes Europe catches a cold," showing the extent to which that city was the heart and soul of the European continent. But in the twentieth century New York was very much to adopt this role, especially in the economic sphere. Ceding economic supremacy to the United States was another cause of the collective anger that could be perceived in Europe in the 1930s. The great depression contributed to further reduce the faith of the Europeans in their political systems. It particularly strengthened the argument that capitalism did not work and that society could not live permanently exposed to the whims of speculators and market changes.

The fact that Russia was not affected by the Great Depression contributed to increasing the popularity of communism. While governments throughout Europe struggled to palliate the effects of the Great Depression, the Soviet Union under Stalin's strong leadership was rapidly transformed into an industrial power. Liberal democracy seemed too weak to stop communism's irresistible rise, only fascism could do this. Fascism proposed a state-regulated economy with closed frontiers that would increase a nation's self-sufficiency and reduce exposure to the ups and downs of international markets. It also showed determination to correct the trend of decline that could be felt throughout Europe, and restore national pride by instilling ideas that would give people meaning and direction. Finally, it had the physical means to stop communism with paramilitary forces, and brutally crush all sorts of opposition by violent means.

Germany, beset by mass unemployment and economic stagnation, quickly became the breeding ground for Nazi expansion. Adolf Hitler's diatribes against politicians who had betrayed Germany, the Communist threat, and the Jews—who were blamed for all evils including the economic crisis—increasingly struck a chord with the average voter. In 1932 the Nazis became the largest party in the German Reichstag. A few months later, Hitler was proclaimed chancellor. Shortly afterward, political parties were banned and the Weimar Republic was replaced by the Third Reich. One of the greatest paradoxes of history is how one of the most advanced and cultured people on earth—that gave civilization figures like Beethoven, Goethe, or Schopenhauer—ended up handing over power to Adolf Hitler. Germany and the whole of Europe are still coming to terms with the consequences of this paradox.

Nazism was an improved and more radical version of fascism. Ideologues like Carl Schmidt advocating that the interests of the nation should be above the rule of law were used by the new regime to unify the country under "one Reich, one people and one Führer," as went one of Hitler's popular slogans. Private enterprise survived but under the strict tutelage of the state, media was efficiently used by the Minister of Propaganda Joseph Goebbels, and freedom of expression was strictly suppressed. Anything that went against the spirit of National Socialism was purged. The regime's cultural policy was clearly defined by a campaign launched in 1933 to publicly burn books that were considered anti-German. Proscribed authors included contemporary figures like Albert Einstein or Heinrich Mann to classic figures like Heinrich Heine, who had prophetically written that, "where they burn books they will too in the end burn people."

Racism was another vital characteristic of Nazism. Hitler and the ideologues of the Nazi Party developed the theory that the Germans were the main representatives of what they called the Aryan race, a superior domineering race. Special legislation was passed to protect this racial purity and purge any elements thought to make it degenerate, like Jews. With the Nuremberg Laws of 1935 Hitler implemented the most radical policy of persecution and elimination of Jews in Germany.

Racism was closely linked to the term lebensraum, a "living space" for the Germans. According to Hitler, Germany ought to occupy more territories for its expanding population, implying not only the recovering of the frontiers of Germany's first Reich, but also conquering lands in Eastern Europe to submit the Slavs, regarded as inferiors, to Aryan hegemony.

The delusions of grandeur and the expansionist ambitions of the Fascists and Nazis were soon to cause international tensions that had not been seen since the early twentieth century. Mussolini, like Hitler, believed in the need to conquer territory for his people. He had also promised to create something that would remind his contemporaries of the splendor of the Roman Empire. All of this led to an aggressive expansionist policy in the Mediterranean and in Africa.

In 1936 a conflict broke out between Italian Somalia and Abyssinia. Mussolini used this as an excuse to invade Abyssinia. For Fascist Italy, it was vital to win this war, because four decades earlier Italian troops had been defeated by the Abyssinians as they attempted to expand their empire into this ancient African kingdom. Within a month after the 1936 invasion, Italian troops triumphantly entered in Addis Ababa and the Abyssinian Emperor Haile Selassie went into exile. Meanwhile in Rome, King Victor Emmanuel III saluted a huge crowd from the balcony of the Quirinal Palace as the new emperor of Abyssinia. Beside him Mussolini addressed the masses, stating that in thirty centuries of history this was one of the most glorious moments: "At last Italy has her empire," he stated.

The initial success of both Fascist Italy and Nazi Germany, as well as the external image of power and organization that they projected contributed to their expansion in Europe. In Portugal Prime Minister Antonio de Oliveira Salazar created the Estado Novo, a single-party, ultraconservative, nationalist regime that granted dictatorial powers to its leader. Spain was the next country to follow this path, but at a much higher cost.

On July 18, 1936, an uprising led by General Francisco Franco put a convulsive end to the Spanish Second Republic and gave way to a bitter civil war. Franco's nationalist troops immediately obtained the support of Germany and Italy, whereas the only official ally of the Spanish republic was the Soviet Union. Young people from all over the Western world joined the International Brigades, paramilitary units set up by the Communist International, in order to assist the Spanish Republic, believing that fascism had to be stopped in Spain or it would expand through the whole of Europe. In this way this war became an international conflict in which the two totalitarian models were confronted for the first time. With Franco's victory, the Fascist-Nazi axis obtained one more triumph. Strictly speaking, General Franco's ideology was Catholic and conservative but his regime in its first decade was clearly inspired by the political philosophies of his two allies.

In the meantime Hitler had taken important steps to strengthen Germany's position in the world and make progress in the creation of the Third Reich that according to him would last for one thousand years. In 1936 he ordered the occupation of the Rhineland, which had been demilitarized under the terms of the Versailles Treaty. Two years later German troops marched into Austria and the union of the two German-speaking nations was proclaimed. The Sudetenland in Czechoslovakia became his next target.

What should be done about Nazi expansion? This question occupied a substantial part of European public opinion in the late 1930s. In Britain, France, and what was left of democratic Europe, appeasement predominated. Prominent figures of the British establishment even showed sympathy toward Hitler, believing that only Nazism was capable of confronting communism. It was also believed that Nazi expansion would stop once the German-speaking territories had been occupied. This is what the leaders of Britain and France believed when they met with Mussolini and Hitler at the Munich Conference in 1938. In a desperate attempt to avoid war, Hitler was granted permission to occupy the Sudetenland. Prime Minister Neville Chamberlain proclaimed after the summit that he had obtained, "peace with honor. I believe it is peace for our time." Nevertheless he was humiliated when in March 1939 the whole of Czechoslovakia was invaded by the Nazis. On September 1, 1939, Nazi troops invaded Poland. Britain then declared war on Germany, France supported the British, and Italy joined the German cause. On one more occasion within slightly more than two decades the great European powers were at war.

Only twenty-five years after the First World War European conflicts led to another world war that was to be even longer and more destructive than the previous one, and its impact on a global scale even larger. If few peoples and countries were immune to the effects of the First World War, this number was reduced much further in the Second World War. To a certain extent Switzerland, Portugal, Turkey, and Spain were neutral, which does not mean that they were not affected by war. Apart from these countries, outside Europe only Afghanistan was strictly neutral. The rest of the countries of the world were either belligerent or occupied, or in some cases both. Latin American republics joined the coalition against the Axis, although most of them did so only in the latter stages of the war, and only symbolically, without the involvement of their armies.

From the beginning the war was fought on a global scale. From Stalingrad to Burma, from North Africa to Normandy, and from the Philippines to Hawaii, people following events in the newspapers or radio on a daily basis would become familiar with the remotest places where crucial battles were fought to determine the result of this war. As historian Eric Hobsbawm wrote, the Second World War was a lesson in world geography.

Just like the previous one, the Second World War could have been short if the German military strategy had worked according to plan. On this occasion, German troops obtained a quick victory on the Western front and managed to invade France and the Low Countries within six weeks. But they underestimated Britain.

In May 1940 Winston Churchill became prime minister. Churchill had been consistently warning since the early 1930s that war against Nazi Germany was inevitable, and that European democracies should stand up to Hitler before it was too late. But this attitude made him very unpopular at a time when appeasement enjoyed widespread support—until events proved him right. At a time when Britain had been left alone to face the Nazi-Fascist axis victory seemed totally unrealistic. The most prudent option would have been to make peace with Germany and acknowledge its power in continental Europe in return for its promise not to interfere in the British Empire, as several members of Churchill's cabinet argued. But this would have implied giving up liberal democracy in Europe and all the values that Britain had traditionally defended. Churchill was convinced that a Nazi victory meant the end of civilization: "A monstrous tyranny never surpassed in the dark, lamentable catalogue of human crime," as he described it. For this reason there was no option but to fight until the end, although initially the prime minister had nothing to offer against German armed superiority but "blood, toil, tears, and sweat," as he stated in his famous speech.

From June 1940 Hitler attempted to force Britain to its knees first with large-scale bombardments on London and other cities. Once he considered that Britain was sufficiently weakened he made a decision that was to pro-long the war and eventually prove catastrophic for the Germans: to open an Eastern Front. On June 22, Operation Barbarossa was launched with the goal of invading the Soviet Union. Hitler aimed at consolidating the Third Reich's expansion with this invasion by which communism would be finally defeated. But despite their initial success, the Germans, just like the French under Napoleon, were soon to realize that the vast Russian territory in winter was unconquerable. From then the on Third Reich was to experience the consequences of imperial overreach. It was fighting a two-front war.

The confrontation between European powers—and the fact that several of them were defeated by Germany—provided a golden opportunity for its ally Japan to occupy some of their possessions in Asia. Japan had been emulating the Western model of growth and expansion for several decades. Now as an ally of the Axis powers it aimed at consolidating its hegemony in Asia. The main obstacle was the United States, and for this reason, on December 7, 1941, Japan attacked the American base at Pearl Harbor. This led the US government to join the fray, while Britain, Australia, and New Zealand also declared war on Japan. Germany, in order to back its Japanese ally, declared war on the United States. In this way, the war, which was originally a European territorial conflict, escalated until it became a global conflict. The Europeans had aimed at spreading their civilization throughout the world but they ended up propagating war on one more occasion.

The United States played a pivotal role in the Second World War. It was the key factor that allowed the allied victory, just as had happened in the First World War. Churchill's comment after finding out that the U.S. had declared war on Japan was sufficiently eloquent: "So we have won after all."

Both Churchill and Charles de Gaulle, the leader of free France, were well aware that without the support of American power they could not win the war. The U.S. provided the allies with the military and economic boost that was necessary in order to defeat the Axis, but Europe was to pay a high price for this: the postwar world would be shaped according to the principles and interests of the United States, not those of the old European powers.

Several months before the fateful attack on Pearl Harbor, the United States was already discussing with Britain what the postwar world order should be. On August 14, 1941, Churchill met for the first time with President Roosevelt, off the coast of Newfoundland. The two statesmen issued a joint declaration, the Atlantic Charter, laying out the policies that they would follow in a post–Nazi world. Among the most important points was the agreement that neither of the two powers would seek any territorial gains. Territorial adjustments should be made in accordance with the wishes of the people concerned, and it was acknowledged that all people had the right to self-determination. Other important points were the agreement to promote the reduction of trade barriers, global economic cooperation, freedom of navigation, and a world of "freedom from fear and want." To a certain extent the Atlantic Charter was an agreement to build a new world order based on ideas and principles that Europe had been promoting since the beginning of its colonial expansion. On the other hand, Churchill was accepting a new international order in which his hallowed British Empire and other European empires could no longer exist, and in which European capitals like London or Paris would have to give up the privilege of governing over peoples in other continents and having the exclusive rights of economic exploitation of overseas territories.

The Allied victory over the Axis demanded an enormous coordinated effort and the sacrifice of many lives. The Atlantic world, which had emerged with the European colonization of the Americas, was never as unified as in the period between 1942 and 1945. The British, Americans, Canadians, French, and other Western countries fought shoulder to shoulder to win this war. They made possible the largest seaborne invasion in history, the landing in Normandy, D-Day, on June 6, 1944, when a Western Front was opened that marked the beginning of the end of Hitler's Europe. In the meantime the Soviet Union pushed German troops back in the Eastern Front, although at a very high price in terms of Russian lives. On April 30, while the allies invaded Berlin, Adolf Hitler committed suicide. Two days before, Mussolini had been executed by Italian partisans. Their deaths, and the official surrender of their two countries, marked the end of the Nazi-Fascist era.

The Second World War lingered on because the Japanese defeat was still pending. With this aim of forcing a Japanese surrender the United States dropped atomic bombs on Hiroshima and Nagasaki in August 1945, bringing the war to an end and simultaneously giving birth to the atomic age.

The Second World War was the most destructive of all wars, a conflict in which the destructive human capacity reached the highest peak. The first consequence of this conflict that must be highlighted is its death toll: over sixty million people lost their lives in this conflict, although the exact figure cannot be known. According to some statistics this figure can be elevated to over eighty million if we include the victims of famines and war-related disease. In the Soviet Union alone around twenty seven million people died. This inspired Stalin's comment that in order to defeat Nazism, "the British gave time, the Americans gave money, and the Russians gave blood." In Germany there were almost eight million dead, and almost six million in Poland. Beyond Europe there were significant casualties throughout the world. In the United States 419,000 were dead. Chinese statistics rank their dead as high as twenty million, whereas Japan lost over 3.1 million people.[*] Particularly high were the casualties among subjects of European empires in Asia. In British India 2.6 million; in the Dutch East Indies around 3.5 million; and over two million in French Indochina. The number of civilian victims was substantially higher than the military ones in this war. Cities and villages became as valid as enemy targets as military bases and battlefields. Women, children, and old people died in the war just as soldiers did. As Antony Beevor wrote, no life was left untouched by the Second World War.[**]

The nuclear bomb was the corollary of the spiral of destructive forces unleashed during this war. It was a North American initiative originally promoted by Europeans and also benefitting from European scientific talent in the U.S. Albert Einstein, together with the Hungarian nuclear physicist Leo Szilard, signed the letter to President Roosevelt proposing that the United States begin researching atomic energy, mainly due to the fact that otherwise it was very likely that Germany would take the lead in this research, with catastrophic results for the Allied cause. With the nuclear era, which the United States inaugurated in 1945, the human capacity to kill and destroy reached its highest limit. It radically transformed warfare, as from then on war became self-destructive.

During this conflict genocide and ethnic cleansing were taken further than ever in history. This was also one of the reasons why the death toll was so high. Concentration camps began to be used by Europeans during war in the colonial world as an efficient method to keep high numbers of enemy population isolated and under control. But during the Second World

---

[*]   Antony Beevor, *The Second World War* (New York: Little, Brown, 2012).
[**] Ibid.

War the Nazis transformed them into extermination camps, centers where undesirable peoples and races could be eliminated in high numbers by the quickest and most sophisticated methods of mass murder, such as gas chambers. Auschwitz, Mauthausen, Dachau, and other Nazi death camps became the greatest symbols of human barbarity. The Jews were the main victims of genocide in this war. Around six million died as victims of Nazi persecution, the majority perishing as a reult of what the Nazis confidentially called the Final Solution: the decision to exterminate Jews in Germany or any conquered territory. The Holocaust constituted the culmination of centuries of anti-Semitism in Europe by the most barbarous methods. Hitler and the Nazis decided to definitively put an end to the Jews in Europe, and they succeeded, if we take into account the fact that Jews virtually disappeared, and Jewish life ended in Germany, Poland, Austria, Hungary, Ukraine, and other countries conquered by the Nazis.

The world found out about the Holocaust when the death camps were liberated in 1945, and later, during the Nuremberg trials, when some Nazi leaders were brought to justice for what were described as crimes against humanity. Genocide had been practiced on many occasions throughout history but never in such a systematic and efficient way. The legacy of the Holocaust left an indelible mark on human history. Germans who had supported the Nazis had to come to terms with the fact that they had, willingly or not, contributed to this horror. Europeans in general were traumatized by the Holocaust. How was it possible that the continent that had reached the highest forms of civilization and development would degenerate to the point of such barbarity? Political theorist Hannah Arendt, herself a Holocaust survivor, explained it as "the banality of evil." Humanity and Europeans in particular have been asking this question without finding a satisfactory answer.

One of the images that are most associated with the end of the Second World War is that of the physical destruction of cities. Dresden, totally destroyed by Allied bombs, offers the most impressive image of destruction. Twelve other major German cities were equally destroyed. In cities like Minsk, Kiev, and Warsaw it was difficult to find a building that had not been destroyed. On the French coast Le Havre and Caen were equally affected. The same happened with Coventry or other industrial cities in the UK.

World War II provoked one of the largest population movements in history. There were eight million people who had been brought to Germany as slave workers, and they were going to return to their countries after 1945. There were population exchanges in Ukraine and Poland, Bulgaria and Turkey, Czechoslovakia and Hungary. As could be expected, Germans in countries like Czechoslovakia were forced to return to their nation of origin.

From 1945 a process of renationalization took place in Europe. Except for Yugoslavia, European nations after 1945 were to be more homogeneous and bound within their borders than ever, as traveling to neighboring nations was discouraged. Nations isolated themselves, reducing to a minimum the exchange of products, ideas, and peoples that had been so important for the continent. In early twentieth-century Europe, the world of yesterday that Stefan Zweig yearned for in his memoirs, it was possible to travel from Lisbon to Warsaw or from Dublin to Athens, crossing frontiers without showing a single passport. This world disappeared in the period between 1914 and 1945. From then on strict frontier controls were implemented and lack of trust among nations was going to make it increasingly difficult for Europeans to travel through their continent. When the Second World War came to an end, the open society which Europeans had once created had all but vanished.

The progressive fragmentation of Europe along national borders that begins in 1914 culminates with the division of the continent into two blocs in 1945. War had made possible a somewhat uneasy alliance between Western democracies and the first communist regime, with the aim of defeating the common enemies: Nazism and Fascism. But the alliance between liberal democracies and the dictatorship of the proletariat was doomed to end once Hitler's Germany had been defeated. The main reason for this was Stalin's determination to establish communist regimes in all territories that were occupied by the Soviet Union during the war. Stalin took advantage of the presence of Soviet troops in all these countries in order to establish communist regimes—and in this way start making true the Bolshevik aspiration of propagating the revolution throughout the world. "Each one imposed his own system as far as his army can reach," opined the Communist dictator.[*]

---

[*]   Tony Judt, *Postwar: A History of Europe Since 1945* (New York: Penguin, 2015).

At the Yalta Conference in February 1945, where Roosevelt, Stalin, and Churchill met in order to discuss the future of Europe after the war, Churchill became alarmed at the enormous power that Stalin had acquired. The price that the allies were going to pay for winning the war was going to be giving up half of Europe to communism. One of the great paradoxes of the Second World War was that the conflict that broke out because of Britain's determination to defend Poland's independence against Germany ended up allowing the Soviet occupation of the country. In 1946 at a famous speech in Fulton, Missouri, Churchill declared that an "iron curtain has descended across the continent." This curtain symbolized the division of Europe into two blocs: a communist bloc under the control of the Soviet Union, and a Western bloc where market economy and democracy would be defended with the support of the United States.

The end of the Second World War also marked the end of Europe's economic supremacy over the world. In 1900 the United States had already become the largest economy, but the year 1945 officially marks the end of the transition of economic power from Europe to the United States. Europe was ruined by the war. The economies of both victors and vanquished were exhausted.

As regards the economic impact, the result of the World War can be summarized in the partial destruction of the European economy. The economies of both the winners and the vanquished were exhausted by the war effort of almost six years. Germany and Italy were going to be the most seriously affected, and the allies demanded a great part of the German industrial production in compensation. Nevertheless, their economies needed much more than German industrial reparations in order to recover. It was enough to compare the state of any city in Britain and France before and after the war to understand the extent to which the countries had been impoverished.

In 1944, under the auspices of the United States, the Bretton Woods Conference took place, in which forty-four allied nations agreed on the rules of the international financial system that was to emerge after the war. After 1945 Britain witnessed the speed with which the pound sterling was substituted by the US dollar as the main reserve currency in the world. The United States had also demanded the liberalization of markets and the opening of economic blocs that were established in colonial empires, and in this way the privileges of the pound sterling and other currencies of the European powers in their colonies came to an end. Shortly after the war was over, John Maynard Keynes was sent by the British government to Washington in order to negotiate a loan from the U.S. with which to refloat the British economy. This journey symbolized the definitive transfer of economic world sovereignty from Britain to the United States.

The decline of Europe as a consequence of the war was particularly evident from a geopolitical point of view. Europe, apart from losing world hegemony, was left divided between two new blocs, those of capitalism and communism.

In 1945 the United Nations was born, with the aim of maintaining peace and security in the world. In its principal organ, the Security Council, five powers were granted permanent member status: the United States, the Soviet Union, Britain, France, and China. The times when international relations were an exclusive affair of the European powers and world peace depended on the decisions of a few capitals in the European continent were definitely over. After five centuries of world hegemony the time had come for Europe to share it with other powers in the world.

More has been written about the two great wars than any other human conflict. The causes of the two World Wars that took place in this recent European dark age have been analyzed in extraordinary depth. But the great question that remains to be properly answered is not why did the First and Second World Wars begin, but rather why were they not anticipated and prevented? Why did the Europeans not foresee their devastating effects?

Chapter 10

Goodbye to All That

The Global Influence of European Intellectual Migration and Exile.

During the first half of the twentieth century, emigration continued to be a basic need for the majority of the peoples of Europe. From Russia to Portugal, and from Norway to Greece, many Europeans spent part or the rest of their lives on other continents. It constituted a way of life, a fate from which there seemed to be no escape. The wave of emigration that swept across Europe in the last decades of the nineteenth century reached its apex between 1910 and 1920, and in some countries it continued well into the second half of the twentieth century. The presence of Europeans in the world was constantly increasing over the first decades of the twentieth century, and as a result the influence of their culture was considerably reinforced in some regions. But what was going to make this massive exodus particularly dramatic was the fact that a substantial part of them left their homeland not for economic reasons, as most European migrants had done for the last centuries, but due to reasons of religion, ethnicity, and politics.

In the nineteenth century Europe experienced an elevation of liberal civilization based on representative parliaments and democratic governments elected by an increasingly wide suffrage. Above all they enjoyed the rule of law, which guaranteed citizens' rights, including freedom of speech, publication, and assembly. European migrants settling in other continents contributed to spread this concept of civilization.

On the other hand, while liberal civilization made progress, from the end of the nineteenth century Europeans began to experience the effects of other movements and ideas that ended up challenging the essence of their civilization, and had devastating effects in the twentieth century. As we have previously seen, nationalism together with liberalism was one of the driving forces of political change in the nineteenth century. Later on its corollary extreme nationalism spread across the continent. Its ideologues made very exclusive definitions of national identity based on history, language, ethnicity, and religion, and advocated the need to defend it from foreign influences. Racism and xenophobia were also increasingly influential in mainstream politics, as was the need to protect pure native stocks from the contamination of inferior races—which was strongly believed by many people in Europe. Rapid economic and social changes gave rise to extremist ideologies on both right and left of the political spectrum. The combination of all these phenomena was to force many Europeans to abandon their homelands in the first decades of the twentieth century. Worst of all, they usually did not have the feeling of leaving a great civilization behind, instead they felt relieved to escape from barbarity.

In 1886 the Statue of Liberty was dedicated in New York, a generous present from the French people to the United States as a testament to their admiration for a great country and the cordial relations they enjoyed in those days. From then the famous statue was to be seen by all emigrants on entering the port of New York. The impact of this emblematic monument went far beyond the most optimistic expectations of its designer, for it became a universal icon of liberty and a symbol of all that the emigrants from Europe and the rest of the world expected from America: freedom to live and work and make their dreams come true, freedom to express themselves, and to practice their religion without fear of persecution for political, ethnic, or religious reasons.

The United States that became the biggest economy in the world in 1900 was constantly demanding labor to maintain its extraordinary rate of growth, as well as a regular influx of new people to occupy its vast territories. The US government and society continued to show a clear preference for European emigration for most of the twentieth century. While the frontiers of the United States were open for the Europeans they remained partially closed for those who came from other parts of the world.* Latin Americans who managed to cross the southern border from Mexico were generally treated as second-class citizens. Even those from Puerto Rico, who were officially US citizens, found it difficult to integrate with their fellow American citizens. For Asians crossing the US frontier, it was even more difficult, particularly for the Chinese. In 1881 President Chester A. Arthur signed the Chinese Exclusion Act, by which entrance of Chinese citizens into the U.S. was strictly prohibited. This law was not repealed until 1943.

The fact that the U.S. was universally considered to be the land of opportunity par excellence and that its frontiers were open to Europeans on the whole explains why such large numbers of emigrants arrived from the old continent. Ellis Island, the country's busiest customs office, received over two million Italians between 1910 and 1920, the decade when migration reached its peak. Over one and a half million people entered the U.S. from Sweden and Norway.** Emigration from Central and Eastern Europe also spiraled in those years and Irish migrants continued to be as numerous as they had been since the 1840s.

Before such a vast influx of European migrants the American government was finally to become increasingly selective, as it could afford to choose the type of immigrant that the country needed from among abundant applications for entry. In 1917 a law forbade the entrance of illiterate emigrants

---

* Archdeacon, *Becoming American.*
** Ibid.

into the U.S. Particularly adverse for migrants from Southern and Eastern Europe was the 1924 law that fixed a maximum quota of people from these countries. After all, the United States was a nation founded by Anglo-Saxons and Protestants, and consequently the proliferation of Italians, Poles, or other immigrants from Catholic or Orthodox Christian nations started to be seen by the ruling elite as a threat to their future identity. In spite of all restrictions imposed after the 1920s, the United States continued to be the favorite destination for Europeans wishing to emigrate. But there were certainly many other options, especially elsewhere on the American continent, where all its countries were open to European emigration.

From the late nineteenth century European migrants were increasingly attracted by large countries that were originally founded by Europeans and were scarcely populated. Canada was a very appealing option for British emigrants, particularly the Scottish. Australia and New Zealand emerged as very attractive alternatives to America for the British, and increasingly more for the Irish. Brazil started to receive migrants from many European countries apart from Portugal, and neighboring Argentina emerged as a paradise for migrants. In all of these countries the influx of Europeans had a great economic and cultural impact, consolidating their identity as offshoots of the European world.

The case of Argentina deserves special attention because in the early twentieth century it became the tenth wealthiest nation per capita and its prospects for growth were phenomenal. Such extraordinary achievements would not have been possible without the contribution of European migration that the Argentine government had been actively promoting since the mid–nineteenth century. Ships full of Europeans from diverse origins continued arriving in Argentine ports until the mid–twentieth century. The presence of immigrants was so numerous that in the 1920s half of the population of Buenos Aires had been born abroad. The majority of migrants in these years were Spanish and Italian, and half a million of them reached this country between 1901 and 1910.[*] But the representation of European immigration was increasingly diverse for the reputation of Argentina as a land

---

[*] Quesada, *La Argentina*.

of opportunity had spread across the whole of Europe. It is proven by the case of Aristotle Socrates Onassis, a young Greek businessman who was eager to leave his country in search of wealth in the 1920s and chose Argentina. In Buenos Aires he managed to make his first million in the tobacco industry and lay the foundations of what was going to become two decades later one of the biggest fortunes in the world.

Ever since the beginning of the era of mass migration in the mid–nineteenth century the network of contacts established by European migrants were scattered throughout the world, strengthening the links between Europe and the other continents. The relationship that the emigrant communities kept with their families in their countries of origin paved the way for the arrival of new migrants that found the process of settling in the chosen country increasingly smooth. In this way European migrants became the most important agents of Europeanization on other continents. Wherever they settled in large numbers, European culture and way of life would become increasingly visible.

The best example of the success of European immigrant networks is undoubtedly that of the Irish in the United States. From the late nineteenth to the early twentieth century the Irish Americans enjoyed their golden age.[*] While the Irish presence steadily increased as a result of constant migration they ceased to be identified with poverty and marginalization, and they were to emerge as a powerful and influential community. Al Smith, a third-generation American who became known as the spokesman for the Irish-American community in the early twentieth century proved how important Irish votes could be in US politics, for he was elected governor of New York on four occasions. His political career culminated as the Democratic presidential candidate in 1928.

Intermarriage among members of the Irish-American community contributed to spread their power in the United States during the twentieth century. The renowned matrimonial alliance of the Fitzgeralds and the Kennedys provides the best example, for the most outstanding member of this powerful family, John F. Kennedy, was the first Catholic president of the United States.

---

[*] Michael Coffey, *The Irish in America* (New York: Hyperion, 1997).

His father, multimillionaire Joseph P. Kennedy, often complained about the tendency of the American press to describe his family as Irish: "What does one have to do to be American?" protested this Bostonian who represented the third generation of Irish-Americans born on American land.* But this was certainly no obstacle for the Kennedy dynasty to reach the highest pinnacles of American society and inspire such admiration among the US population as to be described as America's "Royal Family."

The Italian-American community in the United States experienced similar behavior patterns as the Irish. The city of New York, where the Italian population was strongest, allowed immigrants from Italy to settle with ease and start earning a living. The case of Fiorello La Guardia, a second-generation Italian who became one of the most popular mayors in the history of New York illustrates the success of Italian integration into positions of power. On a more negative note, the notorious Italian mafia—well-known in the public eye thanks to famous gangsters like Al Capone—provided a very good example of the speed and facility with which people, capital, contraband, and vendettas flowed between Italy and the United States.

In Latin America, the networks of emigrants established by the Spanish and the Portuguese contributed to strengthen links with the Iberian Peninsula through the twentieth century, often compensating for political confrontations that emerged in the international sphere. Cuba, the pearl of the Spanish Empire, continued attracting large contingents of Spanish immigrants after obtaining independence in 1898. The life of Angel Castro shows how easy it was for Spaniards to establish themselves in Cuba and prosper in spite of the official anti-Spanish rhetoric. A peasant from the province of Galicia, Castro first went to Cuba in 1898 to fight with the Spanish troops against Cuban insurgents. In 1905 he returned to the Caribbean island, and after years of hard work he eventually became a rich landowner. His life became well known to the wider public shortly after his death, when his son Fidel Castro led the Cuban Revolution in 1959 and became one of the most famous personalities in Latin American in the twentieth century.

---

* Peter Collier and David Horowitz, *The Kennedys: An American Drama* (Claregalway, Ireland: MW Books, 1984).

Mexico became a popular destination for some European immigrants after the 1860s, particularly from France, due to the colonial adventures of Napoleon III in the country. In the early twentieth century European migration was mainly composed of Spaniards, particularly from the late 1930s, when the Mexican government supported the Republican government during the Spanish Civil War and welcomed exiled Spaniards after the conflict. As a result of this, the number of Spaniards living in Mexico almost doubled in the late 1930s and early 1940s. Most of them easily settled into their new Mexican life, and even prospered. The Spanish entrepreneur and philanthropist Eulalio Ferrer is one of the most outstanding examples. Like many exiles from the Spanish Civil War, Ferrer reached Mexico in 1940. Some years later he founded the publicity firm Ferrer, which would become one of the most important in Mexico. After making a fortune, Ferrer became an important philanthropist, promoting cultural projects on both sides of the Atlantic, and obtained numerous awards in his country of origin.

Just like Eulalio Ferrer, many Spaniards and Portuguese emigrated in the 1940s and '50s. They were going to be the last generation of people who attempted "to make the Americas," an expression that became very popular in the Iberian world from the eighteenth century, and just like their ancestors, some migrants were going to be luckier than others in this adventure. But undoubtedly their presence in the Americas made a crucial contribution to the links between the two sides of the Atlantic and raising awareness of the importance of the Hispanic world for Spain and Portugal.

In the twentieth century the presence of Europeans in other parts of the world was going to attract the attention for several reasons apart from emigration. The curiosity for the outer world that originally gave birth to the era of great discoveries in the fifteenth century continued producing extraordinary results for Europe and the world four centuries later. In the early twentieth century European explorers conquered the North and the South Poles. Having reached the coldest parts of the world, the highest peaks were still to be climbed. For centuries climbing the world's highest mountain, Mount Everest, seemed to be a feat that was beyond the limits of human endeavor. But it was finally achieved in 1953. New Zealander mountaineer Edmund Hillary led a British expedition and with the help of the Nepalese sherpa

Tenzing Norgay, he reached the summit of the world. This achievement, at a time when the sun was setting on the British Empire and the era of European hegemony had been left behind, constituted a triumphant epilogue to five centuries of European exploration.

Europe also made great contributions to archaeology as a result of the fascination with ancient civilizations felt by some European travelers in the early twentieth century. In 1914 English archaeologist Howard Carter was financed by Lord Carnavon, a wealthy aristocrat and amateur Egyptologist, to excavate in the Valley of the Kings in Cairo. Then in 1920 Carter and his team discovered the tomb of Tutankhamun, the best preserved of all Egyptian tombs. This astounding discovery notably promoted interest in ancient Egypt and archaeology in general throughout the West.

Archaeology was also what took the storied Lawrence of Arabia to the Near East. T. E Lawrence was doing archaeological research at Damascus when the First World War broke out. From then his passion and knowledge of the Arab people led him to play a leading role in the fight against the Ottoman Empire, transforming him into one of the most influential figures in the modern Arab world.

There was a German version of Lawrence of Arabia, the ethnologist and archaeologist Leo Viktor Frobenius. He assumed the risky mission of promoting the Arab uprising against British rule in the Sudan and Egypt. (But unlike Lawrence, he failed.) Frobenius was to be remembered for his contributions to ethnology and archaeology in his numerous expeditions through Africa. After a Congo expedition in 1904, he advocated the thesis of the African Atlantis, a civilization that flourished in South Africa in antiquity. His research would be widely praised by Africans for having returned their dignity and identity, in stark contrast with a more degrading vision of the African peoples that prevailed with European colonization.

Another major change in the trends of European migratory waves in the early twentieth century was that not only poor and anonymous people were settling in other continents and faraway countries, but also diverse prominent intellectual figures and members of the aristocracy.

The great waves of emigration to other continents had taken place for economic reasons, and consequently the overwhelming majority of emigrants were poor. On the other hand, from the early twentieth century on there were increasing numbers of prominent Europeans who decided to emigrate from Europe and live in foreign countries. They were usually attracted by great opportunities offered by some countries and also by the extraordinarily vital experience implied by living in exotic environs.

The Spanish writer Vicente Blasco Ibáñez, who was to become world famous for his novel *The Four Horsemen of the Apocalypse*, decided to emigrate to Argentina in 1912. After succeeding as a public speaker in the cultural circles of Buenos Aires he decided to travel to the Argentine Pampas with the aim of founding an agricultural colony dedicated to cultivating rice. He named it New Valencia in honor of his home region in Spain. But this ambitious project, in which he employed many immigrants from Valencia, was a dismal failure, and he had to return to Europe in 1914 virtually ruined. Nevertheless, the Argentine adventurer succeeded in the long run with the colony that he founded. It survived and emerged as a dominant business in the rice market.

Another prominent writer, the Danish baroness Karen Blixen, better known by her pen name Isak Dinesen, emigrated to East Africa with her husband Baron Hans Blixen in 1914. Her aim in the British colony was to set up a coffee plantation. The experience was not successful from an economic point of view, as the plantation went bust and Karen Blixen had to return to her country in 1931. Even so, it was a unique experience from a more vital perspective, judging by her memoir *Out of Africa*: "I had a farm in Africa at the foot of the Ngong Hills," starts its enthralling narrative. Isak Dinesen was to describe, with her extraordinary talent as a storyteller, the sense of freedom that Europeans felt in Africa, the pleasures derived from the African rhythm of life and contact with its exuberant nature, a paradisiacal life which a select minority of European adventurers and gentlemen farmers enjoyed in the heyday of colonialism in that part of Africa.

After the end of the First World War, taking up residence far from Europe or the West became fashionable among the most adventurous and bohemian members of the upper middle classes, particularly in France and Britain. This kind of voluntary exile can be attributed to the legacy of war and the fractious atmosphere of the postwar years, when many people, fed up with politics and the miseries of the old continent sought more stimulating and harmonious lives.

The French writer André Gide set out in 1926 on a long voyage to colonial Africa that took him over a year. The result of this experience was his *Journey to the Congo*, a poignant narrative of what he found in the heart of Africa. Like other European writers who had known that part of the world, Gide was appalled by what he saw and made a harsh criticism of colonialism, denouncing the exploitation of the indigenous peoples and abuses that were committed by French companies.

A particularly formative experience that was to have a great impact on his works later in life was that of British author George Orwell's stay in Burma. Orwell, who was born in India in 1899, always felt attracted to that part of the world. For this reason in 1922 he joined the Imperial Police in India and was posted in Burma, where he lived for five years. His difficult experience as a policeman inspired the novel *Shooting an Elephant*, published in 1936. Here he described the thankless task of belonging to the police force and having to repress people who detested colonial authorities. This book was to become one of the most influential Western works criticizing imperialism and colonialism. "When the white man turns into a tyrant, it is his own freedom that he destroys," wrote the noted author.

Traveling and spending time out of Europe was a pastime that rapidly spread among affluent Europeans. Long before this era, it had already been considered an educational, vital experience. In eighteenth and nineteenth century England the so-called Grand Tour became fashionable among young members of the aristocracy, a trip that would allow them to get to know the most emblematic cities of Europe. In the twentieth century, the Grand Tour was expanded beyond the frontiers of the European continent. Jerusalem, Cairo, Alexandria, and Tangier were very popular destinations for those wishing to experience the allure of the East. Others traveled as far as India, the Far East, or even sub-Saharan Africa. After colonizing a great part of the planet, the Europeans were curious to discover it and enjoy all that it could offer. They had very little in common with those adventurers from the early days of colonization, for they always had a well-planned roadmap, stayed at the best hotels, and also had influential contacts that could help them out in case they got into trouble. And above all they were to enjoy better means of transport and communications that made traveling much faster and safer.

In 1872, when Thomas Cook & Son travel agency was set up in England with the aim of arranging foreign trips abroad, it enjoyed a virtual monopoly in this exclusive market for many years, to the extent that Kaiser Wilhelm II contracted its services to visit Palestine in 1898. But by the 1920s travel agencies were well established in Europe's most advanced nations, enjoying the benefits of a rapidly expanding market and helping make traveling abroad a passion, a sign of distinction, and also an existential need for an ever-increasing number of Europeans. In this way they were to lay the foundations of what emerged in the second half of the century as a very powerful industry: tourism.

In stark contrast with the leisurely travelers and those who sought a voluntary exile abroad, the most dramatic aspect of the European exodus in the twentieth century was undoubtedly the one caused by religious persecution. Several centuries after the witch hunts, the Inquisition, and the wars between Protestants and Catholics, secularism had made sufficient progress to guarantee religious freedom in most of Europe. Nevertheless, in the previous century religious persecution was to be once more in European history, a cause for immigration.

Anti-semitism had always been present in Europe. From the middle ages, Jewish communities expelled from several countries in Europe had relocated to other parts of the continent. In most cases these communities achieved a peaceful cohabitation with neighboring Christians and thrived where they were. Nevertheless, anti–Semitism became particularly intensive in several countries from the late nineteenth century. From the pogroms in Russia to the famous Dreyfus affair in France, many conflicts contributed to make the Jews decide that, despite having been living in most parts of Europe from times immemorial, their future in the old continent was very uncertain. For this reason, among the great contingents of European emigrants to America from the 1880s, Jews proliferated. Over two million Jews emigrated to the United States between 1880 and 1920.[*] But the fate of the Jews in Europe

---

[*]   Birmingham, *"The Rest of Us."*

and in the world was going to change radically after the publication of an influential essay by Theodor Herzl in 1897, *The Jewish State.*

Herzl was born in Hungary in 1860 into a Jewish middle class family. After studying at the University of Vienna, he settled down there, where he earned a living as a journalist and literary critic. He was not religious, nor did he demand his wife and children follow Jewish customs. Judging by his appearance and his lifestyle he was not different from any other member of the Viennese bourgeoisie. Nevertheless, the wave of anti-Semitism that swept across Austria and several other countries in Europe led him to reflect on the problems of Jewish identity in this part of the world.

Herzl was in Paris in 1895 when Alfred Dreyfus, a Jewish officer in the French army, was ignominiously imprisoned under the false accusation of spying for Germany. The anti-Jewish feelings that could be perceived in France at the time of the Dreyfus case convinced him that Jews would never be fully accepted in Europe, and that their future could only be secure by the creation of a true Jewish state. But where could this be? In his book, *The Jewish State,* he proposed that the Jews should return to Palestine, where they originally came from.

Herzl's proposal was certainly not original. Zionism, which proposed a return to Zion, the land of Israel, had always been present among the Jewish people. "The next year in Jerusalem," said Jews from time immemorial on celebrating the holidays Yom Kippur or Passover. During the nineteenth century there were several initiatives proposing the settlement of Jews in Palestine. In 1836 an Ashkenazi rabbi from Prussia, Zvi Hirsch Kalischer, contacted the Rothschilds and the Montefiores (a family of Jewish financiers who had settled in London) and sought economic aid from them to set up the Jewish state.* As a result of this type of support the number of Jews in Palestine gradually started to increase. But it was thanks to Herzl that Zionism was going to become an influential movement in Europe.

In 1897 the first Zionist Congress took place in Basel, Switzerland, under Theodor Herzl's chairmanship. From then on, under the chairman's unflinching support, the Zionist movement won an increasing number of

---

* Simon Sebag Montefiore, *Jerusalem: The Biography* (New York: Knopf, 2011).

supporters, not only among the members of the Jewish community and those who sympathized with them but even among those who had always been anti-Jewish.

As Palestine was part of the Ottoman Empire, Herzl decided to request the official support of one of the few people in the world who had sufficient influence with Sultan Abdul Hamid II in Constantinople to ask for his cooperation in the creation of the Jewish state. He approached Kaiser Wilhelm II of Germany, who very much liked the idea, since it seemed to him a good way of getting rid of "the parasites of my empire,"* as he had described the German Jews. Thus, in 1898, on a trip that he made to Jerusalem, stopping over at Constantinople, the Kaiser proposed the project to the Turkish sultan. Nevertheless, as it could be expected, Abdul Hamid bluntly refused to negotiate giving up a part of his empire, however small it might be. "The Jews can spare their millions. When my empire is divided, perhaps they will get Palestine for nothing. But only our corpse can be divided,"** was the Ottoman sultan's angry reply.

While Herzl tried to persuade the rich and powerful, anonymous Jews started to lay the foundation of their future state by emigrating to Palestine. After the Russian pogroms many Jews decided to emigrate to their promised land. In 1883 around 25,000 Jews reached Palestinian territory, and by the early twentieth century there were 28,000 of them out of a total of 453,000 inhabitants. In those years the Jews rapidly expanded through the arid land of Palestine. Due to the proliferation of anti-Jewish demonstrations in Russia, several ships set out from Odessa for the Holy Land. One of them carried a group of Jews of socialist ideology and secular beliefs who had created the Jewish National Fund in order to purchase land on the dunes of the old Arab port of Jaffa, about fifty miles away from Jerusalem. There they founded a city called Tel Aviv (Hill of the Spring) in 1909. Tel Aviv was to be designed by immigrant architects trained in Europe, particularly in Germany, home of the modernist Bauhaus school. A few decades later Tel Aviv emerged as the best example of this European modernist style. Tel Aviv was not only marked by

---

*   Montefiore, *Jerusalem*, p. 376.
** Ibid.

its architecture but also by the secular and socialist ideology of its founders. One of them was a young man named David Ben-Gurion, who was later to be quite influential in the world of Judaism and Middle Eastern politics.

Frustrated by the difficulty of founding a Jewish state in Palestine Herzl started to look for alternatives. Thanks to the influence of the all-powerful Lord Rothschild, in 1903 the British government suggested the possibility of creating a Jewish state in Uganda. Herzl accepted, thinking that being at the heart of Africa would make it easier for his dream to come true than being in the land where the Jews originally came from, but shortly after that he died unexpectedly of a heart attack, and the Ugandan project never took off.

A few years after Herzl's death, Chaim Weizmann took very important steps toward the creation of a Jewish state. A native of Russia, he fled from the persecution of his people, first to Germany and finally to England. There he combined his profession as a chemist with his militant Zionism. In London he obtained considerable support for the creation of the Jewish state in Palestine, including that of Arthur Balfour, who as British foreign secretary committed himself to this cause in 1918. Weizmann discussed his dream with the most influential Englishman in the Arab world: Lawrence of Arabia. Lawrence supported it in principle, as he considered that the Arab world could benefit from a Jewish homeland: "I look upon the Jews as importers of the Western leaven, so important for the countries in the Middle East,"* he commented.

T. E. Lawrence acceded to cross the Arabian desert that he knew so well with Weizmann in June 1918, to introduce him to one of the most powerful Arabs, including Prince Faisal, the future king of Iraq. Faisal accepted the Jews' aim of setting up their homeland, as long as it would be within the great kingdom of Syria, over which he aimed to rule. In this way Weizmann obtained the support from what was then the most powerful nation in the world, and what was even more difficult, some of the main representatives of the Arab world.

He made progress laying the foundations of a future Jewish state in other important spheres. As a scientist he aimed at giving Western knowledge a presence in Palestine. "A Jewish state without a university is like Monaco without a casino" he stated on one occasion. On July 18, 1918, under the

---

* Montefiore, *Jerusalem.*

presence of representatives from the three monotheistic religions and other notables from the city, Weizmann laid the first stone of the building where Hebrew University was going to be.

Palestine, which had been a British protectorate since 1920, experienced a steady increase in population. After the Balfour Declaration, from 1917 to 1925, approximately 90,000 Jews arrived in Palestine. Between 1924 and 1925 another 82,000 joined in, escaping from the chaos and persecution in Russia and also from countries like Poland and Hungary.* With the rise of the Nazis to power in Germany in 1933, Jewish emigration intensified.

Many Jews became aware of the fact that Hitler was going to be much more serious than a temporary outbreak of anti-Semitism, and decided to leave Europe before it would be too late. In 1933, 37,000 of them reached Palestine.** The rapid increase in emigration was going to alter the demographic balance in favor of the Jews. In 1936 there were 100,000 Jews in Jerusalem, in comparison with a combined Christian and Moslem population of 60,000. It was then that the Arab revolts began against the increasing predominance of Jews in the land they considered exclusively theirs. Rising unrest in Palestine led the British government to retract from the original plan of supporting the creation of a Jewish state. In 1939 it announced its intention of supporting a state of Palestine governed by Arabs and Jews, and also set a limit to Jewish immigration. For the European Jews the announcement from the British government could not have been made at a more inappropriate time. As Nazi troops marched over a great part of Europe implementing the plan of Jewish extermination, the Jews were left with only two options to avoid ending up in a concentration camp: to hide or to flee. In this terrible situation the Zionist movement concentrated on promoting illegal emigration to Palestine.

After the end of the Second World War, the news of the Holocaust, in which about six million Jews lost their lives, shocked the world. As a result the creation of the Jewish state enjoyed more international support than ever before. David Ben-Gurion who had become the undisputed leader of the Jewish community in Palestine, increased pressure on the British so that

---

* Martin Gilbert, *Israel: A History* (New York: William Morrow, 1998).
** Ibid.

the state would be created as soon as possible and restrictions to Jewish emigration would be lifted. Before Ben-Gurion, a radical faction called Irgun led by Menachem Begin promoted the armed struggle.

Begin was of Russian origin, like the majority of the Zionist leaders, but he suffered more than any other the horrors of Jewish oppression during the war. After surviving Nazi persecution in Poland he was arrested by the Soviets and sent to a concentration camp. He fled from Russia to Palestine, where he finally arrived in 1942. After enduring so much adversity to reach the Holy Land he was determined not to wait for the British to set up a Jewish state but to fight for it. As a member of Irgun, an underground Zionist organization, he was primarily responsible ordering the bombing of the British headquarters at King David Hotel in Jerusalem, in 1946, where ninety-one people were killed. A few months later the British government announced its intention to abandon Palestine and hand over control of the area to the United Nations.

After the British decision to put an end to its mandate over Palestine, the dream of a Jewish state finally became true. On March 14, 1948, David Ben-Gurion proclaimed the founding of the state of Israel. On the same day he was appointed prime minister, and Chaim Weizmann became president. Over the first three years of its existence, Israel doubled its population, mainly due to immigration from Europe. The majority of immigrants were Holocaust survivors. From Poland and Russia over 200,000 Jews migrated to the Jewish state. In 1950 the Israeli parliament passed the Law of Return, which granted Jews from all over the world the right to emigrate to this new state and become Israeli citizens.

The creation of the state of Israel can be considered the last stage in the history of European expansion throughout the world. The Jews who arrived in this land had very little in common with all those Europeans who had settled in diverse parts of the world on behalf of the great powers over the previous four centuries. Nor were they emigrants or colonialists in the strict sense of the word but members of a community of people that had finally gathered in their land of origin and who were in most cases relieved to leave Europe forever. Nevertheless the founding fathers of the Jewish state came from Europe, the culture in which they had been brought up was European, and the model of society that inspired them was very much European. Those who had received a formal education had done so at European universities and it was there that they had acquired their ideas on democracy, the rule or law, or the market economy that they were going to implement in Israel. Israel was born as a Western state in the heart of the Middle East and in the middle of the Arab world.

While religious persecution provoked the exodus of the European Jews, another phenomenon that proliferated in Europe in the first decades of the twentieth century, political persecution, was to force many eminent personalities into exile.

Russian emigration had increased progressively from the nineteenth century for diverse reasons, but it was the Russian Revolution and the creation of the Soviet Union that provoked one of the greatest waves of exiles that have been seen in history. The first communist regime made it clear from the outset in 1917 that whoever did not support revolution without conditions was an enemy of the people. Many citizens, particularly from the upper echelons of society, were forced to abandon their country in order to earn a living or simply save their lives.

Alexander Kerensky, who took charge of the Russian government after the abdication of Czar Nicholas in February 1917, was an outstanding example of the hard life that awaited the Russians in exile. After the coup d'etat by the Bolsheviks in October 1917, Kerensky, who would have been executed if he had fallen into the hands of the revolutionaries, managed to hide, and shortly thereafter left Russia for Paris, where he began his long life in exile. He lived in the French capital until 1940, when the Nazi invasion forced him to seek a new refuge. On this occasion he decided that the time had come to abandon Europe for good, and he emigrated with his wife to the United States, where he spent the rest of his life.

Many Russians were going to follow a similar path as Kerensky, from nobles who fled with their remaining jewels and the few belongings that they could take with them to humble peasants who were satisfied to leave their country alive. Around two million people left Russia during the revolution and the civil war that lasted until 1921.* Those who were victims of political

---

* Orlando Figes, *A People's Tragedy: A History of the Russian Revolution* (New York: Viking, 1996).

persecution considered themselves exiles, others simple emigrants in search of a place where they could earn a living, and the majority had both political and economic reasons for leaving the country. Although the Russian presence in cities like Paris or London rose rapidly from 1917, the final destination for a high percentage was going to be America, which was far enough from turbulent Europe and offered real opportunities to start a new life.

For obvious reasons, the United States was the favorite destination for the majority, but also Argentina and Canada. In all these countries, a Russian community that was already numerous before the revolution organized itself with the aim of keeping their cultural legacy alive. In 1933, a group of exiled aristocrats founded the Russian Nobility Association, which organized an annual ball that was to become very popular for recreating the old splendor of the Russian nobility among New Yorkers. Russian communities were increasingly politicized from the 1920s, frequently becoming bastions of foreign opposition to the communist regime in their land of origin. After his death in 1970 Kerensky himself could not be buried in any of the Russian churches in New York, because its members refused to grant a burial place to a person whom they accused of provoking the triumph of the revolution. For this reason his body had to be transported to London.

Even though Russian exile was initially synonymous with opposition to the Bolsheviks, the revolution soon started to devour its own sons. After Stalin's rise to power, the rivals who were lucky enough to survive the first purges fled from Moscow. The most famous case was that of Leon Trotsky, who went into exile in 1929. The first stop for the Soviet ex-leader was Kazakhstan, then Turkey, and finally Mexico, where he settled down in 1937. However, not even in this faraway country was he safe from Soviet persecution, and in 1940 he was murdered by a Soviet agent.

Russian exiles continued to proliferate throughout the world and particularly in the United States, where they could espouse the anticommunist cause and a very critical vision of what was happening in the Soviet Union. Exiled dissidents played an outstanding role in this sphere. The most famous of all, Aleksandr Solzhenitsyn, reached the United States in 1974, where he would live until the fall of the communist regime in his country. In that same year, his friend the famous musician Mstislav Rostropovich also went into exile. From America the Russian exile community did not have the opportunity of influencing the Soviet population but they could do it at a more global level, in a way becoming much more powerful enemies of the regime. This was especially the case of Solzhenistyn, who was provided in the U.S. with all necessary means to promote his literature and his opinions about totalitarianism in his country.

In the satellite countries established by Russia in Central and Eastern Europe, many professionals from all walks of life and intellectuals in particular were compelled to go into exile for political reasons. That was the case of the Czech author Josef Škvorecký, one of the spokesmen of the group of dissident writers to which the famous playwright (and eventual president of the Czech Republic) Václav Havel belonged. After the Soviet invasion of Czechoslovakia, Škvorecký and his wife fled to Canada where they spent the rest of their lives.

Another famous case of exile in Eastern Europe was that of the financier, philanthropist, and political activist George Soros. Born in Budapest in 1930 into a Jewish family that suffered the Nazi persecution, he emigrated to England shortly after the Soviet invasion in 1947, well aware that only away from his country and from communism could he embark on a career that would match his ambition. After studying at London School of Economics, Soros moved to New York in 1956. In this city he enjoyed a stratospheric financial career that allowed him to make a colossal fortune. A few decades later, he devoted his fortune to the promotion of open society in Eastern Europe.

Together with Russia and the communist bloc several countries in Europe were affected by exile in the twentieth century. With the rise of fascism and various authoritarian regimes, exiles proliferated from the 1920s. After the introduction of fascism in Italy in 1922, as Benito Mussolini tightened his grip over Italian society, numbers of Italian exiles swelled in neighboring countries like Switzerland or France, and particularly in the United States. Prominent figures like politician and historian Gaetano Salvemini or the diplomat Carlo Sforza opted for exile in the U.S., where they played an influential role in anti-fascist activities among the large Italian-American community. In Portugal, the Salazar dictatorship provoked the exodus of some of the most important personalities from the cultural and political sphere. Initially many of them opted to live in Spain or some other European country, but as the political situation in Western Europe deteriorated, Brazil became the main destination. Former president of the Portuguese Republic Bernardino Machado went into exile there, just as other prominent politicians who contributed to transform the former colony of the Portuguese Empire into one of the main centers of opposition to Salazar.

Spain was to occupy a very special place in the history of European exile during the twentieth century. The Spanish Civil War, one of the most devastating conflicts in contemporary Europe, and the Franco dictatorship with which it culminated, provoked a great wave of exiles.

The Spanish exodus began with the outbreak of the civil war in July 1936—even children were to be affected by it. From the Republican side agreements were reached with various countries in order to send children away to prevent them from suffering the horrors of war. The majority, around twenty thousand, were evacuated to France, and about three thousand went to the Soviet Union. For the latter, living conditions did not improve in the long run as they had the misfortune of having to live in Russia during the Second World War, and very few ever returned to their country.

Exiles from Republican Spain progressively increased as the enemy Nationalist forces gained the upper hand. The great majority initially went to France, where there were 440,000 Spaniards, according to 1939 data. Out of this number many returned to Spain in the 1940s, but around 220,000 were transformed into permanent exiles.[*] Among them, the great majority emigrated to the Americas, especially Mexico and Argentina.

Mexico was the most important country for Spanish exile. The unconditional support that the Mexican government offered to the Republicans from 1936 was going to continue after the war, and for this reason the government in exile was initially established in Mexico City. This country was said to have the largest population of exiled Spaniards. Between 1939 and 1942 twenty-five thousand people entered the country. This presence helped make Mexico one of the most outspoken critics of the Franco regime.

---

[*] Henry Kamen, *The Disinherited: Exile and the Making of Spanish Culture, 1492–1975* (London: Allen Lane, 2007).

The civil war brought the so-called silver age of Spanish culture to a tragic end, one of the most brilliant periods in the country's history from the cultural perspective. Its most outstanding representatives were forced into exile. While many like Gregorio Marañon or Salvador de Madariaga were exiled in Paris and Oxford, England, respectively, others went to Latin America, mainly to Argentina. The philosopher José Ortega y Gasset spent part of the war in Buenos Aires where he had many admirers, but he decided to return to Spain in the mid-1940s. On the other hand, the writers Ramón Pérez de Ayala and Ramón Gómez de la Serna lived in Argentina until the end of the 1950s. As for the writer Francisco Ayala and historian Claudio Sánchez-Albornoz they stayed in this country until the end of the Franco regime. It is quite understandable that so many personalities from the Spanish cultural world chose Argentina for exile, for it was the most advanced of the Spanish-speaking countries with a highly educated elite and plenty of opportunities. Cultural life in Argentina was considerably enriched by Spanish exile.

Mexico also counted on a great community of Spanish intellectuals and representatives of Spanish culture. The eminent film director Luis Buñuel was among them, and he directed great films in this country and left an enduring legacy in its cultural life. Other Latin American countries that received a good number of Spanish exiles were Chile, Venezuela, Cuba, and the Dominican Republic.

"What intolerable suffering living away from ones homeland is,'" wrote the Cordoba-born philosopher Seneca from his Corsican exile. Nevertheless, the life of most Spanish exiles in America was far from intolerable, and they were well compensated for the suffering that they brought from Spain. A good part of the Spanish community in Latin America thrived on the other side of the Atlantic. After all, the war allowed them to find what they desperately needed: a country where there was peace and prosperity. Cultural affinity allowed them to settle easily in their country of adoption, and some of them married locals and left descendants there. One of the most famous victims of the civil war, the poet Federico García Lorca, said on one occasion that the Spaniard does not really know his country until he has traveled to America. Many exiles had the sense of deepening their knowledge of their country after the encounter with the New World that had emerged from the Spanish Empire. Their presence there strengthened the bonds between Spanish-speaking countries whose relationship had been predominantly distant for over a century.

The other great wave of exiles in Europe was going to be provoked by Nazi Germany. From the day when Adolf Hitler became German chancellor and the Nazi Party took power, not only the future of the Jews in Germany was at stake but also that of any German citizen who dared to show opposition to the new regime. As with other totalitarian regimes, the Third Reich left it very clear that whoever did not support it openly would automatically be considered an enemy.

Hitler's rise to power and the establishment of the Third Reich constituted the beginning of a long exile for many Germans. Among the first who decided to abandon his homeland was one of the most prestigious Germans, one who had been described as the greatest scientist in the twentieth century: Albert Einstein.

The great physicist was lecturing in the United States in April 1933 when he received the news that the new National Socialist government had passed a law that forbade the occupation of any official post by Jews, including university chairs. His name was also included in a list of so-called enemies of the regime that was published in the press. From that moment the scientist understood that his life in Germany had come to an end. On returning to Europe he provisionally settled in England with the aim of emigrating to the United States. Shortly after that Princeton University offered him a job, and he crossed the Atlantic and settled in New Jersey, where he would live for the rest of his life. Even after the defeat of Nazism, Einstein, still influenced by the hostility that he felt toward his land of origin, refused to reestablish relations with any German institution. In the world of science and culture many were going to follow his example. In the face of the great upheavals of the old Europe only the New World offered peace and security to live and work.

Not only Jews opted for exile but also many German intellectuals. In 1933 the infamous book-burning campaign took place in Germany, with which the regime aimed at getting rid of what they considered Jewish and anti-German ideas. From Marx and Engels's *Capital* to the works of contemporary authors like Thomas and Heinrich Mann, Stefan Zweig, and Sigmund Freud—all were tossed into the bonfire. Shortly after that the great majority of authors whose books were burned were to abandon their country.

Thomas Mann went first to Switzerland, then in 1939 he emigrated with his family to the United States, which he famously described as "a foreign homeland." After the war he returned to Europe, but he took up residence in Zurich and never returned to his native Germany. His brother Heinrich did not wait for his books to be burned in order to go into exile. After wandering among several European countries, he emigrated to the United States and finally took up residence in California, where he would spend the rest of his life.

A very dramatic case was that of the famous Austrian novelist Stefan Zweig. He lived in Austria when his country was annexed by Germany. He fled initially to England, but like many exiles from Nazism he soon decided to abandon the convulsive old continent and move to America. The Austrian writer arrived in the United States in 1940, but this country that was about to join the war reminded him too much of the European world from whence he escaped. He was attracted by Latin America and for this reason he emigrated to Brazil in 1941.

Stefan Zweig was fascinated by Brazil. "If paradise exists in any place of the planet, it can't be too far from here," he wrote shortly after settling in the city of Petrópolis. The vast South American countryside inspired one of his last works: *Brazil: A Land of the Future.*

In this book the author, so worried by the collapse of old Europe, describes the joy of living in this tropical land that was not polluted by the conflicts of the old world, a country that was so rich and full of opportunities and where an improved version of the Western civilization seemed to emerge. Nevertheless, in spite of the happiness that he showed for living in Brazil, he never overcame the sadness he felt at having witnessed the destruction of the culture into which he was born, and the decline of Europe in the war. For this reason he committed suicide in 1942.

European exile rapidly increased throughout the 1930s and 1940s as Nazi Germany broadened its frontiers. With the invasion of France the last great bastion of liberty in continental Europe was to fall: Paris. After its

353

occupation many French personalities like De Gaulle or Raymond Aron relocated to London. On the other hand, many foreigners who had arrived in Paris seeking refuge from totalitarianism decided to that they would only be safe on the other side of the Atlantic.

From occupied France several eminent intellectual and political personalities fled to America. The famous Jewish political theorist Hannah Arendt managed to escape from a concentration camp and arrived in the United States in 1941, accompanied by her husband, the Marxist poet Heinrich Blücher. The Italian diplomat and antifascist politician Carlo Sforza, who was exiled in Paris from the 1920s, decided to emigrate to the United States in 1940. So did the Europeanist politician and writer Richard von Coudenhove-Kalergi. The list of outstanding figures from cultural, scientific, and political spheres exiled as a result of Nazi expansion was very long, and included names like Alfred Adler, Erich Fromm, Bertolt Brecht, and Kurt Weill.

The fact that many eminent Europeans ended up living in several major cities of the United States during the Second World War contributed to promote the discussion of Europe's future in diverse political circles throughout this country. In 1943 Richard von Coudenhove-Kalergi, the founder of Pan-Europa, an organization that aimed to promote European unification, decided to make good use of his exile in New York to direct a congress there to discuss this ambitious topic. Politicians, academics, and exiled writers were to meet there, among them Thomas Mann, Carlo Sforza, the Greek politician Sophocles Venizelos, and the heir to the Austro-Hungarian throne Otto von Habsburg. Several US congressmen and senators also attended. What all European attendants had in common was the fact that they were far from their countries as a result of the war, and this led them to support von Coudenhove-Kalergi's ideas that had led him to found Pan-Europa in 1922. The Austrian Europeanist had argued for several years that rivalry and war between European nations was the main cause of the old continent's decline, and that in order to put an end to its downward trend European nations should unify.

After the Second World War North American universities also became important centers for the study and research into the old continent's past and future, especially due to the presence of so many Europeans on their faculties.

The fact that they warmly welcomed European scientists, academics, writers, and politicians constituted a great incentive that led many to make the decision to go into exile in this country, and in some cases stay there forever.

Apart from Einstein, who as we have already seen, was employed by Princeton University, the majority of great writers, politicians, and intellectuals who went into exile in the United States collaborated more or less assiduously with its universities. Thomas Mann worked at Princeton, Hannah Arendt taught at various prominent universities, from Berkeley to Yale, Alexander Kerensky was at Stanford, and Richard Coudenhove-Kalergi lectured at New York University. The Spanish eminent biologist Severo Ochoa also arrived in the U.S. with a university contract and rounded out his scientific career there with the Nobel Prize for medicine. His example is not particularly unique, as scientists from several European countries had been emigrating to the United States ever since the 1930s, fulfilling their careers with extraordinary success.

Even among the British, who had no reason to leave their country for political reasons, there were examples of academics who decided to continue their career in the United States, as universities in that country were much more attractive alternatives to austere England under Nazi bombings. The famous philosopher and mathematician Bertrand Russell left his country in 1940, and spent the war lecturing and collaborating in the diverse academic centers of New York.

The great US universities and their research centers had always maintained a strong relationship with Europe. Many of them, especially the most prestigious like Harvard, Yale, or Princeton had Oxford and Cambridge as their model from the time of their founding. Nevertheless from the mid–twentieth century they were going to overtake the great European universities as centers of excellence. The best North American universities were far richer than their European counterparts and increasingly more competitive, for they were open to talent beyond the political, religious, or racial prejudices that were rife in continental Europe. The United States knew how to take advantage of the opportunities offered by the fact that so many European figures from the world of knowledge were to choose their country to emigrate to the 1930s. They were offered generous incomes and the necessary means to do research and promote their knowledge. It is not surprising that many of them were so comfortable in the U.S. that they decided to stay there for the rest of their professional lives.

The attraction of exiled European talent to the United States contributed substantially to displace the center of science and knowledge in the West from Europe to North America. From the 1940s the great American universities outranked the majority of European ones from the top spots in international rankings. The most important scientific discoveries took place in their research centers, and the majority of the Nobel laureates were going to be American researchers, although very often they were Europeans who had obtained US citizenship. Of 314 laureates who won their Nobel Prize for work carried out in the United States since the Second World War, 94 were born in Europe.* Many others were first-generation Americans whose families had emigrated from Europe.

Not only were US universities and research centers to benefit from European intellectual migration but American culture in general. Playwrights like Kurt Weill and choreographers like George Balanchine would enrich the performing arts; great musicians like Igor Stravinsky or Arthur Rubinstein produced masterpieces as naturalized Americans.

European talent was particularly influential in the rapidly expanding film industry. Charlie Chaplin and Alfred Hitchcock, followed by actresses like Audrey Hepburn and Elizabeth Taylor, were among the most prominent British contributions to Hollywood. The German contribution was also extraordinary, with names like Billy Wilder, Fritz Lang, Ernst Lubitsch, and the great star Marlene Dietrich.

The so-called brain-drain to America provoked by totalitarianism and political persecution in Europe from the 1920s continued after the end of the Second World War. Despite the fact that political persecution came to an end in most of Western Europe, no European nation had the economic capacity to compete with the United States in the race for scientific knowledge, and had already lost a substantial amount of talent with emigration. While postwar Europe had little to offer its most talented artists, scientists,

---

★   nobelprize.org

academics, and researchers, the U.S. continued opening its doors and offered European émigrés what they lacked in their countries of origin: economic incentives and work opportunities to make progress. As a result, the United States became the most cherished destination for the talented and ambitious, and American society obtained great benefits from it.

Superiority in the scientific, technical, and cultural spheres constituted an indispensable condition for achieving world supremacy. Europe enjoyed it throughout the era in which its great powers dominated the world, but finally lost it to the United States in the twentieth century. The only consolation that remained for the old continent was that, in the same way that European labor contributed substantially to the transformation of the U.S. into an economic power, the export of European talent was going to enable this country to reach the summit of scientific and technical knowledge and make a substantial contribution to culture in the American Century, as the twentieth century was later to be known.

European migration, particularly to America, continued to be heavy until the 1960s. To a certain extent these last migratory waves constituted the epilogue of European extension beyond its frontiers, for the presence of emigrants in other continents was going to strengthen its legacy and perpetrate Western culture at a time when the sun was setting on European hegemony.

Nevertheless, if emigration in the nineteenth century was a symbol of Europe's great strength in the global sphere, it cannot be interpreted in the same way as the First World War. Mass migration took place in poor countries like Ireland or Poland but also in rich ones like Britain or Germany. That so many citizens from European countries wished to emigrate to other continents was an evident sign that their economies were becoming stagnant and that their societies did not offer as many opportunities to prosper. Great opportunities could be found in the young societies of the New World, where everything was still to be made: Canada, Australia, New Zealand, Argentina, Brazil, Mexico, and particularly the favorite destination of the Europeans, the United States. Long before economic data was going to confirm it, anonymous emigrants seemed to guess that the twentieth century was going to be an American Century and the power of the Western world was to be displaced toward North America.

Emigration caused by the religious and ethnic persecution that took place in the twentieth century weakened Europe and eventually became a sign of its decline. The persecution of the Jews that triggered the Zionist movement deprived several European countries of the contributions of people who had proved particularly talented at finance and wealth creation, and also proved outstanding in the scientific and cultural spheres. Apart from the vacuum left by the Jewish exodus, the impact of the Holocaust questioned many of the achievements of European culture. The fact that a genocide of such magnitude took place in the continent where human rights were born was an evident sign of the degradation that one of its most advanced societies had suffered.

As regards emigration for political reasons, several countries were to suffer the consequences of the intellectual migration provoked by their regimes, for exile of some of the most talented Europeans left a vacuum that could never be filled. The achievements of a continent that was the cradle of democracy and the birthplace of the Enlightenment were largely overshadowed by it.

Chapter 11

Experiences with the Truth

How the Legacy of Imperial Europe Shaped the Postcolonial World.

I n 1929 Mahatma Gandhi decided to adopt the Western practice of writing one's autobiography, "something that no one does in the East," he said. He was driven by a deeper motive than simply explain how he became the leader of the movement for India's independence. He wanted to reveal the spiritual awakening and constant search for truth that would inspire all his actions. For this reason the book was given the title of *The Story of My Experiments with Truth.* Two decades after its publication India was independent and Gandhi had become one of the most inspiring figures for those who sought independence from European empires. But the truth, that truth that Gandhi eagerly sought, led to very different interpretations of how the postcolonial world should be. And the idealism of many of the independence leaders, as we shall see, often clashed against the reality of surviving in a world that had been largely shaped by European culture.

The European colonial world started to be dismantled shortly after the end of the Second World War and had practically disappeared thirty years after. One of the paradoxes of the process of decolonization was that it was not simply the result of colonial revolts or movements for independence in European empires. Within Europe and the whole Western world, very influential personalities demanded the end of colonialism and appealed to an increasingly broad spectrum of the public opinion.

On May 31, 1902, the Treaty of Vereeniging put an end to the Boer War. After almost three years the British managed to win this war, the two Boer republics of the Transvaal and the Orange Free Estate agreed to come under the sovereignty of the British crown. But Britain was to pay a high price for victory. In order to defeat the Boers the British army not only used scorched-earth tactics but even concentration camps. One of the most sinister symbols of war and totalitarian terror in the twentieth century, concentration camps had first been used by Spain during the Cuban War, and also by the United States in the Philippines in 1898, in both cases against enemy insurgents. But in the British case, they were used to control the Boer population in general. Boer prisoners in concentration camps suffered from overcrowding and malnutrition, and many of them died of contagious diseases. News of the terrible living conditions in concentration camps led to widespread public indignation in Britain and denunciations from the Liberal opposition. Consequently, the government appointed a commission led by the Liberal and suffragette Millicent Fawcett, who confirmed that around twenty thousand Boers had died in concentration camps, and this figure represented a thirty percent of the total number of prisoners.

The terms of the peace settlement were not bad at all for the Boers, for they were granted a high level of autonomy. Only nine years later, Britain allowed South Africa to become a self-governing dominion, and it was led by former Boer generals. The conclusion of this costly war was that the British Empire would only be able to survive in the twentieth century by granting a high level of autonomy to most of its peoples. Nationalism, the movement that shook Europe in the nineteenth century, burst into the colonial world with remarkable vigor due to the Boer war. From that time, Britain and the rest of the European empires had to learn how to cohabitate with it and watch it closely in order to survive.

European critics of colonialism and anti-imperialist activists played a very important role in undermining the popularity and internal cohesion of colonial empires. In 1904 the Casement Report was published in Britain. Its author was Roger Casement, an Irish-born British diplomat with considerable experience in the colonial world. As a consul in the Congo Free State Casement had witnessed the most appalling atrocities carried out by Belgian settlers against indigenous peoples. In Congo he met E. D. Morel, a journalist who had been actively denouncing the violation of human rights in Congo in the British press. Together they formed the Congo Reform Association, with the aim of drawing attention to the plight of the Congolese workforce. Its first major victory was when the British government ordered Casement to investigate.

The Casement Report, which was presented in the British Parliament, exposed the abuses of the Congo Free State in detail, including enslavement, mutilation, and torturing of Africans. It concluded that King Leopold of Belgium had not only exploited this African territory for his own private purpose, but had tolerated violence and murder against its people—and the Congolese population had been decimated as a result of it.[*]

European colonial empires were never the same after this report, which was instrumental in putting an end to the Congo Free State. The British prime minister sent the report to his Belgian counterpart, as well as the rest of countries that had signed the Berlin Agreements in 1885, which gave way to the scramble for Africa. Due to the insistence of the Socialist opposition in the Belgian parliament, the government ordered an independent research commission. Finally, in 1908 the Belgian government announced the annexation of the Congo Free State, which formally became a Belgian colony known as the Belgian Congo, and it took direct responsibility for its administration.

---

[*] Séamas Ó Síocháin, *Roger Casement: Imperialist, Rebel, Revolutionary* (Dublin: Lilliput Press, 2008).

Casement, who became known as the father of human rights reports, continued denouncing atrocities against indigenous people in his next posting as consul in Rio de Janeiro. From Brazil he investigated the activities of the Peruvian Amazon Company, and published a report that was almost as devastating as the previous one, detailing the atrocities of the company against the Putumayo tribe. As a result of this the Peruvian Amazon Company was accused of slavery and genocide, and it was closed in 1913.

The world of culture in general and many public intellectuals became very critical of colonialism in the early twentieth century and made significant contributions to turn public opinion against it. This was particularly the case of the great British–Polish novelist Joseph Conrad. In 1902 Conrad published *Heart of Darkness*, based on his experiences in the Congo Free State. This novel, which has been described as one of the great texts of Western literature, evokes the horrors of colonialism through the adventures of Charles Marlow, an English sailor who is recruited by a Belgian company to transport ivory through a river in the heart of Africa. The other personage he described, French businessman Mr. Kurtz, is an example of the corruption and immorality with which Europeans who went to Congo were identified. The novel came to represent an evocation of how disastrously Europeans failed in bringing civilization into Africa.

Other influential writers like Arthur Conan Doyle or Anatole France were also going to contribute to anti-imperialism with their writings and press collaborations. In the academic world anti-imperialist literature also began to proliferate. Particularly influential was the English economist John A. Hobson. Apart from writing against the Boer War and criticizing jingoism, in 1902 he published *Imperialism: A Study*, in which he explained its inextricable link with capitalism. Imperialism was the consequence of the constant search for markets and economic expansion that is implicit in the capitalist system, according to Hobson. The great powers needed colonies in order to create new markets. The fact that the whole system was based on the search for benefits at all costs made it deeply immoral, according to the author.

John A. Hobson's thesis was going to have much impact on all ideological currents that were critical of imperialism. Undoubtedly one of the main reasons why anti-imperialism became a popular cause was due to the rapidly spreading influence of the main ideological currents of left-wing thought: socialism and communism.

The fathers of communism Karl Marx and Friederich Engels devoted their lives to analyzing the evils of the capitalist system. *Capital* explains the historical laws by which capitalism is doomed to failure and will be replaced by communism. Nevertheless, his analysis was based on capitalism in the European countries that he knew, and how the class struggle affected the working class, but he did not analyze its effect on the colonial world. In fact Marx, as well as Engels and many other intellectuals of their age, had a positive opinion of colonialism, as they believed that the propagation of European influence through other continents helped other people overcome backwardness and oppression. Nevertheless, their followers in the twentieth century were going to have a very different opinion about the phenomenon of European imperialism in the world.

Vladimir Ilyich Lenin, the most outstanding of Marx's followers and one of the most influential men of the twentieth century, was a professional revolutionary who devoted his life to prepare the first communist revolution. As well as a revolutionary he was an important theorist of Marxism. Just as Hobson, he interpreted capitalism in the twentieth century as a global phenomenon that great powers propagated through imperialism. For the Russian revolutionary, imperialism could not exist without capitalism.

In 1916 Lenin published an influential work: *Imperialism: The Highest Stage of Capitalism*. In this work he explained how the great powers needed to acquire colonies in order to invest the benefits that their companies accumulated in the local markets, and in this way create new markets. By this process empires had become agents propagating capitalism and reproducing the same system of exploitation in the colonies. The local population in the colonies was exploited by an oligarchy that owned the land, the companies, and the means of production. Cultural and racial differences gave way to even greater abuses in the colonies. Lenin's thesis was going to have an increasing number of followers among the movements for colonial independence and those who looked for alternatives to the colonial order.

Another ideological current of the left that was very critical of imperialism was anarchism. Unlike Marx and Engels, the founders of anarchism, such as Bakunin, Peter Kropotkin, or Proudhon, were going to be very critical of imperialism, as it contributed to promote the social order against which they were fighting. According to the anarchist revolutionary Bakunin, "every people, just as every individual, has the right to be oneself," a principle that was going to lead to many revolts against empires. For Proudhon, who declared that property was robbery, colonialism was a system by which Europeans were propagating through other continents the same property laws that corrupted Western society. For Kropotkin, imperialism was the maximum expression of rivalry and competition between individuals and states that prevented the desired collectivity and the rise of an ideal society in which human beings would cooperate among themselves.

The anarchists, in their eagerness to destroy the established order, became a serious threat to stability in many of the great powers. Their strategy of murdering heads of state and the highest representatives of power had considerable success. Very important leaders both in Europe as in the United States died as a result of anarchist terror, from Czar Alexander II and the Spanish president Antonio Cánovas del Castillo to US presidents Abraham Lincoln and William McKinley, and especially Archduke Franz Ferdinand of Habsburg. These murders often helped change the course of history.

Toward the beginning of the twentieth century the leaders of the European empires were aware of the many factors that threatened their positions, from emerging powers in other countries to independence revolts in their possessions, and obviously ideologies that proposed alternative systems of government. Nevertheless, their biggest fear continued to be their imperial rivals. After several centuries expanding their power through the world, and on many occasions confronting peoples of other races and cultures, the Europeans still feared themselves more than anything else—despite the fact that they belonged to the same race, the same Western culture, and they had the same idea of civilization. For any European power their greatest threat was in other European powers with which they often shared a frontier. The worst enemy did not inhabit faraway lands, but cities on the European continent.

Within less than twenty years after the end of the Second World War, the empires of the European powers were dismantled. From 1947 Europeans abandoned the territories that had been occupied during several decades or even centuries, and in whatever great amounts of human, military, and economic capital had been invested. It is extraordinary that in most cases they did so by peaceful means, after negotiating amicable agreements and transferring power in well-planned ceremonies in which the highest dignitaries from former colonial powers and the new independent nations mutually paid their respects. Cordial diplomatic relations were also usually established with the former colonies. Most difficult of all for the European powers was to come to terms with the loss associated with abandoning a colony that had conferred them wealth, power, and imperial status, although on some occasions decolonization of certain territories constituted a great relief for the powers that had occupied them.

Another reason why in the early 1940s it was difficult to predict that colonial empires would disappear so rapidly was due to the fact that, apart from some exceptions like India, in the majority of colonies the wish for independence was not sufficiently extended. It must also be borne in mind that two of the greatest colonial powers, Britain and France, were on the winning side of the Second World War, and as always happens in war, it could be expected that the victors would expand their possessions at the cost of the losers, but certainly it could not be expected that they would voluntarily give up their territories.

The key to understanding the process of decolonization is in the world order that emerged after the Second World War, and especially the geopolitical interests as well as the mentality of the United States, which was to fight for world supremacy against the Soviet Union.

Decolonization owes a lot to a principle of self-determination that was introduced by the United States in 1919. After its intervention in the First World War, which enabled Britain and France to win, the US government decided that peace and the future world order should be based on its principles and not on European territorial ambitions that had caused so many wars. Self-determination was applied to reconfigure the map of Europe after the First World War and although this principle allowed many peoples to form nations, it did not always have a happy end. Nevertheless, its application to the colonial empires was not to be so immediate.

The first victim of the British Empire as a result of self-determination was Ireland, whose population had been rebelling against British dominance for centuries. The Celtic island was going to be a very good example of the problems caused by self-determination, for while the Irish Free State was proclaimed in 1922, the population of six northern counties that form Ulster decided to remain under British sovereignty. In this way the island was divided.

Another territory of the British Empire that succumbed to independence movements in the 1920s was Egypt. After three years of revolts the British government decided to grant independence to this protectorate in 1924. The rest of the empire continued to be governed in the same way as before the war, although in the case of India, as we shall see, it was going to be increasingly difficult to maintain law and order against the uproar of the independence movement.

In the rest of the colonial world European powers continued exerting their influence without changes, except for the case of Morocco. In 1922 the anti-colonial leader Abd el-Krim led an insurrection against the Spanish presence in Rif. After the proclamation of the Rif Republic it was not possible to recover the control of the protectorate until 1926, when a Franco-Spanish expedition finally defeated Abd el-Krim.

The situation in the colonial world changed drastically after October 1929. The Wall Street crash provoked a crisis in the entire Western world as well as its colonies. The price of commodities and that of many of the colonies' exports dramatically fell, and broad sectors of the population were impoverished as a result. Consequently, many of those inhabitants of the colonies who had supported or at least tolerated European colonization, due to the fact that the modus vivendi depended on them, suddenly turned against it.

The British Commonwealth of Nations was founded in 1931. The Statute of Westminster by which this organization was created stipulated that both Great Britain and the dominions were "autonomous communities within the British Empire, equal in status, in no way subordinate to one another, though united by a common allegiance to the Crown." The Commonwealth seemed the ideal formula for granting independence but at the same time maintaining economic ties and safeguarding the allegiance to the crown of the so-called dominions. But dominion status was only granted to those territories that had been mainly populated by British settlers: Australia, New Zealand, Canada, Newfoundland, and South Africa, as well as the Irish Free State. No other territory was allowed to be a dominion, not even India, despite the fact that this could have been the only way of staving off the increasing support for outright independence among its population.

The origins of the movement for Indian independence can be traced back to the 1880s. In 1885 the Indian National Congress was founded by Allan O. Hume, a retired British officer, and educated Indians who aimed at creating a civil and political platform for promoting reforms within the Raj. Initially composed of seventy-two people, it gradually began to attract members of the Indian middle classes concerned with the state of colonial India. Far from expressing any wish to break away from colonial rule, its overall aim was to hold Britain to its word that the Raj existed for the benefit of Indians. Indians should be properly ruled as British subjects in accordance with democracy, for otherwise they would just be another despotic Asian regime.

Those who upheld such advanced ideas were members of the new Indian bourgeoisie that had thrived in Delhi, Bombay, Calcutta, and other main cities under the British Raj. Most of them had been educated in institutions founded by the British, as well as in Britain. They knew Western culture well and its currents of thought, from liberalism to the increasingly influential revolutionary ideas that emerged from Marxism. They considered themselves ideally suited to represent the overall interests of the India and were determined to defend them as good subjects of the British crown.

By the early twentieth century the Indian National Congress was transformed into a mass party, attracting citizens from diverse backgrounds and acquiring a similar structure to that of the great Western political parties. Home rule, under conditions similar to the white dominions in the Commonwealth, was its initial aim. After the end of the First World War most of its members became frustrated by the fact that the British crown refused to grant them this status, and began to support outright independence. It was against this background that the pacifist lawyer Mahatma Gandhi was elected president. This small unassuming man became one of the main leaders of Indian independence, and the most important personage of India in the twentieth century. He became not only a key figure in the process of decolonization but one of the main advocates of pacifism and an indispensible figure in the spiritual world. This explains why he was known as Mahatma, or "Great soul."

Gandhi was initially an ideal citizen created by the British Raj. Born in 1869 into a middle class family, he studied law at the University of London, and after graduating emigrated to South Africa to work as a lawyer. As a product of the British Empire and an example of its meritocracy, Gandhi had good reasons to be loyal to the Queen and Empire and would have continued to be a good British subject had it not been for his experiences in South Africa. Gandhi was dismayed to discover that Indians in South Africa suffered racial discrimination as much as black citizens. On one occasion he was kicked out of a train for refusing to move from a first class car, for which he had bought a ticket, to the third class compartment, where all those who were not white were meant to travel. After this traumatic experience, Gandhi became an enemy of the British Empire and of European colonization in general.

In 1915 Gandhi returned to India with the aim of devoting the rest of his life to his country's independence. He never wore a Western suit again, and soon the white tunic with which he covered his frail figure (and his sandals) became the main symbols of the anti-colonial struggle. As a pacifist he rejected violence as a legitimate way of pursuing his aims, and he managed to make civil disobedience by peaceful means the method by which the Indian Congress was to fight for independence.

Having failed to obtain home rule or membership of the British Commonwealth, in 1929, under the presidency of Jawaharlal Nehru, the Indian Congress declared independence to be its official aim. Civil disobedience and peaceful resistance became the medium to achieve it. Due to this, India seemed ungovernable in the 1930s. Even so the British authorities refused to even contemplate abandoning the jewel in the crown of the British Empire.

In the rest of the colonial world there was nothing comparable to the Indian National Congress, but there were certainly local elites, who like the Indian middle classes, had benefitted from the best education that European powers could provide, in order to reach the conclusion that that they were just as capable as their colonial rulers to govern themselves. But they still lacked the will and the capacity to fight for independence, for the colonial world did not give the impression of being in decline in the 1930s. On the contrary, it was still expanding, as Japan's invasion of Manchuria in 1931 and the Italian invasion of Abyssinia in 1936 seemed to indicate. Then the outbreak of the Second World War became a major obstacle to the cause of independence for two main reasons: the first was that colonial empires were extremely useful for European powers. Britain and France were a much more formidable enemy because together they controlled a third of the planet. Just as in the previous world war, Britain was assisted by Canadian, Australian, New Zealander, and South African troops, as well as its colonial troops dispersed throughout the world. India contributed with an enormous army of two and a half million soldiers. The second reason was that war led to an outburst of patriotism and a sense of solidarity among all members of the empires that also affected the colonial subjects.

Nevertheless, from 1942 colonial empires were doomed to disappear if the Allies managed to win the war. As we have previously seen when Winston Churchill met U.S. president Franklin D. Roosevelt for the first time in 1941, the British prime minister was desperately hoping to convince the U.S. of the need to enter war on the Britain's side. But he was also aware that this would imply accepting the US leadership of the postwar world order.

Among the main points of the Atlantic Charter, with which this historic meeting culminated, and the two signatory countries agreed on the compromise of not seeking territorial gains from this war. Most important of all, the US president and the British prime minister agreed that territorial changes would take place taking into account the interests of their inhabitants and, above all the right to self-determination of all peoples.

The document reflected the North American vision of international relations much more than the British. Roosevelt was very critical of European colonialism, and he took advantage of his powerful position to demand independence of the colonies, by which empires were to disappear. Churchill, eager to show that Britain was in perfect tune with the U.S., which was his last great hope to win the war, did not want to contradict the president, and he accepted his terms.

The fact that the British prime minister accepted the principle of self-determination prompted much debate in the aftermath of this historic meeting. On returning to London Churchill was asked about the consequences of what had been agreed for the colonies. Churchill played down its importance, commenting that self-determination referred only to Europe.* After all, as he stated on one occasion, he had not become prime minister to preside over the dissolution of the British Empire. But the Atlantic Charter was going to have great influence, particularly from the moment when the United States government entered the war, as it was going to demand that peace should be dictated according to its own terms.

After the end of the most destructive war in history, the victory for Britain and France was to be different from the rest, and their situation was to be so critical that not only did they not obtain any territory, but they soon reached the conclusion that they could not hold on to their colonial empires. This was particularly the case because they were in minority in the new world order. At the new United Nations, Britain and France occupied two of the five permanent seats at the Security Council. The other three corresponded to the United States, the Soviet Union, and China, and one of the very few aims that they had in common was their determination to ensure that there would be no place for European colonial empires in the new world order. For very good reasons, the title of last volume of Churchill's war memoirs was *Triumph and Tragedy*.

Decolonization began in Asia for two reasons: it was the continent where movements for independence had made better progress, and on top of this the colonial powers had been defeated by Japan on several war fronts. Once their inhabitants witnessed how Europeans were defeated, they were no longer willing to go back to live under their sovereignty.

In September 1945, the Vietnamese communist leader, Ho Chi Minh proclaimed his country's independence. After recovering Indochina from the Japanese, the French government had to use part of the money obtained from US loans to send troops to Vietnam and in this way get entangled in a very complicated war. Holland faced the same tortuous and uncertain fate on

---

* Roy Jenkins, *Churchill: A Biography* (New York: Farrar, Straus & Giroux, 2001).

regaining control of its Asian empire. On November 17, 1945, the nationalist leader Achmed Sukarno declared independence for Indonesia, which was widely supported by the inhabitants of Dutch colonies. Holland, which still kept 140,000 troops in Southeast Asia, decided to use them in order to defend what was left of Dutch sovereignty in this part of the world.

Britain on the other hand was going to be much more pragmatic with India than France or Holland with their Asian colonies. It decided that it was better to find a dignified end to its colonial rule rather than have to resort to the use of force to hold onto power. Lord Curzon commented on one occasion that, "As long as we rule India, we are the greatest power in the world. If we lose it, we shall drop straightaway to a third-rate power." Churchill shared this opinion: "The loss of India would be final and fatal to us. It could not fail to be part of a process that would reduce us to the scale of a minor power," he stated in the House of Commons.[*] In spite of all, his successor, Labor leader Clement Attlee, did not hesitate to launch a plan to abandon the jewel in the crown of the British Empire before it was too late. With this aim he appointed Lord Mountbatten as the last viceroy of India. This prestigious Navy commander, related to the royal family, was entrusted with the delicate mission of putting a peaceful end to over three centuries of British presence on the Indian subcontinent.

When the Second World War broke out the Indian National Congress proposed assistance in the war effort and a truce in its demonstrations against colonial rule in return for obtaining independence after the war. But the British government declined, and from then on it was only possible to keep the independence movement at bay by means of strong police repression. On the other hand, while Gandhi's followers fought by peaceful means, other independent factions supported the armed struggle. By 1945 Britain had neither the will nor the capacity to go against a population of four hundred million people.

Lord Mountbatten's mission as the last viceroy of India was not only to negotiate the end of Britain's colonial rule but also to supervise the creation of two new states that were to emerge from the British Raj. Since 1940

---

[*]   Jenkins, *Churchill*.

Muhammad Ali Jinnah, the leader of All-India Muslim League, had been demanding a separate nation for the Muslims of the Raj. Despite Gandhi's opposition, Nehru and other leaders of the Indian National Congress accepted the two-state solution along religious lines. But the most difficult of all was to draw the borders between the two new nations. The Indian Independence Act authorized Cyril Radcliffe, a British lawyer who had never before been to India, to draw the frontiers of Pakistan in the areas where there was a Muslim majority—and at the same time leave as many Hindus and Sikhs in India. On August 14, 1947, India and Pakistan officially came into existence. This was followed by the greatest movement of people in history, involving fourteen million people. Muslims from all over India emigrated to Pakistan, while Hindus and Sikhs who found themselves on the wrong side of the border set out to the new India. The frontier split Punjab and Bengal almost in half. Worst of all was the violence between religious communities provoked by this process, in which over one million died and ten million were dispossessed.[*] Lord Mountbatten had successfully accomplished his mission of putting an end to British colonial rule in India, but neither he nor Nehru nor Jinnah were able to stop the bloodbath and wave of religious and ethnic hatred that followed the proclamation the Indian independence.

Mahatma Gandhi was murdered by an Indian nationalist shortly after the proclamation of independence in 1948. From then on, his pacifism was all but absent in the relationship between the two nations that were born after the end of colonial India. Conflicts between India and Pakistan provoked more deaths after 1947 than all the victims of the fight against British power in three centuries of colonization. It plagues their relationship to the present day.

Both India and Pakistan were to face major challenges in becoming new nation-states, like incorporating princely states that had been practically independent during the British Raj, the incorporation of French colonial enclaves into India, or the annexation of Portuguese Goa. The fact that Pakistan was divided into two separate territories, West Pakistan to the north of India, and East in part of Bengal, was doomed to provoke bitter conflicts.

---

[*] Alex Von Tunzelmann, *Indian Summer: The Secret History of the End of an Empire* (New York: Henry Holt, 2007).

In 1971 the new state of Bangladesh emerged in East Pakistan, after a war of independence that was mainly sparked by Bengali nationalists. The national dreams of visionaries like Nehru and Jinnah came true but at the cost of the Pax Britannica and Gandhi's pacifism.

Shortly after putting an end to colonization in India, the British also withdrew from Palestine, although on this occasion with a great sense of relief. Britain had been the first nation to officially support the creation of a Jewish state, as the foreign secretary Lord Balfour stated in 1917. On the other hand, Lawrence of Arabia had helped instill among the Arabs the dream of creating their own nation. Assuming a compromise with both Jews and Arabs toward the creation of a new nation in Palestine provoked many problems for the British in this region and in the whole of the Middle East.

Palestine grew contentious as Jews arrived in rapidly increasing numbers in the 1930s. In 1936 an Arab revolt broke out, leading the British to back off from its initial promise of creating a Jewish state. On the other hand the British position of limiting Jewish migration in the midst of Nazi persecution in order to prevent clashes with the Arabs was considered inhumane by all those affected. It was bitterly criticized in the international sphere after the crude details of the Holocaust became known. Before such a predicament, the British government announced its wish of putting an end to its mandate over Palestine and hand over to the United Nations the difficult mission of dividing the territory between Jews and Arabs, as recommended by the majority of nations represented in this organization. This contributed to speed up the process by which Palestine was divided and the state of Israel proclaimed. Immediately after the appearance of the first Jewish state, the members of the Arab League (Syria, Transjordan, Iraq, Egypt, and Lebanon) declared war on the new state. Israel quickly gained the upper hand, but this was only the beginning of the Israeli struggle for survival. One of the great conflicts of our era was born.

Britain laid all the responsibility of creating the state of Israel on the United Nations. Nevertheless, for the Arab world the colonial powers, as well as the United States and the West in general, were responsible for creating this new state in a territory that they considered theirs. Nor was the state of Israel going to enjoy much support among all nations emerging from the colonial world, as they regarded this state as an offshoot of the Western world in the Middle East.

In the process of decolonization, the Europeans did not always withdraw voluntarily from their colonies, they were also going to be expelled by force. This was the case of Indonesia, where the Dutch, after four years of futile war against Sukarno's independence troops, had to withdraw. In 1949 Queen Juliana of the Netherlands herself handed over sovereignty of Indonesia to her former foe Sukarno.

French agony in Indochina was even longer. After 1949, Ho Chi Minh's insurgent troops counted on the support of the powerful People's Republic of China. After his rise to absolute power in 1949 Mao Zedong became one of the most feared enemies of Western Europe and the rest of the Western world.

The birth of communist China also demonstrated that communism would not only triumph in industrial nations, as Marx had predicted, but also in agrarian ones. Mao, who set himself the aim of recovering China's power, was not only a determined advocate of decolonization but would also offer to help any peasant movement that revolted against colonization or bourgeois interests. His first opportunity to do it was in neighboring Indochina.

Supported by China, communist leader Ho Chi Minh's troops in the Vietnamese jungle became an unbeatable enemy to France. Moreover, as this war became increasingly unpopular in France, Ho Chi Minh counted on the support of a substantial part of the French left, which saw him as a fighter for a just cause. All this led the French government to negotiate its withdrawal from Indochina in 1954. Deeply influenced by the results of the Korean war, in which the North was occupied by the communists and the South remained under a regime that was supported by the United States, Vietnam was also divided between the North, controlled by Ho Chi Minh, and the South, under the control of Prime Minister Ngo Dinh Diem and supported by the United States. After a nine-year conflict, the French were relieved to hand over to the United States the responsibility of fighting against communism in this region. It ended up being a war that not even the United States could win.

Decolonization rapidly transformed the world order in which Europe had been hegemonic until 1945. In the 1950s several of the nations that had been colonized started organizing themselves in order to defend their interests in the international sphere. An example was the Bandung Congress, celebrated in Indonesia in 1955, where twenty-six decolonized nations convened. Apart from Sukarno, who acted as host, Nehru attended on behalf of India. China proved to be particularly eager to lead this group of nations and was represented by Zhou Enlai. All of them concurred in describing colonization as an evil that ought to be eradicated as quickly as possible. The congress also served the purpose of denouncing Western alliances and to urge all countries from the postcolonial world to stay away from them. Nehru acted as the spokesman for the nonaligned, denouncing the Atlantic Alliance as "the most powerful protectors of colonialism," and he warned that to be part of this organization constituted an intolerable humiliation for an Asian or African country. Among the attendees, one who seemed to pay particularly close attention was Egypt's representative Gamal Abdel Nasser.

Egypt had obtained its independence long before the decolonization process began. After it managed to stand up to British and French power in 1956 and humiliate both, it became the country that best represented the triumph of the principles of the former colonial world over those of Europe.

The Suez Canal, a great symbol of colonial expansion, continued in French and British hands after Egypt's independence, but Nasser did not take long to expel them after reaching power. In 1954 the United States refused to grant a loan to Egypt due to its increasingly close relationship with the Soviet Union and in retaliation the Egyptian president decided to nationalize the canal.

The Suez Crisis constituted a great humiliation for both Britain and France, as it showed that they were no longer great imperial powers. Prime Minister Anthony Eden and President Guy Mollet acted as any of their predecessors would on facing similar crises that could endanger their interests in the world. Every colonial power, particularly Britain and France, had used military force to respond to aggression against their interests, property, or citizens abroad. Nevertheless, in 1956, as the decolonization era was making progress, this policy could no longer be applied, first because in the new world order the interests of the old colonies counted as much as those of the great powers. Second, because European empires no longer ruled over the world, and third because above France and Britain, two superpowers were determined to stop this conflict which they considered a relic from the colonial era.

Another reason why Britain and France could not have won a war against Egypt in 1956 was due to the fact that the operations like those of the Suez could no longer count on the support of their citizens. Unlike other occasions in which the citizens themselves, aroused by the press, had demanded the government defend their national pride at all costs, the opposite happened in 1956. British public opinion was very critical of the decision to involve the country in a war, particularly one that they did not consider fair. French public opinion was also deeply divided. In the postwar era, the majority of Europeans could never forget the price of war, and had ceased to believe in the efficiency of the use of force.

Nasser's triumph prompted other Arab countries to stand up and defend their interests before colonial powers. The sultan of Morocco, Mohammed V, whose country gained independence from France in 1956, claimed sovereignty over several Spanish territories bordering Morocco. In 1956 he took advantage of a revolt against Spanish rule in Ifni and sent Moroccan troops in. The siege of Ifni lasted for several months. In 1958 Spain and France coordinated their armies in a successful offensive by which Spain recovered the colony, at least for a few more years.

France had very good reasons to assist Spain in this campaign against Morocco, even only one year after the defeat in Suez, because the more successful Arab revolts became the more difficult it would be to hold on to its favorite colony: Algeria.

This colony had a very special place in the French Empire because so many French people had emigrated to the North African coast that they had transformed it into a kind of African France. From the 1940s representatives of the Muslim majority began to ask for independence, but the French from both sides of the Mediterranean ignored them. When the French Union was created in 1946, replacing the old French colonial empire, French Algeria was incorporated into European France in a desperate attempt to show that it was not considered a colony but rather an integral part of French territory.* But even this measure failed to quell the support for independence in Algeria.

In 1954 the National Liberation Front began an armed struggle for Algeria's independence. What initially seemed like a local revolt soon escalated into one of the major wars of the decolonization era. The war not only set France against Algerian independence fighters, but also different communities within Algeria. The brutality of the French forces in Algeria turned public opinion in European France against them. Last but not least was the wholehearted support of the Arab world for Algerian independence.

The Algerian War was one of the main causes of the fall of the French Republic in 1958. The return of President de Gaulle to power was seen as the great hope for the European cause in Algeria. "Long live French Algeria," shouted the general during his visit to this territory in 1958. Nevertheless, as he confessed in his memoirs, from the beginning he was pessimistic about the possibilities of France staying there.**

In 1960 Harold Macmillan, who succeeded Anthony Eden as British prime minister, delivered an influential speech at the South African parliament. "The wind of change is blowing through this continent. Whether we like it or not, this growth of national consciousness is a political fact," stated Macmillan. The "wind of change" speech signaled Britain's decision to grant independence to its African possessions in accordance with the new spirit of the times. With this speech Britain placed itself in the vanguard of the decolonization process, and other European powers would have to follow suit or face the dire consequences. Shortly after that, President de Gaulle declared himself in favor of granting independence to Algeria. He who had been a loyal advocate of the French Empire understood that Algerian independence was unstoppable in the era of decolonization, and that his government would pay a very high price for swimming against the tide.

After reaching an agreement with the Algerian National Front, Algerian independence was submitted to a referendum, which an overwhelming majority voted in favor in June 1962. France handed over power to one of

---

*   Harrison, *France and Islam in West Africa.*
**   Tony Judt, *Postwar: A History of Europe Since 1945* (New York: Penguin, 2005).

the leaders of the ANF, Ahmed Ben Bella, an Algerian traditionalist whose first language was French. Almost one million French Algerians returned to France as soon as independence was declared, constituting a serious loss for the new Arab nation in terms of talent and economic capacity.

While the greatest symbol of French colonialism became history, the rest of its huge empire in this continent had also disappeared. France, like the rest of the colonial powers, was initially very reticent to decolonize sub-Saharan Africa, in the belief that their inhabitants were not ready to create independent nations. Nevertheless, toward the end of the 1950s it gave in to the decolonizers' demands.

In August 1958, during a visit to sub-Saharan Africa, de Gaulle had promised in Brazzaville that French colonies would have the opportunity to choose between independence or remaining French. Due to the fact that the overwhelming majority of the territories preferred to govern themselves, the French government launched a rapid process of decolonization. In 1960, nations from Mauritania to Chad, and from Mali to Madagascar were simultaneously reborn as independent.

On that same year, very much influenced by France, Belgium also brought its colonial adventure to an end. For many years the Belgians refused to contemplate the withdrawal from their only colony, but the attitude of their government changed with the late 1950s. The Congolese National Movement, led by the charismatic Patrice Lumumba, intensified its fight for independence. After revolts broke out in Leopoldville in 1959, with hundreds of deaths, the government decided to grant independence to the colony as quickly as possible, in order to avoid getting entangled in a colonial war.

On June 30, 1960, the Belgian independence ceremony took place. The divide between how the colonizers and the colonized viewed their history became evident on this occasion. King Baudouin unwisely paid homage to his grandfather, King Leopold, who had created so many bad memories in the colony. Lumumba, on the other hand, responded in his speech with an acute criticism of colonialism and the evils it had brought to his people.

Despite the need to ensure a peaceful transition, a few days after handing over power, revolts broke out and chaos took over the whole country. Tensions were so serious that the majority of the eighty thousand Belgians who decided to stay on in Congo after independence had to be evacuated by the United Nations. Lumumba himself was murdered shortly thereafter. Mobutu Sese Seko took power after him, setting up the classical model of single-party government that was to predominate in Africa. In 1970 the country was renamed Zaire. Nationalism and hostility toward every symbol of colonization provoked the exodus of companies and foreigners, leading to impoverishment. The country also suffered from acute administrative chaos and corruption. When the Belgians left Congo in 1960 there were only thirty college graduates to cover over one thousand leading posts in the administration.* It constituted a big challenge to fill this gap.

In the meantime, the British Empire in Africa was also going to disappear. Ghana obtained its independence in 1957, as would Nigeria and the rest of the British possessions in West Africa three years later. Much more complex was the decolonization of British East Africa, especially Kenya, which in the last decades had become the favorite place for white settlers.

In order to respond to the spread of revolts against British dominion, the colony established a parliament in which all racial communities were to be represented: blacks, Arabs, Indians, and whites, although the last group retained a majority of seats. This system of democracy, with racial quotas, did nothing but provoke indignation among the nonwhite population. It also contributed to the revolt of the Mau Maus, a group of anti-colonial freedom fighters from the Kikuyu tribe. The British authorities responded to the Mau Mau terror with a declaration of the state of exception in 1952. Order could only be restored in the colony by very unpopular measures like the introduction of concentration camps to control the insurgent population, as had been done during the Boer War. But despite the insistence of the local white population that such measures were justified, the British government was not willing to pay such a high price for remaining in Kenya. In 1960 negotiations were opened for independence. The colony was represented by Jomo Kenyatta, the founding father of Kenya, and one of the great leaders of the postcolonial era.

---

* Martin Meredith, *Fortunes of Africa: A 5,000 Year History of Wealth, Greed and Endeavour* (London: Simon & Schuster, 2014).

Southern European powers liquidated their colonial empires at a slower pace than in the North. The new Italian Republic, eager to strengthen its presence in Europe after fascism, got rid of its colonies with relative speed. In the case of Spain and particularly of Portugal it took them much longer to cease being colonial powers.

General Franco confronted decolonization with considerable pragmatism. He was unwilling to entangle Spain in colonial conflicts. After granting independence to Equatorial Guinea in 1968, and Ifni a year later, an aging Franco confronted the Green March on the Spanish Sahara, launched in 1975 by the astute sultan of Morocco Hassan II. The Spanish government, much more worried about its internal situation, opened negotiations with Morocco and Mauritania, and finally abandoned the colony in 1976. Nevertheless Moroccan and Mauritanian territorial aspirations over the Western Sahara were to be frustrated, for the Polisario Front advocated the territory's independence. In this way not only did European powers face the consequences of the principle of self-determination but also new nations that had claimed this principle to declare independence from the colonial powers. This became one of the many territorial conflicts that emerged as a result of decolonization.

Portugal under the Salazar dictatorship refused to contemplate the independence of any of its colonial possessions, for several reasons. It was a symbol of prestige with which to compensate the marginalization experienced by the former great power at that time. On one occasion, when President Salazar was asked about his plans to decolonize Angola and Mozambique, he answered that it would take place in about "five hundred years."

Nevertheless, to maintain such an extensive empire with scarce resources in the midst of the decolonization process posed a great challenge. In 1961 the Indian government ordered the occupation of the Portuguese colony of Goa, and Portugal could do nothing but complain. After being humiliated in India, it decided to strengthen its grip in the African provinces, especially in Angola and Mozambique.

Angola had half a million European inhabitants in a total population of around five million people. Oil deposits were found in the 1960s, increasing the determination of Salazar's regime to ensure that it would remain Portuguese. But this became increasingly difficult due to the guerrilla activities of the Angolan anti-colonial movement. The same occurred in Mozambique. In order to maintain law and order in these territories the number of troops posted there steadily increased, to the extent that by the end of the 1960s one out of every four men of military age in Portugal was posted in the African possession.

Army discontent in the African colonies was one of the causes of the military coup that brought the Portuguese dictatorship to an end in 1974. Decolonization began with the provisional government of General António de Spínola. But the process was far from peaceful. After the withdrawal of troops, about one million Portuguese abandoned Angola and Mozambique. In Angola, Portugal's exit provoked a civil war between rival factions of the local population, and in the case of Mozambique and Guinea, chaos prevailed as a result of the activities of revolutionary guerillas.[*]

Nationalism rapidly spread across Africa from the mid–twentieth century and it became one of the main ideologies that justified the struggle for independence from colonial rule. Just as European peoples had done in the nineteenth century, the Africans created nation-building identities around factors like language, culture, religion, or race. Apart from the Arabs and black Africans, African whites also attempted to define themselves as a nation, and white nationalism also became another source of conflict in Africa.

The Boers, the first European settlers in Africa, had been cultivating Afrikaner nationalism for two centuries, which allowed them to define themselves as a nation before the foreign and hostile elements that surrounded their South African homeland. According to the ideologues of this nationalist movement, the keys elements that defined their identity were the white race, the Afrikaner language, and their Protestant religion, as well as certain conservative customs that allowed them to define themselves as God's chosen people. All these signs of identity not only set them apart from other races in South Africa, but also from the British.

Afrikaner nationalism led the South African government to establish the controversial apartheid system that racially segregated blacks and Indians, allowing the white minority to retain its power and privilege indefinitely. A

---

[*]   Meredith, *Fortunes of Africa: A 5,000 Year History of Wealth, Greed and Endeavour.*

system that justified racial segregation by the white minority in Africa during the decolonization era could only survive by means of repression. In 1960, the South African government took drastic measures to quell anti-apartheid activities. Sixty-three people were killed by the police during one demonstration. Most of the leaders of the anti-apartheid movement were imprisoned, including a young lawyer named Nelson Mandela.

This racist system would bring South Africa to conflict with neighboring nations, as well as the Commonwealth. After apartheid was condemned by all Commonwealth nations, the South African government reacted by announcing its decision to abandoning the organization. In 1961 South Africa proclaimed itself as a republic with no official links to the British crown. After all, the Boers argued, they had been the first victims in Africa of British colonialism and they ought to take advantage of the decolonization movement to break links with this old colony.

The other nation that emerged as a result of white African nationalism was Rhodesia, and this was to provoke serious problems for the British government. In the colony founded by Cecil Rhodes, the white minority that constituted less than ten percent of the population also established a system of racial segregation. In 1965, Ian Smith, leader of the white nationalist party, the Rhodesian Front, announced his wish to proclaim independence, but the British government demanded the establishment of a proper democracy in which blacks would enjoy the same rights as whites. The Rhodesian Front refused to accept an egalitarian democracy in which the whites would be a minority and therefore lose all power, so Ian Smith unilaterally declared Rhodesia's independence in 1966. The British government had not been defied in such a way by a territory of its empire since the US Declaration of Independence. In fact, Smith himself mentioned the precedent created by the United States in order to justify his decision.

The aspiration of the white people in Rhodesia to maintain their culture and traditions had many supporters in British public opinion, but Harold Wilson's government was not willing to go against the spirit of decolonization and justify a racist regime. For this reason he decided to apply economic sanctions.

For the new Rhodesian nation the main obstacle for its survival was the hostility of neighboring nations and the international community. The United Nations condemned the Rhodesian regime and South Africa was the only country that recognized it as a nation. But the most destabilizing factor for Ian Smith's government was the civil war that broke out between the white minority and Zimbabwe's African Union, led by Robert Mugabe and other groups of indigenous insurgents. The latter enjoyed the support of neighboring countries, which led Ian Smith to the conclusion, toward the end of the 1970s, that his regime could not survive. He negotiated with Mugabe the re-foundation of Zimbabwe Rhodesia, which was officially born in 1979. Shortly afterward, elections were called in which citizens black and white enjoyed the right to vote, and in the new nation (with an over ninety percent nonwhite population), Mugabe was elected.

Ian Smith's aim that decolonization would also benefit South African whites, and that they would be able to continue enjoying the same privileges in a decolonized continent, was a provocation in the 1960s. It ended up being an impossible dream, which succumbed to the overwhelming force of opposition. There was no place for white nationalism in black Africa.

After the fall of white Rhodesia, South African apartheid came next. In the 1980s international pressure bore down on South Africa to end its racist regime, intensifying especially from the United States and Western Europe. Supporters of apartheid argued that the white minority had been responsible for transforming this country into a rich and prosperous nation, unlike all those surrounding it. But in the 1980s, from the perspective of European and Western public opinion, a racist regime that ignored human rights was unacceptable.

The United Nations' economic sanctions on South Africa, together with pressure from Western governments led the South African government to abolish apartheid. In 1991 the first elections took place in which all citizens had the vote. The legendary prisoner Nelson Mandela was elected the first president of the new multiracial South Africa.

The decolonization of Africa was the last great chapter of Europe's imperial decline. Out of those huge empires created by the European powers, by the 1980s only a few enclaves remained scattered throughout the world.

In most cases, the inhabitants of these small enclaves appealed to the right to self-determination in order to remain under the sovereignty of the old colonial empires, rather than be annexed by neighboring nations that claimed sovereignty over them.

Some of these relics of colonial empires were to lead to conflict. In Argentina in 1982, Leopoldo Galtieri's dictatorial regime ordered the invasion of the Falkland Islands. The Argentines had claimed sovereignty over these islands because of their proximity to their nation. But Prime Minister Margaret Thatcher, against US advice, sent in the Royal Navy. After a brief war, British dominion over these islands was restored. This constituted a great victory for the British, and to a certain extent compensated for the humiliation they suffered in the Suez Crisis. Nevertheless, all governments of democratic Argentina that followed the Galtieri dictatorship have continued claiming sovereignty over these islands.

Spain also had to face the territorial claims over the old enclaves of Ceuta and Melilla, which belonged to Spain long before Morocco existed as a nation. Some African nations also disputed the Spanish identity of the Canary Islands, but to no avail, as the principle of self-determination favored Spain in this case.

Where there was clearly no possibility of prolonging European presence was in China, not even under the principle of self-determination. Hong Kong was one of the greatest success stories of the British Empire. The colony, which was established after defeating China in the Opium War, had great importance for British commercial interests. From the mid–nineteenth century the city grew until it became one of the great industrial, manufacturing, and financial centers in Asia. Together with Singapore, Britain's greatest contribution to the development of Asian capitalism was Hong Kong. But what made Hong Kong different from the rest of the European colonies was that this city was occupied by the British as a result of a ninety-nine-year lease agreement with the Chinese government.

For Mao Zedong's regime, Hong Kong was the maximum symbol of Chinese humiliation before European colonization. For this reason Chinese diplomacy was to demand its return to Chinese control as soon as the lease expired in 1999. It was no use to appeal to the principle of self-determination by which the Chinese wished to remain British, as the Chinese government refused to tolerate it, and the British government had neither the desire nor the military capacity to defend it by force.

As soon as the lease expired in 1999, the change of sovereignty was celebrated in Hong Kong at a historic ceremony. Prince Charles, Prime Minister Tony Blair, and Chinese president Jiang Zemin were there, among other dignitaries. As the Union Jack was lowered in this moving ceremony, Britain put an end to centuries of presence in China, while China moved one step forward in its consolidation as a global power.

The negotiations for Hong Kong's change of sovereignty were very complex, as they implied ceding sovereignty of a territory governed by the market economy to a communist power. This was one of the reasons why so many citizens from the colony wished to emigrate. The only great concession that the British government obtained from the Chinese was that the city would enjoy an autonomous status for fifty years, and it would continue to be governed by the market economy. In spite of all, one of the great mass migrations provoked by decolonization was the one that took place in Hong Kong. Over one million people emigrated between 1985 and 1997 at the prospect of the change of sovereignty. The exodus continued after 1999.

Macao, the other great colony in China, had a very similar end to Hong Kong, despite the fact that the Portuguese never signed a lease agreement with China, and in theory they could have continued indefinitely in this territory. Nevertheless, after the "Carnation Revolution," by which democracy was reestablished in Portugal, the government decided to negotiate Macao's return to China. It was agreed that in 1999, with the end of the twentieth century, four centuries of Portuguese colonization of Macao would come to an end. Just as in Hong Kong, the status of one country-two systems was also applied to Macao, which allowed its inhabitants to continue to do business in the same way and live as they had until then. In this way, the end of Portuguese sovereignty in 1999 did not bring drastic changes to Macao's way of life.

The postcolonial world was going to be known as the Third World, as it belonged neither to the First World, composed of Western developed nations, nor to the Second World of nations that were aligned with the Soviet Union. But to the frustration of the United States, or allied former colonial powers, very often members of the Third World were not necessarily neutral in the bipolar confrontation, and in this way it became one more scenario of the Cold War.

The fact that communism was so closely linked to the criticism of colonization made many of the leaders of the postcolonial world regard the Soviet Union and China as their natural allies. The rapid industrialization and modernization of the USSR also helped transform it into an ideal development model for many colonies that were poor and backward.

Decolonization constituted a golden opportunity for both the Soviet Union and China to propagate communism.* Vietnam was the most evident case, where Ho Chi Minh, supported by China, successfully defied France first, and then the United States. The Soviet Union was going to assist many African communist parties or revolutionary groups in their fight against colonialism, or governments that emerged after independence. Soviet support was crucial for the revolutionary forces in the civil war that took place in Angola and Mozambique, and it was thanks to the Soviet Union that both Congo and Benin managed to become Marxist states. The anti-apartheid movement and the African National Congress, led by Nelson Mandela, received Soviet aid. This was used as an excuse for the South African regime to argue that the end of the apartheid would lead to communism.

Anti-communist diplomacy during the Cold War led the United States and several European powers to support African dictators like Mobutu. The theory of the lesser evil, that a dictatorial regime was often the only alternative to a communist takeover, allowed many of the dictators of the postcolonial era to thrive in Africa.

Many of the nations in the Third World that were not attracted by the communist model did not always advocate democracy. The dramatic increase in nation-states in the world after 1947 did not increase the number of democracies in the same proportion, as those promoting liberal democracy from the West would have wished.

What was the best system of government? The leaders of the postcolonial world were going to answer this question in a very diverse way.

---

* Archie Brown, *The Rise and Fall of Communism* (New York: Vintage, 2010).

In the case of India, the Congress Party, with a long experience as a democratic party, made it clear that its country's future was that of a great democracy. After its independence, India, the second most populous country, became the largest democracy in the world. For leaders like Jawaharlal Nehru or Mahatma Gandhi, who had studied for their college degrees in England, and for the middle classes from which they emerged, democracy was the only system of government that seemed legitimate and acceptable. In Pakistan Muhammad Ali Jinnah was just as committed to democracy, but in 1958 military administrations began taking over, eventually leading to a majoritarian Islamic democracy, not to be confused with the liberal democracy model that prevailed in India. In the case of Indonesia, democracy only lasted for a few years, as President Sukarno regarded it as contrary to the country's interests, and in 1958 it was replaced by an authoritarian regime.

In the Middle East, Israel was the only democracy worthy of the name. What prevailed in the Arab countries were authoritarian monarchies or single-party regimes governed by strongmen who reached power in a coup d'etat. In the case of Gamal Nasser, it would be an example imitated in countries like Libya, Tunisia, Algeria, Syria, and Iraq.

In sub-Saharan Africa, democracy was not only virtually absent, but despotic regimes, in the majority of cases, replaced one another by means of violent coups or tribal wars, leading the most brutal dictators to hold power. Uganda's first head of state, Idi Amin, became world famous as the prototype of a ruthless dictator. In the nine years in which he held power he systematically violated all human rights. Mortal victims of the regime reached at least 250,000.

Undoubtedly the most extravagant of all African dictators was the president of Central African Republic, Jean-Bédel Bokassa. An army officer who had served in the French army, he led a coup d'état in 1966 and ruled over his country as an absolute dictator for thirteen years. Not satisfied with his powers as life president, in 1977 he decided to be crowned as Emperor in 1977, at a lavish ceremony in which he spent well over an entire year's budget. His anticommunism earned him the support of the French Republic, but French president Valérie Giscard d'Estaing came to regret the cordial relationship that he established with the dictator, and in 1979 he sent in troops to put an end to his brutal dictatorship, in what became known as the last French colonial expedition.

Another archetypal African dictator was Zaire's president Mobutu Sese Seko. The kleptocratic state established by this dictator allowed him to accumulate a fabulous fortune. Mobutu's support for neighboring Hutus also helped sow the seeds of one of the worst genocides in modern history, the brutal genocide of the Tutsis by the Hutus in Rwanda, in which almost one million people died. This led to an even more catastrophic conflict, the First Congo War, in which Mobutu was overthrown as a result of the invasion by Rwandan forces. Basically the same ethnic rivalries led to the Second Congo War. About twenty armed groups representing different factions fought in this war, and nine African countries became involved, making it known as the African World War. A peace agreement was signed in 2002 and a transitional government was appointed that would bring back stability in the Democratic Republic of Congo, as the country was known since Mobutu. But the conflict caused over 5.5 million deaths, making it the world's deadliest since the Second World War.*

Throughout the first decades of the postcolonial era, the horrors that were visited on the African continent were comparable to those denounced by Roger Casement in the early twentieth century. A century after Joseph Conrad described this part of the world as the furthest point of civilization, it still had not really managed to get there.

Culture and identity also played an important role in decolonization, but the interpretation of these terms was often controversial. History and local customs became very useful tools for independence leaders in order to define their new nations and give them cohesion. The works of historians, archaeologists, and anthropologists were used for extolling a glorious past. In a similar way to European leaders in the nation-building process, leaders of the former European empires used history, culture, religion, and even race as symbols of national pride. National cohesion often emerged as a result of the struggle for independence in which an enemy and all that he represented was rejected. For this reason de-Westernization campaigns were launched

---

*. Brown, *The Rise and Fall of Communism.*

throughout the former colonial world, with the aim of eradicating the legacy of the old colonial powers and eliminating their symbols of power. The most radical in this sphere was the Cambodian dictator Pol Pot, who even went as far as to forbid the use of Western medical advances in his crusade against the West and capitalism.

Nevertheless, postcolonial identity was not always sufficiently strong as to wipe out the colonial legacy and replace the customs of the Europeans. Mahatma Gandhi called upon Indians to return to their local customs and reject all those that were imported from the West in order to find themselves and their true Indian soul. Nehru, on the other hand, was wary of clinging to ancient Indian traditions that had kept so many people poor, and preferred to embark on a process of industrialization and secularization, and to follow the trends of modernization that would bring prosperity and progress into India as it did in the Western world.*

A very important characteristic of British culture that Indians could not afford to reject for practical reasons was the English language. Hindi, the mother tongue of the largest part of the population, was spoken by less than twenty-five percent of the total population. As English was the only common language of communication, the Indian constitution declared it as official language, together with Hindi. An attempt in 1965 to eradicate English and make Hindi the sole official language failed as representatives of minority languages refused to accept it. An Indian could make a career in politics and administration without knowing Hindi, but not without knowing English. In Pakistan English was equally resilient in the post-independence era, and it has been the official language together with Urdu. In Singapore English is the lingua franca, used as the medium of instruction in schools as well as in the administration and courts. As regards Hong Kong, the Chinese government had to acknowledge the prevalence of English, and included it as an official language together with Chinese.

It was clear that English would remain the official language in the former colonies of the British Caribbean, but what seemed more extraordinary was

---

* Ramanchanda Guha, *India After Gandhi: The History of the World's Largest Democracy* (New York: Picador, 2008).

the progress it made in sub-Saharan Africa. From Nigeria to Kenya and from Sierra Leone to South Africa, English not only survived decolonization but actually became the common tongue, particularly in the administration and the business world. It proved particularly useful in countries like Nigeria, where members of several tribes cohabitated without sharing a common language.

In the former French colonies, French became the official language together with Arabic in North Africa or other languages further south. Due to the fact that French was used in politics, diplomacy, and in business it became an instrument for social climbing and self-improvement, and was cultivated by every educated family. The Belgian Congo was renamed Zaire as its main cities adopted African names in order to strengthen its local identity and eradicate every trace of the colonial legacy. Nevertheless, French, the only common language that the population shared, was to be the official language, together with the local languages.

In the African Portuguese colonies, the language of the old empire was also the official one. Even in the small colony of Spanish Equatorial Guinea, Spanish would remain as the common language. The famous comment made by Cardinal Cisneros to Queen Isabella of Castile, that the language was the companion of the empire, not only became true in the Spanish Empire, but in the rest of European empires that were decolonized over one century later. Language became one of the most indelible signs of the European legacy in the world.

As far as customs, social habits, and etiquette are concerned, the leaders of decolonization were going to defend and promote their customs, but they did not always manage to replace those of the colonizers. As regards sartorial customs, Sukarno, Nehru, and Mobutu always dressed as their countrymen did, but on the other hand Ferdinand Marcos and Habib Bourguiba almost always opted for the Western suits. Jomo Kenyatta wisely combined the Western suit with local hats. In the world of business and diplomacy however, Western habits prevailed. Most of the Third World leaders representing their countries in international institutions that the European powers bequeathed would do so in Western suits and following Western etiquette, among other reasons because this was the only truly international etiquette.

Much more challenging was to hide the legacy of Europe in all institutions that define a nation: national parliaments or local assemblies, the judicial system and national courts, schools and universities, the police forces and the army. The army was a very good example of continuity in the postcolonial world. The uniforms, the hierarchical structure and the army discipline was practically the same as that of the colonial powers that had ruled over them, and oppressed them in some cases. The fact that military dictatorships proliferated in many countries strengthened the army as a pillar of the new nations, as it had traditionally been in Europe. Unlike postwar Europe where the army was assigned a very discreet role and citizens tended to reject military values, in the Third World militarism was particularly strong.

Cultural values and moral attitudes experienced substantial changes in many of the new independent states, but the end of colonization did not interrupt the task of most Christian missions. In regions like the Caribbean or sub-Saharan Africa, Christianity had become the religion of the majority of the population and it became a very important channel by which Europeans transmitted many of their beliefs to the peoples of the colonial world.

Nevertheless, an important change brought by decolonization was the rise of Islam. In Arab countries and in Islamic countries like Indonesia, Islam continued to be not just a sign of identity but also a means by which to compensate the colonial legacy and fight against the predominant global Western culture. Apart from experiencing a rise of fundamentalism in the Islamic countries, proselytism also increased. From the Arabic countries a great effort was made to promote the Islamic faith in sub-Saharan Africa. The fact that they tried to describe it as a true African religion, as opposed to Christianity, which had been brought by European colonizers, helped make many Africans opt for the Koran rather than the Bible. Islam also seemed attractive to many peoples who were rebelling against secularism, modernity, and the paths of development marked by the West.[*]

Independence was much more easily obtained in the political than in the economic sphere. Most Third World nations were so heavily dependent on economic links with the former colonial powers that initially it was not

---

[*] Paul Nugent, *Africa Since Independence* (New York: Palgrave, 2004).

possible to cut them off without facing bankruptcy. One of the main aims of the British Commonwealth or the French Community of Nations had been to promote trade links and keep the economic ties among the countries that formed the old empires, and to a certain extent this was achieved in the postcolonial era. Despite the fact that decolonized countries were free to do business with whoever they wished, the legacy of colonization was too strong. In most cases the links with European companies, investors, and financial institutions were crucial to keep their economies afloat.

The only way to truly put an end to the economic influence of a former European colonial power was by the drastic measures of nationalizing European assets and expelling its representatives. Some leaders tried this, with success, like Nasser in Egypt. But in other cases, the price that the country paid for it was its own impoverishment. This is what happened in Zaire with the expulsion of foreign companies. The expropriation of land from white landowners also became very popular in the early days of decolonization. It was practiced in countries like Kenya, Tanzania, and Uganda, and in Zimbabwe Robert Mugabe applied it on a large scale. It was supported throughout the Third World as a way of attaining justice and compensating local tribes for the occupation of land by the whites a century before.

Although economic ties between Western European countries and former colonies remained strong in some cases, competitors emerged from many countries, especially the United States. Decolonization offered great opportunities to American companies in all parts of the world that had been controlled by European empires. Since the 1950s the presence of North American multinationals continued to be increasingly high. Western influence was spread by impressive products from the United States. Hollywood films and Coca-Cola in particular reached the remotest places in the old colonial world.

On the other hand oil made European nations increasingly dependent on many of the former colonial territories. While the industrial powers had been self-sufficient in their first stages of their development, twentieth-century technologies put an end to this energy independence. From then, gasoline became essential for transport, and it made possible the consumer society and the economy in general.

The era of the black gold provided a great source of wealth to many nations of the Third World, which until then had very few resources to subsist. The fact that eighty percent of the oil reserves were found in the Middle East gave the countries in this region an extraordinary economic and political power, especially Saudi Arabia, Iraq, Kuwait, and the United Arab Emirates. For Nigeria or Angola in Africa, or Indonesia or Brunei in Southeast Asia, it constituted not only a formidable source of income but also the main way to project their external influence.

In 1960 Iran, Iraq, Saudi Arabia, Qatar, and Venezuela founded the Organization of Petroleum Exporting Countries (OPEC), with the aim of regulating the price of oil and protecting their common interests. Oil became the Achilles' heel of the economy for Western nations in general, and Western Europe in particular, where there were practically no oil deposits. The Western policy toward the Middle East, where the most important oil exporting countries were, was shaped by the overpowering dependence on oil imports.

Decolonization contributed to accentuate the division of the world between North and South, not only in terms of geography but also of economic development. One of the factors that most Third World countries had in common, even the oil-producing ones, was economic underdevelopment. There were of course notable exceptions like South Africa, Australia, and New Zealand, or Argentina and Chile—all of which had levels of development comparable to northern countries. But the rest, even the oil-producing countries, were characterized by economic underdevelopment, and in some regions like sub-Saharan Africa, extreme poverty.

The fact that poverty and poor economic prospects characterized many of the countries that emerged from colonial empires prompted much criticism of European powers and colonialism in general. What happened to the high ideals of introducing civilization and promoting development that theoretically motivated European settlers? Wasn't poverty the most evident proof of the failure of colonization? Questions like these were asked both in the Third as well as in the First World, where public opinion had turned increasingly critical of the legacy of colonization.

Representatives of European powers responded to these critics by arguing that decolonization had taken place too rapidly and under the constant pressure of the two new superpowers. They also alleged that some of the new countries lacked the economic capacity and the political maturity to survive, let alone thrive as independent nations. The example of a boy who had been given the responsibilities of an adult without knowing how to handle them was often used, not only in Europe but also among many of those who lived or did business in these countries. On the other hand a sense of guilt also prevailed among European policy makers.

In order to tackle poverty and reduce the abysmal differences in economic development that separated the North from the South, developing nations began to offer aid to the Third World. From the 1950s aid programs progressively increased, from economic aid to humanitarian aid, and in some cases, defense. European powers, the United States, and the Soviet Union as well helped countries with which they had a stronger relationship. Western European countries focused their aid programs on former colonies; the United States sent its aid to allied countries that were defined as anti-communist; and the Soviet Union focused its aid programs on satellite countries or those where there were possibilities of establishing a communist regime. In this way, aid served very different purposes, from those who used it to expiate their sense of guilt as a result of colonization, to those who did it with geopolitical and ideological aims. For all providers of aid, this became a very important aspect of their international policy and they were going to compete against each other in order to acquire the greatest influence.

The results of foreign aid varied tremendously. If humanitarian aid was essential to help victims of wars or natural disasters the results of economic aid were to be very debatable. The main challenge was to ensure that the money sent actually reached ordinary citizens and was not mismanaged by an inefficient administration or spent by corrupt governments. In Zaire, much of the money that Mobutu amassed in Swiss bank accounts came from development aid funds. In the light of these allegations Anglo-Hungarian economist Peter Bauer has stated that this was an excellent method of transferring money from the poor in the rich countries to the rich in the poor countries.

For leaders in the Third World, and in fact for every country that had ever been a colony, the models of economic development that inspired them were all those that had originally been experienced in Europe. They all implied mass migration into the urban centers and exploitation of natural resources. As a result, the relationship between the population and the natural surroundings, which was considerably altered from the beginning of colonization, continued deteriorating. The belief in industrialization and urbanization as the only ways of creating wealth spread rapidly through the decolonized world. It was going to attract an increasing number of people to the cities, isolating them from the rural world to which they originally belonged. From Calcutta to Manila, and from Cairo to Lagos, large, densely populated cities emerged that were going to reproduce the problems of cities in Europe and the West at the beginning of the industrial era, but this time on a larger scale and with less control from their governments. Overcrowding in inhumane districts, shanty towns, exploitation of the workers without rights, disease, infant mortality, traffic chaos, mafias and corruption, crime and delinquency—all these evils became present with more or less intensity in most of the great urban centers of the Third World.

As regards the rural world, decolonization did not allow the return to its pristine origins, but very often the opposite. The methods of agriculture, cattle raising, and forestry that had been introduced by the Europeans were inherited by the colonized peoples after independence and continued to exploit the land very much in the same way. The wild areas, the fauna and flora of so many regions, continued to suffer from the trend of destruction initiated by Europeans. European settlers converted hunting into a sport and a business, particularly in Africa and India. The Bengal tiger, the lion, the rhinoceros, the elephant, and so many other exotic animals became highly esteemed trophies, and the sale of hides and ivory were products for which there was a lucrative global market. This reality helped make many Third World countries exploit their fauna with commercial aims, leading some species to the verge of extinction. The West eventually condemned this, leading to international banning of the ivory trade, but often African countries lacked the means to implement it and stop poaching.

Imperialism took place at a time when the idea of exploiting nature for economic purposes was commonly accepted not only by the West but by all civilizations. Third World leaders from Jawaharlal Nehru, Ferdinand Marcos, or Sutan Sjahrir inherited this idea, and in most cases considered it as the best way to reach prosperity. But Europeans had believed in the exploitation of the earth at a time when its resources seemed to have no limit and the available technological means were not so advanced. Nevertheless, in the second half of the twentieth century, many of the nations that decided to create wealth by exploiting natural resources were doing so at a time when these were increasingly limited. Nature could recover from the damages caused by European colonization until the early twentieth century, but this was no longer the case few decades later. The path that led European countries to economic progress was not going to give Third World countries the same results.

The great survivor of the decline of European empires was Russia. It had begun its territorial expansion almost at the same time as Spain and Portugal, and it continued extending its frontiers long after all European empires had fallen in the twentieth century. The Russian Empire was not affected by self-determination, nor did any of the great postwar powers demand that the process of decolonization affect any of its territories. There was an obvious reason for this, for the Soviet Union was a nation-state and not a colonial empire. Also, Stalin, at the height of his powers after defeating Nazi Germany, and with the Red Army deployed throughout Eastern Europe, would not have given up a single inch of Soviet territory. Lenin had anticipated this problem transforming the old czarist empire into the Union of Soviet Socialist Republics. Despite the fact that he fiercely criticized colonialism as an essential part of capitalist imperialism, he never considered the Russian Empire as a product of this phenomenon. Lenin and his successors would argue that the peoples that formed the Soviet Union were not victims of imperialism, but that they had the privilege of belonging to the communist paradise that was being built from Moscow.

Apart from maintaining unity after the Second World War, the Soviet Empire was going to grow by means of establishing satellite regimes in Central and Eastern Europe, and also promoting communist regimes in the Third World. Communism was successfully established first in North Korea and North Vietnam, then in Cuba. In Africa and Asia, the Soviet Union expanded its influence not only by supporting revolutionary forces in all these countries, but also by the traditional method of armed invasion. This was the case with Afghanistan, which was occupied by the Soviet army in 1980.

Of all the empires that emerged from European expansion, the Soviet was the one that collapsed in the most unexpected and quickest way. No one would have dared to predict that the nation that invaded Afghanistan in 1980 would cease to exist only eleven years later.

The Soviet Union did not start to crumble as a result of any uprising within its frontiers, but because of a rebellion in one of its satellite states. Unlike European empires the USSR was challenged due to ideological issues, for the European satellite states had ceased to believe in communism and its peoples could no longer bear the oppression, the inefficiency, or the poverty that it generated.

The fall of the Berlin Wall, on November 9, 1989, started a domino effect, provoking the collapse of all communist regimes in Central and Eastern Europe two months later. The manifestations of discontent with the communist system went up like gunpowder.

The revolutions that took place from Poland to Romania in 1989 not only displayed the enormous problems of communism before the world, but also the weakness and inefficiency of Moscow's government. From the moment the Soviet government renounced the use of its army to crush the insurgents in any of the Eastern European states, the peoples under Soviet rule became aware of how easy it was to set themselves free from the Kremlin. No empire has survived for a long time once its government has given evident signs of weakness, and this was particularly the case in the Soviet Union.

The general secretary of the Communist Party, Mikhail Gorbachev had been a wise statesman who was well aware of the serious problems of the Soviet system. His famous policy of perestroika was an attempt to reform and liberate the system in order to avoid its collapse. But as it often happens to reformist politicians, he ended up being overthrown by the changes that he himself promoted.[*]

After the fall of communism in Eastern Europe, Gorbachev wanted to reform communism and keep the Soviet Union unified, but in the end he did not achieve these aims. Its dismemberment began with the declaration of independence of the Baltic republics of Lithuania, Latvia, and Estonia in the

---

[*] Brown, *The Rise and Fall of Communism.*

summer of 1991. In December Boris Yeltsin, Gorbachev's political rival and first president of the new Russian Federation, signed the Belavezha Accords, which gave way to the creation of several independent republics: to the south, Uzbekistan, Kyrgyzstan, Kazakhstan, Turkmenistan, and Tajikistan were created. In the Caucasus, Armenia, Georgia, and Azerbaijan were born, and in Eastern Europe Moldova, while in the north two large nations emerged: Ukraine and Belarus.

About a third of the territory of the Soviet Empire was lost in 1991.* Most of it had been acquired between 1700 and 1945. The break with the Caucasian republics was relatively easy, as these people of Muslim majority and Islamic customs were so different from those of the Orthodox Russians, and had been the most difficult to integrate into the Russian world. On one hand, what was particularly hard for the Russians was the independence of Ukraine and Belarus, which had formed part of old Russia and contributed to the creation of the Russian identity. On the other hand, far away Siberia, despite the distance that separated it from Moscow and the differences between their peoples and white Russians, was to remain loyal to the metropolis, proving in this way the success of its colonization process.

The disappearance of the Soviet Union did not put an end to the problems of identity and sovereignty in what continued to be the largest country in the world. The Caucasian peoples of Chechnya aimed for independence, and the Russian refusal to grant it caused two wars and a great terrorist threat. Border clashes with Georgia led to a Russian invasion in 2008.

The fall of the Soviet Union was one of the most significant events in the twentieth century. Its disappearance as a world superpower brought the Cold War to an end as well as the ideology that caused it: communism. The great ideological utopia that emerged in Europe in the nineteenth century and became a revolutionary idea of universal influence after 1917, reached a terminal crisis with the disappearance of the first communist state.

The Soviet Union has one of the most extraordinary histories of imperial expansion. Fifteen years after the Russian revolution, the USSR managed

---

* Geoffrey Hosking, *Russia and the Russians: A History* (Cambridge, Mass.: Harvard University Press, 2001).

to transform a backward nation into one of the top industrial powers. And a decade later, in 1945, it reached superpower status, rivaling the United States in the struggle for world hegemony. On the other hand, its fall was also faster than that of any European empire, with the exception of Nazi Germany. The Soviet Empire was dissolved eleven years after it attained its greatest expansion in 1980.

A lot has been written about the achievements of the first communist state. One of the most important was the eradication of illiteracy in a country where over eighty percent of the population could not read or write under the czarist regime. It also allowed the right to education, housing, and health for the entire Russian population, although the quality of the last two was often precarious, particularly in the regime's final two decades. In the promotion of the principle of equality and the eradication of differences due to wealth and social background, the Soviet Union reached further than any other system.

On the other hand its legacy regarding liberty and human rights was disastrous. Terror was the inseparable companion of the Soviet state throughout its seven decades of existence, reaching unbearable levels during the time of Stalin. As a result of the famous book *The Gulag Archipelago*, by the dissident writer Aleksandr Solzhenitsyn, the world could find out about the reality of the forced labor camps where so many of the convicts faced a tragic end. After the fall of the Soviet Union, it became known that the work of the prisoners in the Gulag generated around a ten percent of Soviet production.[*] A regime that claimed to stand against all sorts of slavery ended up benefitting from slave labor.

The data about the victims of terror and repression in the Soviet Union from 1917 varies a lot. According to the *Black Book of Communism*, published by several academics in 1997, the number of deaths could reach a minimum of twenty million.

As communism spread around the world similar methods of violent repression were used, although some leaders applied them with more rigor. This was particularly the case of the founding father of the People's Republic of China, Mao Zedong, who learned from the Soviet Union that violence

---

[*]   Brown, *The Rise and Fall of Communism.*

on a grand scale was necessary in order to consolidate a communist regime. Around sixty-five million Chinese people died from repression in Communist China according to the *Black Book*. In Cambodia, the number of deaths caused by Pol Pot's regime was around two million people, which constituted twenty percent of the population. Vietnam was responsible for about one million deaths and North Korea around two million. As regards the Marxist regimes in Africa, its victims were around 1,700,000 deaths; and in Latin America, 150,000.

Communism, a movement that aimed at setting human beings free from all forms of injustice caused the death of over ninety million people in the twentieth century.* Communist expansion ended up being more lethal than any other imperial movement with which it can be compared, including European colonialism. There is no reliable data that allows us to have an accurate figure for the number of deaths caused by European colonial expansion from the fifteenth century. It is evident that the victims of crimes, executions, and forced labor, as well as slavery and genocide associated with colonialism, would reach several million and affect a wide range of peoples throughout the world. But no colonial regime developed such systematic, repressive structures, nor did it manage to eliminate so many people within such a short time span.

Despite the fact that communism was born as a European ideology, it never really took root in Europe. Communism was incompatible with the characteristic individualism of the Western culture, the traditional aspiration of the peoples of Europe to own private property, the wish to enjoy freedom without state supervision, and of course, the revered freedom of expression. This is one of the reasons why the communist revolution initially only succeeded in Russia, which is a Eurasian country, and the attempt to expand it to Central and Eastern Europe ultimately failed. For let us not forget that the collapse of communism was caused by the 1989 revolutions in Europe.

On the other hand communism was Europe's most successful ideological export of the twentieth century, judging by the success it had on other

---

*   Stéphane Courtois, et al., *The Black Book of Communism: Crimes, Terror, Repression* (Cambridge, Mass.: Harvard University Press, 1999).

continents, particularly in Asia. The fact that China, the most populous country and a great civilization, became communist gave this ideology formidable clout. But this ideology had also been in crisis since the death of Mao Zedong, and faced serious threats to survive. In the 1980s China began experimenting with a partial introduction of the market economy in order to avoid the system's collapse, but discontent continued spreading, particularly among the urban generations that demanded democratic reforms and less repression. This led to the Tiananmen Square protests in summer 1989, in which several hundred people were killed by police forces. Unlike the USSR and its European satellites, the Chinese government did not hesitate to use all forms of repression to ensure the survival of the regime. On the other hand China learned from the collapse of the Soviet Union and speeded up a process of economic transformation into what was called a socialist market economy. In this way capitalism was to return to China, but under the control of the state and the supervision of the Communist Party.

The Chinese model of the socialist market economy would inspire neighboring Vietnam, which gradually opened itself to market forces and tourism. North Korea, on the other hand, remained loyal to communist orthodoxy and could only survive at the cost of becoming one of the most isolated countries in the world. Equally dramatic was the situation of communism in Latin America in the 1990s. From the 1960s communism in Cuba had succeeded thanks to Fidel Castro's charismatic leadership and Soviet aid. Once Soviet subsidies and economic aid ended, Cuba entered into a critical period, leading to a dramatic impoverishment from which it is still suffering. As these two cases showed, communism as a revolutionary ideology capable of exerting influence in the global sphere was dead.

The dismemberment of colonial empires was much faster than could have been expected in 1945. It was also, on the whole, remarkably peaceful from the perspective of the colonizing powers. There is no precedent in history of imperial governments voluntarily dissolving themselves as European powers did in the postwar period, although it is true that holding on to the possessions would have had catastrophic results in many cases.

After 1991 the geographic division of the planet into three worlds ceased to make sense. Russia, which represented the Second World, began to approach the First World by attempting to establish a democracy and a market economy. As a result the term "Third World," in reference to all those countries that were away from the first two Worlds was also obsolete, at least from the geostrategic point of view. The fall of Russia had a considerable impact on the Third World countries. All those countries that had sought inspiration from the Soviet model entered into a critical stage.

The disappearance of the last European colonial empires led to an extraordinary increase in the number of sovereign nations in the world. Africa evolved from just two independent nation states in 1920 to over fifty in the 1970s. The nation-state, that great European invention of the seventeenth century, was to be particularly useful for dismantling empires, although the process of forming nations and consolidating states in the postcolonial world was often going to be very complex and provoke plenty of turmoil. The postcolonial world caused more conflicts, and very often more deaths than the process of building empires. This was clearly the case in India, Indochina, and the Middle East.

With decolonization a third voice emerged in the global sphere, that of the Third World, predominantly characterized by a strong anti-European and anti-Western feeling. Despite its theoretic independence from the bipolar confrontation, several Third World countries became Cold War pawns as both the superpowers and Western Europe vied to maintain their influence in this part of the world.

The fall of the last great European empire, that of the Soviet Union, precipitated the end of the division of the world into three blocs. From that point, we could no longer talk of the Third World, but of a developed world, where the old European powers were, and another, the developing world, to which most former colonies belonged. To acquire the status of a developed nation it was necessary to follow the trends of economic progress and institutional and political stability that had been set by Europe and the rest of the Western world. This is how the majority of former Third World countries understood it, and many of them were going to follow these trends with such determination and efficiency that they managed to incorporate themselves into the world of global prosperity. The shadow of imperial Europe is very long.

Chapter 12

The European Dream

How Europe Transformed itself into a Union that Exerts Universal Attraction.

B etween 1914 and 1945 Europeans experienced the worst nightmares in their history, and they almost destroyed their civilization. But in the second half of the twentieth century they lived the most extraordinary dream that allowed the emergence of a unified Europe.

For those who were old enough in 1945 to have lived through the two world wars, the conclusion was obvious: Europe had been destroyed by war. War among European nations ought to be eradicated, and nationalism, the cause of all these wars, should be decisively overcome. The fact that Europe was divided into two blocs of alliances, dependent on the support of the two new superpowers, also led to the conclusion that Europe could not continue divided into nation-states, as it had traditionally been. The recovery of the

European economy and its position in world affairs could only be achieved as a result of a process of supranational unification. The national frame of mind ought to be substituted by a European one.

The idea of European unity is quite old in European history. From the eighteenth century several philosophers, men of letters, and even some statesmen had argued that the division of Europe into nation-states simply responded to economic and political interests, but that European culture and civilization were above national divisions. The philosopher Immanuel Kant in his essay *Perpetual Peace* advocated a Europe in which there would be a federation of states with no standing armies and nations would happily trade with each other rather than fight futile wars. After the First World War, the idea of European unification ceased to be utopian and won the support of influential figures. In 1923 Austrian philosopher and politician Richard von Coudenhove-Kalergi published *Pan-Europa*, in which he proposed a plan for European unification. The Pan-Europa movement held its first congress in Vienna in 1926, and it was attended by prominent figures like Aristide Briand, Albert Einstein, and Sigmund Freud.

From 1945 the political and economic unification of European nation-states was no longer a utopian idea, but a necessity. It began to be considered as the only way by which Western Europe could reemerge from its catastrophic state. "We must build the United States of Europe," stated Winston Churchill at a memorable Zurich speech in 1946. The fact that one of the most influential statesmen in the world pronounced himself in favor of European unity was a major boost for this cause. Two years later, Churchill was invited to act as chairman at the Congress of Europe, organized by the new European Movement with the aim of discussing how to launch the process of European integration.*

Churchill's involvement in this historic congress at The Hague in 1948 contributed to its success. From sixteen countries came 750 delegates, including statesmen like Konrad Adenauer and such future heads of government as Harold Macmillan and François Mitterrand. Also attending were those later to be known as the fathers of Europe, like Jean Monnet,

---

* Jenkins, *Churchill*.

Paul-Henri Spaak, and Salvador de Madariaga. Very general ideas about how to promote European unification were discussed at this congress, but above all it acted as a catalyst. From that point what could be described as the European political and diplomatic elite in the postwar era began to associate the future of their continent with its unification.*

Some of the resolutions adopted at the Hague Congress materialized shortly thereafter among the first institutions to promote a unified Europe. In 1949 the Assembly of the Council of Europe was created, the first Pan-European parliamentary assembly, although it still did not have real power. The College of Bruges, the first Pan-European postgraduate center, was founded shortly afterward with the purpose of preparing new generations of European college graduates to work in a unified Europe.

The United States also made an important contribution to European economic unification through the plan for European reconstruction known as the Marshall Plan. In 1948 the U.S. Congress approved a plan for economic aid to the countries affected by the war. One of the conditions was that the European states receiving this aid should advance toward closer economic cooperation. This gave birth to the Organization for European Economic Co-operation in 1948.

Shortly after came the founding stage of what was to be known as the process of European integration: Jean Monnet, a French businessman and civil servant who went down in history as the father of the European Union, proposed a revolutionary idea of merging French and German coal and steel industries under a supranational authority. As a result of this the two industries would not only multiply their productive capacity by benefitting from economies of scale but also definitively put an end to the risk of war between the two countries. Coal and steel were then the two essential products that were needed for waging war, and if they were put under the responsibility of a supranational authority, war became literally impossible.

It is remarkable that those who really set in motion the process of European integration were not world-famous, larger-than-life figures like the wartime leaders, but modest people who worked mainly behind the scenes.

---

* Judt, *Postwar.*

This was particularly the case of Monnet, an unprepossessing Frenchman who was originally a wine merchant and had never been elected to public office. Nevertheless, he had worked for the French government during the two world wars coordinating the allied war effort, and this allowed him to acquire a vision of intergovernmental cooperation that most of his contemporaries lacked.[*]

Monnet had to use all his persuasive capacity to convince the members of the French government of the advantages of such an unconventional alliance with a former foe. Foreign Minister Robert Schuman clearly understood the historic importance of such a treaty. On May 9, 1950, the famous Schuman Declaration was delivered, in which the French foreign minister declared:

"Europe will not be built at a stroke, nor constructed in accordance with some overall plan: it will be built upon concrete achievements which first create a de facto solidarity."

German Chancellor Konrad Adenauer was equally enthusiastic about the advantages of this Franco-German initiative, well aware that the only way of overcoming what was then known as the German problem was by the creation of a European Germany. For this reason, as he explained in his memoirs, he fully agreed with the plan as it was the beginning of a federal structure of Europe.[**]

Belgium, Holland, and Luxembourg, as well as Italy, were also attracted by the Schuman Declaration and decided to pool their coal and steel industries with France and Germany. In this way, in 1951 the European Coal and Steel Community was created by six European countries.

The next major step in the process of European integration was taken on March 25, 1957, when the Treaty of Rome was signed, by which the European Economic Community and the European Atomic Energy Community were created. As a result of this the Common Market emerged, with the six EEC member states agreed to trade among themselves without any

---

[*] François Duchêne, *Jean Monnet: The First Statesman of Interdependence* (New York: W.W. Norton, 1994).

[**] Charles Williams, *Adenauer, The Father of the New Germany* (Hoboken, N.J.: Wiley, 2000).

barriers, and applied a common external tariff to other countries trading with them.

These European Communities were not only pooling the main industries and their economies together but also embarking on a process of political unification. In order to supervise this process four supranational institutions were created: the European Commission, which was the executive body; the Council of Ministers, represented by national governments; a European Parliament; and a European Court of Justice. These four supranational institutions were responsible for implementing decisions about the European Community, exerting parliamentary control, and legislating in accordance with the European Community law that was to prevail over the law of the member states. In this way, a European supranational entity emerged that was above member states. This was totally unprecedented in European and world history.

One of the reasons why the initial stages of the European Economic Community were so successful was due to the fact that the economic circumstances were particularly favorable to promote free trade and create a tariff union. From 1950 the Western European economy emerged from the ashes, giving way to what was known as the affluent era: over two glorious decades of economic growth without precedent in modern history.[*] In 1957 at a Conservative Party rally, Prime Minister Harold Macmillan painted a rosy picture of the British economy and way of life, stating that: "Most of our people have never had it so good." Such optimistic comments were rife among political leaders in Western Europe, in view of the dramatic rise in living standards that was taking place in the postwar economic boom. How could this be possible in a continent that had been virtually destroyed by war a decade earlier?

The Marshall Plan laid the foundations of the economic recovery in Western Europe. The injection of capital from the United States to European countries after 1948 allowed them to recover rapidly from the ravages of war. As a result of the Marshall Plan, products and services in the 1950s

---

[*] John Kenneth Galbraith, *The World Economy Since the Wars: A Personal View* (London: Sinclair Stephenson, 1994).

experienced twenty-five percent growth.* Toward the mid-1950s industrial production already reached thirty percent above what it was when the Second World War broke out. These extraordinary figures not only had an impact on European affluence but on the United States and the Western world in general. The Marshall Plan had been launched with the double aim of preventing economic crises leading to communism among the recipient countries, and also to continue exporting US products to Western Europe where the most important trading partners were. For all these reasons economic prosperity in Western Europe was absolutely vital for US interests.

The postwar economic boom filled the coffers of nations in Western Europe, and in this way contributed to the birth and expansion of the welfare state, another of the great European contributions to the contemporary world, which played a crucial role in contemporary Europe.

The origins of the welfare state can be traced back to nineteenth century Germany. Chancellor Otto von Bismarck introduced the first old age social insurance system in the 1880s, mainly to stave off socialist unrest. Similar measures were taken by fascist regimes from the 1920s. But it is the Beveridge Report that lays the foundations of the welfare state in its present form in Europe. The British economist William Beveridge published a report in 1942 in which he identified five giant evils in society: squalor, ignorance, want, idleness, and disease. The state ought to use public money raised through taxation in order to tackle these five evils and guarantee a minimum living standard for all citizens. Equality of opportunities should be fostered regardless of wealth, social circumstances, or health.

The National Health Service, to be commonly known as the NHS, was launched in Britain in 1948, providing free universal health care to all citizens. By the same principle free education was offered to all citizens, unemployment benefits to all workers, and the right to receive a pension after the age of sixty-five or when a worker was no longer fit for work. The welfare states spread across Western Europe from the late '40s. Britain, Germany, France, and the rich industrial nations in the North provided much better conditions than Southern Europe, but all Western European governments

---

* Galbraith, *The World Economy Since the Wars*.

without exception accepted the principle that citizens ought to have the right to free health service, education, unemployment benefits, and old age pension, and that it was the duty of the state to ensure that enough public money was available to make this possible.

The welfare state was undoubtedly one of the great achievements of the postwar era in Western Europe. It proved that the state was finally responding to the principle that all citizens were equal. Above all it constituted an efficient remedy to the evils associated with poverty that were so widespread in Europe. From then on, images of grinding poverty in working class districts or rural areas became a thing of the past. Europe consolidated a new model of society that was more egalitarian, and in which no one was excluded due to lack of means. As a result of its success the welfare state emerged as the main alternative to communism in eradicating poverty and promoting equality in society. Soon the Western European model of society began to exert universal attraction. Initially very few countries could afford to replicate it, as it required a very prosperous economy and a strong and well-coordinated state. Nevertheless, from the 1950s governments throughout the world were drawing inspiration from Western European countries in their attempt to create fairer societies and eradicate poverty.

From the 1950s European citizens not only benefitted from the welfare state but also from technological advances that made life easier and more enjoyable. Inventions like the refrigerator and the washing machine transformed domestic life. Television started to reach European homes and became a great source of entertainment. The automobile, which from the 1950s could be afforded by those with more modest means, revolutionized transport and enabled the development of the urban periphery in major cities. All these benefits of the modern era were accessible to the masses thanks to consumer credit, another benefit of what became known as the consumer society, a new social model in which individual happiness was based on the capacity to satisfy a great amount of material needs.

The 1950s were the beginning of a new golden age for the bourgeoisie. This social class, characterized by high levels of education and success at the most important professions in urban centers, had emerged in Europe in the late eighteenth century. Its spread in numbers, wealth, and political power constituted an enduring social revolution, which was replicated with success in North America. The vitality and stability that it provided in societies, the values it represented, as well as the wealth it generated are some of the factors that explain its success. In the interwar years, the bourgeoisie was impoverished and discredited by trade union movements, believing the Marxist theory that the bourgeoisie, together with capitalism, were doomed to disappear, but in the 1950s it experienced a remarkable revitalization. This was not only due to the economic boom and the optimism it generated, but mainly because of its remarkable growth. Traditionally the bourgeoisie, as the middle stratum in society, had been very small. But in the 1950s as a result of free education, an increasing number of members of the working class gained access to the jobs and professions that had been reserved for the bourgeoisie. Egalitarianism and greater social mobility led to the creation of a broad middle class, more numerous and open than ever before. This became a factor of stability in Western Europe that was greatly admired by the external observer, which explains why so many governments throughout the world aimed at consolidating a solid middle class.

The world of arts and culture also experienced an extraordinary rebirth from the 1950s. This was largely thanks to a new principle that spread across Europe, that it was also the duty of the state to use public funds in order to promote culture among citizens. The most exclusive genres like opera, or those that attracted smaller audiences, like the theater, very much benefitted from it, whether they were Laurence Olivier's theatre in England or Samuel Beckett's modernist works. In 1960 French president de Gaulle appointed the novelist and intellectual André Malraux as minister of culture, a political post that was increasingly influential in Western politics, for culture was regarded as far too important to be simply regulated by market forces or popular tastes. Culture was a pillar of civilized society. Apart from enriching citizens intellectually it was also an industry that generated plenty of wealth. This is the message that Western Europe was transmitting the world since the 1950s, and from then it was to inspire many countries in their attempt to promote arts and enhance their cultural heritage.

It was in this period that Paris reemerged as the great capital of culture, when the influence of Jean-Paul Sartre, Simone de Beauvoir, and Albert

Camus reached its apogee. The new cultural trends were existentialism and structuralism. Communism continued to exert great attraction among many noted representatives from the world of culture, from Pablo Picasso to Sartre, who defined Marxism as the dominant idea of that era and its secular religion. Nevertheless, toward the end of the 1950s, in the post-Stalinist era, some of the most influential critics of communism emerged in Europe. Raymond Aron, Karl Popper, and Isaiah Berlin began to be increasingly influential. The fight against the proliferation of nuclear weapons attracted many prominent figures from the world of culture and academia, from Bertrand Russell to Salvador de Madariaga. Western European intellectuals led a new trend of pacifism, warning against the dangers of militarism in the nuclear age.

After the end of the Second World War, Marxist economists predicted the end of capitalism in Europe, arguing that the historic period of capitalism was over and that it was entering its terminal stage. However, from the 1950s the economy in Western Europe indicated quite the opposite. The market economy had managed to recover, giving evident signs of being in better shape than ever before. While Eastern Europe under a Marxist economy lived in austerity and scarcity, Western Europe flourished under the market economy.

In this very favorable context European integration continued making progress. In 1960 Britain and six other countries wishing to promote free trade in Europe created the European Free Trade Association. It was an alternative to the European Community, created by those countries that were not interested in any other form of unification along supranational lines, and for this reason refused to join the EC. The EFTA created great expectations among those joining it, nevertheless by the end of 1961 British prime minister Harold Macmillan reached the conclusion that Britain could no longer afford to stay out of the EEC, as it included its most important trading partners. In December 1961 Britain applied for membership of the European Community. This application was a major boost to the process of European integration. It left clear that unification along supranational lines, advocated by the European Community, was going to prevail. Nevertheless, British entrance into the EC had to wait. In January 1962 French president de Gaulle announced his government's intention to veto British application to the EC. He argued that Britain lacked a genuine interest in this organization and that it would act as "a Trojan horse of the United States.'"

De Gaulle not only blocked the first enlargement of the European Community, he also clashed with the president of the European Commission, Walter Hallstein, in relation to the model of European integration. Hallstein advocated reforms in order to strengthen the European Community executive and grant it budgetary independence. He proposed that the European parliament have more extensive budgetary powers, and was particularly in favor of introducing a system of majority voting in the Council of Ministers. All these aspirations particularly annoyed de Gaulle, who strongly believed that the only possible Europe was that of individual European nations; any attempt at establishing supranational institutions that should challenge in any way the independence and sovereignty of the nation-states ought to be stopped. At a press conference in 1962 de Gaulle launched a verbal attack on the Commission and ridiculed Walter Hallstein's plans. He mocked the Commission functionaries as stateless people and the technocratic jargon they used as *volapuk* (gibberish). "At present there is and can be no Europe other than a Europe of states, except of course a Europe of myths, fictions, and pageants," he stated.**

The clash between de Gaulle's concept of a Europe of nations and Hallstein's belief in a supranational Europe reached a critical point in 1965, when the president of the European Commission proposed the replacement of unanimity with a majority system in the Council of Ministers. This implied that the member states in the minority would have to tacitly accept what the majority decided. De Gaulle considered this an affront to French national interests and he announced that the French representative would not attend the next Council of Ministers meeting. This provoked the so-called "empty chair crisis." This first major crisis in the European Community was eventually solved a year later when the Luxembourg Compromise was reached. De facto veto power

---

★   William Hitchcock, *The Struggle for Europe: The Turbulent History of a Divided Continent 1945 to the Present* (London: Profile, 2004).

★★   Ibid.

was given to all members that could be used on topics that were deemed to be crucial to their national interests. It was basically an agreement to disagree.

As regards de Gaulle's veto on British entry, this was not solved until his resignation. Enlargement of the European Community finally took place in 1973, when Britain, as well as Ireland and Denmark, became members. This enlargement coincided with the oil crisis, which plunged Europe and the Western world into recession. As a result of this crisis, which put an end to over twenty years of steady economic growth, little progress was made in European integration during the 1970s, when governments were too busy dealing with the twin problems of inflation and unemployment.

On the other hand, a very important decision was taken in the 1970s to promote Europe's political unification. The European Parliament was one of the main dreams of the great Europeanists. It had been created in 1958, with members selected by EC member states. Initially it was simply a consultative assembly with virtually no legislative powers and its members were not elected by the citizens. In this way it very much justified the increasing criticism that European integration was an elitist conspiracy by which the European Community had been created without directly asking the citizens of its members states. One way of tackling this democratic deficit was by electing the European Parliament by universal suffrage. This decision was eventually implemented in 1979.

The first European elections took place in 1979, giving citizens of the nine EC member states the opportunity to elect their representatives in the same way that they did in national or regional elections. For the first time in history a supranational parliament had been elected. Europe had invented a system of universal attraction: democracy and the institution where it was mainly exerted—national parliaments. But now it was creating something new, the supranational parliament, showing that democracy would not only be exerted within the boundaries of the nation-state but it could go beyond them. Democracy could also be exerted in the supranational sphere within a group of nations as long as they shared an institutional and legal framework and the same democratic culture.

The same year in which the European Parliament was first elected by universal suffrage, Jean Monnet died. The father of Europe, as he had been known in European Community circles had published his memoirs a few years before, which are an invaluable source-book to understand the revolutionary idea of political and economic integration, and how the development of the European Community took place. Two principal ideas underpin his tireless campaigning on behalf of Europe: that Europe would be built not on the basis of visions and generalities but on practical achievements, and that common institutions not intergovernmental cooperation were the key to a durable European Community. He believed that it was only through institutions, as repositories of experience and shared values, that human beings accumulate wisdom and transmit it for future generations.[*]

He was well aware that some statesmen and nations would be reluctant to support his concept of European unification. As someone who had worked closely with the British government he was well aware of the reasons for its initial reluctance to join the European Community. But he also learned a lot from British pragmatism and he was confident that Britain would play a leading role in the European Community if they were capable of creating an organization that really worked. "We do not make coalitions among states, we unify people."[**] This statement is the one that best reveals the essence of Monnet's European dream.

The 1980s were a golden decade in the history of European integration. Several factors made this possible, first of all the recovery of the Western economies, which allowed governments to focus on the most ambitious ideas. The second factor was political leadership. French President Francois Mitterrand and German Chancellor Helmut Kohl were both convinced Europeanists, which allowed the Franco-German axis to lead the European Community more than ever. Jacques Delors, who presided over the European Commission throughout this decade, proved to be its most successful president, determined to transform the European Community into an organization that allowed Europe to exert global influence.

In 1980 Greece joined the European Community. Five years later Spain and Portugal were accepted as members. The Europe of the twelve then

---

[*] Jean Monnet, *Memoires* (New York: Knopf, 1978)
[**] Ibid.

implemented the next step in its economic unification: the single market that would go one step beyond the Common Market. The Single European Act, signed in 1986, officially launched this new single market with its four freedoms that EC citizens would enjoy: free movement of goods, free movement of persons, freedom to provide services, and finally freedom to move capital.

Few months after the Single European Act was signed, on May 29, 1987, the flag of the European Community was hoisted for the first time in Brussels to the sound of Beethoven's *Ode To Joy*. The European flag, a circle of twelve five-pointed stars on a dark blue background was then to proliferate in official institutions throughout the EC. This was one of the measures taken in order to create what became known as a people's Europe. The European Community had been excessively identified with political and economic decisions agreed upon by political leaders and implemented by civil servants. The average citizen felt no identification with it and felt suspicious of what was derisively described as "merchants' Europe." For this reason it was necessary to make it appeal to the populace. In this sphere symbols like the flag and the anthem were considered important. A new passport was issued to citizens of the European Community. All of these measures aimed at helping the citizens identify with this new supranational entity that represented them in a similar way to the state to which they belonged.

For this reason, parallel to the Single European Act, important initiatives were taken to promote social integration among citizens, along the lines of the welfare state, like the European Social Fund. The EC not only aimed to narrow the gap between the rich and poor but also between the richer and the poorer states in Europe. This is what motivated the creation of the so-called structural and cohesion funds, by which the less developed regions would be granted funds to improve their infrastructure and economy.

While the Western half of Europe enjoyed times of prosperity and took major steps in its process of unification, the Eastern half seemed to be disintegrating at an alarming speed. Under the leadership of Mikhail Gorbachev in the Soviet Union, major changes were to take place in the Soviet bloc, prompted by evident signs of crisis. In 1985 Gorbachev launched his policy of perestroika, and urged the countries of the Soviet bloc to implement similar reforms. In parallel, movements like Solidarity in Poland proliferated, all with the common aim of putting an end to communism in their countries.

On November 9, 1989, the fall of the Berlin Wall was broadcast to the world. The images of the main symbol of the division of Europe being pulled down by the citizens of Berlin took the world by surprise and gave way to even more extraordinary events. The collapse of the Berlin Wall had a domino effect which provoked the collapse of communism in Europe within two months. Poland, Hungary, Czechoslovakia, and Bulgaria experienced nonviolent revolutions by which communist regimes ended peacefully. In Romania and Yugoslavia the end of the communist regime took place by more traumatic means. Communism in the Soviet Union lingered on for one year. In 1991 communism was not only abolished but its disappearance also provoked the end of the Soviet Union. Russia recovered not only its name but also many symbols of its prerevolutionary identity including the city name of St. Petersburg and its Europhile sentiments. Throughout the last days of the Soviet Union Gorbachev had spoken about "our European common house, to which Russia and all European nations belonged."

Two models had cohabitated in Europe from 1945: liberal democracy and market economy in the West and socialism in the East. The disappearance of the Soviet bloc left it clear that the Western model of liberal democracy and market economy were going to prevail. The Western strategy of defiance toward the Soviet bloc, which President Ronald Reagan adopted wholeheartedly, helped speed the end of communism, as his most loyal ally Margaret Thatcher pointed out. But once the Soviet bloc disappeared the European powers and the EC had to act fast in order to fill the vacuum it left and respond to this great opportunity to expand their influence. For over four decades European citizens had felt like "the kidnapped West," as Czech novelist Milan Kundera described it. This is the reason why they treasured the European Community as a symbol of freedom and prosperity.

Once the great Western powers decided to support the reunification of Germany, on 1990 the European Council meeting in Dublin decided that the former GDR would be incorporated into the Community. A more challenging issue was how to help the former communist nations in Europe in their transition to democracy and how to respond to their wishes to join the European Community. All of these issues confirmed the need to speed up European integration in both the economic and political spheres, and ensure that the EC emerged as a global actor capable of responding to the challenges of the post–Soviet era.

The Maastricht Treaty was a turning point in European integration. It laid out the path to an economic and monetary union, and it also introduced all necessary institutional and political changes for the creation of a political union. The overall aim was to prepare Europe for the final stage of the process that had begun in 1957 with the Treaty of Rome and allow Europe to finally emerge as a key player in the global stage. From then the European Community was to be known as the European Union, more in accordance with the unified institutional structure that it was creating. The name also aimed at instilling a sense of unity among its citizens, similar to what they felt toward the states to which they belonged.

Maastricht opened the way to the monetary union and the appearance of a single currency, with which Europe's economic unification was to culminate. The advantages of a currency union were considered to be the following: elimination of exchange rate risks and costs for traders within the EU; greater convergence for travelers, a strengthening of collective discipline in the fight against inflation, and finally, affirmation of European identity in international relations. But to implement it there was a need to overcome the most difficult obstacles. Currencies are one of the most powerful symbols of national sovereignty and their replacement by a European currency seemed to skeptics more a political than an economic aim, prompted by utopian dreams of European unity. One of the most outspoken critics was Margaret Thatcher, who as a result of her opposition to the single currency became the most outstanding representative of the eurosceptics: all those who were opposed to supranational integration of Europe or were suspicious of the Brussels institutions.

The monetary and currency union implied that such economic powers as Germany, with strong currencies like the deutsche mark, would share a currency with the poorest economies, like that of Greece. The experiment could only succeed if the stronger economies would subsidize the weak ones and keep strict control of their monetary policies. For this reason the

European Council announced that only those countries fulfilling the convergence criteria of a specific, limited level of inflation, interest rates, and budget deficits would be allowed to join.

In 2002 the euro was officially born. Eleven countries out of a total of fifteen that fulfilled the convergence criteria were to share this new European currency. Britain, Denmark, and Sweden decided to stay out of this project, and Greece was allowed to join the eurozone in 2001. A central bank in Frankfurt had also been set up with the equivalent responsibilities of national central banks in relation to issuing currencies and monetary policy. Despite all doomsayers that had predicted administrative chaos and economic collapse once the euro was in circulation, quite the opposite was the case. For the first time in history some of the oldest nations in history were to share a currency.

The single currency was a giant step in the history of European integration. The euro was the culmination of the process of European economic integration. Just as it had happened with nation states in the process of national unification, the monetary union increased the sense of unity among EU citizens. Traveling around EU countries without the need to change currency and trading with other European nations in the single currency seemed a revolutionary step, which largely contributed to the exchange of peoples and capital in Europe.

Above all, the single currency marked the emergence of the European Union as an economic hegemon and one of the main players in the world economy. The euro emerged as one of the leading international currencies, rivaling not only the Japanese yen but also the US dollar. The dollar had dominated the international economy from 1945 until 2002, when this position began to be challenged by the new European currency.

Many factors explain why a new European single currency was capable of threatening the dollar's dominance from the outset. The euro was backed by the greatest commercial power, as the EU had become, with the largest market in the world—almost five hundred million consumers. France, Germany, Holland, Italy, and Spain, which were among the twelve largest economies in the world at that time, were all sharing this currency. Member states of the eurozone also enjoyed the benefits of a broad international network, created through centuries of expansion. Last but not least was the international admiration earned by the

European Union for having managed to merge the main European economies to make a single currency possible among former rival nations.

Soon the euro emerged as an alternative to the dollar as a currency reserve. From 2002, out of approximately 150 countries in the world that have their currency exchange rates fixed to a currency reference, fifty-one percent began to use the euro. In 2003 Russia increased its reserve of euros up to twenty-five percent, as did China. In 2005 Chinese president Jiang Zemin stated that they were planning to change their currency reserves to euros for two reasons: "First because we believe in multipolarity and second because it will be good business."* An even bigger threat to the dollar's sovereignty arrived with the rumor that OPEC countries were contemplating the possibility of switching the pricing of oil into euros.** The dollar's weakness in comparison to the euro was the main reason that led some OPEC countries to consider this move. There were also political reasons as most OPEC countries were more inclined to contribute to an international economy in which a European currency dominated, rather than the US dollar.

The single currency had a great impact from both the economic and the political point of view. The fact that the monetary policy of the majority of EU states was no longer implemented by national central banks but by the European Central Bank in Frankfurt played a very important role strengthening the cohesion of the European Union, and its global role.

While the single currency became a reality the EU had also been preparing for the greatest enlargement in its history. From the early stages of European integration the European Union had always had a good number of countries applying for membership. This is probably the best proof of its success. Like the most exclusive private clubs the EU kept a long waiting list of prospective members and it had the privilege of setting very high membership criteria to select its applicants. By the early 1990s what was then an EU of twelve members was preparing to double its size. In view of the applications for membership it could transform itself into an EU of over thirty members and a population of over five hundred million people.

---

* Mark Leonard. *Why Europe Will Run the 21st Century* (Madrid: Taurus, 2006).
** Ibid.

Expanding into countries that had been members of the Soviet bloc constituted a great challenge not only because they were poorer economies than the average EU member, but also due to their short experience with liberal democracy. In 1993 the so-called Copenhagen Criteria were laid out, which defined whether a country was eligible to join the European Union. These included institutions to preserve democratic governance, human rights, and a functioning market economy. A total of fifteen countries were to fulfill these criteria between 1995 and 2005, when the last enlargement took place. These included the Baltic states, former Soviet satellites like Bulgaria or the Czech Republic, and Mediterranean islands like Cyprus and Malta.

As the frontiers of the EU reached Russia and the Black Sea it became essential to answer the question that was not strictly clear from the geographic point of view: what is the eastern frontier of Europe? Should the EU encompass countries that are not fully European? The issue was raised for the first time in 1987 when Morocco applied for membership in the European Community. It was rejected on the grounds that it was not a European state, and for the first time the article of the Treaty of Rome was invoked that stated that only European states are eligible for membership. Shortly after this issue was debated in relation to the Turkish application, which was initially rejected but then accepted. Turkey's credentials as a European nation were dubious from both the geographic and the cultural point of view, and this is the reason why its application was so controversial. The democratic credentials of Turkish institutions were also to provoke much skepticism, particularly at a time when Turkey was moving away from Kemalism and experienced a worrying descent into authoritarianism.

Could Russia join the European Union? As a Eurasian power, proud of its former superpower status, it was obvious that this question did not require an answer as Russia had no intention of becoming an EU member. Nevertheless, it was clear that former Soviet republics like Ukraine, Georgia, or Moldavia, which were geographically European, were potential candidates that could join the EU at any time. In this way an EU that had reached twenty-eight members by 2013 could potentially increase its membership to well above thirty.

By the time the last enlargement took place, the frontiers of the EU covered a very substantial part of the European continent, a territory that was larger than the Roman Empire, Charlemagne's Empire, or Napoleon's Empire. From the times of ancient Rome to those of Nazi Germany several sovereigns and heads of state had dreamed of ruling over the whole of Europe. None of them achieved it, but EU policy-makers and representatives were getting very close to making this dream come true. What was most extraordinary was that unlike all other attempts to conquer the whole of Europe, the EU had done this peacefully and not by putting any pressure on Europeans—on the contrary, by exerting an irresistible attraction on the peoples of Europe.

Europe's influence in the world had not only grown as a result of its growth into a community of over five hundred million people, but also due to the growth of what became known as the eurosphere: a broad range of countries that were not only transformed by European investment, economic cooperation, or foreign aid, but also politically influenced by the EU and shaped by its values.

From the postwar period European leaders were worried that Europe was living uncomfortably between two superpowers, but as they were primarily concerned with regional interests, ceased to have a global policy. For a long time the European Community did not have the necessary consensus among its leaders to design a global policy, nor did it have the institutional mechanisms. From the 1970s the first measures were implemented within the European Community to allow its birth as a global actor. European Political Cooperation was initiated, by which European Community foreign ministers were to meet on a regular basis and reach common resolutions before key issues in international affairs. Such mechanisms allowed the European Community to apply sanctions against nondemocratic regimes like those in Spain, Portugal, and Greece. This became a very efficient way of promoting democratic transitions in these countries as the three of them wished to join the European Community. It also allowed the EC to condemn the actions of rogue states like Libya and contribute to its international isolation. Since the 1990s the European Union started to create what could be described as a proper foreign and security policy, with an institutional structure and representatives.*

Under the Treaty of Amsterdam the European Union post of high representative for foreign and security policy was created. The Spaniard Javier Solana became the first high representative. A decade later in 2009, the European External Action Service was launched, a new European diplomatic service. On one occasion, U.S. secretary of state Henry Kissinger is rumored to have asked, "Who do I call if I want to speak to Europe?"—highlighting the lack of leadership and institutional representation in the European Union. With this new post the EU international policy finally had a representative.

The Achilles' heel of the European foreign policy and security project was the lack of a proper European army. This became evident during the war in the former Yugoslavia. That war set Serbia against Bosnia and other nationalities that had lived together peacefully in Yugoslavia until 1991. It constituted one of the most shameful moments in the history of contemporary Europe, as the heart of the continent fell victim on one more occasion to the evils of ethnic cleansing and extreme nationalism. It was the United States and NATO (the North Atlantic Treaty Organization) that put an end to the war in Bosnia. NATO was also crucial to ending the war in Kosovo, which culminated with the NATO bombings in 1999 and the withdrawal of Yugoslavian and Serbian troops from this territory.

As a result of this adverse experience European leaders were determined to develop a military branch and rapid deployment force capable of intervening and preventing armed conflicts from getting out of control. The European Security Strategy was launched in 2003, under the slogan, "A secure Europe in a better world," defining the purposes of humanitarian intervention that would justify sending European troops abroad. In 2003 troops were sent to Macedonia to prevent the conflict escalating into another ethnic-nationalist war like those in the Balkan region the previous decade. After the success of the US and NATO intervention in Bosnia and Kosovo, control of Bosnia was handed over from NATO to the European Union in 2004. On that same year EU forces were to be sent to distant lands. In

---

* Hitchcock, *The Struggle for Europe.*

response to a petition from the UN secretary general, fourteen hundred troops were deployed in Democratic Republic of the Congo.* This was very much an example of the military running a humanitarian intervention to justify the deployment of EU troops. Rather than minding only its self-interest and sending troops to protect assets or key economic interests abroad, the EU was focusing on international pacification and the defense of human rights.

In spite of all the EU efforts to develop a proper European army, the EU did not have the capacity to send more than 85,000 troops abroad, which seemed an insignificant figure in comparison to the United States, which could easily send 400,000 wherever they were needed. Nevertheless this constituted no impediment for an efficient defense policy in accordance with European principles and interests. The aim of EU policy-makers was to prepare Europe for defense and security in the twenty-first century, in which conventional wars were no longer fought and traditional large armies had ceased to be necessary. In the new world order emerging after the 9/11 terrorist attacks, the major threats to world peace came from international terrorism and rogue states supporting them, or acquiring weapons of mass destruction for expansionist plans. Small but highly specialized army units supported by intelligence services—with the most sophisticated technology to tackle cyberterrorism and other threats of the new Internet era—were the keys to a successful defense policy.

The EU's defense policy in the twenty-first century seemed increasingly different from the American. The US decision to launch an invasion of Iraq in 2003 on the grounds that the dictator Saddam Hussein possessed weapons of mass destruction not only led to a confrontation between both sides of the Atlantic but also led to one of the most dramatic rifts among EU member states. The war in Iraq led to the division between what US defense secretary Donald Rumsfeld described as new Europe (those who supported the war) versus old Europe. In this instance the European Union abstained from intervention, and those member states that supported the United States, like Britain, Spain, Portugal, and Poland, intervened on an individual basis. Americans are from Mars, Europeans are from Venus was

---

* Leonard, *Why Europe Will Run the 21st Century.*

shorthand to explain what political scientist Robert Kagan believed about European reluctance to use force in contrast to the United States.* However much Americans insisted on the need for preventive attacks against rogue states, or as a self-defense strategy, Europeans insisted that military intervention could only be justified in order to defend EU resolutions and make international law prevail.

There was certainly plenty of war-weariness behind Europe's defense policy. For centuries Europeans had been masters in the art of war, if it could be called an art. But they had also suffered the consequences of war more than any other continent. Rather than following von Clausewitz's treatise on war they preferred Kant's perpetual peace. In this aspect Europe was clearly setting a trend in the twenty-first century, as the overwhelming majority of national governments in the world no longer believed in war as a legitimate way of solving conflicts.

Above all the EU in the early twenty-first century implemented innovative ways of exerting its influence in the world that went well beyond traditional tools of foreign and security policy. As the European Union consolidated itself as the premier commercial power its leaders also applied more sophisticated mechanisms to influence other countries. In 2004, after the last major increase in membership, the European Neighborhood Policy was launched with the aim of promoting cooperation and development among countries that could be considered the EU's neighbors, including all those in North Africa, the Middle East, Eastern Europe, and North Africa. The overall aim of this policy was to bridge the huge gap in development and prevent the emergence of a dividing line between a rich Europe and poor and unstable countries in neighboring regions. The EU aimed at contributing to their development by signing a wide range of agreements to foster economic, political, and cultural cooperation. Those countries developing the most solid links with the EU would be granted association status, which included tariff-free access to the single market. Others would simply receive some kind of financial assistance, but all agreements with neighboring countries would be conditional on their

---

* Robert Kagan, *Paradise and Power: America Versus Europe in the Twenty-first Century* (London: Atlantic Books, 2003).

commitments to economic and political reforms, improvements in the sphere of rule of law, and human rights.

In 2011 the European Commission announced what was described as a new and more ambitious European Neighborhood Policy. Despite the fact that this new program was launched in the middle of the global crisis it was backed by more than 1.2 billion euros in new funds, bringing the total to about 7 billion spent on this program. The new policy highlighted the strategy of giving more funds in exchange for more reform, in this way increasing the incentives of recipient countries to improve their democratic credentials.

The influence of the EU was reaching much further through its aid programs. Over the last decades of the twentieth century aid from Europe to the underdeveloped world, or peoples in distress, steadily increased. A feeling of responsibility toward former colonies or a bad conscience about the legacy of colonialism may explain this. It could also be considered as a mechanism of self-defense, for improving living conditions in underdeveloped countries and also prevent the problems associated with mass migration. Aid not only came through official channels as a result of government agreements but also through non-governmental organizations, or NGOs. The EU, greatly influenced by the moral conscience of its member states took responsibility for providing aid so eagerly that it became the planet's biggest aid donor. In the year 2000 the EU signed the most ambitious aid program at the city of Cotonou in Benin. A total of seventy-nine countries from Africa, the Caribbean, and the Pacific were to benefit from it. Well aware that money from aid programs had often ended in the wrong hands and failed to have the expected impact on beneficiaries, the EU signed comprehensive partnership agreements to guarantee their effectiveness and ensure that they complied with its development plans. It also moved beyond focusing on the main aim of eradicating poverty and linked it to broader aims like the promotion of sustainable development, democracy, and regional integration.

In 2013 a new aid program was launched, Agenda for Change. On this occasion it focused on the poorest and most vulnerable nations in the world, and it aimed at focusing on very specific assistance but at the same time it was associated with the millennium goals discussed at the UN and released in a report two years later. The EU helped forty-nine countries through this program, most of them in sub-Saharan Africa. As a result of all these aid programs the EU has been able to help alleviate some of the most dramatic humanitarian crises, from victims of droughts in Ethiopia and the Sahel to those of the armed conflict in Syria and Mali.

Both the European Neighborhood Policy as well as the mentioned aid programs have allowed the influence of the European Union to expand in a very significant way in the Eurosphere, the area of the world that is clearly under Europe's influence and where the EU is the main external factor of change. Over one hundred countries form this Eurosphere, it includes all those that have the EU as their most important trading partner, as well as those that depend on EU credit or foreign aid.*

Another reason for the increasing influence of the EU in the world was the fact that its model of regional integration was expanding. Since the 1990s economic cooperation agreements proliferated throughout the world, which were clearly inspired by the European Union. In 1991, Argentina, Brazil, Paraguay, and Uruguay signed the Treaty of Asunción, by which the Southern Common Market was created, most popularly known as Mercosur. The aim of Mercosur was to create a free-trade area and a common external tariff among its member states, just as Europe had originally done in the fifties. It soon started to enlarge in South America, as Bolivia, Chile, Peru, Ecuador, and Suriname became associate states.

In 1994 the United States, Canada, and Mexico signed the North American Free Trade Agreement (NAFTA), with the aim of creating a trilateral trade bloc. It was an initiative to respond to the challenge of the European single market. Long before North America, CARICOM had been established in 1973 in the Caribbean, with the aim of promoting economic integration among its states.

Unlike NAFTA or CARICOM, which were purely economic agreements, Mercosur aimed at fostering political integration. It included a democratic clause, which played a very important role fighting against dictatorial tendencies in Latin America. In 2017 Venezuela's membership was revoked due to the establishment of a dictatorial regime there.

---

* Leonard, *Why Europe Will Run the 21st Century*.

Asia was also evolving along these lines. The Association of Southeast Asian Nations (ASEAN) had been formed in 1967 by five southern Asian nations as a regional intergovernmental organization, but by 2007 its members agreed to move closer to a political union similar to that of the EU. At the opposite end, India, Pakistan, and five other nations founded the South Asian Association for Regional Cooperation (SAARC).

Regional integration has even made progress in the twenty-first century in the world's most backward continent. In 2001 the African Union was created in Addis Ababa, by fifty-five countries with the principal aim of accelerating the economic and political integration of the continent. At a summit in Cairo in 2004, members of the Arab League discussed the plan of creating an Arab Union, by which all Arab countries would merge into a political union, and they also discussed the project of a Pan-Arab parliament and a single currency.

As we have seen, the aims of regional organizations vary from those that merely aimed at establishing a free-trade area to those contemplating political unification along supranational lines. But all of them have been inspired by the European model, and it is the success of the European Union that has led them to move in this direction.

Just as it happened in Europe, once regional integration begins it is difficult to stop, as it becomes increasingly indispensible for the needs of every nation. Of course many of these regional organizations can collapse or be dismembered in the same way that kingdoms and empires have disappeared in the past. But even so, regional organizations are here to stay, as for most of them this is the only formula by which they can play a relevant role in the twenty-first century.

About five centuries ago, Europe invented the nation-state. It gradually expanded first in Europe, then in America, until in the twentieth century it became an indispensible element in international relations. For any people in the world the only way of being visible and earning international respectability was to form a nation-state. In the twentieth century, Europe invented a new political organization above the nation-state. The EU could be defined as a supranational state or simply as a network of nations ruled by common institutions.

Of course a world of regional organizations should not necessarily be better than one formed by nations. Inward-looking regional blocs waging commercial war against each other could lead to conflicts that are as serious as those caused by nations. But this is not the type of regional integration that the EU represented. On the contrary it has provided a model for promoting cooperation and creating wealth in a region, and at the same time contributing to global development and prosperity. It has also set an example of how to tackle the great challenges of the new millennium, like environmental sustainability and global warming, against which individual nation-states are virtually powerless.

One of the reasons why the EU emerged as a model that inspired and shaped so many nations is due to its internal social development. Since the fifties Western Europe had promoted a model of society that combined individualism and personal freedom, two pillars of the Western way of life, with the eradication of poverty and promotion of equal opportunity. This was possible thanks to the development of the welfare state, which as we have previously seen, after its initial success in the fifties continued steadily expanding through Europe. This played an important role in the emergence of what political scientist Jeremy Rifkin defined as the European dream.[*]

Until the mid–twentieth century the only social model that was attractive enough to be described as a dream was the American dream in the United States. This dream was based on the belief that any citizen living in the United States could realize any personal ambition, usually the acquisition of wealth or material possessions. Regardless of social background or ethnicity, a citizen could live the American dream as long as he worked hard enough and showed determination to succeed. The American dream attracted millions of immigrants to the United States. It became a pillar of the American way of life that was admired throughout the world, and it played a very important role in the transformation of the United States into the largest economy in the world, and allowed the country to live up to the Jeffersonian idea of being an empire of liberty.

---

[*] Jeremy Rifkin, *The European Dream: How Europe's Vision of the Future Is Quietly Eclipsing the American Dream* (Cambridge, England: Polity, 2005).

By the late twentieth century a new dream emerged in the Western world, this time it was the European dream. It was based on the idea that all citizens, regardless of social background or ethnicity, could make their dreams come true in European society, but furthermore they would also enjoy the benefits of living in a society that provided both quality of life and security. While the American dream is associated with wealth, the European dream has more to do with the quality of life. It refers to all that there is in life that is not measured in material possessions, like the enjoyment of leisure, availability of a rich cultural life, and above all personal transformation. Also the enjoyment of a healthy life, in harmony with nature, and feeling secure as a result of the absence of crime and social tensions that could prevent citizens from walking freely on the streets of any city. The European dream was also based on the idea that every citizen had a place in society and would therefore be looked after regardless of personal success of failure. The European social model provided a safety net that would allow citizens enjoy a minimum living standard. The European dream enabled citizens to liberate themselves from nightmares associated with falling on hard times, as all working citizens enjoyed the benefits of the welfare state.

Whereas the American dream was better at promoting economic growth in society, the European dream created a more harmonious one. It avoided the problems of a society divided between extremely rich and poor, a lifestyle based on what was derisively called the rat race, where people worked from dawn to dusk in stressful, meaningless jobs. Well aware that the economy could no longer afford to be based on unlimited material growth and extraction of limited natural resources, the European dream also promoted sustainable development.

The European dream contributed to enhance the EU's global presence because it had a universal appeal. Governments throughout the world were studying the European social model and the values underpinning it, hoping to reproduce it in their countries. Of course, just as it happened with the welfare state many countries could not afford it, but nevertheless it was still set as a long-term aspiration.

The other evidence for the European dream's universal appeal was emigration. Europe had been a continent of emigrants until the twentieth century. But since the fifties the trend was reversed, Europeans not only ceased to emigrate to other continents but the continent began to attract migrants from all over the world. Initially only the great industrial powers and the richest countries in Western Europe appealed to emigrants, but as wealth spread around Europe, as well as the benefits of EU citizenship, migrants proliferated through the continent. By the nineties practically every member state of the European Union was attracting immigration. By the early twenty-first century fifteen out of twenty-eight member states had an immigrant population of over ten percent. Between 2010 and 2013, 1.4 million migrants arrived in the European Union every year. In 2016 the number of people living in the EU who were citizens of non-member states was 20.7 million.*

On the other hand, the European Union in the early twenty-first century was facing the most serious challenges of its history. The global financial crisis that broke out in 2008 seriously affected the whole of Europe to the extent that it made the pillars of its financial and political institutions tremble. The greatest economic crisis since 1929 began with a mortgage market crisis in the United States and it escalated into a major international banking crisis. Corporate greed in an increasingly deregulated financial world, and proliferation of easy credit were the two major causes. Europeans were particularly vulnerable to it, as they had been living for decades in the culture that made it possible. Since the fifties Europeans had grown used to living on credit. Governments also promoted this culture of indebtedness in order to deliver all that the welfare state promised. Political parties in all of Europe competed against each other offering government programs that could provide better public services, better pensions, schools, and health systems, without increasing taxation. All of this was made at the cost of increasing government deficits, until the national debt became unsustainable. This was particularly the case with Greece, which provoked such a crisis in the eurozone that it seriously threatened the survival of the European monetary union. Not only euro members and the whole of the European Union were concerned with this, but all other great economic powers.

---

*   eu. europa.eu/eurostat/statistics

Their economies had become so interdependent that the disappearance of the euro could lead to a new global crisis. The European Union was not only an essential trading partner for the United States and Japan, but also for the BRIC countries (Brazil, Russia, India, and China), four emerging, newly industrialized countries that were to play a leading role in the world economy. All of them had benefitted from commercial exchange with Europe. They all kept currency reserves in euros, China in particular. Losing a currency and a market of over five hundred million consumers with some of the best purchasing power in the world was certainly a dire prospect. As the eurozone weathered the financial storm not only were European citizens relieved, but also the members of the leading economic powers.

The global financial crisis showed the dark side of the European dream. The latter was heavily dependent on high levels of government spending that were no longer sustainable. Nor was the welfare state affordable any longer. Indebtedness was nothing new in European history. A quick look at Europe's financial history shows that for any power there is a clear correlation between indebtedness and decline.

Spain under the Habsburgs had fourteen bankruptcies between 1557 and 1697. Prerevolutionary France spent sixty-two percent of its budget to pay debts shortly before the French Revolution. Britain entered a critical stage as an imperial power in the 1930s, when it was spending about forty-four percent of its budget for interest on its debt. Public and private indebtedness increased in Europe while its growth rate decreased. Eurozone countries grew 3.4 percent in the 1970s, 2.4 in the 1980s, 2.2 in the 1990s, and only 1.1 percent from 2001 to 2009.[*] To survive, it would have to undergo serious reforms.

Before the crisis, the long-term sustainability of the welfare state had become a subject of intense debate among policy-makers. The EU represented 25.8 percent of the world's GDP and fifty percent of global social welfare spending, with only seven percent of the world's population.[**] Europe on the

---

[*]   Niall Ferguson, *The Ascent of Money: A Financial History of the World* (New York: Penguin, 2008).

[**]   eu. europa.eu/eurostat/statistics

whole seemed to be drowning under the cost of its welfare bills. In spite of this the peoples of Europe on the whole did not demand a drastic change of direction.

The culture of indebtedness and reliance on the state for all basic needs of human existence had contributed to this situation. European people in the early twenty-first century had very little in common with their ancestors. Rather than cultivating thrift and hard work, and making sacrifices for a better life, they insisted on clinging to privileges that could no longer be afforded. Citizens' rights were constantly discussed in the public sphere, but not their duties. Any civilization in which citizens showed more concern with extracting its benefits than contributing to it was doomed to collapse.

The European dream was also threatened by those who did not share the culture and values that made it possible. Most European countries had taken pride in the development of multiculturalism and the fact that as a result of mass immigration people from different races and cultures were happily cohabitating with native Europeans. But the myth of multiculturalism collapsed under Islamic terror.

After the 9/11 terrorist acts in the United States, Al Qaeda, with its intention to bring the Western world to its knees, spread terror around Europe. Madrid suffered a devastating terrorist attack in 2004, in which 192 people died, followed by an attack on London a year later. Then came the Jihadist group Daesh, a self-styled Islamic state that managed to control large swathes of territory in Syria and Iraq, killing numerous innocents in major European cities, particularly in Paris.

What seemed especially surprising was that the majority of those arrested in relation with Islamic terrorism in Europe were not people who had recently arrived on the continent, but sons of emigrants from Muslim countries who were born in Europe and grew up there. Unlike first generation of immigrants who felt gratitude toward European countries welcoming them, the second and third generation rejected European culture. It was from among them that terrorists were recruited. In its rise to world hegemony, Europeans had fought a great number of enemies, but now the enemy was within its borders.

Against this background of a eurozone economic crisis, refugees fleeing into Europe and away from Islamic terrorism, the prestige of the European

Union was seriously undermined to the extent that its very survival was at stake. The European Union became the scapegoat for all problems faced by the peoples of Europe; referenda emerged as the way to hasten its end. In 2005 France and Holland voted against the treaty establishing an EU constitution. As a result, the first attempt in history for several nation-states to be governed by one constitution had failed.

But undoubtedly the biggest threat to the survival of the European Union came in 2016, with the Brexit referendum. The news that the majority of British citizens voted against remaining in the European Union was the biggest shock in the history of European integration. The fact that Britain, one of the three major economies of the EU and a country that had played the most important role shaping modern Europe, decided to abandon the EU contradicted the essence of European unity and jeopardized many of its achievements.

"Eppur si mouve." ("Yet it moves.") This is the phrase attributed to the Italian physicist Galileo Galilei after he was forced by the Pope in the seventeenth century to recant his claims that the Earth moves around an immovable sun. In a similar way, after all the adversity faced by the European Union in what can be described as a lost decade, and in spite of all doomsayers eager to announce its death, the European Union was still moving forward.

In the midst of the global economic crisis and at a time when the United States had become increasingly isolationist, the European Union continued to show a determination to shape the world as a major global player, especially when the values in which it believed were challenged beyond its frontiers. This was the case as a result of the Arab Spring and particularly during the Libyan Civil War, which broke out in 2011. European peoples had supported the revolutionary wave that spread across the Arab world in 2011. It was described as the Arab Spring in allusion to several revolutionary experiences in Europe, like the 1848 revolutions, described as the springtime of nations, the Prague Spring of 1968, or the 1989 revolutions in Eastern Europe. On this most recent occasion social media contributed to the swift propagation of popular revolt from Tunisia to Syria, and in Egypt and several other Arab countries, in some cases toppling dictatorial regimes. In the case of Libya, Colonel Muammar Gadaffi decided to use his power to crush dissent at all cost, leading to the outbreak of a civil war.

The EU had the option of remaining indifferent toward the Libyan Civil War, as the rest of the great powers did, including the United States, or intervening in favor of the rebel forces. French president Nicolas Sarkozy took the initiative to ensure a UN mandate to intervene in Libya. Finally a coalition of EU forces led a military operation against Gaddafi. A few months later, Gaddafi's dictatorship succumbed. This was an example of a rightful and efficient European intervention, backed by the United Nations. The fall of this brutal dictatorship, which had been one of the most dangerous enemies of the West, gave the Libyans the opportunity to march toward a system in which the values of democracy and the rule of law espoused by Europe would prevail.

In 2012, in the middle of the financial storm in the eurozone, the European Union was awarded the Nobel Prize for Peace for "having contributed for over six decades to the advancement of peace and reconciliation, democracy and human rights in Europe." Peace, which so many people in Europe and the world took for granted in the twenty-first century, was no minor achievement, and it had been the cornerstone of the EU's policy both within its frontiers and beyond them.

In one of his famous postwar speeches Winston Churchill had stated that Europe should be "as free and happy as Switzerland is today." Europeans seemed to have followed Churchill's recommendations over the following decades. Throughout history Switzerland had skillfully managed to isolate itself from all European wars and focus on creating a prosperous society in which citizens could feel free and happy. Since the fifties both large and small nations in Europe seemed to be inspired by the Swiss example, making peace and internal development the cornerstone of their happiness.

More than five centuries after Europeans began their expansion through the world, the spirit of Columbus, Vasco da Gama, and Cook, and their desire to open new horizons beyond their frontiers, seemed to have vanished. The ideas that had guided the foreign policy of the great powers from Philippe II to Wilhelm II did not appeal to policy-makers. Europeans had forgotten about their aspirations of building world empires and defending interests wherever they were challenged abroad. Instead they focused on building urban centers and great shopping malls, and defended themselves from any internal challenge that affected their daily lives.

More than navigators, missionaries, imperialist statesmen, or migrant self-made men who had inspired past generations, Europeans at present seem to follow Voltaire's famous maxim of cultivating one's own garden. Europeans felt that in a modern world that was largely made by them, their role was more in their internal development and setting an example by developing an ideal model of society.

In a globalized world in which emerging powers enjoyed increasing influence, Europe continued exerting universal attraction. While the entire planet had been opened to tourism, Europe was still the favorite tourist destination for a very high percentage of travelers. Out of the ten most visited countries, five were European: France, Spain, Italy, the UK, and Germany. Out of the twenty most visited art museums in the world, fourteen were European. Out of the top 980 universities in the world 400 were European. Europe and the UK in particular shared the leadership in university ranking with the United States.

This evidence also explains why the European Union had become a leader in a new type of power that was crucial for exerting influence in the contemporary world: soft power. Political scientist Joseph Nye, who first defined this term, described soft power as the ability to shape the behavior of others through appeal and attraction. It was a more subtle and ultimately effective way of exerting influence than through the traditional spheres of military or economic power. According to several think-tanks analyzing influence and global presence in terms of soft power, the European Union ranked the highest; six out the ten countries with the most soft power were European.

In this way the EU was in a very strong position to continue shaping the world in the early twenty-first century. As an organization formed by several former great powers it was very much a satiated power, no longer interested in the struggle for supremacy, as the emerging powers were, but simply contributing to a world order in which peace and stability would prevail. More than any other power the EU had proved to have a global conscience, tackling international terrorism or the actions of rogue states, and above all responding to the greatest challenges, like sustainable development and global warming. It had also developed a transformative power that can be defined as the capacity to bring about change in an efficient way. For all these reasons the EU had become the tool with which Europeans could continue influencing the world in a positive way and even be considered as humanity's last best hope.

Conclusion

The Pillars of a Global Civilization

The relationship between civilizations has changed a lot from the days of the first encounter between Hernán Cortés and the Aztec ruler Moctezuma or that between Lord Macartney and Chinese Emperor Qianlong. Even when Korean dictator Kim Jong-un defies President Donald Trump, or Syrian dictator Bashar Hafez al Assad or Iranian president Hassan Rouhani pose major challenges to the Western world, potential clashes between civilizations are mitigated by the interests of a global civilization that is quietly rising above all others.

A global civilization has emerged in the twenty-first century. Many of its members from different parts of the world will not acknowledge that they belong to it. Just as their ancestors did, they continue feeling that they are different from other peoples because of their race, culture, religion, language, and many other factors, but even so, they have a closer relationship with each other than ever and as a result of it they have a lot in common. They all live under an international market that provides many of the essential products that they consume in their daily lives. The house where they live and the urban landscape surrounding them are the products of technologies and design techniques that have become available across the world. They also share very similar daily experiences. Global brands not only solve their daily needs and consuming habits, but they even provide their leisure activities. An extraordinary sign of convergence is to find members of different civilizations who have read the same books, watched the same films, and even support the same football team.

One of the great achievements of our era is that there is a peaceful interchange among peoples from different cultures, learning from each other, studying their history and ideas and thus enriching each others' lives. Traveling facilities, progressively available to most citizens, allow them to visit other countries and interact with members of this global civilization. Knowledge of English and other European languages that have become global also contributes to this interaction.

Above all, what makes us become aware of our membership in a global civilization is that we share the same access to information through the Internet and apply very similar methods for acquiring knowledge, which is unprecedented in history. This is mainly thanks to the United States. Major commercial brands with which we identify, the emergence of computer technology, and the Internet are all North American: Microsoft, Dell, Apple, Google, Facebook, Twitter. But it was Europe that opened the path that led to the Internet era. Europe inaugurated this era of modernity and introduced the method of thinking that makes this extraordinary convergence possible.

The members of this global civilization live in an international society in which their countries are represented in the United Nations. Rules are based on regulations made by institutions deriving from this organization, in which European ideas have considerable weight. Liberal democracy has become not only the most widespread political system but also the one that enjoys more international respect, despite the fact that several powerful countries reject it. Concepts that were born in Europe, like the rule of law, press freedom, and human rights have also earned broad global support.

The map that is used to teach geography all over the world, and which also has guided travelers, was mainly created by Europeans. In its most common version, the European continent appears in the center, surrounded by the rest of the Earth. The reason for what other continents may consider a Eurocentric vision of the planet is simply because Europeans made the first geographic discoveries and they also made the most important contributions to cartography.

The curiosity to discover other worlds has been one of the most common characteristics of the peoples of Europe, not only from the fifteenth century, but even from antiquity. Already in the fourth century BCE, Greek historian Herodotus attributes the expansion of the Greek people across the Mediterranean to an adventurous spirit and an eagerness for discovery—something other people lacked. "Every year we send our ships with great danger for our lives and at great expense to Africa, in order to ask: Who are you? What are your laws? What is your language? But they never send a ship to ask us."

Every European power left important marks of their culture, values, and political system on the empires created by them. There are on the other hand notable differences between colonial empires that were to mark the nations emerging from them.

In British America, the individualism of the first settlers, their sense of community and their determination to participate in government affairs contributed to the emergence of a solid democracy when the United States was founded. Similar characteristics of the populations that settled in Canada, Australia, and New Zealand allowed British democratic traditions and institutions to be reflected in these countries. On the other hand the Iberian empires were characterized by the hierarchical and bureaucratic structures of its administration, leaving very little scope for the citizens' participation. This among other factors explains why countries in Latin America have struggled so much to consolidate democracy. Countries emerging from the French Empire have had similar problems in general, despite the fact that a concept of citizenship was promoted in which all were theoretically equal, regardless of race or background. Russia proved a very different case, where the autocratic system and quasi-feudalism by which the country was ruled pervaded all its territories.

In the case of the Spanish and Portuguese empires in America, intermarriage allowed to a certain extent the cohabitation of the Indian peoples with Western culture. This was not the case with the British Empire in America, where the families of the first settlers pushed the Indian peoples toward the West until they were practically exterminated.

We can therefore see the great differences between imperial legacies that mark nations until the present.

In spite of all differences among the empires that we have examined in these pages, all gave evident signs of sharing a common history and a cultural heritage. All great powers were aware of representing European civilization in its expansion. They were also convinced of being this civilization's best representatives, and they believed that the more territories they occupied the bigger the benefit would be for the whole of humanity.

The main incentive for building colonial empires was economic. This led to the creation of commercial routes that linked the main cities of Europe with the rest of the world, and the expansion of the market economy through all continents. In order to govern and regulate the economy of these empires it was also necessary to create a legal system, which led to the spread of the European judicial system, based either on Roman law or British common law. The rule of law is one of the most important of European exports. Another characteristic that empires shared was superior science and technology. Markets and networks created by Europeans allowed scientific and technological advances to open their way throughout the world, from the compass and the printing press to railways and the telegraph.

The culture of the European world, its ideas and beliefs, were also going to be reflected in the empires, starting with Christianity. The cross was a very important symbol in the Iberian empires as well as in the French Empire. In the Russian Empire, each settlement was accompanied by the construction of a church. In the British Empire, Christianity was more a personal issue for the settlers than for the colonial government, but even so it made Christianity equally relevant. In all empires, the church—Catholic, Protestant, or Orthodox—took advantage of Europe's imperial expansion to evangelize. Christian missions converted Christianity into one of the great religions of the world. Their educational work with indigenous people played an essential role transmitting European culture.

The idea that the white race was superior was present in all empires, even in those promoting intermarriage. This belief explains many of the atrocities that were allowed to take place in the colonial world. It served as an excuse to justify abuses, killings, and genocides, and also to propagate slavery and transform this scourge into a lucrative international business.

On the other hand, it was through the empires and networks established by great European powers that the most important ideas determining progress in the modern world have been spread. One of the basic ones was the idea that all men are equal regardless of race, politics, or religion. The ideas about equality, liberty, and the rights of men—born in the eighteenth century—revolutionized both the European and the colonial world. These ideas led to the abolition of slavery. The Europe that globalized the slave trade eventually forbade it and imposed its prohibition on other civilizations.

The concepts of liberty and equality among citizens were the ideological pillars that led to the dismantling of empires and founding of new nations, from the United States in 1776 to those emerging from the decolonization process. The idea that colonization was unfair and immoral was present among those who suffered it but also among some people belonging to the colonizing nations, from Bartolomé de las Casas to Robespierre. From the eighteenth century, Europe was an ideological school for independence leaders. From Benjamin Franklin to Jawaharlal Nehru, many leaders of modern nations obtained from the Europeans ideas about the type of nation and society that they wished to build. In the drafting of constitutions, the creation of political systems, and models of society, Europe was the main ideological source. From liberalism to nationalism, from socialism to communism, all these ideas that were born in Europe were spread throughout the planet via the empires and through channels that were opened during colonization. Europe also inaugurated a process of industrialization and subsequent modernization that has gradually become worldwide.

Europeans have been the most committed emigrants in history. Imperial expansion and its legacy made this possible. Europeans migrated in great numbers to both territories of their empires, as well as nations emerging from them, those in the Americas in particular. The largest American nations were populated by Europeans. Their trajectory as nations and their economic development would not have been so outstanding without them, nor would the link had been so strong with the other side of the Atlantic. This is particularly the case of the United States.

The end of the European era was atypical in the history of empires. European hegemony did not end as a result of an enemy invasion, nor because of a culture from a new power that replaced its own, but rather by conflicts caused by its own nations. They were primarily responsible for bringing the era of European hegemony to an end. The struggle for supremacy in Europe that takes place from 1870 to 1914 can be interpreted as a final attempt by the great powers to decide which one of them should exert undisputed world hegemony once they had managed to control a substantial part of the world among them. They were exclusively concerned with rivalry from other European powers, as it seemed that they were the only ones with sufficient military and economic might to defy them. On the other hand they failed to understand that their hegemony could also be threatened by emerging powers beyond the European continent that had followed the same trends of development. In fact the only nations beyond the European continent that managed to defeat a European power and expand at its expense was a Western power, the United States, against Spain in 1898; and also a Westernized power, Japan against Russia in 1904. Had it not been for the confrontation between its own countries the European era could have continued for much longer, just like their empires.

In the early twentieth century independence movements were not sufficiently strong to destabilize their empires, with the exception of India and Ireland. In the same way that nothing seemed to herald Europe's meteoric rise in the fifteenth century, it seemed inconceivable in the early twentieth century that Europe's fall would be so dramatic.

But on the other hand, the relationship between European powers and their empires did not finish with independence, as we have seen. The links with postimperial nations continued to be very strong, first due to the legacy of European culture, secondly because of economic and trade links, and finally as a result of emigration from former colonies. Postimperial Europe was an example of the cohabitation between different cultures that must be present in every open society.

The history of the last five hundred years could have been much more peaceful if all Europeans had stayed in their homelands. Many conflicts and a lot of human suffering could have been avoided. But there is also the possibility that history would have been even more convulsive without the spread of European civilization. Taking into account the expansive instinct that has characterized civilizations in general, many regions of the world would have been occupied by other peoples if Europeans had not arrived first.

How would the American continent have evolved if it had been colonized by the Chinese, the Japanese, or the Arabs instead of the Europeans? What would Africa's modern history have been if instead of being split between European powers it would have been taken over by the Arabs from the north? How would Eurasia have evolved if the Mongols had managed to hold onto their power into modern history? Let us imagine that India would have been colonized by another Asian power instead of the British, or that one of its peoples would have managed to dominate the rest of the Indian subcontinent. Obviously the history of civilizations, including Europe's, would have taken very different paths of progress, and at present the values that prevail in the majority of nations would be very different.

The almost five centuries of European hegemony have left an indelible mark. The decline of old European powers gave way to the rise of the United States as a superpower, a country built and populated mainly by Europeans and under the inspiration of ideas that were born in Europe. Americans have always refused to be identified as an empire or to have imperial aspirations. They prefer to see themselves simply as a great nation that is richly endowed in all aspects and has managed to acquire superpower status. Nevertheless, just like the European powers in their prime, the United States has been guided by the principle that the expansion of its power and influence was good for the peoples of the earth and that it was their duty to propagate the "empire of liberty" that Thomas Jefferson yearned to create. Both the government and the U.S. army have had to comply with the obligations of being a hegemonic power in a similar way to how the great European imperial nations are paying for their hegemony in the past.

The United States has made an essential contribution to the continuity of the Western hegemony. But once the signs of decline as a superpower have become visible, the term "post-Western era" has started to be used as the center of the world trade is shifting from the Atlantic to the Pacific Ocean. Nevertheless, this post-Western world that is looming in the horizon will not be under the control of a new non-Western superpower, as there is no specific civilization capable of dominating the rest. Cooperation and interaction rather than competition and rivalry will become a necessity in the post-Western world, as all countries in the world face similar problems of sustainability and also share the same knowledge and almost the same technology to face them.

In today's international society the central elements that define it and by which it is structured have been provided by Europe. The most predominant are first of all the market economy and free trade. Second, democracy. Third, complementary elements that make it work: the rule of law, press freedom, and human rights. Finally, scientific and technical progress. These have also become Asian, African, or Middle Eastern ideas, but only by adoption. The more they have adopted Western techniques, principles, and ideas in the rest of the world the stronger the legacy of Europe becomes. Of course there are nations and peoples that reject the market economy, refuse to govern themselves by democracy, and cling to superstitions and traditions rather than science and empiricism, but so far these are usually in a minority and are incapable of making their alternatives prevail in the international sphere.

European culture more than any other gained ascendancy in this global civilization. Humanism, which places the human being at the heart of everything, is present in every society making progress. Empiricism guides scientific and technical research. Universities, another great Renaissance invention, were refined in nineteenth century Europe to educate the young all over the world. Only Europe has produced global languages. The international language above all others is English, and Europe has also been the source of other global languages like Spanish, French, and Portuguese. European customs and etiquette prevail, particularly in the international sphere, from wearing a suit and tie to eating with a knife and fork on a table, to sitting on chairs. The global civilization rests on pillars that have been provided by Europe.

Europe is therefore an essential reference for the overwhelming majority of the nations on earth. Out of the 193 countries represented in the United Nations, more than two thirds have belonged to European empires at some stage of their history. To a certain extent Europe represents in this global civilization the equivalent to ancient Greece and Rome for European civilization. In the same way that Europeans cannot understand their history without tracing back their origins to Greece and Rome, the inhabitants of the present global civilization need to refer to Europe in general or specifically to one of its former great powers to understand themselves and the world surrounding them. Some of them may be proud of the European heritage, others may reject or even abhor it, but whether they like it or not, this global civilization cannot be explained without Europe's contribution. People from other cultures will also refer to Europe as a source of inspiration to face political or economic challenges and advance toward modernity, for the European model of society is one that has inspired more admiration, and the one that more governments have tried to imitate. Last but not least, Europe, where the nation-state was born, has also created a model of supranational political and economic integration that will have universal appeal in the global age.

The world order in the early twenty-first century is increasingly multipolar. The United States has given up many of its responsibilities as a superpower. President Donald Trump, at present, defies many of the Jeffersonian and Wilsonian principles that have guided US international policy. China, led by President Xi Jinping shows staunch determination to attain world hegemony at all costs. Russia under Vladimir Putin is also determined to consolidate its role at the cost of the West. Smaller powers benefit from the prevailing disorder in which international rules no longer seem to apply. Sharp power is on the rise, which helps authoritarian powers to coerce others and manipulate opinion abroad. In this context Europe has an essential role to play; not only does it have a moral duty to continue influencing this world, which more than any other power or civilization it has helped create, but it also has considerable strength to carry it out.

The European Union is at present the second largest economy in the world. It is in a prime position when it comes to global trade, as it is the largest single market. Several of its member states are among the twenty wealthiest in the world and rank among the highest in the human development index. After suffering the consequences of extreme nationalism the EU has created the most innovative model of integration between states, which has allowed the emergence of a European identity. The latter is particularly important at a time when Europeans will have to defend the best of their legacy in the world.

The European Union is a satiated power; its member states have neither the wish nor the capacity to exert world dominance nor to impose their values on other cultures. They aspire to do something more useful for themselves and for the rest of the world: to ensure that the ideas and principles that bring real progress to this global civilization will prevail. It is also in the best position to keep the world order from falling into the Thucydides trap, in which a rising power challenges an incumbent, leading to war. It is true that none of the great powers aim at conquering other peoples' territories, but would rather conquer markets and peoples' minds. Open war might not necessarily take place in the twenty-first century, but the world order can easily degenerate into an atmosphere of bitter rivalry and chaos that would undermine many of the achievements of this global age.

The EU has continuously strived to defend a world order in which peace and cooperation prevail. It has also shown more determination than any other power to confront the most serious challenges of the twenty-first century, such as global warming, international terrorism, or problems associated with widespread poverty and underdevelopment.

Another worrying phenomenon of the present is how democracy, the government by the people, is degenerating in several countries into an *ochlocracy*, or mob rule, in which different factions pursue their aims by whatever means they can in order to obtain majorities, often in opposition to the rule of law, or even worse, at the cost of truth. Press freedom is corrupted by fake news. It has never been easier to promote lies. In this context, Europe once more has a special mission to preserve one of its greatest contributions to the world: democracy and the model of society that makes it work efficiently.

From the Renaissance to the Enlightenment, and from the era of revolutions to European integration, Europe has created economic, political, and cultural conditions capable of unleashing the most extraordinary human creativity. It has reached the highest forms of civilization and offered human societies solutions for its most complex problems. With its lights and shadows, its triumphs and tragedies, it had been a beacon of light for humanity.

For a long time Europe has lacked a grand narrative, not only one that explains what the European Union has achieved, but more important, what Europe has represented in modern history and how eminent Europeans have shaped it. I hope these pages have contributed to this purpose.

Bibliography

Abernethy, David B. *The Dynamics of Global Dominance: European Overseas Empires, 1415–1980* (New Haven, Conn.: Yale University Press, 2000).

Akçam, Taner. *A Shameful Act: The Armenian Genocide and the Question of Turkish Responsibility* (New York: Metropolitan, 2007).

Archdeacon, Thomas J. *Becoming American: An Ethnic History* (New York: Free Press, 1983).

Aron, Raymond. *Penser la guerre: Clausewitz; l'age européen* (Paris: Éditions Gallimard, 2017).

———. *Peace and War: A Theory of International Relations* (New York: Routledge, 2003).

Ansprenger, Franz. *The Dissolution of Colonial Empires* (London: Routledge, 1989).

Armitage, David. *A Declaration of Independence: A Global History* (Cambridge, Mass.: Harvard University Press, 2007).

Barzun, Jacques. *From Dawn to Decadence, 500 Years of Western Cultural Life: A Cultural History of Europe* (St. Louis: Turtleback Books, 2001).

Beevor, Antony. *The Second World War* (New York: Little, Brown, 2012).

Beasley, William. *Japanese Imperialism, 1894–1945* (Oxford, England: Oxford University Press, 1990).

Birmingham, Stephen. *"The Rest of Us": The Rise of America's Eastern European Jews* (Boston: Little, Brown, 1984).

Blixen, Karen. *Out of Africa* (London: Penguin, 1990).

Bouche, Denise. *Histoire de la colonisation française* (Paris: Fayard, 1991).

Braudel, Fernand. *A History of Civilizations* (London: Penguin, 1991).

Brook, Timothy. *Vermeer's Hat: The Seventeenth Century and the Dawn of the Global World* (London: Vintage, 2008).

Burckhardt, Jacob. *The Civilization of the Renaissance in Italy* (Whitefish, Mont.: Kessinger, 2010).

Burk, Kathleen. *Old World, New World: The Story of Britain and America* (London: Abacus, 2007).

Burke, Edmund. *Reflections on the Revolution in France* (Oxford, England: Oxford World Classics, 2009).

Burns, E. Bradford. *A History of Brazil* (New York: Columbia University Press, 1993).

Butel, Paul. *Histoire des Antilles francais, XVIIe-XXe siècle* (Paris: Parrin, 2002).

Carr, Raymond. *Spain 1808–1975* (Oxford, England: Oxford University Press, 2000).

Carlyle, Thomas. *The French Revolution: A History* (Oxford, England: Oxford World Classics, 2000).

Casas, Bartolomé de las. *A Short Account of the Destruction of the Indies* (New York: Penguin Classics, 1999).

Calvo, Alex & Qiaoni, Bao. "Forgotten Voices from the Great War: The Chinese Labour Corps," *The Asia Pacific Journal*, 13(49).

Chamberlain, M. E. *Decolonization: The Fall of the European Empires* (Hoboken, N.J.: Wiley-Blackwell, 1999).

Champlain, Samuel de. *Le Voyages de Samuel de Champlain au Canada, de 1603 à 1618* (London: Forgotten Books, 2017).

Chateaubriand, François René de. *Mémoires d'outre tombe* (Paris: Grasset, 1996).

Churchill, Winston. *A History of the English-Speaking Peoples*, Vols. II and III (London: Cassell, 1982).

———. *My African Journey* (London: Standard Publications, 2007).

———. *The River War* (London: Standard Publications, 2007).

———. *The World Crisis, 1911–1918* (London: Penguin, 2005).

———. *The Second World War, Vol. VI: Triumph and Tragedy* (London: Penguin, 2005).

Clark, Kenneth. *Civilization: A Personal View* (New York: HarperCollins, 1980).

Clarke, Pe. *The Last Thousand Days of the British Empire: Churchill, Roosevelt, and the Birth of the Pax Americana* (London: Penguin, 2008).

Clausewitz, Carl von. *On War* (Oxford, England: Oxford World Classics, 2008).

Coffey, Michael. *The Irish in America* (New York: Hyperion, 1997).

Collier, Peter & David Horowitz. *The Kennedys: An American Drama* (Claregalway, Ireland: MW Books, 1984).

Conrad, Joseph. *Heart of Darkness* (London: Penguin, 1994).

———. *Nostromo* (London: Penguin, 1994).

———. *Lord Jim* (London: Penguin, 1994).

Condorcet, Nicolas de. *Esquisse d'un tableau historique des progrès de l'espirit humain. Ouvres completes* (Paris: Nabu Press, 2010).

———. *Réflexions sur l'esclavage des nègres. Ouvres completes* (Paris: Nabu Press, 2010).

Cook, James. *The Voyages of Captain Cook* (London: Wordsworth Classics, 1999).

Cooper, Robert. *The Post Modern State and the World Order* (London: Demos, 1996).

Cole, Juan. *Napoleon's Egypt: Invading the Middle East* (London: Palgrave Macmillan, 2007).

Crowley, Roger. *Conquerors: How Portugal Forged the First Global Empire* (London: Faber and Faber, 2015).

Darlymple, William. *Return of a King: The Battle for Afghanistan, 1839–42* (London: Bloomsbury, 2013).

Darwin, John. *After Tamerlane: The Rise and Fall of Global Empires, 1400–2000* (London: Bloomsbury, 2008).

Davies, Norman. *Europe: A History* (Oxford, England: Oxford University Press, 1996).

Diaz del Castillo, Bernal. *The Conquest of New Spain* (London: Penguin, 2003).

Dickens, Charles. *American Notes* (London, Penguin Classics, 2004).
———. *Martin Chuzzlewit* (London: Penguin Classics, 2004).
Duchêne, François. *Jean Monnet: The First Statesman of Interdependence* (New York: W.W. Norton, 1994).
Dunn, Mary. *William Penn: Politics and Conscience* (Princeton, N.J.:Princeton University Press, 1967).
Eccles, W. J. *The French in North America, 1500–1783* (East Lansing: Michigan State University Press, 1990).
Elliott, John H. *Empires of the Atlantic World: Britain and Spain in America 1492–1830* (New Haven, Conn.: Yale University Press, 2006).
———. *El Viejo Mundo y el Nuevo (1492–1650)* (Madrid: Alianza Editorial, 2000).
Ferguson, Niall. *The House of Rothschild, Money Prophets, 1798–1848* (London: Penguin, 1999).
———. *Empire: How Britain Made the Modern World* (New York: Penguin, 2004).
———. *The Cash Nexus: Money and Power in the Modern World, 1700–2000* (London: Penguin, 2001).
———. *The Ascent of Money: A Financial History of the World* (New York: Penguin, 2008).
———. *Civilization: The West and the Rest* (London: Penguin, 2011).
———. *The Square and the Tower* (London: Allen Lane, 2017).
Fernández-Armesto, Felipe. *Millennium: A History of the Last Thousand Years* (New York: Scribner, 1995).
———. *Civilizations: Culture, Ambition, and the Transformation of Nature* (New York: Free Press, 2001).
———. *Columbus* (Oxford, England: Oxford University Press, 1991).
———. *The Americas: The History of a Hemisphere* (London: Weidenfeld and Nicolson, 2003).
———. *Amerigo: The Man Who Gave His Name to America* (New York: Random House, 2006).
———. *1492: The Year the World Began* (San Francisco: HarperOne, 2009).
Ferro, Marc. *Colonization: A Global History* (London: Routledge, 1997).
Fieldhouse, D. K. *Economics and Empire, 1830–1914* (London: Palgrave Macmillan, 1984).
Figes, Orlando. *A People's Tragedy: A History of the Russian Revolution* (New York: Viking, 1996).
———. *Natasha's Dance: A Cultural History of Russia* (New York: Metropolitan, 2002).
Flynn, Dennys; Giráldez, Arturo; Von Glahn, Richard. *Global Connections and Monetary History, 1470–1800* (London: Ashgate, 2003).
Forastié, Jean. *Les Trente Glorieuses, ou la Révolution Invisible de 1946 à 1975* (Paris: Poche, 2011).
Foreman-Peck, James. *A History of the World Economy: International Economic Relations Since 1850* (London: Harvester, 1993).
Franklin, Benjamin. *The Autobiography of Benjamin Franklin* (New York: Henry Holt, 1916).
Frankopan, Peter. *The Silk Roads: A New History of the World* (New York: Vintage, 2017).
Frieden, Jeffry. *Global Capitalism: Its Fall and Rise in the Twentieth Century* (New York: W.W. Norton, 2006).
Fukuyama, Francis. *The End of History and the Last Man* (New York: Penguin, 2012).
Galbraith, John Kenneth. *The Affluent Society* (New York: Penguin, 1963).
———. *The World Economy Since the Wars: A Personal View* (London: Sinclair Stephenson, 1994).
Gandhi, Mohandas. *An Autobiography or The Story of My Experiments with Truth* (London: Penguin, 2000).

Games, Alison. *Migration and the Origins of the English Atlantic World* (Cambridge, England: Cambridge University Press, 1999).

García Cárcel, Ricardo. *La Herencia del Pasado, las Memorias Historicas de España* (Barcelona: Galaxia Gutenberg, 2011).

Gibbon, Edward. *The Decline and Fall of the Roman Empire* (London: Penguin, 1998).

Giddens, Anthony. *Europe in the Global Age* (Cambridge, England: Polity, 2006).

Gide, André. *Voyage au Congo* (Paris: Poche, 2007).

Gilbert, Martin. *Israel: A History* (New York: William Morrow, 1998).

Glendinning, Victoria. *Raffles and the Golden Opportunity* (London: Profile Books, 2012).

Glover, Jonathan. *Humanity: A Moral History of the Twentieth Century* (London: Cape, 1999).

Goldstone, Jack. *Why Europe? The Rise of the West in World History 1500–1850* (Boston: McGraw-Hill, 2009).

Gobineau, Joseph Arthur. *Essai sur l'inegalite des Races Humaines* (Paris: General Books, 2012).

Grotius, Hugo. *The Free Seas* (Indianapolis: Liberty Fund, 2011).

Guha, Ramachandra. *India After Gandhi: The History of the World's Largest Democracy* (New York: Picador, 2008).

Haggard, H. Rider. *King Solomon's Mines* (London: Penguin, 1996).

Halkuyt, Richard. *The Principal Navigations, Voyages, Traffiques and Discoveries of the English Nation* (London: Nabu Press, 2011).

Harrison, Christopher. *France and Islam in West Africa, 1860-1960,* Cambridge University Press, 1988.

Hastings, Adrian. *The Church in Africa, 1450–1950* (Oxford, England: Oxford University Press, 1994).

Hastings, Max. *Catastrophe 1914: Europe Goes to War* (Glasgow: William Collins, 1914).

Havard, Gilles. *Histoire de l'Amérique Française* (Paris: Flamarion, 2008).

Herman, Arthur. *To Rule the Waves: How the British Navy Shaped the Modern World* (New York: HarperCollins, 2004).

Hitchcock, William. *The Struggle for Europe: The Turbulent History of a Divided Continent 1945 to the Present* (London: Profile, 2004).

Hobsbawm, Eric. *The Age of Capital: 1848–1875* (London: Michel Joseph, 1975).

———. *The Age of Empire: 1875–1914* (London: Michael Joseph, 1992).

———. *The Age of Extremes: A History of the World, 1914–1991* (London: Michael Joseph, 1994).

Hobson, J. A. *Imperialism: A Study* (Ann Arbor: University of Michigan Press, 2007).

Hobston, John. *The Eastern Origins of Western Civilization* (Cambridge, England: Cambridge University Press, 2004).

Holland, R. F. *European Decolonization, 1918–1981* (London: Palgrave, 1985).

Hosking, Geoffrey. *Russia and the Russians: A History* (Cambridge, Mass.: Harvard University Press, 2001).

Hsu, C. Y. Immanuel. *The Rise of Modern China* (Oxford, England: Oxford University Press, 2000).

Huntington, Samuel. *The Clash of Civilizations and the Remaking of World Order* (New York: Simon & Schuster, 2011).

Israel, Jonathan. *The Dutch Republic: Its Rise, Greatness, and Fall, 1477–1806* (Oxford, England: Oxford University Press, 1998).

James, C.L.R. *The Black Jacobins: Toussant L'Ouverture and Santo Domingo Revolution* (New York: Vintage, 1963).

James, Lawrence. *Raj: The Making and Unmaking of British India* (London: Abacus, 1997).

Jenkins, Roy. *Churchill: A Biography* (New York: Plume, 2002).

Johnson, Paul. *Intellectuals, From Marx and Tolstoy to Sartre and Chomsky* (London: Harper Perennial, 2007).

Judt, Tony. *Postwar: A History of Europe Since 1945* (New York: Penguin, 2005).

———. *Reappraisals: Reflections on the Forgotten Twentieth Century* (London: William Heinneman, 2008).

Kagan, Robert. *Paradise and Power: America Versus Europe in the Twenty-first Century* (London: Atlantic Books, 2003).

———. *The Return of History and the End of Dreams* (London: Atlantic Books, 2008).

Kaldor, Mary. *The Disintegrating West* (London: Hill and Wang, 1978).

Kamen, Henry. *Empire: How Spain Became a World Power, 1492–1763* (New York: Harper Perennial, 2004).

———. *The Disinherited: Exile and the Making of Spanish Culture, 1492–1975* (London: Allen Lane, 2007).

———. *Early Modern European Society* (New York: Routledge, 2000).

Keay, John. *China: A History* (New York: HarperCollins, 2008).

Kennedy, Paul. *The Rise and Fall of the Great Powers: Economic Change and Military Conflict from 1500 to 2000* (New York: Fontana Press, 1989).

Kissinger, Henry. *Diplomacy* (London: Simon & Schuster, 1994).

———. *On China* (London: Penguin, 2012).

———. *World Order: Reflections on the Character of Nations and the Course of History* (London: Penguin, 2016).

Klein, Herbert. *A Population History of the United States* (Cambridge, England: Cambridge University Press, 2004).

Landes, David. *The Wealth and Poverty of Nations: Why Some Are So Rich and Some So Poor* (London: Abacus, 1998).

Lapierre, Dominique and Collins, Larry. *Freedom at Midnight: How England Gave Away an Empire* (New York: Simon & Schuster, 1975).

———. *O Jerusalem!* (New York: Simon & Schuster, 1988).

Lawrence, T. E. *The Seven Pillars of Wisdom* (Radford, Va.: Wilder, 2011).

Lenin, Vladimir Ilyich. *Imperialism: The Highest Stage of Capitalism* (London: Penguin, 2010).

Leonard, Mark. *Why Europe Will Run the 21st Century* (Madrid: Taurus, 2006).

Lévy, Bernard-Henri. *Les Aventures de la Liberté* (Paris: Grasset, 1991).

Litalien, Raymonde. *Champlain: The Birth of French America* (Montreal: McGill-Queen's University Press, 2004).

Livingstone, David. *Missionary Travels and Researches in South Africa* (London, PQ Books, 2015).

Loti, Pierre. *Au Maroc* (Paris: Broché, 2000).

Lovell, Julia. *The Great Wall: China Against the World, 1000 BC–AD 2000* (New York: Grove Press, 2007).

———. *The Opium War: Drugs, Dreams and the Making of Modern China* (New York: Picador, 2011).

Lucena Giraldo, Manuel. *Naciones de rebeldes* (Madrid: Taurus, 2010).

———. *Francisco de Miranda La aventura de la política* (Madrid: Edaf, 1990).

Lynch, John. *The Spanish American Revolutions, 1808–1826* (New York: W.W. Norton, 1986).

McCue, Jim. *Edmund Burke & Our Present Discontents* (London: Claridge Press, 1997).

BIBLIOGRAPHY

Machiavelli, Niccolò. *The Prince* (New York, Penguin Classics, 2011).

MacMillan, Margaret. *Paris 1919: Six Months That Changed the World* (New York: Random House, 2001).

Madariaga, Salvador de. *Hernán Cortés* (Madrid: Espasa, 1977).

———. *Bolivar* (London: Hollis and Carter, 1952).

———. *De Colon a Bolivar* (Madrid: Espasa, 1981).

———. *El Auge y el Ocaso del Imperio Español en América* (Madrid: Espasa-Calpe, 1977).

———. *España, Ensayo de Historia Contemporánea* (Madrid: Espasa-Calpé, 1979).

Malthus, Thomas. *An Essay on the Principle of Population* (New York: Penguin, 2012).

Marrus, Michael Robert. *The Unwanted: European Refugees in the Twentieth Century* (London: Temple University Press, 2002).

Mazower, M. *Dark Continent: Europe's Twentieth Century* (London: Penguin, 2008).

McCue, Jim. *Edmund Burke and Our Present Discontents* (London: Claridge Press, 1997).

McNeill, John Robert. *Atlantic Empires of France and Spain: Louisbourg and Havana, 1700–1763* (Chapel Hill: University of North Carolina Press, 1985).

McNeill, W. H. *The Rise of the West: A History of the Human Community* (Chicago: University of Chicago Press, 1963).

Mintz, Sidney W. *Sweetness and Power: The Place of Sugar in Modern History* (New York: Penguin, 1986).

Mill, James. *The History of British India*, vol. 1 (London: Baldwin, Cradock & Joy, 1817).

Monnet, Jean. *Memoires* (New York: Knopf, 1978).

Montesquieu, Charles de. *Persian Letters* (New York: Penguin, 1973).

Morison, Samuel Eliot. *The European Discovery of America: The Northern Voyages* (Oxford, England: Oxford University Press, 1971).

Morris, Ian. *Why the West Rules—For Now: The Patterns of History, and What They Reveal About the Future* (London: Profile, 2010).

Nugent, Paul. *Africa Since Independence* (London: Palgrave, 2004).

Nietzsche, Friederich. *Thus Spoke Zarathustra* (New York: Sterling, 2012).

Oates, Charles G. *Matabeleland and the Victoria Falls: The Letters and Journals of Frank Oates, 1873–1875* (London: Jeppestown Press, 2007).

O'Brien, Patrick & Prados de la Escosura, Leandro. *The Costs and Benefits of European Imperialism from the Conquest of Ceuta, 1415, to the Treaty of Lusaka, 1974* (Madrid: Revista de Historia Economica, 1998; vol. 16, no. 1).

Oliveira Marques, A. H. de. *History of Portugal* (New York: Columbia University Press, 1972).

Orwell, George. *Shooting an Elephant* (London: Penguin, 1950).

Osborne, Roger. *Civilization: A New History of the Western World* (New York: Pegasus, 2008).

Osterhammel, Jurgen. *The Transformation of the World* (Princeton, N.J.: Princeton University Press, 2009).

Page, Martin. *First Global Village, How Portugal Changed the World* (Lisbon: Casa das Letras, 2002).

Paine, Thomas. *Common Sense* (London: Penguin, 2004).

Stéphane Courtois, et al. *The Black Book of Communism: Crimes, Terror, Repression* (Cambridge, Mass.: Harvard University Press, 1999).

Parekh, Bhikhu. *Colonialism, Tradition, and Reform: An Analysis of Gandhi's Political Discourse* (London: Sage, 1999).

Pakenham, Thomas. *The Scramble for Africa: The White Man's Conquest of the Dark Continent from 1876 to 1912* (New York: Random House, 1991).

Parker, Geoffrey. *Military Revolution: Military Innovation and the Rise of the West, 1500–1800* (Cambridge, England: Cambridge University Press, 1996).

Pepys, Samuel. *The Diary of Samuel Pepys* (New York: Modern Library, 2003).

Peyrefitte, Alain. *The Immobile Empire* (New York: Vintage, 2013).

Pocock, Tom. *Battle for Empire: The Very First World War, 1756–63* (London: Michael O'Mara, 1998).

Pomeranz, Kenneth. *The Great Divergence: China, Europe, and the Making of the Modern World Economy* (Princeton, N.J.: Princeton University Press, 2000).

Raleigh, Sir Walter. *The Discovery of Guiana* (Whitefish, Montana: Kessinger, 2009).

Ravenstein, E.G. *A Journey of the First Voyage of Vasco da Gama, 1492–1499* (Cambridge University Press, 2010).

Reid, T. R. *The United States of Europe: The New Superpower and the End of American Supremacy* (London: Penguin, 2004).

Reynolds, David. *One World Divisible: A Global History Since 1945* (London: W.W. Norton, 2000).

Riendeau, Roger. *A Brief History of Canada* (Markham, Ontario: Fitzhenry & Whiteside, 2007).

Rifkin, Jeremy. *The European Dream: How Europe's Vision of the Future Is Quietly Eclipsing the American Dream* (Cambridge, England: Polity, 2005).

Roberts, Andrew. *Napoleon the Great* (London: Allen Lane, 2016).

Robinson, Ronald, J. Gallagher, and A. Denny. *Africa and the Victorians: The Official Mind of Imperialism* (New York: IB Tauris, 1965).

Rogan, Eugene. *The Arabs: A History* (New York: Basic, 2009).

———. *The Fall of the Ottomans: The Great War in the Middle East* (New York: Basic, 2015).

Russell, Bertrand. *A History of Western Philosophy* (London: Union Paperbacks, 1987).

Said, Edward. *Orientalism: Western Conceptions of the Orient* (London: Penguin, 1978).

———. *Culture and Imperialism* (London: Vintage, 1994).

Saenz de Quesada, Maria. *La Argentina: Historia del País y de su Gente* (Buenos Aires: Sudamericana, 2001).

Sassoon, Donald. *The Culture of the Europeans: From 1800 to the Present* (London: HarperCollins, 2006).

Sebag-Montefiore, Simon. *Jerusalem: The Biography* (New York: Knopf, 2011).

———. *The Romanovs: 1613–1918* (New York: Alfred A. Knopf, 2016).

Seeley, John Robert. *The Expansion of England: Two Courses of Lectures* (Cambridge, England: Cambridge University Press, 2010).

Smith, Adam. *The Wealth of Nations* (New York: Bantam, 2003).

Spengler, Oswald. *The Decline of the West* (New York: Knopf, 1926).

Síocháin, Séamas Ó. *Roger Casement: Imperialist, Rebel, Revolutionary* (Dublin: Lilliput Press, 2008).

Stanley, Henry. *How I Found Livingstone: Travels, Adventures, and Discoveries in Central Africa, Including Four Months' Residence with Dr. Livingstone* (London: Wordsworth, 2010).

———. *Through the Dark Continent: Or, The Sources of the Nile Around the Great Lakes of Equatorial Africa and Down the Livingstone River to the Atlantic Ocean* (London: Adamant, 2000).

Taylor, A.J.P. *The Struggle for Mastery in Europe: 1848–1918* (Oxford, England: Oxford University Press, 1987).

———. *Europe: Grandeur and Decline* (London: Penguin, 1985).

Tocqueville, Alexis de. *The Ancien Régime and the Revolution* (London: Everyman's Library, 1988).

———. *Democracy in America* (New York: Penguin, 2003).

Thomas, Anthony. *Rhodes: The Race for Africa* (New York: Thomas Dunne Books, 1997).

Thomas, Hugh. *Rivers of Gold: The Rise of the Spanish Empire, from Columbus to Magellan* (New York: Random House, 2004).

———. *The Golden Age: The Spanish Empire of Charles V* (New York: Penguin, 2011).

———. *The Slave Trade: The Story of the Atlantic Slave Trade, 1440–1870* (New York: Simon & Schuster, 1997).

———. *The Conquest of Mexico* (London: Hutchinson, 1993).

Tunzelmann, Alex Von. *Indian Summer: The Secret History of the End of an Empire* (New York: Henry Holt, 2007).

Vargas Llosa, Mario. *The Celt's Dream* (London: Faber and Faber, 2012).

Wasserstein, Bernard. *Barbarism and Civilization: A History of Europe in Our Time* (Oxford, England: Oxford University Press, 2009).

Watson, Peter. *Ideas: A History of Thought and Invention, from Fire to Freud* (New York: Harper Perennial, 2006).

———. *The Modern Mind: An Intellectual History of the 20th Century* (New York: Harper Perennial, 2002).

———. *The German Genius: Europe's Third Renaissance, the Second Scientific Revolution, and the Twentieth Century* (New York: Harper, 2010).

Whitaker, Arthur. *The Western Hemisphere Idea: Its Rise and Decline* (London: Forgotten, 2017).

Williams, Charles. *Adenauer, The Father of the New Germany* (Hoboken, N.J.: Wiley, 2000).

Zakaria, Fareed. *The Post-American World* (New York: W.W. Norton, 2008).

Zeldin, Theodore. *France, 1848–1945: Politics and Anger* (Oxford, England: Oxford University Press, 1987).

Zweig, Stefan. *The World of Yesterday* (London: Pushkin Press, 2015).

———. *Messages from a Lost World: Europe on the Brink* (London: Pushkin Press, 2011).

———. *Brazil: A Land of the Future* (Riverside, Calif.: Ariadne, 2017).

Acknowledgments

I would like to express my gratitude to several people who have contributed to the publication of this book. I would first of all like to thank Charlie Viney, my literary agent, for representing me and my work with such extraordinary skill and professionalism. He has been an invaluable source of advice ever since we met. Secondly, I am indebted to Claiborne Hancock who has given me the privilege of being edited by Pegasus Books. I would like to thank Jessica Case for her support in the editing process; finally, Nicki Kennedy and her colleagues at the Intercontinental Literary Agency for their effort to internationalize this book as far as China.

Several colleagues from the academic world have enriched me with their ideas on how to grasp such a vast topic as the European era of supremacy. I would particularly like to thank Hugh Thomas, Lord Thomas of Swynnerton for his wise comments on a few chapters that he read. It was a great privilege to benefit from his wisdom and historical perspective on such interesting topics and it is regrettable that he did not live to see this book published. For this reason it is dedicated to his memory.

ACKNOWLEDGMENTS

As always, my parents have been very supportive and made useful comments on the final draft of the book. I would specially like to thank my wife Catherine for her loyalty, forbearance, and the good humor with which she has put up with my literary vocation. Last but not least, I express my gratitude to my children, Eduardo and Sandra, my pride and my joy, for their enthusiasm, encouragement, and inquisitive spirit. One advantage of writing this book has been to spend many evenings with them at home, and as a result they have become more knowledgeable of their European roots than most of their contemporaries.

Index

INDEX

INDEX